SHAKESPEARE
and Dramatic Tradition

S. F. JOHNSON

(Photo by Hilda Bijur)

SHAKESPEARE
and Dramatic
Tradition

Essays in Honor of S. F. Johnson

EDITED BY

W. R. Elton

AND

William B. Long

DELAWARE

NEWARK: University of Delaware Press
LONDON AND TORONTO: Associated University Presses

Associated University Presses
440 Forsgate Drive
Cranbury, NJ 08512

Associated University Presses
25 Sicilian Avenue
London WC1A 2QH, England

Associated University Presses
P.O. Box 488, Port Credit
Mississauga, Ontario
Canada L5G 4M2

The paper used in this publication meets the requirements
of the American National Standard for Permanence of Paper
for Printed Library Materials Z39.48-1984.

Library of Congress Cataloging-in-Publication Data

Shakespeare and dramatic tradition.

Includes index.
1. Shakespeare, William, 1564–1616
—Criticism and interpretation.
2. Johnson, S. F. (Samuel Frederick),
1918–   . I. Johnson, S. F. (Samuel
Frederick), 1918–   . II. Elton, William R.,
1921–   . III. Long, William B.
PR2976.S334   1989   822.3'3   87-40242
ISBN 0-87413-333-5 (alk. paper)

Printed in the United States of America

Contents

PART 3: *Traditions*

Preface

This volume is a tribute to Samuel Frederick Johnson, Professor of English and Comparative Literature at Columbia University (1954–84), and now emeritus. His career as a distinguished Renaissance scholar is marked by acknowledgments in more than seventy books, many of these based on some hundred doctoral dissertations he directed. In addition to his teaching and publication, his influence has been transmitted by such dissertations, and by his students now placed in every part of the country. The duality of his position as research-oriented historical scholar and perceptive literary critic may be linked to the two distinguished directors of his own Harvard dissertation: the Renaissance editor, Hyder Rollins, and the scholar-critic, Harry Levin. (The dissertation itself, *Early Elizabethan Tragedies of the Inns of Court*, 2 vols., 1948, has just been published by Garland.) Such complementary literary approaches are reflected, amid a variety of methods, in the contents of this *Festschrift*. These contents in turn reflect Johnson's own professional interests: Shakespeare; the Renaissance stage; opera; and English and continental drama, from medieval cycles through the late seventeenth century.

W. R. E.

SHAKESPEARE
and Dramatic Tradition

PART I
Shakespeare

A Garden in Belmont

The Merchant of Venice, 5.1

Harry Levin

Comedy, at its most typical, has generated an urban and bourgeois—not to say a mercantile—atmosphere, in keeping with the sharpness of its satiric tone. Shakespeare transcends that pattern by characteristically harking back to nature and by sounding what C. L. Barber has taught us to call a festive note. Money gets mentioned less often in Shakespeare's other and later plays than in his fledgling adaptation from Plautus, *The Comedy of Errors.* Within its classical tradition love was envisaged as a casual, if not a venal, relationship. Conflicts tended to develop between the pantaloon or *senex iratus,* the angry old man clutching his moneybags, and the young lovers abetted by servants cleverer than their masters. Comedy in Shakespeare's romantic vein, which embraces a good many heterogeneous elements, tends to seek and find a retreat amid the countryside, in some green world or pastoral surrounding where mundane complications may be happily resolved. Such is the vitalizing influence of the forest in *A Midsummer Night's Dream* and *As You Like It,* of the Bohemian sheepcote in *The Winter's Tale,* and of the enchanted island in *The Tempest.* The respective comic spheres of city and country are uniquely interlinked in *The Merchant of Venice.* In *The Tempest, The Winter's Tale, As You Like It,* and *A Midsummer Night's Dream,* the vicissitudes of rustication set aright the discontents of court. The court that holds jurisdiction over *The Merchant of Venice,* of course, is not regal but legal.

That does not make it any less dramatic, inasmuch as England's central institution, the law, has incidentally served as a matrix for the drama. Among its original sponsors were lawyers at the Inns of Court, who produced the first English tragedy, *Gorboduc,* where the dumb shows were made vocal by the parleys of opposing counsels. It could not have been an accident that the first English comedy, *Fulgens and Lucres,* was self-characterized in juridical terminology as a "process." A trial, being a verbal agon before an audience, presents a kind of theatrical performance. Dramatists were apt in exploiting its possibilities, and very notably the Jacobeans, who rose to such climactic courtroom scenes as Jonson's in

13

Volpone and Webster's in *The White Devil*. Shakespeare had his own reasons for bypassing the notorious arraignment of Prince Hal, and he showed a particular sympathy for trials in which the defendant was a woman and a queen: Hermione and Katherine of Aragon. But circumstance could not have provided him with a more striking confrontation of values, styles, and personalities than what takes place in the fourth act of *The Merchant of Venice*. Given the suspense relieved by such a climax, anything that followed ran the danger of anticlimax. Spectators have been known to walk out after the exit of Shylock, and there have been productions wherein the fifth act was drastically curtailed or else omitted altogether.

Critics with an eye to more modern stages, like Gustav Freytag and Harley Granville-Barker, have been inclined to view Shakespearean drama as inherently a three-part form. Its pseudo-classical five-act structure, which seems to have been rather unevenly superimposed, means more in print than it does in the theater, though its amplitude could have licensed the playwright to double and redouble his plot. Even so, since its denouements can be foreseen quite early, particularly in the comedies, the story-line may slacken after the third act. Slack can be taken up by directly completing the story and thereupon devoting the fifth act to a divertissement, as in *A Midsummer Night's Dream*. The situation would be much the same in *Love's Labor's Lost*, if Shakespeare had not overturned it with a last-minute shock. In *The Tempest* he postpones the conclusion by eking out the fourth act with a masque. In *The Merchant of Venice* the predicated business has virtually terminated with the courtroom scene. He employs a brief aftermath to plant his motivation for the sub-subplot of the last act, the displacement and replacement of the rings. Without this contrivance there would be no action left; and despite it there have been actors, audiences, and commentators who have regarded the rest as a superficial and expendable letdown. Act 5 may be less of a "graceful winding up," in Hazlitt's phrase, than it is—in A. W. Schlegel's—"a musical afterpiece."

Generally, Shakespeare's underplots move parallel to his main plots, as with the revenge of Laertes in *Hamlet* or the sons of Gloucester in *King Lear*. In the comedies, where the theme so repeatedly involves wooing, the couples are reduplicated at different levels: Bassanio and Portia never far from Gratiano and Nerissa, the four transversely paired as knight and squire or mistress and waiting-woman, plus Lorenzo and Jessica on a plane connecting the two plots. Those two plots are aligned with an antithetical series of contrasts between the pettifogging commercialism of Venice and the leisurely grace of Belmont, between man's justice and woman's mercy, between adversary and amatory relations, hatred versus love. In yoking such antitheses together, Shakespeare took the risk of letting Shylock run away with the play, just as Falstaff jeopardizes the equilibrium of *2 Henry IV*. The pound of flesh and the three caskets are even-handedly balanced in the subtitle of the first quarto. The title role is hardly that of a hero, though it has sometimes been confused with Shylock's; as a matter of fact, the entry in the Stationers' Register appends an alternative title, "the iewe of Venyce." The merchant Antonio speaks no more than 188 lines, less than Bassanio (339), Shylock (361), and Portia (578), who comes fourth after Rosalind (721), Cleopatra (670), and Imogen (591) among Shakespeare's most articulate heroines.

Shylock's part, then, is not much longer than Bassanio's and much shorter than Portia's; he appears in but five of the twenty scenes. A succession of histrionic stars managed to extend it by acting out and sentimentalizing the episode reported by Solanio and Salerio in choric mockery: his outcry on returning from the banquet to discover that Jessica has eloped and taken some of his hoard along. The stellar potentialities in the conjunction of Shylock and Portia gained this play an outstandingly rich history of performance, more frequent during certain periods than any other Shakespearean vehicle with the exception of *Hamlet*. Yet it seems to have gone unperformed through the seventeenth century, possibly because its mixed emotions were unpalatable to neo-classical tastes. In Viscount Lansdowne's mangled and coarsened version, *The Jew of Venice* (1701), Shylock has to be played as a comic butt—a twist which prompted Shakespeare's first editor, Nicholas Rowe, to confess that he thought the personage had been "design'd Tragically by the Author." Rowe's perception of "a savage Fierceness and Fellness" would be realized by Charles Macklin, who preempted "the Jew/That Shakespeare knew"—as Pope put it—for almost fifty years. That archvillain would be romanticized by nineteenth-century Shylocks from Edmund Kean to Henry Irving, whose "patriarch of Israel" provoked the derision of Bernard Shaw.

Heinrich Heine's testimony might have betrayed some hereditary bias, but he claimed to have witnessed a blonde Englishwoman weeping sympathetically over the downfall of Shylock and consequently ranked *The Merchant of Venice* among Shakespeare's tragedies. An increasing pathos in the interpretation could be correlated with a broadening tolerance for Jews. Shylock's hard heart would be softened to a maudlin degree in the Yiddish theater, and Arnold Wesker has recently attempted to depict him in amicable collusion with Antonio. Nonetheless it must be noted that, ever since Hitler made so catastrophic an issue of antisemitism, the play has figured less prominently in both the repertory and the classroom. Meanwhile scholars like E. E. Stoll, considering historical attitudes toward ethnicity and usury, had recaptured an image of the Jewish moneylender that Shakespeare knew—or rather, did not know, since there had been no English Jewry for 300 years. Out of the stereotypes he created a curmudgeon, sinister and grotesque by turns, yet a human being. Swinburne, confounding Shylock with Lear, could proclaim him "more sinned against than sinning." Where could the balance between those states be determined, if not in a lawcourt? He has been on the defensive after the elopement: "If you prick us, do we not bleed" (3.1.64)? He takes the offensive before the tribunal: "Hates any man the thing he would not kill" (4.1.67)?

The poetic justice of the hearing is accentuated by a vernacular echo. It was Shylock, hatching his machination, who soliloquized about Antonio: "If I can catch him once upon the hip . . ." (1.3.46). It is Gratiano, after the switch in judgment, who gloats and jeers: "Now, infidel, I have you on the hip" (4.1.334). It brings home the irony of hoisting the engineer in his own petard, when Portia—her plea for compassion having fallen upon deaf ears—resorts to a legalism more literal-minded than Shylock's. Vengeance has been his seething and mounting objective: revenge against racial persecution, revenge against financial rivalry, revenge against a twofold personal loss. Shakespeare would be coming to closer grips with that barbaric motive in probing Hamlet's compunctions. Ethically *The Merchant of Venice*, like *The Atheist's Tragedy*, is an antirevenge play. G. L. Kittredge used to maintain that Shakespeare portrayed no villain so malign but that he had a case, and it is the losing case for Shylock that makes the play so controversial. There are wavering moments when the Christian comedy might almost have turned into a Jewish tragedy, observed the Variorum editor, charting the shifts of interpretative sympathy. But the sexual game, the light-hearted banter, and what Coleridge termed "the lyrical movement" of act 5 would be heartlessly *de trop* if we recognized Shylock as the protagonist.

Sir Arthur Quiller-Couch believed that it had been underrated, that it constituted "the most delightful part of the play." Though act 4 is unquestionably the showpiece, its high tensions call for a resolution. Where the urbanized lagoons of Venice are precincts of sharp practice, which Jonson would elaborate in *Volpone*, the bucolic terra firma of Belmont represents "a place where life is heightened," according to Anne Barton. Temperamentally and geographically it borders on *Twelfth Night*: "This is Illyria, Lady." Portia's villa is a haven lighted by the chromatic glow of Veronese, after the hustle and bustle of the Rialto. Shakespeare commutes in artful alternation from the one locale to the other: twelve of the scenes are set in Venice, eight in Belmont. Venice repairs to Belmont in the wake of the suitors' "secret pilgrimage" (1.1.120). The successful suit of Bassanio, with an undertone of ambiguity, is compared to the Argonauts' mythical quest for the golden fleece (1.1.170; 3.2.241). Moving in the opposite direction, Belmont makes an incursion into Venice when Portia goes to the rescue; penetrating that ambience as a dea ex machina, she must assume the guise of a man and a barrister. Her juristic exploit cannot be scrutinized very professionally. The terms of the bond, like those of her father's will, as Granville-Barker has pointed out, are the stuff of fairy tales. "Shylock is real while his story remains fabulous."

Shakespeare's "all-combining mind"—the formulation is Henry Hallam's—could have found his themes of extortion and courtship already combined in what seems to have been his principal source, a novella from *Il Pecorone,* the collection of tales by Ser Giovanni Fiorentino. The tale about the pound of flesh and the loophole for avoiding that penalty had been told many times in the European Middle Ages and can be traced as far afield as the *Mahábhárata.* But the lady of Belmonte in the Italian romance is a rich widow who must be successfully bedded and who has a stratagem for staving off all except the last of her swains. Shakespeare obviously needed something more courtly and more presentable on the stage. Within Giovanni's framework, held together by the Venetian loan, he substituted a folktale that again had many far-ranging analogues and was probably familiar to him through its inclusion in the *Gesta Romanorum.* Among those fascinated by the three caskets was Freud, who predictably saw them as symbols of women's bodies and hence analogous to the judgment of Paris and other myths that hinge upon triple choices. The paradox that allows the basest metal to form a receptacle for the prize fits in well with a recurrent Shakespearean theme, the distinction between appearance and reality, moralized in such maxims as "All that glisters is not gold" or "O, what a goodly outside falsehood hath!" (2.7.65; 1.3.102).

In the *Gesta Romanorum* the chooser of the golden casket is promised "that he deserveth," and it is the silver one which promises "that his nature desireth." In the lottery of Portia's destiny the moral symbolism has been reversed; gold is associated with desire and silver with desert (2.1.15). The inscription on the leaden casket in the old fable reads: "Who so chooseth me shall finde that God hath disposed to him." Such religious quietism differs profoundly from the Marlovian challenge that ultimately attracts Bassanio: "Who chooses me must give and hazard all he hath" (2.7.9). Quiller-Couch, remarking that "a predatory young gentleman such as Bassanio would not have chosen the leaden casket," begs the question; for a character necessarily consists of whatever he does and says, and this is Bassanio's most important act or statement. True, he started out by speaking as a fortune hunter, anxious to wive it wealthily in Belmont like Petruchio in Padua. But Belmont, unlike Padua, is fabulous terrain. Broaching his intention to restore his depleted fortunes, he mentions Portia's inheritance, her beauty, and her virtue in that order (1.1.161–63). Though it may be a long shot, he is truly a gambler. So is Antonio, whose ventures threaten to be much unluckier than his friend's, since—having wealth and life itself to lose—it is he who gives and hazards all he has, both his purse and his person.

It has been speculated that when Portia welcomes Bassanio, she reveals the password: "pause a day or two / Before you *hazard* . . ." (3.2.1 f.). This is of a piece with the tempting conjecture that the cautionary song "Tell me where is fancy bred," which accompanies his appraisal, hints at the proper choice through its rhymes with "lead": "bred," "head," and "nourished" (63–65). Portia, however, though she frankly confesses her preference for Bassanio, is sworn to silence on the sphinxlike riddle by the conditions of her father's will—a document almost as stringent as Shylock's bond. In her poignant awareness of each casket's responding message, she must constrain strong feelings while the Princes of Morocco and Aragon are going through the rite. They have been preceded by at least half a dozen, as we learn from the witty and sophisticated prose of her expository scene with Nerissa, where the candidates are reduced to caricatures of their several nationalities. Paternal stricture not only condemns them to dismissal, but forbids them the consolation of marriage elsewhere. It stretches the long arm of coincidence when Bassanio, the third suitor whom we witness, is both the first she has liked and the first to opt for lead. The gamble is moralized by his expressed distrust of "outward shows" (73). Yet under the circumstances, and in view of the alternatives, she seems even luckier than he.

Small wonder that when the casket disclosed her fate, one of the famous Portias, Ellen Terry, kissed it and sprinkled rose leaves. The complexity if not the inconsistency, the moods and changes of her character have aroused diverse opinions. Portia was "not a very great favourite" with Hazlitt; she was "the most perfect of [Shakespeare's] creations" for H. H. Furness. Her name refers us back to Cato's daughter, Brutus's wife, a Roman model of perfection (1.1.166). Since it is she who solves a dilemma baffling to everyone else, she is demonstrably the most intelligent person in the courtroom. Yet, while ardently accepting Bassanio as "her lord, her governor, her king," she has described herself as "an unlesson'd girl, unschool'd, unpractic'd" (3.2.165, 159). Unlike Jessica, who is embarrassed about enacting a breeches part, she exuberantly throws herself into the garb and bearing of a lawyer. Like Saint Joan—Shaw's, not Shakespeare's—she can enter a man's world and straighten out its confusions. Her chats with Nerissa are acutely critical of the male sex. Yet, under her "father's imposition," this brilliant woman can neither choose nor refuse her future husband (1.2.26). Such apparent contradictions lend the role a matchless range: enchantress, chatelaine, gossip, hoyden, jurisconsult, prankster, lady-love. It offers the actress, as Hamlet does the actor, an opportunity to play many parts and to dominate the cast.

The amenities of Belmont harbor no escape from the extortions of

Venice. Bassanio has no sooner passed his test and been certified as the Lord of Belmont by Portia's ring, than Salerio arrives posthaste with the news of Antonio's jeopardy, and the plots converge in the second scene of act 3. Amid the goings and comings and the adverse reports from high seas, the three-month contract has fallen due all too suddenly. Lorenzo and Jessica have likewise gravitated to Portia's sanctuary and will become its temporary lord and lady during her absence. Here too they will recounter Launcelot Gobbo, whose defection parallels Jessica's—from Shylock's "sober house" to the "shallow fopp'ry" of the merrymakers (2.5.35 f.). Launcelot had introduced himself with the kind of set piece made popular by the clown of Shakespeare's troop, Will Kempe, recalling the farewells of Launce and his dog in *The Two Gentlemen of Verona* and foreshadowing the Porter's monologue in *Macbeth*. Like the Porter, Gobbo acts out a little morality play, in this case a dialogue between Conscience and the Devil. The ethical quandary is complicated because his conscience bids him stay, while the fiend exhorts him to depart—from a house which Jessica will identify with hell (2.2.1 ff.; 2.3.2). When they meet at Belmont he rallies her about her conversion, jesting that it will help to "raise the price of hogs" (3.5.24).

Playing the preacher, he has been threatening her with the scriptural doom for "the sins of the father," unless she plead bastardy (1 f.). He had anticipated her unfilial trickery by an initial trick upon the elder Gobbo, who—notwithstanding his blindness—recognized his "own flesh and blood" (1.2.92). Shylock is hated by Antonio's friends for his repeated lament over the lovers' getaway: "My own flesh and blood to rebel!" (3.1.34, 37, 38 f.). In his vindictive code of an-eye-for-an-eye, this could be a providential avengement upon his scheme to exact the pound of Antonio's flesh, while neglecting the blood. Jessica's rejection may be contrasted with Portia's acceptance of her defunct father's legalisms. Rather than undergo the ordeal of the caskets, Lorenzo has merely to catch the casket of jewels tossed down by Jessica (2.6.33). Shylock's immediate reactions, as reported, verge on sheer bathos. Since he equates his daughter with his ducats, and her apostasy with his precious stones, the Venetian boys seem justified in jeering at his outcries (3.8.15 ff.). When we see and hear him at first hand, he is oscillating grotesquely between grief over his losses and joy over Antonio's, equating his lost diamond with the curse upon his race, and calling simultaneously for the return of the booty and for Jessica's demise (3.1.85–90). These monetary reductions cannot seriously have been meant to engage our sympathies.

Yet, when he learns that Jessica has frivolously bartered away his turquoise ring for a monkey, Shakespeare accords him one touch of common humanity, wryly voiced: ". . . I had it of Leah when I was a bachelor. I would not have given it for a wilderness of monkeys" (121–23).

For an instant we are startled by a glimpse of Shylock as a loving husband, even as we glimpse the ghost of a dutiful daughter in Lady Macbeth's hesitation at Duncan's fatal bedside: "Had he not resembled / My father as he slept, I had done't." Jessica has been criticized severely as a minx, a shameless hussy, the most undutiful of daughters, and Lorenzo has fared no better for supposedly leading her astray. Thematically she reverses the dark legend of the Jew's daughter, utilized to decoy Christian youths toward their ritual murder, which flowers into a miracle in the narration of Chaucer's Prioress or the ballads about Saint Hugh of Lincoln. Shakespeare had a nearer precedent in Marlowe's *Jew of Malta,* where Abigail revolts against her plight, is converted to Christianity, and becomes one of her father's innumerable victims. Barabas, the latter, can be taken as the cynical measure of Shylock's credibility, since his monstrous vendetta is wholly animated by the lust for gold and for the power it confers. His amoral and esthetic paean—"O girl! O gold! O beauty! O my bliss!"—is grimly echoed by Shylock's jeremiad over his daughter and his ducats.

Jessica would suffer by comparison with the pathetic Abigail, if *The Merchant of Venice* were a tragedy. But since it was framed to be a comedy, albeit with a difference, she need not be blamed for surviving to grace the charmed circle of Belmont. Since Shakespeare has treated her sympathetically, we ought not to treat her antipathetically unless we are prepared to censure him. When her prototypes—in works of fiction that must have influenced him—help themselves at the expense of their usurer-fathers, they are turning ill-gotten gains into merited dowries. Her scriptural precursor was Rachel, in the book of Genesis, stealing the paternal effigies. Jessica's flight is essentially a liberation and not a desertion, though it may not seem to be so in the light of latterday broad-mindedness. From a strictly historical viewpoint, she has been an infidel, born and bred outside the one true faith, and therefore ineligible for salvation. Yet the Christians seem to accept her as an *anima naturaliter christiana;* and Gratiano, with a pun on *Gentile,* declares her "a gentle, and no Jew" (2.5.51). Her baptism, the prerequisite of marriage to Lorenzo, will assure her progress through this world into the next. Such presumptions may not jibe with ours, and certainly do not accord with Shylock's. Antonio's high-minded stipulation, that "he presently become a Christian," is not likely to have been received as a spiritual favor (4.1.387).

With due respect for intellectual background, we should not overstress it to the neglect of dramatic foreground. In characterizing a Jewish outlook and idiom, Shakespeare drew concretely on the Old Testament here and there. But it asks for too much from Belmont, in any excepting the most loosely general terms, to argue that act 5 is imbued with the spirit of the New Testament. A current tendency of criticism, and of production as well, seeks to invest even Shakespeare's lighter comedies with an aura of solemnity. Though *The Merchant of Venice* is by no means light in its implications, it still adheres to the nature of the comic genre by indulging the pleasure principle, which is destined to enjoy the final triumph. Though Jessica and Lorenzo cannot be absolved from the taints of frivolity and extravagance, these are qualities that thrive in the purlieus of high comedy. Lorenzo's metaphor, "For the close night doth play the runaway," has been acted out in the haste of their miniature balcony scene (2.6.47). United with her in the security and serenity of Portia's country estate, he will retrospectively evoke that runaway evening:

> In such a night
> Did Jessica steal from the wealthy Jew,
> And with an unthrift love did run from Venice
> As far as Belmont.
>
> (5.1.14–17)

The verb *steal* is his ambiguous acknowledgment that, in their stealthy departure they have burglarized Shylock's ghetto dwelling. And Jessica, in her gently mocking rejoinder, linking crime and religion with love in a metaphysical conceit, will take note of Lorenzo's gallantry, "Stealing her soul with many vows of faith" (19).

The bitterest blow to fall upon Shylock has been their "unthrift love." Wider than the religious distance between them is the opposition between that inveterate miser and this pair of spendthrifts who can lavish fourscore of his austerely hoarded ducats upon a single frolicsome occasion. Comedy, opposed to the asceticism of hoarding, sides implicitly with the hedonism of spending: with the handout as opposed to the hold-in. Liberality, in Aristotelian ethics, is defined as a mean between the extremes of avarice and prodigality. Prodigality, though rather a vice than a virtue, can be construed as the amiable weakness of beautiful people. Bassanio has embarked upon his speculative adventure because his debts have become "something too prodigal" (1.1.129). Shylock tolerates his hospitality, contrary to ethnic principles, so that he may ambiguously and ominously "feed upon / The prodigal Christian" (2.5.14 f.). Antonio, when facing his apparent losses at sea, is prematurely and unjustly stigmatized by Shylock as "a bankrout, a prodigal" (3.1.44 f.). Gratiano, embroidering on the parable, has likened the fortunes of love to those of a maritime enterprise:

> How like a younger or a prodigal
> The scarfed bark puts from her native bay,
> Hugg'd and embraced by the strumpet wind!

This fickle metaphor proceeds to veer about and present, for a crucial interval, a portent of failure:

How like the prodigal doth she return,
With over-weather'd ribs and ragged sails,
Lean, rent, and beggar'd by the strumpet wind!

(2.6.14–19)

There can and will be further and happier fluctuations in the long run. The
wind, ancillary to the bitch-goddess Fortune, will change again. In the
mean time enough has been adumbrated to prepare the way for a season of
homecoming, forgiveness, and fatted calf.

The setting for that reunion has been located by most editors in "the
avenue before Portia's house"—*avenue* in its horticultural aspect.
Theobald would specify "a Grove or Green place"; and the script makes
clear that the resident lovers are waiting there to welcome the returning
parties on, we might well imagine, a terrace of some sort. A garden, we are
never allowed to forget, symbolizes the conceptual norm of Shakespeare's
imagery. "Our bodies are our gardens," says Iago. Flowers provide an
emblematic language for Ophelia's madness, weeds for Lear's. A literal
gardener, in *Richard II,* propounds an allegorical object lesson in state-
craft for "our sea-walled garden," England. The Wars of the Roses break
out when Yorkists and Lancastrians angrily pluck their floral emblems in
the Temple Garden. Jack Cade's rebellion peters out when the rebel leader
is run to earth in a peaceful Kentish garden. The Duke of Burgundy points
a concluding moral in *Henry V:* vanquished France is "this best garden of
the world," whose cultivation should bring peace and plenty—a hopeful
prospect not to be attained. Since it is past nightfall in Portia's garden, no
attempt is made to describe the foliage; when Oberon evoked the wild
thyme and nodding violets on the bank where Titania lay asleep, the
resulting sensation was as tactile and olfactory as it was visual. Here the
main problem for Shakespeare was to convey an impression of nighttime
while the performance was taking place in the daytime.

It may have neutralized disparities for Lorenzo to begin the scene by
observing "The moon shines bright" (5.1.1). This is the starting point of
the lyrical nightpiece together, "In such a night as this . . . ," invoking
classic myths of moonlit assignations. Its counterpart in *Romeo and Juliet*
is an *aubade,* the duet between lovers parting at dawn, under the dialec-
tical patronage of the lark and the nightingale. The literary examples cited
by Lorenzo and Jessica, which derive from Chaucer and Ovid, prove to be
more ominous than encouraging. Troilus and Cressida would become the
most problematic of Shakespeare's couples. Pyramus and Thisbe he had
lately been reducing to burlesque in *A Midsummer Night's Dream* and
transmuting into tragedy in *Romeo and Juliet*. Dido, if she was one of
Cupid's saints, had become a martyr. Medea was a *femme fatale* with a
fearsome record, whose nocturnal rendezvous with Jason was not a tryst

but a spell of ghoulish witchcraft. When Berlioz was writing his libretto for *The Trojans,* he would stray from its Virgilian source to his cherished Shakespeare and base the lyrics for his love duet on this exchange of Jessica's and Lorenzo's. Since the singers are Dido and Aeneas, they cannot instance themselves, but they can invoke—more appropriately than Thisbe and Medea—Venus and Diana. One set of role models is twice called upon. "In such a night," Lorenzo whispers,

> Troilus methinks mounted the Troyan walls
> And sigh'd his soul toward the Grecian tents,
> Where Cressid lay that night.
>
> (3–6)

This is much less auspicious than the operatic allusion, since she has betrayed him with Diomedes, and he is full of jealousy and sorrow, whereas Aeneas pictures the lover awaiting his beloved in the joyous expectation of fulfilment:

> *Par une telle nuit, fou d'amour et de foie,*
> *Troïlus vint attendre aux pieds des murs de Troie*
> *La belle Cresside.*

The auspices look better, but the outcome will be tragic, whereas the omens in *The Merchant of Venice* are passing clouds in a benevolent sky. When Rosalind, disguised as a pert youth, instances "the patterns of love" in *As You Like It,* she too cites Troilus along with the equally ill-starred Leander. Her sardonic point is that, although they died, it was "not for love." Love may be a universal experience, but it can be less exalting than such romantics as Orlando naively profess. So Jessica and Lorenzo, having striven to "out-night" one another, terminate their litany with an exchange of good-humored mutual reservations (23). Functionally, as the stagewise Granville-Barker could show, their antiphonal stanzas have sustained the continuity while Portia and Nerissa were changing back from lawyers' robes to feminine attire.

Jessica and Lorenzo are symmetrically interrupted by the messenger Stephano, with his alibi for the arrival of Portia after her pretended pilgrimage, and by the redomesticated Gobbo, mimicking the posthorn that has heralded the coming of Bassanio. There is a brief interlude of anticipation, filled by Lorenzo:

> How sweet the moonlight sleeps upon this bank!
> Here will we sit, and let the sounds of music
> Creep in our ears. Soft stillness and the night
> Become the touches of sweet harmony.
>
> (54–57)

What stays visible, upward not earthward, is seen in configurations of darkness and light: the sky and the stars, "the floor of heaven" and the "patens of bright gold" (58, 59) that shine through it. These are synesthetically transposed into aural images; and if the singing of angelic choirs is inaudible to mortal ears, like the music of the spheres, corporeal musicians can be summoned to "wake Diana with a hymn" (66). The moon—another amorous predecessor, sleeping with Endymion—must by now have discreetly passed behind a cloud (109). The intensive lyricism of this act, composed wholly in verse, with sound effects and an orchestral nocturne, makes it an appropriate sounding board for Shakespeare's tribute to "the sweet power of music" (79). Jessica's confession, "I am never merry when I hear sweet music," contributes to the bittersweet mood of the play (69). And Lorenzo's ensuing eulogy draws upon both Orphic and Pythagorean traditions to affirm the civilizing functions of harmony and to portend a harmonious resolution. Some of the critics' efforts to put him down as a mere wastrel should be weighed against his humane criterion:

> The man that hath no music in himself,
> Nor is not moved with concord of sweet sounds,
> Is fit for treasons, stratagems, and spoils . . .
> Let no such man be trusted.
>
> (83–88)

Shylock happens to be such a man, who, in his suspicion of the masked revellers, has admonished Jessica against "the drum / And the vile squealing of the wry-neck'd fife" (2.5.29, 30). And though for him the bagpipe exemplifies an irrational dislike, it could likewise represent the harsh cacophony of his own temperament (4.1.49, 56).

The scenes at Belmont, on the other hand, are counterpointed by melodious fanfares and enhanced with musical accompaniment at two turning points: Bassanio's decision and Portia's reentry. It is significant that although Shakespeare fondly and frequently alludes to music throughout his work, he uses the word itself in *The Merchant of Venice* more often than anywhere else: fifteen times, eleven of them in the last act alone. Browsing through Professor Spevack's concordance affords a convenient and suggestive method of tracing Shakespeare's thematic concerns, as they have been verbally orchestrated. Among the other words we note that reach their highest frequency in this play are *Jew* (69 times), *bond* (39), *ring* (38), *choose* (35), *judge* (24), *flesh* (23), *Christian* (22), *forfeit/forfeiture* (19), *casket* (13), and *hazard* (11). The incidence is high with *law* (19), *justice* (15), and *mercy* (13), yet not as high as in *Measure for Measure*, where comparable issues are at stake (29, 26, and 16 respectively). All of these are key words instrumental to the plot, denoting its situations and interactions. The excessive repetition of the brusque mono-syllable *Jew,* rasping across the rift that divides the dramatis personae, emphasizes the alien status of Shylock and the routine contempt of his interlocutors. But the iteration of *music* comes as an extra embellishment, not less welcome because it transposes the mode.

After the discords of Venice we arrive at the concord of Belmont. The Venetian masque was hastily dropped with the suburban flight of act 2; the celebration over the offstage marriages in act 3 had to be put off for the litigation of act 4. Ordeals are duly overtaken by revels, with the grand finale of act 5, carrying out the mischievous scenario that Portia has spontaneously devised while pursuing her legal career. Day is the time for affairs of business, night for escapades of imagination. It is dark when she enters, but not too dark, no more than "the daylight sick" (5.1.124). Her colloquy with Nerissa, like the preceding repartee of Jessica and Lorenzo, trips along from images of light to those of sound. Relativistic com-parisons—beginning with the moon and the candle, moving on to the lark and the crow and other birds, and culminating in the day and the night—lead into a brittle sequence of sententious quips.

> How far this little candle throws his beams!
> So shines a good deed in a naughty world.
>
> (90 f.)

This motif of glimmering through the darkness, figuratively as well as physically, pervades the entire scene. "Everything in its season" is the burden of her remarks, signalizing both the round of the seasons and their seasoning effect upon those who have weathered them (107 f.). Gradually she is discerned and greeted by Lorenzo, just as the trumpet announced the entrance of Bassanio's party. Gradually picking up her train of thought, he hails her with a trope of solar brilliance. She acknowledges the stan-dard compliment with a standard quibble on *light,* connoting loose be-havior as well as illumination, and thereby interjecting a coquettish hint of marital infidelity (129–31).

He proceeds to introduce the guest of honor, Antonio, who has cele-brated his acquittal by crossing from Venice to Belmont: "the man . . . / To whom I am so infinitely bound." Bassanio has always been *attached* to Antonio; moreover, he is now doubly *indebted* to him, in the deepest conceivable sense; and Portia's reply adds a trenchant reminder of the contract in the recent law case:

> You should in all sense be much bound to him,
> For as I hear he was much bound for you.
>
> (134–37)

The energy of the monosyllables is reinforced by the parallellism of the lines, the catchword occupying the same position in both and controlling the transposition from "him" to "you." We are reminded of Shylock's laconic and equivocal answer to Bassanio at the very outset: "Antonio shall become bound, well" (1.3.6). At the height of his pride, when he had all but succeeded in fatally binding Antonio, Shylock rebuffed Bassanio's appeal by asserting his own independence: "I am not bound to please thee with my answers" (4.1.65). His insistence on the bond reechoed through the court, accentuated by that device which the rhetoricians term *epistrophe,* the repeated locution at the end of a line. "Is it so nominated in the bond" (259)? Could any rhetorical question have been more implacable? Shylock's household wisdom was summed up when he ordered Jessica to shut the doors:

> Fast bind, fast find—
> A proverb never stale in thrifty mind.
>
> (2.5.54 f.)

But, for better and worse, she will not bind and he will not find. He has no more luck in shutting out the world, in holding Jessica and his goods bound fast, than he will have in entrapping Antonio. She has not loved her father, as Cordelia loves Lear, "according to my bond"; she rejects, like Goneril and Regan, "the bond of childhood," her family ties; yet Jessica's recoil has been warranted by overriding considerations.

Portia's gracious reception of Antonio is cut short by the farcical outburst between Nerissa and Gratiano. As the young lawyer Balthazar, she has demanded Bassanio's ring for her fee. Gratiano has been his emissary in reluctantly yielding it up; and his corresponding transaction with Nerissa, as the sham law clerk, has been effectuated behind the scenes. It is fitting—and it builds up the humorous progression—that Portia should stand above the battle judiciously, until Gratiano's self-defense exposes her misplaced confidence in Bassanio. His effort to allay her mock-suspicion sets them off on what might be called a blank-verse *pas de deux.* "Sweet Portia," he pleads,

> If you did know to whom I gave the ring,
> If you did know for whom I gave the ring,
> And would conceive for what I gave the ring,
> And how unwillingly I left the ring,
> When nought would be accepted but the ring,
> You would abate the strength of your displeasure.

Since she is actually the person to whom he gave the ring, she well knows for whom and for what it was given, and with what reluctance. It is he who is ironically unaware that she knows, that she was the civil doctor, and that she has the ring—whose erstwhile disappearance is deftly stressed by the terminal syllables in a rising succession of conditional clauses. But she can also out-ring him, epistrophe for epistrophe, as fluently as she has out-matched the spokesmen of masculine jurisprudence:

> If you had known the virtue of the ring,
> Or half her worthiness that gave the ring,
> Or your own honor to contain the ring,
> You would not then have parted with the ring.
>
> (192–202)

Momentarily it seems as if Shakespeare were inviting the director to become a choreographer. The dancing is more formal in the finales of many other comedies, and the Elizabethan theater regularly featured song-and-dance afterpieces known as "jigs." But I recall a eurythmic blocking of this passage where Portia turned her back and promenaded the stage, followed at several paces by Bassanio, each of them taking a single step per line and pausing at every repetition of *ring.* At a more psychological level, the gamesmanship resembles the last-act maneuvres in *The Marriage of Figaro,* another garden scene at night both in the comedy of Beaumarchais and the opera of Da Ponte and Mozart, where the men are absurdly hoodwinked by the mistaken identities of the women.

Gratiano has operated as a zany to Bassanio, the jocular subaltern who goes through the same motions as his mentor with a parodic exaggeration. From the beginning he elected to "play the fool," when Antonio declared his own part to be "a sad one" upon the world's stage (1.1.79). Bassanio rebuked that "skipping spirit" for being "too wild, too rude, and bold of voice" (2.2.187, 181). Gratiano's conversational style, "an infinite deal of nothing," bears a generic resemblance to that of Shakespeare's other free-speakers: Mercutio, Berowne, Benedick, and in another key Hotspur (1.1.112). In Gratiano's *contretemps* with Nerissa, he parries her suspicions about the missing ring by describing its recipient—herself in her disguise—as "a little scrubbed boy" (5.1.162). Her tactic is to push the accusation, which no one could appreciate better than she, that this boy was a woman: "The clerk will ne'er wear hair on's face that had it" (144). Portia's equivocations to Bassanio go farther, and express a resolve to get even by a reciprocal adultery: "I'll have that doctor for my bedfellow"— that doctor being, in actuality, her virginal self (233). Nor does she deny herself anything in saying: "By heaven, I will ne'er come in your bed / Until I see the ring" (190 f.). Such conjugal tests continually and increasingly bring home to us the awareness that these marriages have yet to be consummated, that bed lies ahead.

It is Antonio, Antonio unbound, lone bachelor in the presence of three couples newly united by "love's bonds," who intervenes to halt the flirtatious charade (2.6.6). Typically, he characterizes himself as "th'unhappy subject of these quarrels" (5.1.237). It was he who opened the play on a note of sadness: "In sooth I know not why I am so sad" (1.1.1). In linking his free-floating anxiety with the fortunes of his ships at sea, Salerio and Solanio then painted an incidental picture of his mercantile position. That might well have served to diagnose a justifiable premonition, but Antonio rejected the motive, as he did the suggestion of love. Conscious of his moody role, like Jaques, who would expatiate upon their simile of the *theatrum mundi,* he cultivates a special melancholy of his own. Among his cohort of friends, who warmly attest his moral and fiscal worth, he reserves a unique affection for Bassanio. "I think he only loves the world for him," Solanio remarks (2.8.50). When Antonio philosophically accepts the unrelenting decree, he addresses his farewell to Bassanio, requesting him to tell his new wife about it,

> And when the tale is told, bid her be the judge
> Whether Bassanio had not once a love.

(4.1.276 f.)

This is the point at which Bassanio, seconded by Gratiano as usual, wishes that his wife could be traded for Antonio's life, prompting dryly appropriate comments from Portia and Nerissa and a caustic aside from Shylock reflecting against his new son-in-law: "These are the Christian husbands" (295). Portia—who is the judge right now—has beforehand, on the basis of Lorenzo's report, accepted Antonio as "the bosom lover of my lord" (3.4.17). Modern readers have sometimes scented a homosexual relation. That supposition would not explain why Bassanio courted Portia, or why Antonio backed the courtship so generously. "Greater love hath no man than this . . ." But the mortal sacrifice envisioned by the Gospel of Saint John altogether transcended sexuality. Though Antonio is not a saint, he seems to live vicariously, ready to die for the happiness of another. *The Merchant of Venice* does not strain the issue of love versus friendship, as do *The Two Gentlemen of Verona* and the *Sonnets,* though it may put some strain on our credulity.

   Yet if we suspend our disbelief in the vagaries of male impersonation, we ought not to balk too much at milder improbabilities. Shakespeare had the convention of boy actors so well in hand that he liked to mock it, and Portia gayly seizes the chance to burlesque the other sex: "these bragging Jacks" (3.4.77). Helena, her opposite number in *All's Well That Ends Well,* likewise scores a professional success, after disguising herself as a physician, and wins her errant husband's ring through a less innocent wile than Portia's, the bed-trick. The loan of a ring was among the traditional devices for misunderstanding in *The Comedy of Errors.* Jessica's romance with Lorenzo is colored with touches of the carnivalesque. Since the actual wooing of Portia must be conducted as a ceremonial, there has been little opportunity for open flirtation until this final episode. Portia has been more and more effectually in charge, pulling all the strings like Rosalind in *As You Like It*. Nominally she may have deprecated herself as an unschooled girl and made Bassanio lord and master of her person and property with the gift of the ring. But—mistress of it once more—she makes a fool of him by her fifth-act joke, after having outwitted the males by her fourth-act verdict. There should be no feminist capitulation for her, as there was for Katherina in *The Taming of the Shrew*.

When Antonio pleads with Portia, offering "to be bound again" as security for his friend, she precipitates the denouement by producing the bone of contention (5.1.251). It is she who presides over the recognition scene, clearing up the misunderstandings and handing out the prizes. Antonio's argosies have come safe to harbor after all, though how she obtained the good news will remain her secret forever. And, when Nerissa informs Jessica and Lorenzo of Shylock's bequest, Lorenzo's response is becomingly biblical: "Fair ladies, you drop manna in the way / Of starving people" (294 f.). Threats of cuckoldry are dissolved in jests, for Bassanio and Gratiano, with the disclosure that their shadowy rivals have been their own wives incognito. Within two hours the night—such a night!—will be over. To suggest that these lovers might just as well stay up through another day, and thus delay the consummation further, is no more than teasing. Conventionally, the happy endings of comedy have been formalized by revelry, by feasts or dances with a mating or betrothal in view: from the *gamos* of Aristophanes, with its phallic procession, to the tutelary blessing of the god Hymen for the four assorted couples in *As You Like It*. Here, since the weddings have already taken place, it is high time for the privacy of the bridal chamber.

There, between the postponed embraces, the spouses can complete their "inter'gatories," mutually filling in the details by reverting metaphorically to the cross-questioning of the courtroom (298). As they retire into the villa, two by two, extinguishing the candles in the garden, Antonio remains the lonely celibate, observably less at home in Belmont than in Venice. Like the melancholy Jaques—and not unlike the unpartnered Bunthorne in *Patience*—he is the odd man out, who must conclude: "I am for other than dancing measures." The dialogue has waxed increasingly erotic, charging the air with double entendres, and the saltiest diction has been Gratiano's. Under the misapprehension that Nerissa may have regained the ring by dalliance with her alter ego, he has sworn to "mar the young clerk's pen" (237). Revelation is metamorphosis; that boy—it transpires—was a girl, his girl; and his attitude shifts from aggressiveness to protectiveness. Yet he lapses, with his ultimate couplet, into another genital innuendo:

> Well, while I live I'll fear no other thing
> So sore, as keeping safe Nerissa's ring.

(306 f.)

In this context it might not be improper to remember the fabliau of Hans Carvel's ring. That became available in English through the ribald poem of Matthew Prior, adapted from the *Contes* of La Fontaine; but it could be read during the Renaissance in versions by Rabelais, Ariosto, and others; and it is one of those facetious anecdotes that was bound to be passed along by word of mouth. Therein an old and cold jeweller takes a young and promiscuous wife. He is advised by the Devil how to curb her promiscuity: by permanently keeping his third finger encircled within her. Gratiano, to be sure, may imply that there are other and better ways of accomplishing that purpose. Shakespeare's own high-spirited wordplay loses no occasion for reminding us that men are males, that women are females, and *vive la différence!* The last word is the key word that brings us back to the digital symbol of the conjugal bond. The ring itself, the tie that binds, has also been proposed as a legal fee, in a milieu where ducats are worth their weight in daughters and where a pound of flesh could be the contractual consideration for three thousand ducats. Thus, as Barbara Lewalski has argued on other grounds, "The ring episode is, in a sense, a comic parody of the trial scene."

In concern over Portia's and Nerissa's rings, we have nearly forgotten Leah's ring and what it signified to her husband if not her daughter. Why have these revels been staged, if not to put Shylock out of our minds, to awaken us from the throes of a nightmare? Yet, with Shakespeare, the query always lingers: which is the reality, which the dream? Shylock the killjoy must be scoffed out of court; Shylock the spoilsport must be exorcised from the realm of comic euphoria. We ought not to sentimentalize this self-chosen scapegoat. Olivia can afford a soft valediction for Malvolio in *Twelfth Night:* "He hath been most notoriously abus'd." But he must go, and go he does, impenitently and ineffectually vengeful: "I'll be reveng'd on the whole pack of you." We waste no grief on him—why so much grief over Shylock? "He doesn't cast a shadow sufficiently strong," in Edwin Booth's opinion, "to contrast with the sunshine of the comedy." Other actors, however, have tried to exalt him into a tragic hero. Erich Auerbach would situate him at the borderline, an odd pariah originating in farce, voicing certain humanitarian ideas that have acquired a deeper resonance during later centuries, yet finally capitulating as a "duped devil" ("geprellter Teufel") before the "careless Olympian serenity" ("achtlos olympische Heiterkeit") of fairytale motifs and tender blandishments.

"To make him a tragic hero . . . ," Auerbach has written, "clashes with the whole dramatic economy." Others would contend that, through the figure of Shylock, such a clash is built into the drama. Dr. Johnson praised "the union of two actions in one event." So did Bertolt Brecht, though from quite another dramaturgical standpoint. Unity, which Brecht might not have emphasized, depends on Shylock's total exclusion from act 5. He is not even named, except for Portia's mention of "the rich Jew" and the reversion of his fortune "after his death" (292 f.). Yet, because the characterization has conveyed so powerful an impact, his shadow has continued to haunt the sunny purlieus of Belmont. In the French adaptation performed by the actor-director Firmin Gémier, Shylock chilled the honeymoon by making an untimely reappearance in Portia's garden. To his conventional attributes—the hooked nose, the forked beard, the red curls, the jewelled fingers, the pantaloon's cap, the tribal gabardine—Gémier added a hangman's noose. The intrusion was an unwarrantable distortion, but it all too heavily underlined a besetting Shakespearean point: that happiness, in one way or another, is seldom unconnected with suffering. Joy cannot be unconfined, when such joylessness can still be humanly instigated. But to pursue that insight, as Barber suggested, would require an additional play.

And significantly, in spite of its carefully planned conclusion, this play has given rise to a train of sequels, most of them dedicated to the vindication of Shylock. A sense of unfinished business seems to have led the Irish playwright St. John Ervine to a disillusioning postlude, *The Lady of Belmont,* wherein—though Shylock makes a painless financial comeback—the wedded lovers succumb to boredom or resort to adultery ten years afterward. Maurice Schwartz, in *Shylock and His Daughter,* grounded upon a post-Nazi Hebrew novel, relocated characters within the ghetto of Venice and tried to work out an uneasy reconciliation. One of the objections to comedy, and to most fiction, is that real human beings can never count on living happily ever after. Since this truism is intimated by *The Merchant of Venice,* it looks beyond its genre. Some may perceive in it, with W. H. Auden, "as much a problem play as one by Ibsen or Shaw." Such approaches, while sharpening its focus, have narrowed its range. Granted, the problems it raises for us were too easily, and factitiously, solved by the ideologies and conventions of Shakespeare's day. His gift for humanizing and intensifying his subject matter projected it into an unforeseeable future, so that we can now look back at it and consider it timely. By the same token, it is subject to continuing vicissitude, and no problem it broaches can expect a final solution.

Mixed Prose-Verse Scenes in Shakespearean Tragedy

Jonas Barish

My innocuous title may not be quite so innocent as it looks. It conceals at least one booby trap. For setting aside the problem of what constitutes a scene—by which I here mean any chunk of action that feels like a unit, whether or not it corresponds to what classical printers and editors would have called a scene—what is prose? what is verse? and how do we recognize a mixture of the two?[1]

These questions take us into a minefield. Paul Bertram, in his recent study, *White Spaces in Shakespeare,* has reminded us sharply of the extent to which our standard editions depart form the original texts in the matter of lineation, especially in their regularizing of what appear in folio or quarto as short lines of verse or simple prose into ordered pentameters, often echelonned across the page in bits and pieces, assigned to two or more speakers, so as to produce the neatly patterned look desiderated by neoclassic editors.[2] Our editions also contain numerous instances of the conversion of verse into prose, though Bertram rather neglects these. Bertram does not on the whole reckon seriously enough with the frequency with which most of us would endorse without protest the long-standing editorial consensus on such matters. In *Romeo and Juliet,* to take one instance, we have some striking sequences of verse—always so printed by modern editors—that appear in both Q2 (the basic text) and F as prose: the Nurse's reminiscences about Juliet's childhood for one, Mercutio's Queen Mab fantasy for another. In neither of these cases can we miss hearing the iambic rhythm. We even hear it distinctly as pentameter, despite the fact that the eye is traveling over what typographically appears to be prose. The Nurse's speech, when reordered, contains a few rough lines amid the regular ones, but most of it is so plainly stamped as blank verse that it would be absurd to treat it otherwise merely in obedience to what may have been a blundering copyist, or a thick-eared scribe, or a heedless compositor. The same goes doubly for Mercutio's speech. Later, in the musician's scene following Juliet's mock death, we have the reverse situation: a passage nowadays always printed as prose, which in the early texts appears as verse, but verse so disjointed and invertebrate—so hopeless, indeed, *as* verse—that one is forced to assume either mischief or incompetence on the part of one agent or another in the line of transmission. In short, although Bertram may be largely correct in saying (with respect to his own favored specimen from *Antony and Cleopatra*) that "the Folio mixture of verse and prose provides our only authoritative source for the rhythms in which the speeches may be realized" (p. 30), it is also as clearly the case that neither the Folio nor the good Quartos, important and even primary as they are, may be taken as gospel. Pope's comment on the Folio editors, that "prose from verse they did not know,"[3] cannot indeed be altogether wrong.

If this is so, if we may not blindly trust *either* the original text *or* the editors from Pope onward who have labored to regularize and to pentameterize the verse, whom do we trust? What is the court of last appeal? The answer must be, I believe, our own ears, with whatever danger of subjective variation that may imply. What we hear as verse, however printed, must be felt as verse, so laid out on the page, and so recited. What we will not find, necessarily, when we apply this text, are the neat columns of pentameter lines sought by Pope and his followers, still less the beautiful marching across the page of fractions of a verse line distributed among two or more speakers. What we *will* find is the occasionally light, occasionally insistent iambic beat, which must be honored as such. Bertram's own prize exhibit from *Antony and Cleopatra* seems to me to speak as eloquently against his conclusion as it does for it. That is, it seems strongly to invite the very editorial regularizing that Bertram regards as officious tampering. Consider:

Cleopatra. Where is the Fellow?
Alexas. Halfe afeard to come.
Cleopatra. Go too, go too: Come hither Sir. *Enter the Messenger as before.*
Alexas. Good Maiestie: *Herod* of Iury dare not looke vpon you, but when you are well pleas'd.
Cleopatra. That *Herods* head Ile haue: but how? When *Anthony* is gone, through whom I might commaund it: Come thou neere.
Messenger. Most gratious Maiestie.
Cleopatra. Did'st thou behold *Octauia?*
Messenger. I dread Queene.
Cleopatra. Where?
Messenger. Madam in Rome, I lookt her in the face: and saw her led betweene her Brother, and *Marke Anthony.*

(1621–35)[4]

Now it seems to me that from the very beginning of this we sense a distinct iambic pulse. "Whére is the Féllow? Hálfe afeárd to cóme" constitutes a perfect iambic line (with or without an initial trochaic substitution). To try to make it sound like prose would be absurd. And so with most of the passage. Consider, for instance: "That *Hérods* héad Ile háue: but hów? When Ánthoný is góne, through whóm I míght commáund it." Or, even more emphatically: "Mádam in Róme, I lóokt her ín the fáce: and sáw her léd betwéene her Bróther, ánd *Márke Ánthoný*." Regardless of whether we *see* these speeches as verse, and regardless especially of whether we attempt to cut them into strips of pentameter, we feel the iambic pulsation, which persists in the lines that follow until we reach a point at which the Folio itself is printing the scene as verse. I am not at all sure therefore that the editorial convention that converts these lines into verse for the eye does not have considerable justification. If it tends to lay things out too neatly, it also has the virtue of alerting us to the underlying rhythm.

If we inspect the ten lines from the 1860s Cambridge edition declared by Bertram to be unscannable as iambic pentameter, we find that in fact all are respectably iambic. Three, however, are hexameters, two are tetrameters, and three are trimeters. Since late Shakespearean verse, among its other irregularities, abounds in hypermetric lines and in short lines, there is no need to be unnerved by these syllabic variations or to regard them as eccentric. As for the remaining two lines, both scan normally with only insignificant departures from iambic strictness: line 1662–63, "For the móst part tóo, they are fóolish thát are só," contains an extra light syllable in its first foot, and an elision ("they'are") in its third foot, while line 1680–81, "I haue óne thing móre to áske him yét good *Chármian,*" contains another elision ("I'haue") and a feminine ending (or perhaps a sixth foot, counting *Charmian* as trisyllable). Neither presents the slightest difficulty, and only a zeal for iambic straitjacketing could disqualify them as perfectly staple instances of blank verse.

It may be that from time to time in the edited texts we find patches of what Stephen Orgel has termed "typographical fantasia,"[5] but that may mean no more than that editors are imperfect creatures working over puzzling materials and subject to error. The fact is, as Fredson Bowers has shown with magisterial amplitude and meticulousness, that patient analysis reveals a number of repeated patterns in the handling of short lines in the early texts and in the way short lines combine to form standard pentameters.[6] An implicit system seems to be at work, and the editorial custom of relineation, however often faulty in detail or excessive in its application, corresponds to something real in Shakespearean writing. Given the lateness of *Antony* in the canon, I would view the present scene as a fairly normal stretch of late Shakespearean verse, not as a "mixture of verse and prose." It seems doubtful that any of it could be rendered convincingly as prose, since to do so would require strenuously *avoiding* the iambic rhythm that rules it pretty much throughout. Whether parts of it were left *looking* like a mixture when set on the page because of Shakespeare's own inattentiveness or that of the compositor or intervening copyist, it is probably impossible to know. And what Philip Brockbank says concerning G. B. Harrison's Penguin edition, which reproduces F's lineation slavishly, would apply to the situations we are concerned with. Folio lineation, in *Coriolanus,* at least—or, more precisely, the lineation of Compositor A—"shows a reluctance to detach words from clauses at the end of a line, and . . . each line pauses on a punctuation mark. Because it attends to syntactical units rather than to metrical ones, it conveys the speech movement with clarity and emphasis (it is not hard to imagine actors' parts written out in this fashion), but it forfeits the measure."[7] Or, in other words, excessive coincidence of the line unit with the syntactic unit tends to slur over metrical considerations. The grammar of a speech may be made more distinct, but some of its music may be lost. And this would apply no less, one would think, to places where prose and verse come together, and where we find genuine ambiguities, where neither the text nor the reader's ear affords certainty, where Shakespeare seems to be working in a kind of limbo or intermediate region between prose and verse, where we cannot say with confidence which of the two we are encountering at a given moment.

Such moments of indeterminacy tend to occur most often in mixed prose-verse scenes, but the alternations in such scenes may also be fairly clear-cut, however the text is printed. In the opening moments of *Julius Caesar,* the tribunes, Murellus and Flavius, are scolding the holiday-making citizens in a taut, angry blank verse, while the commoners answer them in a deliberately jocose, slack-jawed prose:

> *Murellus.* You sir, what Trade are you?
> *Cobbler.* Truely Sir, in respect of a fine Workman, I am but as you would
>   say, a Cobler.
> *Murellus.* But what Trade art thou? Answer me directly.
> *Cobbler.* A Trade Sir, that I hope I may vse, with a safe Conscience,
>   which is indeed Sir, a Mender of bad soules.
> *Flavius.* What Trade thou knaue? Thou naughty knaue, what Trade?
> *Cobbler.* Nay I beseech you Sir, be not out with me: yet if you be out Sir,
>   I can mend you.
> *Murellus.* What mean'st thou by that? Mend mee, thou sawcy Fellow?
> *Cobbler.* Why sir, Cobble you.
>
>   (13–25)

And so forth. Here we have a sharp collision between the stinging utterance of the verse speakers and the looser, more ambling utterance of the other. Although Murellus's and Flavius's speeches are given (or seem to be given) as prose in the Folio[8] and belong to a text generally regarded as exceptionally clean—printed from tidy copy, perhaps a scribal transcript of authorial foul papers later used as a promptbook—[9] recent editors, rightly I believe, and especially in view of 5–13 and 33–34, prefer to treat them as verse. Shakespeare seems consciously to be alternating short speeches in prose and verse, so that the actors who speak them and the readers sounding them in their minds' ears must bring out the distinction. I would not call this a case of indeterminacy, but merely of the neglect of someone in the line of transmission to set down clearly what Shakespeare had in mind—perhaps Shakespeare himself.

Something similar occurs, I think, in scene 2 of *Antony and Cleopatra.* Here Cleopatra's maids, together with others of her household, are questioning the Soothsayer. The scene, lasting until Cleopatra's entrance (80–155), appears entirely as prose in F, again the only text. Yet all modern editions, correctly as I think, find a deliberate contrast between the giggling jocosity of Iras and Charmian, in prose, and the portentous, oracular blank verse of the Soothsayer. Enobarbus, the chameleon character, or split personality, who can inhabit both Roman and Egyptian worlds comfortably but is ultimately torn apart between them, speaks only twice in the course of the scene, first in verse, to command the servants to bring more wine. The second time, after the wine has presumably done its work, an Egyptianized Enobarbus lapses into prose himself, so continuing into the following scene through the bulk of his dialogue with Anthony until cut short by Antony's firm order, "No more light Answeres" (275). The text of this play, despite a good deal of alleged mislineation (which may *be* mislineation) is also generally thought to have been set up from Shakespeare's own manuscript. If so, and if the compositor did his work properly, then it would appear that Shakespeare himself failed to insert the right signals in his manuscript. He failed to instruct the rest of us what rhythm (if any) he was following in his own mind and wished to hear reproduced by his actors. As an instance of how readily Shakespearean prose can crystallize into blank verse even when no such thing is apparently intended, we may cite Charmian's first speech. It opens in a hectic prose, but concludes, "Oh, that I knewe this Husband, which you say, must change his Hornes with Garlands"—a powerfully iambic utterance, scannable as a pentameter line followed by a three-foot line.

In other cases a more fluid situation seems to prevail, as in the scene in *Titus Andronicus* between the mad Titus, his brother Marcus, and the Clown carrying pigeons to the Emperor. Titus's verse is here answered in prose by the Clown, thus establishing an instant contrast between the speech rhythms of the two. But a kind of contamination of each character's speech by that of the other also takes place. Titus and Marcus fall into prose at one point because the Clown has been addressing *them* in

prose. In another moment it is the Clown's prose that undergoes contamination, or is pulled by attraction into the orbit of Titus's verse. Titus is
demanding to know if Jupiter will do him justice. The Clown, misunderstanding, hears "Jupiter" as "gibbeter" or "gibbet-maker." Titus repeats
his question urgently: "But what sayes *Iupiter* I aske thee?" (a four-foot
iambic line). The Clown replies, "Alas sir I know not *Iupiter:* I neuer
dranke with him in all my life" (1951–53). Modern editors (following
Capell)[10] print this last speech as prose, but in Q1 (the basic text) as well as
in F, it comprises two lines of verse: "Alas sir I know not *Iupiter,*" an
acceptable blank verse line with one light syllable omitted from the first
foot, and "I neuer dranke with him in all my life," a perfect blank verse
line in all respects. It is followed in the Clown's next speech by a single line
in which the caesura does duty for an unstressed syllable in the fourth foot
(a common enough situation in Shakespearean blank verse, as Bowers has
pointed out [pp. 96–97]). Here is a case where Bertram's rule, coupled with
another, ought to apply, where the authority of the early text, *when it
coincides with* the evidence of our ears, ought to carry the day.

We have, then, in Shakespeare's first surviving tragedy, a mixed prose-
verse sequence in which the customary division into verse for the noble
characters and prose for the Clown breaks down, as each character
adopts, momentarily, the rhythm associated with the other, a phenomenon
we may think of as Shakespearean fluidity, where it is the ebb and flow of
the rhythmic tide that seems to govern the choice for any individual
speech rather than any preordained assignment of one mode or another to
one or another character.

An example of what I am calling indeterminacy appears in *Romeo and
Juliet*. At the beginning of 2.4 (1105 ff.), Mercutio and Benvolio, in the
street, are speculating as to Romeo's whereabouts. Their opening lines are
printed as prose in F, as verse in Pelican and Riverside, as prose in New
Arden. If we consult the quartos, we find that two crucial lines appear as
verse in the authoritative text, Q2 ("Why that same pale hardhearted
wench, that *Rosaline,* / Torments him so, that he will sure run mad"),[11]
while two other lines, even more crucial from our point of view, appear as
verse only in Q1: "*Tibalt,* the kinsman to old *Capulet,* [/] Hath sent a
Letter to his Fathers house" (1111–12), which I find impossible to hear as
anything but two sturdy pentameters. Q1 is, of course, a bad quarto. But as
such, it is presumably based on a memorial reconstruction, and I would
guess that what we have here is what someone in the theater, whether
player, prompter, or stagehand, actually heard, or perhaps spoke. And if
this much is granted, then the opening speech may also be plausibly recast
as two lines of verse, with a second short line: "Where the deule should
this *Romeo* be? came hee not home to night?" (1106–7), to be followed by
a single line from Benvolio—"Not to his Fathers, I spoke with his man"—

which we could hear as a pentameter with caesural suppression of the stressed syllable in the fourth foot and an anapestic fifth foot. The passage as a whole, then, might plausibly be set as verse. Yet the fact that a few of its lines are a bit wobbly and that it leads directly into a stretch of no-nonsense prose might reasonably prompt some hesitation.

A conceivable reason for leaving it all in prose might be the fact that once these preliminaries are concluded, what follows moves into prose so unarguably. But then a counterconsideration might be alleged from the end of the scene. After the young men's badinage, their taunting of the Nurse, and Romeo's instructions to her, and shortly after a substantial verse speech from Romeo (1281–87), both Q and F strikingly fail to mark as verse the following speech from the Nurse: "Is your man secret, Did you nere heare say two may keep counsell putting one away" (1290–91). Here the rhymed pentameter couplet settles the status of the speech beyond any doubt, yet the early texts seem unaware of the fact; both set it as prose. Failing us in such an obvious case as this, they can hardly be trusted as authoritative guides to the more delicate cases.

Interesting in a slightly different way is the later public scene in which Tybalt kills Mercutio. Here the flickering back and forth between prose and verse occurs so rapidly and unpredictably that it is hard to keep track of. Benvolio commences with four lines of undoubted verse, two of them misprinted as prose in Q2 and F. Mercutio then delivers himself of his mocking set piece in prose concerning Benvolio's supposed quar-relsomeness. With Tybalt's entry (1465) we shift briefly into verse in all editions, but whereas Riverside, following Q2, preserves prose unbroken from this point on, Pelican tries to return to verse for Mercutio's answer: "And but one word with one of vs? [/] couple it with something, make it a word and a blow" (1470–71). The Pelican editor hears this speech as two blank verse lines, plausibly enough, though the first line is short one foot, and the second squeezes a few hypermetric syllables into its regulation ten. The editor is obviously unnerved by the fact that the pattern seemingly established in Tybalt's opening words is so quickly subverted by a return to prose. But this is precisely the sort of thing that happens often in Shakespeare in such stretches. Prose now proceeds unchallenged until verse reasserts itself in Benvolio's futile attempt at pacification (1481) and in the exchange between Romeo and Tybalt, strongly enough indeed to draw Mercutio into its field of force, leading him too to versify along with them until he breaks out irrepressibly with his scornful baiting of Tybalt: "Good King of Cats," etc. Romeo and Tybalt themselves, clearly programmed as verse characters only for this scene, pull Mercutio back into their own orbit again until the moment in which he is wounded, when he once more erupts, now for the last time, in what we may feel to be his "natural" medium of scoffing prose. Unstable as this passage may seem to be in the suddenness and speed of its switchings back and forth and in the impartiality with which two of its characters speak now prose now verse, editors have rarely tampered with it, since its very instabilities seem so cleanly defined and so appropriate to the psychic energies of the speakers.

Hamlet contains a number of mixed scenes, especially those in which Hamlet, rapidly donning his antic guise following the arrival of Polonius, or Ophelia, or the assembled court, lurches abruptly from verse into prose. The shifts are usually well marked, as in the "Ha, ha: Are you honest?" (1758) harshly addressed to Ophelia, or his announcement to Horatio, "They are comming to the Play: I must be idle. Get you a place" (1946–47), where "idle" has the force of "incoherent, void of sense, delirious," assigned it in the *Oxford English Dictionary*. Ophelia's mad scene in act 4 weaves a crazy quilt of distracted prose, ballad fragments, blank verse (from Gertrude), prose (from Claudius), and a hovering between verse and prose from Laertes. Laertes starts in verse ("How now? what noise is that?" etc. [2906]), continues so, though without verse marking in F ("Had'st thou thy wits, and did'st perswade Reuenge, it could not moue thus"), then shifts into prose along with Ophelia, only to revert at length to verse: "Thought, and Affliction, Passion, Hell it selfe: / Shc turnes to Fauour, and to prettinesse" (2939–40). Here we have another rapid alternation, and an irregular and unpredictable rather than a carefully measured one. Rhythmic and arhythmic modes seem scrambled almost indiscriminately corresponding to the distracted state of the participants, with Laertes being first drawn into and then pulled out of the orbit of Ophelia's distraction, as Mercutio is drawn into the tensions of the interchange between Tybalt and Romeo in their confrontation in the marketplace.

Two fairly striking instances of indeterminacy occur in *Othello,* the first from the scene in which Iago and Desdemona match wits while awaiting Othello's arrival on Cyprus. This episode has often attracted disfavor because of its "excessive" length and the allegedly unattractive spectacle of Desdemona bandying words with Iago while fearful for Othello's safety, perhaps also because the virtuous and high born Desdemona is assigned the "humble" medium of prose while the malicious Iago speaks the "noble" language of verse. Iago's couplets of mock praise appear in italics in both Quarto and Folio texts, but two of his warm-up speeches are set as verse in Q1, as prose in F:

Come on, come on: you are Pictures out of doore: [/] Bells in your Parlours: Wilde-Cats in your Kitchens: [/] Saints in your Iniuries: Diuels being offended: [/] Players in your Huswiferie, and Huswiues in your Beds (879–83).

And again, when asked how he would praise Desdemona,

I am about it, but indeed my inuention [/] comes from my pate, as
Birdlyme do's from Freeze, [/] it pluckes out Braines and all. [/] But my
Muse labours, and thus she is deliuer'd (899–902).

The textual situation gives little help here. Both Q1 and F have a claim to
independent authority; both are usually reckoned substantive texts. And
editors have found a certain eclecticism not merely desirable but necessary: New Arden adopts Q1 as its copy text, but admits numerous readings from F; Pelican and Riverside both take F as their copy text but
include plentiful readings from Q1 (about 190 in the case of Pelican, over
three hundred in the case of Riverside). My own impression is that the first
of the disputed passages may be allowed as verse, a loose and irregular
verse to be sure, heavily larded with hypermetric syllables, with a rolling
rhythm that breaks away from the firm iambics practiced elsewhere in the
play. But it fits well with the mood of the moment; it goes naturally with
Iago's misogynist couplets. The second passage by contrast seems to me
to wear the air of prose and to look stiff and uncomfortable in its blank
verse dress. True, the second line ("comes from my pate, as Birdlyme do's
from Freeze") sounds like a good pentameter line by itelf, but not when
introduced by the lame tetrameter that must precede it, following which it
rings much more naturally as prose. I myself would not even regard this as
a case of indeterminacy, except for the fact that so many redoubtable
others have disagreed, the New Arden, Pelican, and Riverside editors
among them: all have preferred the quarto reading, perhaps in order to
preserve Iago as a consistently verse-speaking character in this scene.

The other instance occurs in the eavesdropping scene in act 4. I begin it
at the point where Othello conceals himself and Cassio comes in. With
Cassio's answers, the iambic rhythm begins to crumble. Extra syllables
creep in; the lines shorten. By the time we reach 2505 ("Do ye triumph,
Romaine? do you triumph?") we have just about lost the iambic pulse. I
hear this line itself as a near perfect *trochaic* pentameter, though it might
also be heard as basically anapestic, with only three and a half feet. It is
succeeded by an answer from Cassio (2506–8), and two slightly later
answers (2514–16 and 2518–21), printed as verse in Q1 and F but as prose
by both Pelican and Riverside, correctly in my view. (Ridley, in New
Arden, prints the first of the three speeches as verse, the others as prose.)
Here we have an analogy to the musician's scene in *Romeo and Juliet*.
That is, though these lines are set up as verse in F, it is difficult to hear
them as anything but prose, the more so since most of the conversation in
which they are embedded is also prose. What we have is a kind of in-
between stretch in which the previously well-knit verse disintegrates, so
to speak, *into* prose, which finally takes over for the remainder of the
scene, up to the arrival of the Venetian ambassadors. During the transition

it is not always possible to know whether a given line of print represents prose or blank verse. Certainly, "Alas poor Rogue, I thinke indeede she loues me" (2497) is a sound iambic line, but what of the exchange in 2499–501? "*Iago.* Do you heare Cassio? / *Othello.* Now he importunes him / To tell it o're; go too, well said, well said." Here is a place where the visual patterning of the text by eighteenth-century and later editors has produced one of those misleading white spaces deplored by Bertram. Only by some wrenching can we hear lines 2499–500 as a line of blank verse: "Do you heare Cassio? Now he importunes him." It would make better sense to treat Othello's enraged aside as unrelated metrically to Iago's question. But editorial bewilderment is understandable. Whether through conscious design or through genuine uncertainty on his own part, Shakespeare seems once again to be composing in a kind of intermediate zone between verse and prose, to be drifting, and to be content to be drifting, in a misty mid-region or no-man's-land between those fixed poles, to the bafflement of those who would insist that he cleave to one pole or the other.

Finally, among a number of places in *King Lear* that might be mentioned in the same connection, we may point to the climactic mad scene on the heath, especially that part of Lear's raving monologue that begins, "Behold yon simpring Dame, whose face betweene her Forkes presages Snow" (2563–64). F and Q both print this as prose, down to the end of the speech, "Giue me an Ounce of Ciuet, good Apothecary sweeten my immagination: There's money for thee" (2572–73). But editors have found these lines troublesome. Dr. Johnson printed them as verse except for the last five lines, and so does Harbage for Pelican. "Tucker Brooke thinks the whole speech is good honest prose," reports Kenneth Muir (New Arden),[12] who himself prints it all as verse, as does Evans for Riverside. Again, one sympathizes with all parties. Most of the disputed lines scan comfortably as iambic, but half of them are short, containing only two or three feet. In fact they alternate for some distance fairly regularly between five-foot lines and short lines. Now this same pattern can be detected, and in fact has been detected by modern editors, in the earlier portion of the same speech, beginning, "I, euery inch a King" (2554). This earlier portion, however, is set in F as verse, but verse containing half a dozen or so awkward six-foot lines (even one with seven feet), which lie heavily on the tongue and clog the mind's timekeeper. When relineated, the lines fall into the pattern of five- and three-foot lines observable through the printed prose of the latter half of the speech. This leaves only the final five lines as doubtful, and a case can be made for hearing them as either prose or iambic verse. If, however, following Muir we hear them as verse, we find we must start off with an overloaded first line, which destroys the half-line following a full pentameter line that has by this time become the staple for this speech: "Beneath is all the fiends." And from this point on, if we start trying to cut the rest of the speech into standard blank verse, we run into uncouthnesses at every step. But whatever may be done with these re-calcitrant lines, we should note that like those in the scene from *Othello* just glanced at, they form the hinge of a scene that is gradually swinging *from* verse *into* prose.

Timon of Athens, like *King Lear,* contains a good deal of prose, most of it in the first half. Prose appears in the opening scene with the arrival of Apemantus, who has a kind of prima facie claim to be regarded as a prose character, up to the moment of Timon's retreat to the woods. Somewhat in the manner of Casca in the initial sequence of *Julius Caesar,* or Enobarbus in the early scenes of *Antony,* Apemantus stands for cynicism and dissent. He strikes a note of satiric discord against the sugary harmonies of Timon and his friends. Yet even in his first appearance we find marked indeter-minacy. The scene that commences with his entrance begins in verse; so much is unmistakable. And it ends in prose; so much is also unmistakable. But in between we are in flux. Timon's ringing blank verse question in 225–26, "Why dost thou call them Knaues, thou know'st them not?" initiates a series of short speeches, mostly single lines or half-lines, that we cannot confidently label either prose or verse. Sequences of such short speeches indeed form a recurrent source of indeterminacy throughout the canon. In line 230 the Jeweller asks, "You know me, *Apemantus?*" (an acceptable half-line of blank verse, if we wish to term it such), to which Apemantus retorts, "Thou know'st I do; I call'd thee by thy name," an unexception-able blank verse line that Pelican and Riverside treat as prose, presumably because it occurs amid a flurry of short-line speeches, though the iambic beat remains perceptible, and at times pronounced, in much of the se-quence. To Timon's next observation, "Thou art proud *Apemantus?*" Apemantus returns, "Of nothing so much as that I am not like Timon." Here the iambic beat persists, though slightly weakened by the admission of two unstressed syllables (along with a presumptive elision of "I'am"). This is the kind of situation in which an actor might easily throw the weight onto the iambic accent or away from it. What should he do here? I suspect he should preserve it, but not too thuddingly, since it is in the process of abating. In the next interchange, the same situation: a half-line query from Timon, "Whether art going?" followed by Apemantus's brutal riposte, "To knocke out an honest Athenians braines"—a four-foot iambic line with two hypermetric syllables. And so it proceeds, with a gradual unravelling of the iambic fabric countered by an occasional fitful resump-tion of it, as in the following sequence, where the rhythmicality is most approximate until the final phrase: "*Timon.* How lik'st thou this picture *Apemantus?* / *Apemantus.* The best, for the innocence. / *Timon.* Wrought he not well that painted it. / *Apemantus.* He wrought better that made the Painter, and / yet he's but a filthy peece of worke" (238–42). Here we waver on the borderline of blank verse only to finish thumpingly with it at the end: "and yet he's but a filthy peece of worke." At such moments we seem to be up against a kind of Shakespearean constant, a tendency for prose to drift toward the iambic pattern even when it is most clearly intended as prose. A writer who has composed as many thousand lines of blank verse as Shakespeare has (and whose verse, moreover, is coming increasingly to resemble prose in its irregularity) can hardly help falling into it even in places where he may not be aiming at it: "What cares these roarers for the name of King?" (*Temp.*, 24–25), "Looke, th'vnfolding Starre calles vp the Shepheard" (*Meas.*, 2068–69), [13] etc. No wonder that Dover Wilson used to speak of "verse fossils" in Shakespeare's prose dialogue, going so far as to base a theory of revision on them.[14] In our present scene, at all events, the verse disintegrates, slowly but incxorably, until it ends, uncontrovertibly and perhaps to our relief, in "good honest prose."

Apemantus, even this early in the play, cannot properly be called a prose character. But someone thought he was—perhaps Shakespeare, perhaps the compositor. After the initial greeting between Timon and Alcibiades, Apemantus's contemptuous growl, beginning "So, so; their Aches contract, and sterue your supple joints" (296–97), is printed as prose in F but as verse in editions since Capell, even though (to defend the Folio reading) only the line just quoted, "Aches contract, and sterue your supple joints," can be accounted a solid blank verse line, it being followed in modern editions by two hypermetric lines, one of them extremely prosy and awkward, "that there shouldest be small loue amongest these sweet knaues." When Timon leaves with his retinue, Apemantus stays behind to continue sparring with two unnamed lords. Again we move into or remain in a limbo between prose and verse, with verse initially maintaining the upper hand.

> *1. Lord.* What time a day is't *Apemantus?*
> *Apemantus.* Time to be honest.
> *1. Lord.* That time serues still.
> *Apemantus.* The more accursed thou that still omitst it.
> *2. Lord.* Thou art going to Lord *Timons* Feast.
> *Apemantus.* I, to see meate fill Knaues, and Wine heat fooles.
> *2. Lord.* Farthee well, farthee well.
> *Apemantus.* Thou art a Foole to bid me farewell twice.
>
> (307–16)

Here each of Apemantus's stinging replies restores or reinforces iambic regularity. Of his four speeches, three constitute perfect blank verse lines. Interestingly, the Pelican editor, Hinman, who sets the passage as prose, nevertheless marks the preterite syllable of "accursed" with an accent ("èd"), as though unconsciously to make the line conform visually to what his ear hears, an impeccable pentameter line with a feminine ending.

The next scene presents a comparable situation, except that here F prints as verse what modern editors have had trouble deciding on:

> [*Timon.*] They say my Lords, *Ira furor breuis est.*
> But yond man is verie angrie.
> Go, let him haue a Table by himselfe:
> For he does neither affect companie,
> Nor is he fit for't indeed.
> *Apemantus.* Let me stay at thine apperill *Timon,*
> I come to obserue, I giue thee warning on't.

(370–76)

Editors have found this passage confusing. Cambridge and Pelican treat Timon's portion as prose, New Arden and Riverside as verse. But then Cambridge and New Arden print Apemantus's lines as verse, Pelican and Riverside as prose. Not only is there no agreement in the case of either speech in itself, there is no clear line of *dis*agreement that extends to both speeches. Listening again to the passage, we hear only one line that can pass muster as iambic pentameter: "Go, let him haue a Table by himselfe." But we also hear the kind of logical distinction that Shakespeare utilizes freely in prose, very sparingly in verse: "For he does neither affect companie, / Nor is he fit for't indeed." We could, strainingly, read the first of these lines as blank verse, but it would require a false accent on the first syllable of "affect," as well as an unnaturally heavy emphasis on the last syllable of "companie," while the final half-line (with its elided "for't") seems designed deliberately to *thwart* iambic reading. Apemantus's answer more convincingly might be scanned as verse, assuming an unsounded light syllable at the start of the first line and an elision ("to'obserue") in the second.

It is likely of course that we are here dealing with a manuscript still in the formative stage. We may suppose that had Shakespeare finished the play such indeterminated passages would have been clarified. Such passages have in fact been taken as *evidence* that the play was left incomplete. Evans in Riverside, for example, cites the "misarrangement of verse and prose and of prose as verse" as reason for thinking that the play was "abandoned by Shakespeare in an unfinished state" (p. 1474). But we have seen enough of such vacillation, or indeterminacy, in other places to beware of leaning too hard on it as evidence for one kind of copy or another. Considering how often Shakespeare moves in this twilight zone, especially in transitional passages, we would be rash to conclude that it reflects anything but his normal method of composition. That method may indeed include a sporadic indecisiveness as to whether he wishes prose or verse for a given sequence; it may also be that a high incidence of such moments points to a less than usually finished manuscript. But comparative incidences would need to be established.

Coriolanus provides a somewhat similar situation: a text evidently set from Shakespearean autograph, yet not from fair copy, so that while it may represent the play at a more advanced state of composition than that of *Timon,* it contains enough uncertainty to suggest that the playwright would have clarified certain passages had he copied out the text himself. As Brockbank in New Arden, commenting on later attempts at regularization, puts it, "It . . . seems likely that . . . Shakespeare [at various points] hesitated between prose and verse and left the text undivided. . . . The edited version [i.e., that of Pope, Rowe, and Steevens] cannot here be justified either as an approximation to copy or a recovery of the author's intention; it is rather an interpretation of an intention imperfectly achieved. Shakespeare, the implicit claim has it, would have transcribed into verse had he been making fair copy; but being free to emend, he would have made a better job of it than his editors. Certain infelicities . . . are the expected inheritance from autograph first draft" (p. 12).

But similar infelicities, if we wish to call them such, are also to be found in plays *not* stemming from autograph first copy. It may be that the formula, "hesitated between verse and prose and left the text undivided," explains some of the indeterminacies found at *all* epochs of Shakespeare's career. It may also account for some of the bewildering oscillations between prose and verse we can find even when individual speeches seem clearly stamped as one or the other, when prose intrudes unexpectedly into a scene of verse and then as unexpectedly disappears, or when verse plays the intruder for a brief moment and then melts away. Why, for example, amid the prose boasting of Gregory and Sampson at the beginning of *Romeo and Juliet,* do we find (in F but not in Q) two lines printed as verse: "Me they shall feele while I am able to stand; / And 'tis knowne I am a pretty peece of flesh" (31–32). Evidently whoever was responsible for F heard two lines of blank verse here; given a little pushing they can be made to scan tolerably well. But lodged in the middle of a passage unmistakably *not* verse and appearing only in a derivative text, they have no claim to priority over the reading in Q. Yet they illustrate once again the ease with which Shakespearean prose can take on the rhythms of iambic verse and the possibilities for confusion that can result. Similar misunderstandings may well have happened in places where they are less easy to detect.

Enough, perhaps has been said to make a simple point: that we still need to do more clearing of the ground before we can claim authoritatively to distinguish prose from verse, and that indeed there may be places where such a distinction is next to impossible, where we may be confronting an indeterminacy in Shakespeare's own mind, if not a deliberate *technique* of indeterminacy used in certain equivocal situations, in which we are not really meant to hear, or in any case do not hear, except as the actor requires us to hear, either the clear rhythms of blank verse or the irregularities of prose.

NOTES

1. This essay represents an enlarged and altered version of a paper done originally for a seminar on Shakespeare's Prose at the 1984 meeting of the Shakespeare Association of America, in Cambridge, Mass. The seminar focused on the tragedies and tragicomedies, for which reason I continue to limit myself here to a consideration of prose in the tragedies, not doubting, however, that much of what can be said in this connection will apply to plays of other genres.

2. *White Spaces in Shakespeare: The Development of the Modern Text* (Cleveland, Ohio: Bellflower Press, 1981), pp. 18–36, 65–68, and passim.

3. Cited in Bertram, *White Spaces,* p. 20.

4. Quotations (unless otherwise specified) refer to *The Norton Facsimile: The First Folio,* ed. Charlton Hinman (New York: W. W. Norton, 1968), and parenthetical line numbers to the through-line-numbering utilized by Hinman. I have written out speech prefixes in full.

5. Review of Bertram, in *Renaissance Quarterly* 36 (1983): 304.

6. "Establishing Shakespeare's Text: Notes on Short Lines and the Problem of Verse Division," *Studies in Bibliography* 33 (1980): 74–130.

7. Brockbank, ed., *Coriolanus,* New Arden (London: Methuen, 1976), p. 13.

8. At least that is what T. S. Dorsch, ed., *Julius Caesar,* New Arden (London: Methuen, 1955), p. 4 (textual note on lines 15 and 18), thinks, though it is not clear to me that the lines in question would look different if the F compositor had meant them as verse.

9. Dorsch, *Julius Caesar,* p. xxiv.

10. Including the editor of the most recent edition, Eugene M. Waith, in The Oxford Shakespeare (Oxford: Oxford University Press, 1984).

11. *Romeo and Juliet, Second Quarto, 1599,* ed. W. W. Greg, Shakespeare Quartos in Collotype Facsimile, no. 6 (Oxford: Clarendon Press, 1949), sig. E2.

12. (London: Methuen, 1952, reprint, 1957), p. 176, note on 4.7.120–35.

13. I owe these examples to Professor Emeritus Arthur King of Brigham Young University, who plucked them out of thin air when the present topic was under discussion at the Cambridge seminar.

14. See, *inter alia,* his edition of *As You Like It* (Cambridge: Cambridge University Press, 1926), pp. 94–98.

Coriolanus and a Shakespearean Motif

Elizabeth Story Donno

Dumb presagers of my speaking breast
Sonnet 23

With the study of rhetoric an essential part of school and university education and with a plethora of rhetorical manuals available, together with educational treatises like those of Eliot and Ascham, it was expected that writing of any sort—whether historical, homiletic, or imaginative—would display the rhetorical character proper to the genre. Yet early on there developed objections to the "craft"—to use Leonard Coxe's term—first in the anti-Ciceronian, then in the pro-Ramist movement, though both of these were directed to the abuse of rhetoric rather than to the art itself.

The most challenging of the attacks by far came from the ranks of religious reformers but, given doctrinal differences, with an expected diversity of emphasis. The Gospels provided a sound basis for a general belief that speech should be revelatory of the self rather than an instrument of persuasion, for was it not twice written that out of the abundance of the heart the mouth speaketh (Matt. 12 : 34; Luke 6 : 45)? Appearing in related form in the Old Testament, the belief gave rise to the locution of a heart that speaks or thinks: "For as he thinketh in his heart so is he" (Prov. 23 : 7); "The heart of fools is in their mouth, but the mouth of the wise is in their heart" (Ecclus. 21 : 26; cf. Pss. 4 : 4, 45 : 1).[1] Accordingly those who "flatter with their lips" are said to speak with a "double heart" (Ps. 12:2).

The idea, as Tilley amply records, also assumed proverbial dress: "What the heart thinks, the tongue speaks"; "The tongue of the wise man is in his heart," plus a number of other examples, including the misogynistic extension, "A woman's heart and her tongue are not relatives." Since it could also be said to have classical endorsement, if in a somewhat generalized form when contrasted to the specific of rhetorical tricks, the notion came to have the status of a moral precept; as Ascham, humanist, rhetorician, and staunch Protestant, observed in his influential *Schoolmaster:* there should be no divorce between the tongue and the heart.

Given Shakespeare's mastery of the technical devices of rhetoric with an enormous repertoire (well catalogued in Sister Miriam Joseph's *Shakespeare's Use of the Arts of Language,* 1947), it is all the more interesting to note his recognition and use of this antirhetorical reaction. Generally presented in only a few lines of text, the precept becomes in his hands a kind of index to character, its brevity accounted for by the audience's awareness of its moral and psychological import. The frequency of allusion to it in the plays, together with its association with a range of characters—good, mixed, or evil—comes to seem even more significant when considered in the light of his last tragedy, where the precept acquires a thematic focus. My purpose in this essay is to show, first, how it functions as a "motif" consequent upon the frequency with which it appears in plays of great diversity—in tragedy, comedy, history, and pastoral, if not in play unlimited—and in accord with a multiple moral range of characterization, and then to show how it functions as the prime factor in determining the character of Coriolanus.

*   *   *

In wooing Katherine of France, King Henry, though avowedly having "no cunning in protestation," gives her the reason for one's trusting to a heart that speaks:

> A speaker is but a prater . . . but a good heart, Kate, is the sun and the moon, or rather the sun and not the moon; for it shines bright and never changes, but keeps his course truly. (*Henry V,* 5.2.158–64[2])

In his farce the *Taming of the Shrew,* Shakespeare early on makes use of the precept in delineating what may be called the "true" character of another Kate, the "wild-cat" Katherina. Initially she is presented as intolerably curst and froward, "an irksome brawling scold," even as Petruccio is, by his own arrogant admission, a fortune hunter seeking to find some one "rich enough" to be his wife (1.2.67). When it comes to asking for Kate's hand, he admits to her father that his absolute "peremptory" nature will clash with her proud-mindedness, but he also predicts that their two extremes will cancel each other out and at that time he will yield to her even as she yields to him (2.1.131–36). He also astutely perceives that if Kate is curst, it is for policy (2.1.292), and accordingly he "politically" sets about to cure her froward behavior. First he employs allopathic measures ("Say that she rail, why then I'll tell her plain / She sings as sweetly as a nightingale" 2.1.170–71), which he follows up with more rigorous homeopathic measures (*similia similibus curentur*), killing her, as the servants acknowledge, "in her own humor" by being "more shrew than she" (4.1.85–86; 180). That this double cure has worked is attested by Kate's final speech, lessoning the other wives.

In the penultimate stage of Petrucchio's boisterous homeopathic treatment, it may be noted how Shakespeare points up Kate's real nature, and that nature is admirably honest and direct. Having borne with the many distressing, even tumultuous situations—the delayed appearance of the bridegroom, so shockingly attired, at the wedding ceremony, the forefeited repast, the rough and miry trip to his villa, the starvation diet, the (two) sleepless nights—Kate finally erupts in protest. Here she speaks as she feels and as it is her true nature to do: for her, there can be no (long) disjunction between her tongue and her heart:

> I am no child, no babe;
> Your betters have endur'd me say my mind,
> And if you cannot, best you stop your ears.
> My tongue will tell the anger of my heart,
> Or else my heart concealing it will break,
> And rather than it shall, I will be free,
> Even to the uttermost, as I please, in words.
>
> (4.3.74–80)

Though in a quite different emotional key, we find the same recognition of the psychic pain resulting from the suppression of one's true feelings in the second scene of *Hamlet*. Here Hamlet gives voice to his revulsion at the "wicked" speed of his mother's incestuous marriage and concludes this, his first soliloquy, with the poignant line, "But break my heart, for I must hold my tongue." After the appearance of the Ghost, he speaks only "wild and whirling words" to his companions even as later he puts on an antic disposition to cloak his true feelings. Summoned to his mother's closet, he first utters a brief soliloquy in which he admits that he could act contrary to his true nature ("Now could I drink hot blood") and for the occasion admits to a duplicity of speech:

> O heart, lose not thy nature! . . .
> I will speak daggers to her, but use none,
> My tongue and soul in this be hypocrites—
>
> (3.2.393–96)

Clearly this compulsion to speak from the heart, dramatically compatible with a character in farce and in tragedy, also lends itself to mysogynistic humor of the fabliau type. In the *Merry Wives of Windsor,* the jealous Ford, disguised as Master Brook, appeals to Falstaff to test his wife's fidelity—for a fee. With his customary audacity, Falstaff promises the "jealous wittoly knave" that he will do so and inform him of the fact that very night. Ford vents his jealous rage in soliloquy, directing it first at his wife, then at all her sex:

Cuckold! Wittol! Cuckold! . . . I will rather trust a Fleming with my butter, Parson Hugh the Welshman with my cheese, an Irishman with my aqua-vitae bottle, or a thief to walk my ambling gelding, than my wife with herself. Then she plots, then she ruminates, then she devises; *and what they think in their hearts they may effect, they will break their hearts but they will effect.* (2.2.299–308, my italics)[3]

Ford is of course also sounding a frequent note in the conventional characterization of women. Even the sprightly Rosalind concedes this. When she learns that Orlando has arrived in the Forest of Arden and that Celia has seen him, she assails her with multiple queries as to how he looked, what he said, where he was going, what he was doing there, demanding an answer "in one word." The protesting Celia instructs her to cry "holla" to a tongue that "curvets" so "unseasonably"; but Rosalind, who has already made clear that though caparisoned like a man she does not have a "doublet and hose" in her disposition, responds with what for the sixteenth century would be a purely rhetorical question:

> Do you not know I am a woman? When I think,
> I must speak. (3.2.249–40)

Aware of the heart-tongue motif as it must have been, a contemporary audience watching *King Lear* would not, I suggest, have considered Cordelia's reaction to the love-test in quite the same light that later critics have. Coleridge, it may be remembered, explained it as "some little faulty admixture of pride and sullenness"; others have frequently added the term "obstinacy" to this description. When one is conscious of the motif, the psychological focus shifts from *what* she does not say to *why* she does not say it. Her reaction, admittedly, functions as a precipitating factor that sets the plot in motion, but given the motif's moral import, the audience could be expected to take her few speeches here as indicative of her true character.

As the eldest, Goneril is the first to say her piece, and the oxymoron in her declaration—after five lines of hyperbole—creates an almost mocking effect:

> A love that makes breath [voice] poor, and speech unable:
> Beyond all manner of so much I love you.
>
> (1.1.60–61)

Hence Cordelia's aside, "Love, and be silent." Regan then takes her turn, relying on only a slight disparagement of Goneril's words for rhetorical advantage, "In my true heart / I find she names my very deed of love; / Only she comes too short . . ." (1.1.70–72). Cordelia, again in an aside, comments, "I am sure my love's / More ponderous than my tongue." And to Lear's expostulations after she refuses to emulate her sisters and so says nothing, she responds, "Unhappy that I am, I cannot heave / My heart into my mouth" (1.1.91–92). In place of the total filial love her sisters profess, she announces that when she is married, her husband will have half her love, the other half by implication still her father's. Lear then asks in what following on the words of the two sisters proves a particularly ironic question, "But goes thy heart with this?"

> *Cordelia.* Ay, my good lord.
> *Lear.* So young and so untender?
> *Cordelia.* So young, my lord, and true.
>
> (1.1.105–7)

To the fulsome speeches of her sisters in this scene, Cordelia's reaction might well be summed up as that of Troilus on reading Cressida's letter:

> Words, words, mere words, no matter from the heart.
>
> (5.3.108)

Neither so young nor so true as Cordelia, Cleopatra nevertheless acknowledges that there is a distinction between tongue and heart when she chides Antony on his "mouth-made vows" (1.3.30). Yet she herself is adept at paltering when the occasion demands it. After the Egyptian fleet has yielded and Antony is raging at the Circean witch who has, he thinks, sold him to Octavius, she takes up Charmian's suggestion of locking herself in the tomb and sending him word that she is dead. Her directions to Mardian are designedly histrionic:

> go tell him I have slain myself;
> Say that the last I spoke was "Antony,"
> And word it, prithee, piteously.
>
> (4.13.7–9)

Mardian appears to Antony as he is concluding that there is nothing left to do but to end his life, and the eunuch's words are sufficiently piteous to work their effect; at the same time they point up Cleopatra's equivocal nature:

> the last she spake
> Was "Antony, most noble Antony!"
> Then in the midst a tearing groan did break
> The name of Antony; it was divided
> Between her heart and lips.
>
> (4.14.29–33)

Equally revealing of character is the description Antony earlier gives of Octavia as she prepares to leave her brother and go with him to Athens. Cherished by Octavius, she is noted, according to Agrippa and Maecenas, for her beauty, virtue, and modesty, though in Enobarbus's terms of a "holy, cold, and still" deportment. Her sole function is to ensure the tenuous political and fraternal alliance between Octavius and Antony. As brother and sister make their farewells, the weeping Octavia wishes to tell him something but *only* in his ear; Antony's account of that moment perfectly renders the delicate poise of her competing loyalties:

> Her tongue will not obey her heart, nor can
> Her heart inform her tongue—the swan's down feather,
> That stands upon the swell at the full tide,
> And neither way inclines.
>
> (3.2.47–50)

Two scenes later Antony reports to her the sources of division between the two competitors. In addition to thousands of "excusable" actions, Octavius has waged new wars against Pompey, made out his will and read it publicly, spoken scantly of Antony and when he could not but pay him honor did it grudgingly or did it "from his teeth," the colloquial flavor of Antony's words reenforcing the notion of a very politic Octavius.

By such small touches, Shakespeare points up the positive though sometimes slightly equivocal aspect of his characters, whatever the genre they appear in. A last instance of this sort comes from *Much Ado About Nothing,* where Benedict, though a "profess'd tyrant" to the female sex and an "obstinate heretic" to beauty (1.1.169, 234), is characterized in this positive way. He has, in the words of the genial Don Pedro, a "heart as sound as a bell, and his tongue is the clapper, for what his heart thinks, his tongue speaks" (3.2.12–14). But does it? His merry flytings with Beatrice ("My Lady Tongue") and their flippant, often barbed exchanges function rather to mask their true feelings. Only after the shock of Claudio's public renouncing of Hero do they admit to their love for each other in a near-simultaneous admission that marks the complementarity of their characters. But Beatrice's "Kill Claudio" ringing through the church elicits his vehement refusal to do so, thus prompting in turn her derisive charge, a counterpart to his "Lady Tongue":

> Manhood is melted into cur'sies, valor into compliment, and men are only turn'd into tongue, and trim ones too. (4.1.319–21)

In the opening scene Leonato urged the three visitors, Don Pedro, Claudio, and Benedict, to stay in Messina longer than the promised month. On repeating that invitation to Claudio and Benedict in his presence, Don Pedro had genially commented, "I do swear he is no hypocrite, but prays from his heart." To the biblically attuned in the audience, his remark would seem an echo of the words of Jesus to the scribes and Pharisees:

> Ye hypocrites, well did Isaiah prophesy of you, saying, This people draweth nigh unto me with their mouth, and honoreth me with their lips, but their heart is far from me. (Matt. 15:7–8)

When he comes to characterizing certain less genial figures, Shakespeare links the divorce of tongue and heart to the notion of hypocrisy that is, of course, its concomitant. Duplicity of utterance to varying degrees becomes in his hands a sure means of indicating a faulty, mixed, or evil nature. This is clearly an easier dramatic technique than to build to a positive sense of character by adducing the merit of honest speech (as modern critical responses to his last tragedy, discussed below, readily attest). Yet he does so with a similar economy: the somewhat faulty Lucio in *Measure for Measure,* for example, reveals that verbal deceit is for him a conscious motive, no less when slandering the Duke than when trifling with maids:

> 'tis my familiar sin
> With maids to seem the lapwing [that is, to delude], and to jest,
> Tongue far from heart. . . .
>
> (1.4.31–33)[4]

In *Richard II,* Shakespeare presents the character of Lord Aumerle, Richard's (as well as Bolingbroke's) "tender-heart'd cousin" as subtly mixed. Aumerle is very much aware of the distinction between what the heart thinks and the tongue speaks, but for politic reasons he handles the distinction with a certain flexibility. Following on the banishment of Mowbray for life and Bolingbroke for ten years reduced to six, the king is curious to know what tears were shed when he parted from Bolingbroke. Aumerle owns there was none on his part except a drop caused by the northeast wind to grace the admittedly "hollow" parting. To the king's question as to what was said in parting, he acknowledges that the prompting of his heart inhibited his speaking while at the same time teaching him "to counterfeit" a grief so excessive that it appeared inexpressible:

> And for my heart disdainéd that my tongue
> Should so profane the word [Farewell], that taught me craft
> To counterfeit oppression of such grief
> That words seem'd buried in my sorrow's grave.
>
> (1.4.12–15)

Coming as it does at the outset of the play, the speech suggests a certain deviousness in his character, which from one angle of interpretation marks his later actions. Aumerle's early adherence to the precept by subterfuge contrasts with the later invocation of it on the part of Richard's former groom of the stable: pressed to leave the dungeon at Pomfret Castle before the arrival of the king's murderers, he discloses his feelings in the single line, "What my tongue dares not, that my heart shall say" (5.5.97).

Aumerle's father, the Duke of York, may also be said to exhibit aspects of an equivocal if not devious character, since his actions so frequently are at odds with his words. In spite of having voiced his objections to the king's seizing of John of Gaunt's estates to finance the Irish wars, he agrees to take over his political function and act as regent during his absence in Ireland. Again in spite of having voiced his objections to Bolingbroke's unauthorized return and his armed following, he agrees on pragmatic grounds to "remain as neuter." Yet it is he who announces "plume-pluck'd" Richard's surrender of his crown. Trusting to providential sanction for the fall of Richard and the rise of Bolingbroke (5.2.37–38), York declared fealty to the new king and pledged himself for the surety of his son, who has now been degraded from ducal rank for the alleged complicity in Gloucester's murder. Yet he "lost" that title, his father admits, "for being Richard's friend" (5.2.42). When he discovers Aumerle's involvement in the conspiracy to kill Henry and restore Richard to the throne, he at once rushes off to Windsor Castle to denounce him. Aumerle rushes after him, followed by the Duchess.

The domestic interlude of a family divided against itself that they then play out before the king has elements of irony and of farce. Arriving first, Aumerle wins an immediate pardon on the grounds of an "intended" as opposed to a "committed" fault. On rushing in, York opposes this so vehemently that the king grants the pardon a second time, now on the grounds of the father's "goodness." He is again calling for the death penalty when the Duchess comes in, this third arrival eliciting the king's bemused comment that the "scene" has altered; no longer is it a "serious thing." With York continuing a counterpoint of denials against the prayers of wife and son, the Duchess proclaims the duplicity of his appeal:

> Pleads he in earnest? Look upon his face:
> His eyes do drop no tears, his prayers are in jest,
> His words come from his mouth, ours from our breast.
> (5.3.100–102)

Her later charge (107) that York's prayers are "full of false hypocrisy" is tacitly confirmed by the king's pardon of Aumerle for yet a third time.

Although critics have granted the theatrical effect of this scene, its function has been questioned and its inclusion regretted by some. But it does function, I think, in suggestive ways: (1) it offers a comic lull before the horror of the murder scene; (2) it provides a parallel to the earlier situation, when acting as a judge rather than as a father, Gaunt agreed to the banishment of Bolingbroke (1.3.237–38); (3) it points up Aumerle's continued loyalty to Richard in contrast with York's new-found allegiance to Henry; and (4) in the consequent disrupting of familial bonds, it becomes but an extreme instance in the sequence of disloyalties and betrayals that leads to the long horror of civil war.

Shakespeare uses the motif in delineating two hero-villains, the first from fairly early on in his career, the second fairly late, and it is interesting to note the difference in the handling of the motif in the two instances. A brilliant Machiavellian, Richard III manipulates his victims by means of his verbal skill even as he openly acknowledges its deceptive power. To achieve the—one would think—impossible task of wooing Lady Anne, bereft of her husband and his kingly father by Richard's hand, he projects himself as a soldier who heretofore has disdained to weep or supplicate:

> I never sued to friend nor enemy;
> My tongue could never learn sweet smoothing word;
> But now thy beauty is propos'd my fee,
> My proud heart sues, and prompts my tongue to speak.
>
> (1.2.167–70)

When she begins to relent and would know his heart, he replies that it is figured in his tongue, a reply that is at once candid and beguiling: to the audience it seems candid—after all, they have already been primed by Richard's initial determination to prove a villain—to Anne it seems, and is, beguiling.

Even as Richard's seeming candor about himself disarms his victims, so, too, does his realistic appraisal of the world he bustles in. Admitting its depths of deceit to the young prince wishing he had more uncles to welcome him, he acknowledges that the "outward show" of a man "seldom or never jumpeth with the heart" (3.1.10–11). Thus the greater irony in the council scene when Buckingham, Richard's "other half" but later to be cast off, declares that the two of them know "each other's faces" but not each other's hearts; this is as events prove. A more immediate irony is provided forty lines later when Hastings, soon to be beheaded, reveals that he takes Richard at face value:

> I think there's never a man in Christendom
> Can lesser hide his love or hate than he,
> For by his face straight shall you know his heart.
>
> (3.4.51–53)

His short shrift follows.

With Macbeth and his lady, real rather than seeming candor is an essential element in their relationship, certainly at first, more fitfully before the murder of Banquo, and never again after the banquet scene. But the essential element in their relation with others is a controlled dissimulation, insofar, that is, as the protagonists prove capable of it. After reading Macbeth's letter with the account of the Weird Sisters, Lady Macbeth leaps immediately to considering the means necessary to make him king. Interrupting these reflections is the pat arrival of the messenger to announce that Duncan will be at the castle that evening, a coincidence prompting her to set forth her "fell purpose" in soliloquy. With Macbeth's entry she declares her state of transport and enjoins him to adopt a deceptive decorum:

> bear welcome in your eye,
> Your hand, your tongue. . . .
>
> (1.5.64–65)

By the critical day of the banquet, Macbeth, now crowned, no longer depends on his lady's encouragement in arranging for the murder of Banquo and Fleance. He even, deceptively, instructs her to pay special honor to Banquo that very night:

> Present him eminence both with eye and tongue. . . .
>
> (3.2.31)

His reply to her hint that Banquo's lease of life is not eternal is that she should remain innocent of any knowledge until the deed is done. What accounts for this estrangement? Is it that Macbeth is already aware he has stepped in so far that he no longer need rely on her support—an assumption belied by the banquet scene—or is it that he senses she is already drifting toward a loss of control ("Nought's had, all's spent . . ."), though that, too, seems belied by the banquet scene? He greets the guests with the somewhat curious remark that while he will mingle with them, Lady Macbeth will keep her chair of state until "in best time" she will give them welcome. Yet she does so immediately, employing a clever *occupatio*, declining to say what in fact she does say:

> Pronounce it for me, sir, to all our friends,
> For my heart speaks they are welcome.
>
> (3.4.7–8)

What the hearts of the two offer indeed is "welcome," the repetition of the word ending each of their first three speeches, as Kittredge noted, indicating how insistently they are seeking a social bond to legitimize their status.

Though hypocrisy is the means the two rely on in pursuing their diabolical ends, it is Macbeth's open recognition of this fact that keeps him within the bounds of sympathy. When he is having second thoughts about the murder of Duncan, Lady Macbeth overcomes his scruples; he becomes "settled," resolved to "mock the time" even as earlier she had charged him to "beguile the time" (1.5.63), declaring:

> False face must hide what the false heart doth know.
>
> (1.7.82)

Again in the scene before the banquet when she has exhorted him to be "bright and jovial" after his admission to terrible dreams, he rallies again, acknowledging the necessity of a hypocritical front: "we / Must . . . make our faces vizards to our hearts. / Disguising what they are" (3.2.32–35).

Finally, in the soliloquy before the approach of the English soldiers supported by the rebelling nobles, Macbeth, "sick at heart," reflects on what he has to look forward to—not love, honor, and troops of friends but a compelled and therefore hollow obedience—mouth-honor:

> Curses, not loud but deep, mouth-honor, breath,
> Which the poor heart would fain deny, and dare not.
>
> (5.3.27–28)

Such instances should perhaps be sufficient to show Shakespeare deftly introducing the motif of tongue and heart into quite different kinds of plays. Its double edge serves to suggest different aspects of character and its being familiar to his audience permitting him to do so in brief compass. With his last tragedy it becomes a governing factor of characterization.

* * *

Though the firmly articulated structure of *Coriolanus* has been much admired, the character of the protagonist has not. In fact, some find his political viewpoint and the manner in which he gives expression to it so offensive that only with difficulty, if at all, is he included in the roster of Shakespearean tragic heroes. Such an archidolater as A. C. Bradley, while acknowledging the play a tragedy ("for the passion is gigantic, and it leads to the hero's death") separates it out from the "supreme" examples as of a totally different order, a judgment with which other critics have concurred.[5]

Yet some have studied this starkly beautiful play in ways that point to aspects that go beyond the question of the merits or appeal of its titular hero. As a result of these studies, Shakespeare may be seen to have provided a rich thematic context in which to present his protagonist with relentless clarity. In an essay that provided Hutchings with the title of the article cited above in note 5, F. N. Lees looks at the play from the aspect of political philosophy, arguing that the Aristotelian statement, "He that is incapable of living in a society is a god or a beast," provides a fitting comment for it; to support its relevance for the sixteenth century, he then cites a version of this statement appearing in Bacon's essay "On Friendship": "Whosoever *is delighted in solitude* [my italics] is either a wild beast or a god" (1625).[6] From a Renaissance perspective Lees's stress on the Aristotelian requirement for social concord in a *polis* or city state is altogether apt: a translation of the *Politics* was available in 1598, and for such a voracious reader as Shakespeare seems to have been might well have provided, in Lees's words, "seed for the good ground" of his imagination. The citation from Bacon, however, is a case of special pleading, for one must reckon with Bacon's use of the version he gives. In the opening sentence of his essay, he takes occasion to remark on the mixture of "truth and untruth" that it encompasses in so few words; the statement, in fact, serves as a point of departure for his following animadversions, and these relate not to political ideas but to the merits of friendship, as the title indicates. Furthermore, one may wonder whether "delight in solitude" can fittingly account for the anguish of Coriolanus's banishment or the fierceness of his revenge. It is true, on exiting from Rome he likens himself to a lonely dragon in his fen, but when we next see him he is in the "goodly" city of Antium seeking vengeance on Rome through fellowship with a rival military hero.

An additive if not a corrective to this emphasis on political philosophy is provided by a concern for the period in which this semilegendary hero lived. In a most useful study, Paul A. Cantor has stressed the different chronological perimeters Shakespeare set himself to portray in *Coriolanus* and in *Antony and Cleopatra:* the one focusing on the small but now (following on the expulsion of the Tarquin kings) republican city which fostered a military ethos in order to maintain itself among hostile neighbors and which instituted its first tribunate in order to give some degree of power to the rebelling plebeians; the other focusing on a triumphant Rome at the height of its imperial domination. Each of these heroes, Cantor observes, has his specific historical milieu: "Each embodies the way of life characteristic of the regime under which he lives; each achieves the perfection of the virtues and the extreme of the vices characteristic of his era."[7] To evoke so sharply two such distinct periods and two such distinctive protagonists, whose passions are as great as they are different, must be accounted a remarkable feat of historical projection on the part of the playwright.

A third aspect of the play that has come to notice is Shakespeare's use of a topical issue; this is seen in a linking of early Rome and its economic problems of scarcity for the plebeians and of revolution for the patricians to the current social problems in Elizabethan and Jacobean England. Economic as well as religious causes had prompted several rebellions in the sixteenth century, and in 1607 (perhaps the year preceding the composition of *Coriolanus*) there were risings in Northamptonshire, Leicestershire, as well as in Shakespeare's own Warwickshire, consequent upon scarcity and high prices.[8] When Shakespeare reduced the grievances of the plebeians from Plutarch's double basis of usury and dearth to the single one of scarcity of corn, he was, Geoffrey Bullough concludes, responding to a topical issue (pp. 458–59).

The disjunction between what the heart thinks and the tongue speaks, which, as we have seen, became for Shakespeare a kind of motif in projecting character, also represents a topical issue in its reflection of the antirhetorical attitude that developed in the course of a rhetorically attuned period. In this his final tragedy he employs it as a means of particularizing his hero's integrity in his persistent, if overinsistent, belief that speech should mirror the speaker's true response to the occasion. Coriolanus's own use of language in differing situations manifests this: at times laconic to the point of curtness, at times copious to the point of pleonasm. His adherence to a nonmanipulative use of language is in sharp contrast to the attitudes not only of the tribunes who oppose him but also to those of the patricians who support him, most particularly the adroit Menenius and the indomitable Volumnia; their differing attitudes concerning the use of language become determinants in the tragic conflict. Thus Hutchings concludes his survey of interpretations with the comment that the "heart of *Coriolanus* lies in a conjunction of its concern with social cohesion and its stress on appropriate language" (p. 48). In general this seems right. But, significantly, Coriolanus is also opposing the dissembling and duplicity that may be required to make speech "appropriate" to the occasion. His view of language pits him not only against the demands of politic considerations but also against those of his friends, his family, and even Rome itself (though it does, as we have seen, align him with a popular Elizabethan view).

A number of commentators have explained the character of Coriolanus by placing him in the category of the blunt, plain-speaking soldier, though the characteristics of such a stock figure do not easily meld with Shakespeare's presentation of his other soldier-heroes. One thinks of the "witchcraft" in Othello's account to Desdemona of his battles, sieges, and fortunes, or the splendid stylistic range of an Antony, "triple pillar" and "greatest soldier of the world." Related to but different from the stock figure of the blunt soldier is that of the plain-speaking civilian. This topos also has a long tradition in the period, notably instanced at its outset in Wyatt's first satire ("My own John Poins," with its assertive catalogues beginning "I cannot . . ."; "I am not . . ."). But like other topoi, this, too, lends itself to reverse application, nicely illustrated in the figure of Kent whose "occupation" it is to be "plain." As Cornwall aptly observes:

> This is some fellow
> Who, having been prais'd for bluntness, doth affect
> A saucy roughness, and constrains the garb
> Quite from his nature. He cannot flatter, he,
> An honest mind and plain, he must speak truth!
> [If] they will take 't, so; if not, he's plain.
>
> (*King Lear,* 2.2.95–100)

Nonetheless, despite the possibility that such a plain-speaker may only be posturing, the pose itself evokes the conception of one who speaks not from his mouth but from his heart, or, as Menenius says about Coriolanus: "His heart's his mouth: / What his breast forges, that his tongue must vent" (3.1.255–56).[9] Carried one step further, the conception also evokes the individual who presents not an ostensible but a true self to the world, reversing Wyatt's satiric formulation, "rather than to be, outwardly to seem" and endorsing Hamlet's declaration to his mother, "Seems, madam? . . . I know not 'seems'. . . . These [his inky coat and suits of solemn black] indeed seem, / For they are actions that a man might play" (1.2.76, 83–84). Coriolanus, too, when he is urged to assume the gown of humility and ask for the votes of the populace, objects to such actions as alien to his nature; it is a "part" that he will blush "in acting" (2.2.144–45). He uses this theatrical metaphor at several critical points but most notably in this the first of the two crises when he is persuaded to act contrary to his principles. Both of these crises are decisive, the one leading to his banishment, which he does not anticipate; the other to his death, which he does.

Initiating the first is the popular fervor that we are told he arouses in Rome following on his remarkable feats of valor at Corioli: the dumb thronging to see him, the blind to hear him speak, matrons, ladies, and maids showering him with their gloves, scarves, and handkerchiefs, the nobles bowing as to Jove's statue. This report given by a nameless messenger (2.1.260–66) contrasts with the derisive version of the same scene that the representative of the people, the tribune Brutus, gives:

> All tongues speak of him, and the bleared sights
> Are spectacled to see him. Your prattling nurse
> Into a rapture lets her baby cry
> While she chats him. The kitchen malkin pins
> Her richest lockram 'bout her reechy neck,
> Clamb'ring the walls to eye him; . . .
>
> . . . .
>   Our veil'd dames
> Commit the war of white and damask in

Their nicely gauded cheeks, to th' wanton spoil
Of Phoebus' burning kisses. Such a pother,
As if that whatsoever god who leads him
Were slily crept into his human powers,
And gave him graceful posture.

(2.1.203–8, 213–19)

When the scene is being readied for the senate to select a consul, the two officers laying out the cushions comment on the nature of Coriolanus's attitude toward the populace. Again alternative views are presented. The Second Officer sees it as a "noble carelessness," his reason being that many great men who flattered the people were never loved, and many were loved but for no reason; therefore if the people know not why they love, then they hate upon no better ground.[10] To the First Officer, however, Coriolanus's adversarial stance is not simply the "carelessness" of patrician rank; in his view Coriolanus actively seeks the hatred of the people, and he observes that "to seem to affect the malice and displeasure of the people is as bad as that which he dislikes, to flatter them for their love" (2.2.21–23).

Having been named consul, Coriolanus must, in accord with custom, don the napless vesture of humility and entreat the "voices" of the people. In demurring from an exercise so repugnant to him, he puts it as a request, "Please you / That I may pass this doing"—a manner of speech he uses on only one other occasion and that is in rallying Cominius's soldiers when they have retired from the field ("Please you to march . . ."). Yet he consents and declares he will "practise" the insinuating nod (the verb conveying also the sense of duplicity), doff his hat in feigned deference, and so counterfeit the "bewitchment" of a demagogue.

But this counterfeited appeal is only briefly successful, the citizens, except for one who simply takes it as "his kind of speech," judging it a mockery. Consequently, the two tribunes are able to incite their followers, whom it is clear they had earlier primed to oppose Coriolanus's election, each of them chiding: "As you were lesson'd"; "As you were fore-advis'd." By further priming, they intend to exculpate themselves from the ensuing revocation, for they instruct their followers to noise it about that they had agreed to Coriolanus's election as consul only because of *their* injunctions: "we labour'd," "after our commandment," "lay the fault on us," "spare us not," "we read lectures," "we did commend," "our putting on." To the tribunes, the "voices" of the people should be merely echoes of their voices and their words.

When the tribunes stop his passage to the market place, Coriolanus's response is to harangue the senators and patricians at length for ever having acceded to the instituting of the tribunate, urging finally that its power be thrown in the dust. Declaring this to be "manifest treason," the tribune Brutus pronounces summary judgment on him, immediate death from the Tarpeian Rock. In the fray that follows, the patricians are able to "beat in" the mutinous people, and when the "rabble" reappear, Menenius is able to cajole them into proceeding by due process.[11] On this occasion Coriolanus is taken aback at his mother's disapproval, given her usual attitude toward the people, and demands to know why she wishes him milder: "Would you have me / False to my nature? Rather say I play / The man I am" (3.2.14–16). Her response is that one can be too "noble" when "extremities speak": at such times honor should combine with policy.[12] Enjoining him to turn again to the people, she makes clear that in her view language is a manipulative technique; it need not—perhaps should not—reveal a heart that speaks:

> Now it lies you on to speak
> . . . not by your own instruction,
> Nor by th' matter which your heart prompts you,
> But with such words that are but roted in
> Your tongue, though but bastards and syllables
> Of no allowance to your bosom's truth.
>
> (3.2.52–57)

For Volumnia, action is eloquence (3.2.76); words are subordinate to performance, which here entails staging a contrived scene—Coriolanus appearing with bonnet in outstretched hand, his knee bussing the stones, his head bowing in all directions, and his speech the language of apology and conciliation. In short, it entails playing a part: "Must I," he asks, "With my base tongue give to my noble heart / A lie?" Yet since the situation involves others than himself, he agrees to perform, though sensing correctly that it is such a "part" that he will never "discharge to th' life" (3.2.101–6).

After having primed the populace as to how it is to react, the tribunes deliberately set out to chafe him, knowing full well that "then he speaks / What's in his heart" (3.3.28–29). Quickly enraging him with the charge of "traitor," even as Aufidius is to do later, they pronounce the sentence of instant banishment; to this Coriolanus gives the splendidly impassioned, highly romantic retort, "I banish you! . . . thus I turn my back. / There is a world elsewhere!"

Some commentators interpret Coriolanus as exhibiting a "natural antipathy" to eloquence,[13] but this is, I think, to miss the topical issue that there should be no divorce between the tongue and the heart, the posited ideal representing a moral as well as an aesthetic concern for a harmony of the two, "thought and word," "word and deed."[14] Consequently, a critic who finds fault with the protagonist in this play just because the "inward man is virtually a duplicate of the outward" has ignored an important and, in my opinion, supremely important, aspect of the play.[15]

Rather than exhibiting an antipathy to eloquence, Coriolanus displays a range of styles and an energetic and vigorous mode of expression.[16] Earlier, mention was made of his terse, laconic manner. Greeted on his first entry, "Hail, noble Martius," he answers, "Thanks" (1.1.163), and some fifty lines later when the messenger, reporting on the warlike state of the Volscians, calls for him, he responds, "Here" (1.1.222). Yet between these two monosyllabic answers, almost all of the lines are given to him, and while his speeches provide necessary exposition about the rebelling plebeians and the concessions granted them, they add up to nothing less than an abusive tirade. It was thus a bold stroke on Shakespeare's part to introduce his protagonist in so unappealing, even repelling fashion, though it has the merit of allowing him at the very outset of the action to project what is to be his fate and the reason for it: "Trust ye? / With every minute you do change a mind, / And call him noble that was now your hate, / Him vile that was your garland" (180–83).

The other patricians are also abusive of the people—Volumnia, openly after her son's banishment; Menenius, who designates them "rats" of Rome and "multiplying spawn," calls the tribunes a "brace of unmeriting, proud, violent, testy magistrates (alias fools)" and "old crabtrees," his point of view being that "We call a nettle but a nettle, and / The fault of fools but folly." Still, he lessens the effect of his malice ("What I think, I utter") by a palliatory manner, taking particular refuge in his reputation as a "humorous" type, like Prince Hal a man of all humors. Even the sage Cominius refers to the "dull tribunes" and the "fusty plebeians." But among these patricians it is the soldier Caius Martius Coriolanus who supremely commands not only the eloquence but also the heroics of vituperation. In the second part of the play, such heroics are much reduced, most significantly by his progressively reducing speech to mere essentials.

Though they were able to beat in the plebeians, the patricians offered few and utterly futile words on Coriolanus's behalf, having given way like beasts and cowardly nobles (as Menenius later puts it) to the crowds hooting him out of the city (4.6.122–24). Coriolanus himself offers a dignified and consolatory farewell to family and friends as he goes into exile. Arrived at the goodly city of Antium, disguised in mean apparel, he admits that were it not for his disguise, women (with spits) and boys (with stones) would—justifiably—slay him in "puny battle." This speech, sometimes interpreted as a crass comment on his earlier triumph, can surely be taken as Coriolanus's first open acknowledgment of what war means to the victimized:

> 'Tis I that made thy widows: many an heir
> Of these fair edifices 'fore my wars
> Have I heard groan, and drop. Then know me not. . . .
>
> (4.4.2–4)

In the marvelous scene that follows, when he reveals himself to Aufidius, Coriolanus first speaks with noble candor of his "extremity": it is "not out of hope / . . . to save my life" but "To be full quit of those my banishers, / Stand I before thee here." Next by skillfully modulating his words, he allows for Aufidius's refusal:

> But if so be
> Thou dar'st not this, and that to prove more fortunes
> Th' art tir'd, then, in a word, I also am
> Longer to live most weary, and present
> My throat to thee and to thy ancient malice. . . .
>
> (4.5.93–97)

Then with a counterturn, he goads him with a blunt recital of the harms he has done to him and to his country. His speech brings Aufidius's immediate consent to join him in his revenge on Rome—partly out of admiration, partly out of emulation, as it proves. Such immediate consent gives instant confirmation to Coriolanus's words in his earlier soliloquy beginning, "O world, thy slippery turns":

> so fellest foes,
> Whose passions and whose plots have broke their sleep
> To take the one the other, by some chance,
> Some trick not worth an egg, shall grow dear friends
> And interjoin their issues.[17]
>
> (4.4.18–22)

Among the Volscians, Martius, as he is now properly called, reassumes his martial stature: "made on," so a servant reports, "as if he were son and heir to Mars" (4.5.196–97). The soldiers fly to him, as if by "witchcraft," but even as Aufidius acknowledges that Martius indeed "bears all things fairly," "shows good husbandry for the Volscian state," and "fights dragon-like," he is even then designing how he may recoup his own military reputation. After Menenius's unsuccessful embassy to the camp outside Rome, Aufidius again admits that Martius keeps a "constant temper" (5.2.92), while in the view of the Second Watch, "he's the rock, the oak, not to be wind-shaken" (5.2.108–9). To Menenius, having seen him in his chair of state, "He wants nothing of a god but eternity, and"—with proleptic irony—"a heaven to throne in." But it is Cominius's description that most aptly sums up the change in Martius; it is, in fact, not so much a "change" as a reverting to his earlier antirhetorical stance that speech should reveal what the heart prompts. Unable to respond as he would, he speaks but a single word and that scarcely audible. "I tell you, Cominius says,

> he does sit in gold, his eye
> Red as 'twoud burn Rome; and his injury
> The gaoler to his pity. I kneel'd before him:
> 'Twas very faintly he said "Rise," dismiss'd me
> Thus, with his speechless hand.
>
> (5.1.63–67)

This speechless gesture links movingly with Martius's earlier greeting of Virgilia in 2.1 as "my gracious silence" and with the stage direction before he acquiesces to Volumnia: *"Holds her by the hand silent"* (5.3).

In spite of his "constant temper," Martius shows consideration for his two former compatriots, sending a letter to Cominius after his embassy and preparing one in advance of Menenius's because as he says to him, "I lov'd thee," and as he explains to Aufidius because he wished "to grace" him. His resolve to reject further embassies is immediately thwarted by the appearance of his family, eliciting his instinctive response, "I melt, and am not / Of stronger earth than others. . . . / Great nature cries, 'Deny not,'" but this he at once opposes with the defiant claim, "I'll never / Be such a gosling to obey instinct, but stand / As if a man were author of himself / And knew no other kin" (5.3.28–29, 33–37). When his wife and mother speak to him, Martius's admission, apparently in an aside, is again in the theatrical terms that reveal his distaste for "seeming": "Like a dull actor now / I have forgot my part and I am out / Even to a full disgrace" (5.3.40–42). Conscious that Volumnia will offer "colder reasons," he beseeches her not to speak. Yet he listens in silence to her fifty-odd lines of harangue constraining him to choose between "mercy" and "honour." It is, he recognizes, a choice that will prove "most mortal" to him, and so it does.

In this tightly constructed play with its prevailing military ethos and its context of competing political forces, the actions of the protagonist lead inexorably to his fate.[18] Yet in the last two scenes Shakespeare introduces ironic touches. Martius, who earlier "fled from words" (2.2.72), is expected by Aufidius "to purge himself with words," a point that is endorsed by the Third Conspirator, who urges immediate assassination "ere he express himself or move the people." Yet in spite of, or because of, the truce now in effect the Volscians split the air with noise to welcome him and tear their base throats "with giving him glory." He enters the city— marching with the Commoners.

In reciting Martius's malefactions to the city lords, Aufidius includes the altogether apposite charge that as general he had not held a counsel of war to obtain the consent of the Volscians for withdrawing the troops. Since Volumnia has argued for his extending a "noble grace to both parts" (or, in Martius's words, for framing "convenient peace" in place of "true wars"), the charge can be taken in either of two ways: as evidence of his former arrogance or as evidence of an impulsive response to Volumnia's appeal.[19]

In connection with these two possible interpretations, it is worthwhile to note Shakespeare's introduction of the motifs of pity versus wrath, those specifically Homeric (hence "classical") topoi. There is the incident in act 1 where Martius, refusing the princely gifts his general offers, asks for freedom for the poor Volscian in whose house he has slept. He explains that he had seen him taken prisoner but then, before he could come to his aid, Aufidius came within his view, "And wrath o'erwhelm'd my pity" (1.9.80–84). There is the crucial reverse situation in act 5 when as the result of the "prayers" of Volumnia (5.3.171) "pity" overcomes his wrath with the consequent saving of Rome and his own consequent death; there is in all its irony the premeditated act of Aufidius, when together with his conspirators, he attacks Martius out of "rage" (5.6.135), an excusatory "impatience," the Second Lord calls it. Lastly, in one of Shakespeare's—it must be admitted—more hurried endings, there is Aufidius's final encomium of the murdered hero, beginning "My rage is gone, / And I am struck with sorrow."

With the extremes of pity and wrath counterposed, Martius's single decision to halt the war should, I think, be seen not as a return to his former arrogance but as a reflection of the passionate nature of his character that was forcefully presented early on in the play: his impetuosity at Corioli. When the common soldiers retreat like "hares" and "geese" before the Volscians and ignore his charge to follow him within the gates, he is shut in "alone / To answer all the city" (1.4.51–52). Though believed slain, he reappears, "bleeding" and "assaulted by the enemy," a sight that stirs the soldiers to turn defeat into victory. Meanwhile in another part of the battlefield Cominius is allowing his soldiers to retreat when Martius appears, looking as if he had been "flay'd." Despite his wounds, he beseeches his general to set him against Aufidius and his Antiates and is permitted to select his own command. Here he directs his appeal to the soldiers in a series of conditionals (1.6.66–75), one of which is surely reflected in his later knowing submission to Volumnia, "If any . . . think his country's dearer than himself. . . ."

Critics have commented that at the end of the play, though Rome has been spared, the political situation for both Romans and Volscians is no better than before. Yet Shakespeare has beautifully established a historical perspective. This is well pointed up when one recalls Volumnia's assertion that action is eloquence. To this Coriolanus's military valor throughout brilliantly attests, but the truth of her assertion must also include the *death* of the hero. His inability to tolerate the disjunction between what the heart prompts and what is required by expediency defines his political ineptitude under the conditions of a warring, quite primitive, Rome. Still, it is a Rome on its way to greatness, and in that historical process the tragic figure of Coriolanus comes to have, as Hutchings aptly puts it, a "mythic" value.

NOTES

1. Compare the proverbial charge, "to lie in one's throat," also frequent in Shakespeare. Morris Palmer Tilley, *A Dictionary of the Proverbs in England in the Sixteenth and Seventeenth Centuries* (Ann Arbor: University of Michigan Press, 1950; reprint New York: AMS Press, 1985), T268.

2. All references, until otherwise noted, are to the Riverside edition of Shakespeare, ed. G. Blakemore Evans (Boston: Houghton Mifflin, 1974).

3. See *Much Ado* (3.4.80–86), where Margaret makes mocking reference to this metaphor when teasing Beatrice:

You may think perchance that I think you are in love. Nay, by'r lady, I am not such a fool to think what I list, nor I list not to think what I can, nor indeed I cannot think, *if I would think my heart out of thinking,* that you are in love, or that you will be in love, or that you can be in love, (italics mine).

4. In "The Convention of 'Heart and Tongue' and the Meaning of *Measure for Measure*," *Shakespeare Quarterly* 5 (1954): 1–10. John L. Harrison discusses this motif as part of the overall design of the play.

5. For a survey of differing interpretations of *Coriolanus*, together with pertinent analyses, see W. Hutchings's article, "Beast or God: The *Coriolanus* Controversy," *Critical Quarterly* 24.2 (1982): 35–50.

6. "*Coriolanus,* Aristotle, and Bacon," *Review of English Studies* n.s. 1 (1950): 114–25.

7. *Shakespeare's Rome: Republic and Empire* (Ithaca: Cornell University Press, 1976), p. 15.

8. These are detailed in Geoffrey Bullough's *Narrative and Dramatic Sources of Shakespeare* (London: Routledge and Kegan Paul, 1964), volume 5.

9. I use the Arden edition, ed. Philip Brockbank, 1976, throughout.

10. Cantor (*Shakespeare's Rome,* pp. 74–75) perceptively notes that in Rome a military hero who was willing to court the favor of the plebeians and use their support against his fellow patricians could make himself sole master of the city, and he cites the example of Caesar: "Once the plebeians ["the tag-rag people"] begin following a powerful patrician against the advice of their own tribunes (*Julius Caesar* 1.1), or, more importantly, once the patricians cease to quarrel among themselves but take their disputes to the plebeians for arbitration (*JC* 3.2), the Republic is doomed."

11. The descriptive stage directions quoted here—"beat in," "rabble"—are generally acknowledged to be Shakespeare's.

12. Again, Wyatt's first satire provides an analogue:

I cannot learn the way.
And much the less of things that greater be,

That asken help of colours of device
To join the mean with each extremity.

(ll. 59–62)

13. See, for example, Maurice Charney, *Shakespeare's Roman Plays* (Cambridge: Harvard University Press, 1961), p. 34, and Paul Jorgensen, *Shakespeare's Military World* (Berkeley: University of California Press, 1956), pp. 298–99.

14. See T. McAlindon's interesting chapter, "Words, Deeds and Decorum," in *Shakespeare and Decorum* (London: Macmillan, 1973).

15. Huntington Brown, "Enter the Shakespearean Tragic Hero," *Essays in Criticism* 3 (1953): 287.

16. Some of the vigor of Coriolanus's speech, as Brockbank points out (*Coriolanus*, p. 68), is the result of his turning nouns into verbs or participles: "had I come coffin'd home" (2.1.175); "Lov'd me . . . / Nay, godded me indeed" (5.3.10–11); "my true lip / Hath virgin'd it e'er since" (5.3.47–48).

17. This, Brockbank notes, recalls Hamlet's "even for an egg-shell" speech (*Hamlet*, 4.4.46–56), but in the case of Coriolanus he considers that in seeking to revenge himself on Rome, he brings "his reflections to an ignominious climax." Yet one may also note that Hamlet's assertion—"Rightly to be great / Is not to stir without great argument. / But greatly to find quarrel in a straw / When honor's at the stake"—is at one with Coriolanus's heroic stance.

18. Perhaps one explanation for the lowered response to Shakespeare's final tragedy rests on the division of opinion about what constitutes its climax, some believing it to be when Coriolanus determines to revenge himself on Rome, others when in sparing Rome he is false to the Volscians. But the one action is the inevitable concomitant of the other. Brockbank has said of Coriolanus; "The integrity of the soldier destroys the integrity of the man" (Arden edition, p. 50), but it is just as true to say that the integrity of the man destroys the integrity of the soldier. It is this tragic inevitability that surely gives to the play much of its classical feeling.

19. Plutarch says that some of the Volscian army "misliked" what he had done; others were well pleased at the peace, while some who misliked it said he was not to be blamed for yielding to such a "forcible extremitie" (printed in Bullough, *Narrative Sources*, 5:541).

Ovid and *The Winter's Tale*
Conflicting Views toward Art

Mary Ellen Lamb

The recent upsurge of attention to Ovid as a source for Shakespeare's works demonstrates that despite the extensive writing already devoted to Shakespeare's sources, there is more to be done.[1] This is particularly true of *The Winter's Tale*. Critics have noted the Ovidian source for Autolycus and Paulina, the two figures for the artist added to the basic plot adapted from Greene's *Pandosto*.[2] What critics have not noted, however, is the extent to which the differing perceptions of Ovid represented by Autolycus on the one hand and Paulina on the other involve *The Winter's Tale* in the ongoing debate about Ovid at that time, unexpectedly present in the contemporary attacks on theater. The use of these Ovidian artist-figures to appeal to the conflicting readings of Ovid in the Renaissance shifts the defense of theater from art itself to its reception by an audience. An understanding of the Ovidian source of *The Winter's Tale* is central to a new perspective on the often-discussed view of art in this play.

The implied audience for *The Winter's Tale* derives from the Renaissance reader of Ovid, faced with two coexisting and conflicting perceptions of Ovid's work, allegorical and literal. For centuries, Ovid's *Metamorphoses* had been interpreted allegorically to contain moral lessons, laboriously set forth in complicated commentaries.[3] By the Renaissance, however, many readers had become sceptical of allegorical interpretations; and unmoralized and even erotic imitations of Ovid by Shakespeare, Marlowe, Marston, and others stripped Ovid of his cloak of respectability to raise the question of the worth, moral or otherwise, of his highly improbable tales.[4] Through its use of conflicting perceptions of Ovid in Paulina and Autolycus, *The Winter's Tale* poses the question of the worth of art. By calling upon its audience to apply the Renaissance reader's tolerance of contradicting perceptions of Ovid, *The Winter's Tale* rests its own defense.

The two opposing views of Ovid as urbane wit or moral philosopher correspond to the two views of the artist represented by Autolycus and Paulina. Does the artist bandy about ridiculous tales for his own amusement or financial self-interest, like Autolycus? Or does the artist teach lessons of moral worth, like Paulina? Autolycus's ballad of the maid turned into a fish "for she would not exchange flesh with one that loved her" (4.4.281–82)[5] is conventionally Ovidian and, according to the literal terms in which Autolycus presents it, amusingly fraudulent. Autolycus, at least, is under no illusions about any hidden truth in the ballads he sells, any more than he believes his own disguises. Palming off patently absurd tales on country clowns is one of his several performances enacted to swindle money from a gullible public. His performances, as empty of pretense to moral worth as his ballads, point to a perception of theater as morally bankrupt. An entirely different view of theater is dramatized by the reenactment of Ovid's Pygmalion myth, as Hermione's "statue" slowly comes to life before the astonished court. This scene, together with the sixteen-year performance in which Paulina has pretended Hermione is dead while managing Leontes' rites of repentance, is finally redemptive, at least for Leontes and possibly for the court audience as well. Just like the myths of the moral Ovid depicted in the commentaries, Paulina's "lies" are beneficial to the soul.

The two views of art dramatized through Paulina and Autolycus resonate through *The Winter's Tale* itself, for these conflicting perceptions are, in the end, self-reflexive. *The Winter's Tale* poses this question: is it merely an "old tale," fully as silly, with its oracles and Bohemian seacoasts, as it appears to be? Are we gullible country clowns for buying tickets? Or, despite its evident artifice, can it "redeem" us, or at least show us some higher truth of value in our lives? Finally, these two perspectives extend beyond theater to the nature of reality itself. Is Autolycus (and the early, unreformed Leontes) correct in perceiving identity as a series of empty performances in a world of moral chaos? Or can we share Paulina's belief in a sacramental reality controlled by a careful Apollo? The choice in *The Winter's Tale* to select the two figures for the artist from Ovid reflects the extent to which Ovid was inextricably implicated in these issues. Thus, the charges leveled against the theater are explored through Autolycus, while Paulina represents an alternative view of the kinds of truth offered in plays and, finally, in reality as well.

Autolycus's name, obtrusively Ovidian among traditional pastoral names like Dorcas and Mopsa, calls attention to itself and to its source. His description of himself as a "snapper up of unconsidered trifles" because he was "littered under Mercury" derives unmistakably from the moral commentaries on Ovid's Autolycus from book 11 of the *Metamorphoses*.[6] Fathered by Mercury upon a mortal woman at almost the same time that Apollo engendered his "twin" brother Philammon, Autolycus (or "Awtolychus," as Golding calls him) appropriately represents false art. While the art of his brother Philammon, who "in musicke arte excelled farre all other, / As well in singing as in play,"[7] delighted without deception as befitted the son of Apollo, Autolycus inherited his father's unscrupulous nature:

> . . . a wyly pye,
> And such a fellow as in theft and filching had no peere.
> He was his fathers owne sonne right; he could mennes
> eyes so bleere,
> As for too make ye black things whyght, and whyght
> things black appeere.

(11.360–63)

The commentators embroider on Autolycus's ability as a trickster. Natale Conti relates two incidents, one about his theft of a valuable horse, replaced with a mangy ass, and the other about his abduction of a beautiful bride, for whom he substituted a toothless old hag.[8] Bersuire moves Autolycus's trickery from a physical to a spiritual plane in one of the few moral commentaries on the myth, in which he likens Autolycus's ability to make black seem white to the devil's ability to color over sins, a skill pronounced in flatterers and heretics.[9] In contrasting those upright persons born under the sign of the sun to those of questionable morality born under the sign of Mercury, Sabinus finds contemporary relevance to the myth, for he claims that nothing is so common in his day as to see the songs of Mercury "in aulis & in Judiciis forensibus" in law courts and in palace courts (Aa6). Finally, Fraunce also stresses the dangerous eloquence of those born under the sign of Mercury:

> Such as be Mercuriall, are commonly not very rich. yet they finde out now and then conceits and deuises to drawe money out of the chests of princes & mighty men. . . . If, by chance, his Legierdumaine be perceiued, he can so fincly smooth vp al by facility of discourse, that he neuer is vtterly disgraced by the mighty men. (pp. 96–97)

These commentaries may well have affected Autolycus's function in *The Winter's Tale,* for his own attribution of his dishonesty to his astrological sign, his being "littered under Mercury" (4.3.25), demonstrates their influence over common interpretations of Ovid's myths. The implications of Autolycus's trickery extend beyond his actual thefts to disclose a spiritual corruption, shared at crucial points by the court characters Leontes and Polixenes. This connection between Autolycus and the court, present in the commentaries, extends beyond his courtly affectations to glance at the validity of courtly roles and courtly language.

Paulina's connection with Ovid is through the submerged myth of Pygmalion, which bears clear resemblances to the coming-to-life of Hermione's "statue" in act 5. Pygmalion was a sculptor who fell in love with his own creation; Venus pitied his love and gave life to his statue, which became a warm, breathing woman. Through its resonances with the Pygmalion myth, Paulina's play can be seen to present a positive view of dramatic art as containing valuable higher truth, while Paulina herself can be seen as representing that other view of the artist in the Renaissance, a "maker," whose earthly creativity imitates the divine. And there are strong intimations of divinity in Paulina's art, as in a hushed chapel, she enjoins her audience to "awake your faith" (5.3.95). Working to fulfill Apollo's oracle, Paulina enacts divine will on earth to the benefit of other mortals: her art is not solely human; it partakes of the divine. In this respect, Paulina's role as an artist resembles Pygmalion's. Pygmalion's art, like Paulina's, is a human enactment of divine will. Pygmalion himself has no power to transform his statue into a woman; it is Venus, taking pity on him, who causes the actual metamorphosis.

An apparent difference, however, between the Pygmalion myth and Paulina's play is the presence of an audience. While it is Hermione who "comes to life," the real changes are meant to take place in the hearts of Leontes and the members of the court audience. However, just as Shakespeare's Autolycus was formed in part from the commentaries surrounding the myth, so the use of the Pygmalion myth in *The Winter's Tale* is formed by commentary of a particular kind of special relevance to Shakespeare's play. The Pygmalion myth, so clearly about art, became part of the debate on theater, particularly involving the effect of theater on an audience. Heywood, for example, cites it in defense of theater:

> Painting, likewise, is a dumb oratory; therefore may we not as well by some curious Pygmalion, drawe their conquests to worke the like love in princes towards these worthyes, by shewing them their pictures drawn to the life, as it wrought the poore painter to bee inamoured of his owne shadow? (B3v)[10]

Gager used the Pygmalion story to show the evil effect of art on an audience, as he argued against letting boys wear women's clothing:

> For men may be ravished with love of stones, of dead stuffe, framed by cunning gravers to beautiful womens likenes, as in Poets fables appeareth by Pygmalion.[11]

Gager and Heywood share a common assumption, that art must be judged by its effect on an audience; they only disagree as to whether that effect is likely to be good or bad. In the terms in which this myth is presented in this debate, as well as in the myth itself, the statue scene in *The Winter's Tale* bears a close likeness to the Pygmalion myth: the nature of art is determined, finally, by the way the audience responds to it.

The question of how an audience responds to a work of art is particularly germane to the Pygmalion myth; for this tale, more than others, contrasts especially sharply the diametrically opposed perceptions possible to Ovid's works. At that time it represented both transcendent myth and smutty joke. The simultaneous humor and eroticism of Pygmalion's fondling a statue in his bed only to find the statue a living woman proved irresistible to John Marston, whose *Metamorphosis of Pigmalions Image* (1598) is unabashedly pornographic. This transformation of seemingly cold women to willing bed partners underlies Shakespeare's own reference to the Pygmalion myth in *Measure for Measure* when Lucio taunts Pompey, "What, is there none of Pygmalion's images newly made women to be had now, for putting the hand in the pocket and extracting [it] clutched?"[12] The moral ambivalence of Renaissance responses to the Pygmalion myth, present also in the moral commentaries on the tale,[13] renders it an ideal vehicle for the complex exploration of the value of art, as will be shown below.

The choice of two artist figures closely connected with Ovid draws this play directly into the debate about theater, for Ovid was under attack on the same grounds: explicitly for his immorality, his instruction in vice; less explicitly for the claim of "allegory," some saving kernel of truth conveyed in his improbable tales; and finally (although not directly mentioned) for his essentially rhetorical, dramatic view of man's identity. Such was the significance of Ovid in the propaganda by the enemies of the theater, in fact, that some critics became confused and mistakenly attributed dramatic works to him. In the *Anatomie of Abuses*, Phillip Stubbes claimed that "*Augustus* banished *Ovid* for making Bookes of love, Enterluds, and such other amorous trumperie;" and I. G. made the same mistake.[14] In Ben Jonson's *Poetaster*, as well, the character Ovid is banished for writing a morally questionable play for private performance.[15]

For Stubbes and I. G. (Jonson's position is complicated),[16] Ovid represented the immoral artist deserving banishment from the commonwealth. His banishment served as classical precedent for their own government to censure writers of immoral literature and, in particular, of plays. In fact, the city of London had already expelled players to beyond the city limits in 1575, but enemies of the theater wanted still more stringent controls and, finally, the elimination of theaters entirely. Thus, Stubbes, I. G., and also writers like Gosson and Greene all refer to Augustus's decision. This connection between Ovid and theater is particularly explicit in Henry Crosse's diatribe: "Many well-governed Common-wealths . . . supplanted and beate down Theaters and common Play-houses . . . [just as] *Ovid* for his wanton *Ars Amandi* was exiled by Augustus."[17] In his defense of theater, Lodge implicitly addresses this issue in his criticism of Augustus's decision: "I like not of an angry Augustus which wyll banish *Ovid* for envy, I love a wise Senator, which in wisedome wyll correct him and with advise burn his follyes" (B3).[18] This perception of Ovid as banished from Rome because of the immorality of his works is all the more striking because it represents a choice at variance with what Ovid himself hints in his *Tristia,* that like the innocent Actaeon, he was punished for accidentally witnessing something the powers-that-be desired to be kept secret. This latter version was recognized and cited by other Renaissance writers, such as Thomas Nashe, who were sympathetic to literature.

Ovid's *Ars Amatoria* also played a central role in the propaganda against the theater, for it provided a *locus classicus* for the goings-on among theater audiences, confirming the worst suspicions of the theater's foes. According to Ovid, the theater was a particularly likely place to pick up women:

> But it is especially at the theater you should lay your snares; that is where you may hope to have your desires fulfilled. Here you will find women to your taste: one for a moment's dalliance, another to fondle and caress, another to have all for your own . . . the theater's the place where modesty gets a fall.[19]

Ovid's passionate approval of Romulus's decision to reward his troops with permission to carry off the Sabine women from a theater only made matters worse; and Gosson conflated these passages with Ovid's next passage, actually located at a racetrack, which details techniques of picking up women. Following Ovid point by point, Gosson remarks the exact same behavior at contemporary theaters, concluding that the theater is "a generall Market of Bawdrie" (C2). He brings the subject up again in *Playes Confuted in Five Actions* (c. 1582) (G5ᵛ–G6), and so does John Northbrooke's *A Treatise wherein dicing, dauncing, vaine playes or enterluds . . . are reproued* (1577) (I1v–12). In an unfortunate passage that one critic accurately calls "inept," Thomas Heywood's *Apology for Actors* praises the rape of the Sabine women in his defense of the power of the stage.[20] It is likely that the very perception of the Renaissance stage as "an appointed place of Bauderie" was to some extent filtered through a reading of Ovid.[21]

In so stressing the Ovid of the *Ars Amatoria,* the enemies of the theater were implicitly denying the validity of the other view, the moral Ovid of the commentaries on the *Metamorphoses.* While the *Metamorphoses* is not often mentioned by name, its presence hovers around the arguments about allegory, particularly allegory of classical myth. In a passage revealing his common disapproval both of myth and theater for their distance from literal truth, Gosson, for example, ridicules the traditional levels of interpretation of myth.[22] In his reply to Gosson, Thomas Lodge insists on the traditional hidden meanings in classical myths, including Ovid's.[23] Increasingly, Ovid's moral lessons were dismissed with his myths. Why indulge in these verbal decorations? Why not just tell the moral and dispense with the story altogether? purists were inquiring by the time of *The Winter's Tale*.

This dismissal of allegory, the means by which readers had found moral meanings in myths for centuries, touches directly on what, in the view of at least one prominent critic, was the real animus behind attacks on theater: truth, the real truth, God's truth, did not require phrases, allegories, or any kind of fancy language. God's truth is simple, ideally communicated from God to man's soul without the medium of words at all. A sophisticated manipulation of language indicates equivocation or worse, not eloquence in any true sense. From this perspective, literature—the beauty of its language, the complexity of its vision, ancient myth or contemporary play—was irrelevant or worse. If, as defenders claimed, myths hide a kernel of truth within the husk of the story, why not dispense with the husk entirely and convey the truth, the kernel, pure, unadorned, uncorrupted, enimently digestible?[24] To the standard defense of drama offered, in this case by John Harington, that plays "may make men see and shame at their own faults," Stubbes had already replied, "Oh blasphemie intollerable!" (L7), while Gosson's *Schoole of Abuse* advised that for moral instruction, an audience should repair to a sermon instead.[25] To those who perceived language and the reality it conveys as a matter of literal and unequivocably simple truth, the defenders of myth and drama were utterly unconvincing. From the perspective of literal truth the complexity of works by Shakespeare and Ovid must yield to the simplicity of a country sermon. The two views of reality—the one complex, in flux, resisting exact definition, revealed in language functioning in part on a nonliteral level, the other simple, unchanging, its parameters exactly defined, revealed in literal speech—could not be reconciled. These opposing views of reality are explored in *The Winter's Tale*.

The Winter's Tale also explores the corollary to these differing perceptions of truth. Just as God's truth was thought to be simple, stable, directly communicable, so was man's identity. Just as the use of any art in decorating language was suspect, so any deliberate crafting of words or behavior in life was the equivalent of lying. For this reason, many antitheater tracts revealed a horror of performance for its own sake. Playing roles threatened one's single, God-given identity; acting enabled one to appear what one was not.[26] Gosson foments on this subject in *Playes Confuted in Five Actions,* to argue that even morally acceptable plays, like Buchanan's play of Herod, teach how "to counterfeit and so to sinne" (E6). His perception

of stage-playing as lying, "by outward signes to shew themselves otherwise then they are" (E4v) reveals the belief that what actors are, their
"true" identity, is simple and separate from what they play. Like Gosson,
Crosse also claims that merely watching plays, no matter how moral they
may be in themselves, teaches an audience how to perform; and learning
to perform, to play a role, is in itself deleterious to the soul: at the theater
"a man will learne to be proud, fantasticke, humorous, to make love,
sweare, swagger, in a word closely doo any villanie" (P4v). Except perhaps in the negative connotation of Gosson's translation of the title of the
Ars Amatoria as the "craft" rather than the "art" of love, Ovid is not
mentioned in this material. But the *Ars Amatoria,* which teaches the
reader how to fashion behavior to appear to be in love, that even love, that
most private of emotions, should be fashioned by art, is equally vulnerable
to these charges. In Ovid's works are fulfilled the worst fears of those who
distrusted the effect of watching a performance on the stage. For Ovid, as
for Shakespeare, man is finally an actor creating a role for himself in his
public reality.[27]

The terms of Shakespeare's engagement in the debate over theater were
perhaps sparked by one of his earliest critics, who had warned his readers
of a "Shake-scene" in London.[28] The debate about Ovid and theater
explicitly involves Robert Greene, author of *Pandosto,* the major source
for *The Winter's Tale.* In *Greenes Vision,* one of his several "deathbed"
renunciations of his art, Greene explicitly identifies himself with Ovid as a
sinful writer deserving banishment. Greene explores the possibility of
moral value in literature by presenting two stories, one slightly ribald tale
recounted by a vision of Chaucer, and one laced with moral declamations
recounted by a vision of Gower. Both tales depict a jealous husband's
sudden and unfounded suspicions of his innocent wife's chastity; both
tales depict the husband's subsequent cure. Greene finally denies the
moral worth of either story and adopting the simple view of reality and of
art endemic to antitheater tracts, gives himself up wholly to theology,
secure in the knowledge that "there is no wisedome, but the knowledge of
the law of the Lord" (H2v). In condemning both versions of this tale of a
jealous husband, Greene condemns by implication his own *Pandosto,* also
a narrative about a jealous husband's cruelty toward his faithful wife
written at about the same time as *Greenes Vision.* Shakespeare's choice of
Pandosto as his major source for *The Winter's Tale* represents his own
attempt to work the story through one more time, to test it for moral
worth.

Through Autolycus and Paulina, *The Winter's Tale* examines the very
problems surfacing in the debate over theater, particularly as that debate
implicated Ovid. It explores the morality of theater, especially as measured by its effect on an audience; it explores the kinds of "truth"

available to the "old tales" and dramatic performances; it explores the effect of perceiving language and reality solely in terms of literal rather than complex truth. These issues, all raised for Ovid as well, gain definition from the literary context surrounding Ovid in this period, from the complicated process by which readers selected the appropriate "Ovid" with the awareness of another "Ovid," equally viable. Like Ovid's myths, the theater's valuation depends largely on its audience's belief, with a thoroughness and complexity surpassing theater's most avid defenders as well as its most vehement foes.

As he is portrayed in *The Winter's Tale,* Autolycus embodies several of the evils feared by those who attacked the theater. His entrance marked by a merry song about stealing sheets and tumbling with his "aunts" in the hay, he neatly fits the figure of the immoral artist. While his ballads peddled to the country characters are more conservative, some straight-laced types would no doubt have also disapproved of "Two Maids Wooing a Man," and worried over its effect on susceptible young ladies who might sing it. But the audience for this ballad complicates the question of the moral effect on art, for Dorcas and Mopsa are hardier types than the highly impressionable audiences assumed in the antitheater tracts. Their first reaction to Autolycus and his wares is, admittedly, discouraging as they slip snide accusations at each other over their respective relationships with the Clown. But the song, "Two Maids Wooing a Man," seems if anything to resolve their conflicts. Its approximation to their real-life situation seems to soothe their jealousy, and the Clown also seems calmer as he offers, "Wenches, I'll buy for you both" (4.4.313). The good country people remain good country people, and their laughing, quarreling, and wooing are not, finally, significantly or permanently altered by Autolycus one way or another.

But the question of the moral effect of art is not so easily dismissed. Autolycus possesses tremendous stage appeal, and his entertaining high jinks capture the hearts of many audiences, although some critics seem immune to his charm.[29] From the moment he steps into act 4 singing about his "pugging tooth," his exuberant immorality adds new liveliness to the play. Played with any skill, his catalogue of the tortures awaiting the Clown is broadly comic: "He has a son, who shall be flayed alive, then 'nointed over with honey, set on the head of a wasps' nest" (4.4.785–86) is, if properly delivered, very funny. Even though we know his petty thefts deprive sympathetic pastoral characters, his own delight in his misdeeds is contagious: "Sure the gods do this year connive at us, and we may do anything extempore" (4.4.676–77). But this very appeal poses a problem. Looking on as Autolycus pilfers the Clown's purse, party to his glee, we the audience are drawn into an innately conspiratorial relationship with him. Our very laughter implicates us, in a sense, in what we tolerantly resist calling his "crimes." This presentation of Autolycus may have been influenced by the source for his pranks, for this same disparity between appropriate moral judgment and emotional appeal is characteristic of Greene's *Second* and *Third Part of Conny-Catching*.[30] While its introduction conveys deep and even hysterical abhorrence of conny catchers as "vultures," "harpies," and "vipers," its title page calls their misdeeds "merry tales," revealing the narrator's sympathy, even clearer in the episodes themselves, with the rogue rather than with the victim.

Through Autolycus, *The Winter's Tale* also explores the kinds of truth available to literature, for his ballad of the fish, as stated above, points to the absurdity of ballads, Ovidian myths, and by extension, improbable tales like *The Winter's Tale* itself. "How a usurer's wife was brought to bed of twenty money-bags at a burden, and how she longed to eat adders' heads and toads carbonadoed" (4.4.263–66), one of his other ballads, devalues Ovidian tales even further by placing a metamorphosis into one of the cheapest, most sensational kinds of literature of the day, tales of births of deformed babies and cattle. To Autolycus, these ballads are clearly lies, for he deceives the country audience with his repeated affirmations of their literal truth. He presents "evidence" for the truth of the ballad of the usurer's wife by providing the signatures of the midwife, "one Mistress Taleporter," and five or six other women present. The ballad of the fish is similarly "proven" by the signatures of five justices and "witnesses more than [his] pack will hold" (4.4.285). Autolycus further asserts his own credibility by asking rhetorically, "Why should I carry lies abroad?" (4.4.272), neglecting the obvious motive of profit. The peasants' belief in the ballads is laughably absolute: "Bless me from marrying a usurer!" (4.4.269), Dorcas exclaims; while Mopsa's blind faith in the written word, "I love a ballad in print, a life, for then we are sure they are true" (4.4.261–62), unintentionally satirizes the sale of printed imaginative literature in general.

The conversation between Autolycus and the peasants about the "truth" of these obviously false ballads seems to defend the claim of those who argue against the theater because of its lack of truth. *The Winter's Tale* is from this perspective, like Autolycus' ballads, a lie sold to the gullible for profit. But, like the accusations in the antitheater tracts, the terms in which Autolycus and the peasants measure "truth" are limited to the most literal level. The ballads themselves cannot be so easily dismissed, even if we doubt the midwives' signatures. For all of their absurdity from a literal point of view, they appeal to a deeper reality, an "allegory" as the pamphlets would say. Certainly in the world of comedy, as opposed to that of religious tracts, a woman who refuses to return the love of an appropriate suitor is a kind of "cold fish," lacking full humanity. The ballad of the usurer's wife is likewise a "moral" tale as it points to the dehumanization that occurs when money is overvalued, its painful consequences often appearing in the next generation.[31] This scene seems to pose the following question: is it possible that a work proceeding from low self-interest might still contain some higher truth, quite apart from the intention of the author or performer? The gap between intention and result surfaces at other times in the play, for example when Autolycus exclaims, struck by the sight of the Clown and Old Shepherd dressed in their new court finery, "Here come those I have done good to against my will" (5.2.124–25). Perhaps something of the sort is possible for Autolycus's ballads as well.[32] But since the play itself does not develop this nonliteral level of meaning in the ballads, this question about the kinds of "truth" available in imaginative literature is left open-ended.

Finally, Autolycus embodies the worst fears of the enemies of theater about the pernicious nature of performance. Autolycus does not limit his theatrical skills to the forceful hawking of his wares; he dons disguises throughout act 4 for the sole purpose of cheating the country people of their money. We see him act out a beggar—but he is not really a beggar; he just pleads for the Clown's help so he can pick his pocket. We see him as a peddler—but he is not primarily a peddler; he really sells ballads and trinkets so that he can pick pockets. We see him as a courtier—but he is not really a courtier; he is pretending influence to gain a bribe from the shepherd and his son. The complete lack of any connection between surface accoutrements and inner reality becomes evident in his description of himself as a courtier solely in the terms appropriate to an actor portraying the part:

> Whether it like me or no, I am a courtier. Seest thou not the air of the court in these enfoldings? hath not my gait in it the measure of the court? receives not thy nose court-odour from me? reflect I not on thy baseness, court-contempt? . . . I am courtier *cap-a-pe*. (4.4.730–36)

The Clown is as taken in by Autolycus's assumed roles as his ballads because he perceives "truth" of identity, as of art, in exceedingly literal terms: a man picks his teeth, so he is a courtier. And Autolycus in his way is no different. As Autolycus abjures honesty and trust, those qualities that establish any connection between role and reality, with the sneer, "Ha, ha! what a fool Honesty is! and Trust, his sworn brother, a very simple gentleman!" (4.4.596–97), his reality becomes as simple, as impervious to nuance or tone, as the Clown's. He is, quite simply, lying and so to his mind is anyone else who is acting out a role. Autolycus is entirely unmoved by Perdita's graceful performance as Queen of the Whitsun Festival. To him, she is merely Florizel's "clog" (4.4.679), and Florizel's desire to abandon all he has to fly away with her is merely "a piece of iniquity"

(4.4.678). For Autolycus, roles, like ballads, are either true or false (usually false); the world is literal and hollow, devoid of value, its inhabitants divided into "easy marks" and con men.

Autolycus's world view becomes critically important to the play when it is shared by other characters. At first impressed by Perdita's performance as Queen of the Whitsun Festival, Polixenes falls into a rage when his son vows to marry her. In his anger, he describes Perdita as "a fresh piece / Of excellent witchcraft," "a knack," "an Enchantment" (4.4.423, 429, 435). So similar to Autolycus's, these epithets convey his view that she has been using her seductive wiles to lure Florizel into loving her; that she has been "acting" her role to gain power and money through the prince; that her apparent love for Florizel is merely a cunning ruse, an assumed role (not unlike Autolycus's performances, if Polixenes had known about them) to gain profit. But while the views of Perdita's acting are similar, the emotional response is not; and Polixenes' "moral" outrage shows the extent to which he expects literal truth at this point in the play.

This ugly view of Perdita is untrue to our experience of her in act 4. Her role, partially forced on her by the Old Shepherd, is appropriate and necessary for the feast. While she herself entertains doubts about assuming the role of Queen as she fears "this robe of mine / Does change my disposition" (4.4.134–35), her "acting" in no way compromises her truth or her love for Florizel; it only frees her to express it more fully, as she imagines Florizel "quick, and in mine arms" (4.4.132). Her neat response to Camillo's compliment reveals a keen sense of play:

> Camillo. I should leave grazing were I of your flock,
>   And only live by gazing.
> Perdita. Out alas! You'd be so lean that blasts of January
>   Would blow you through and through.
>
> (4.4.109–12)

But it is her remarkable flower speech describing daffodils, primroses, oxlips, "violets, dim, / But sweeter than the lids of Juno's eyes / Or Cytherea's breath" (4.4.120–22) that is her tour-de-force. This highly finished artifact, drawn from the Ovidian myth of Proserpina, delights without any intention to deceive.[33] Her playful use of Ovidian myth stands in dramatic contrast with Autolycus's Ovidian ballad passed off as "truth." It is ironic that the speaker of this elegant verse refuses to allow gillyvors, improved by human means, in her garden; but her suspicion of gillyvors is of a piece with her suspicion of her own "borrowed flaunts" (4.4.23). Her consciousness of herself as acting seems to help rather than to hinder her poetic skill.

Autolycus's reductive perspective, shared for a time with Polixenes, is experienced most fully by Leontes.[34] Perdita's performance so admired by

Polixenes before his condemnation of her supposed sexual guile recalls an earlier dramatic tableau. Hermione's marvellous speech to Polixenes, spoken at her husband's own behest, was just as socially appropriate. Like Perdita's flower speech, her light-hearted threat to detain Polixenes as a prisoner, if not as a guest, is elegant and playful. While this her crowning argument is not literally true, it truthfully expresses her desire to extend her hospitality for awhile longer. This nonliteral use of language does not offend anyone but Leontes, for it characterizes court talk: the play opens with a witty exchange in which the courtier Archidamus similarly "threatens" to give Camillo "sleepy drinks" to dull his awareness of any deficiences in Sicilian hospitality (1.1.13). Yet Leontes is impervious to her grace. He is similarly unmoved by her elegant self-defense at her trial, which is, like her invitation to Polixenes, a set public speech, consciously invented and performed for an audience. Leontes perceives her speeches *only* as performances, as lies. His distrust of public roles and nonliteral speech plunges him into a reductive worldview like that of Autolycus. As Autolycus perceives Perdita only as "a piece of iniquity," so Leontes grossly distorts his view of Hermione to a "bedswerver," "slippery," "As rank as any flax-wench" (2.1.93; 1.2.273, 277). Soon he perceives his entire court as made up of actors out to deceive him, and he becomes a player himself as he schemes to set Camillo to poison his formerly best friend Polixenes. From the time Leontes suspects his wife's chastity, his perception of playing as lying evokes a literal sense of reality in which all roles are lies: "Go play, boy, play: thy mother plays, and I / Play too" (1.2.187–88); to Camillo: "we have been / Deceived in thy integrity, deceiv'd / In that which seems so" (1.2.239–41): I / Remain a pinch'd thing: yea, a very trick / For them to play at will" (2.1.50–52). His suggestion that Camillo "might'st bespice a cup, / To give mine enemy a lasting wink" (1.2.316–17) makes of Archidamus's "sleepy drinks" a chilling reality.

Thus, *The Winter's Tale* points to the danger of taking play too literally. The over-literal interpretation of language and role plummets Leontes, for one, into a world in which he perceives no truth, in which everyone is seen as acting out a lie in word and deed. The set "performances"—Hermione's courtly invitation to Polixenes and Perdita's eloquent flower speech—amply demonstrate the beauty and innocence possible to nonliteral language. But *The Winter's Tale* does not stop there, balancing a somewhat hysterical distrust of "lies" against these graceful displays of wit. Instead, the final scene, in which Hermione's "statue" comes to life, immensely complicates the play's stand on art.

So much has already been said about the statue scene. It is now perhaps a commonplace that Paulina's brilliant stage managing, the culmination of a sixteen-year performance, is highly effective, and that the result of this entire long drama is nothing less than the regeneration of Leontes' spiritual state.[35] As the impact of Paulina's art moves out beyond Leontes, beyond the court, to us the audience, linked as we are in our mutual ignorance that Hermione did not, in fact, die at the end of act 3, what is affirmed for us? That with repentance comes redemption, that full measure may not be demanded of all our mistakes, that some divine ordering principle silently shapes our lives? This optimistic perspective does not encompass the entire play. Instead, it yields to form part of a larger mode of perception that this scene and indeed the entire play moves us toward. As we, with the court, hold our breath while Hermione descends, living and breathing, from her pedestal, we simultaneously participate in the wonder of this miracle while we recognize that we have been tricked. We had been explicitly given to believe that Hermione had died. Not only had Leontes ordered that the "dead bodies of my queen and son" (3.2.235) be brought to him before being buried in a common grave, but her appearance to Antigonus in a dream convinced that trustworthy gentleman that "Hermione hath suffer'd death" (3.3.42). By falsely leading us to believe that Hermione had died, the play breaks with theatrical convention and, while there is no doubt that Paulina's deception has been beneficial to Leontes, we may hold in suspension our double perception of the statue scene as miracle and fraud.[36]

The implicit resonances of the Pygmalion myth in the last scene defy the tone of the scene, pure, elevated, a moving reunion between wife and husband, mother and daughter.[37] What use could these references have? Are they meant to introduce squalid obscenity into this poignant moment? to impugn Hermione's chastity? Obviously, Hermione is above reproach in this last scene. But her very name perhaps points to a deep Ovidian cynicism. As a passage containing her name in the *Ars Amatoria* makes clear, Ovid, like Autolycus and the early unreformed Leontes, could sometimes present fidelity between husband and wife, faithfulness between friends, as the overromantic wish of a naive fool:

> Friendship and constancy are both but empty names. You cannot with safety tell your friend all the charms of the woman you adore; if he believed what you said of her, he would straightway become your rival. But, you will argue, the grandson of Actor stained not the couch of Achilles. . . . Pylades loved Hermione with a love as chaste as that which Phoebus bore for Pallas, or as the love of Castor and Pollux for their sister Helen. But if you count on miracles like that, you might as well expect to cull apples from the tamarisk, or to gather honey in the middle of a river.[38]

Hermione's long-suffering chastity perhaps can exist only in a play like *The Winter's Tale,* which constantly points to its own lack of realism, its resemblance to an "old tale." Perhaps, according to this cynical view,

Hermione's fidelity and continuing love for Leontes is as impossible in this real world as the seacoast in landlocked Bohemia.

These cynical undertones do not, however, destroy the wonder of the moment when Hermione embraces her husband and blesses her daughter. Her love remains miraculous. But these dissonant associations point to alternatives to how we interpret what we see. They work against the acceptance of the statue scene, or indeed *The Winter's Tale* itself, as literal "truth" or even as transcendent vision. But, just as Autolycus's ballads contain some higher truth beyond the literal level despite any awareness or intention of his, so the miracle of harmony and forgiveness presented in *The Winter's Tale* cannot be dismissed as an "old tale," either. Any decision about what to "believe" must be made with the consciousness of the complexity of reality, the continuum of alternatives simultaneously possible and contradictory, if we are not to be country clowns or urban cynics. Oddly enough, the model for this kind of belief is presented by the Clown in his own transformation into a "gentleman born" when he swears that Autolycus is courageous ("tall") and sober:

> I'll swear to the prince thou art a tall fellow of thy hands and that thou wilt not be drunk; but I know thou art no tall fellow of thy hands and that thou wilt be drunk: but I'll swear it, and I would thou would'st be a tall fellow of thy hands. (5.2.163–68)[39]

Not only does *The Winter's Tale* refuse to resolve the contradictory views of the artist presented through Paulina and Autolycus, but the play further complicates each of the two attitudes towards art. Finally, *The Winter's Tale* shifts the question, "What kind of value can an obviously untrue tale possess?" from the tale to the audience. Just as Ovid's Pygmalion myth can be read as an example of redemptive cooperation with a divine power or as an obscene story of a whore, so *The Winter's Tale* can be interpreted as an absorbing play of regeneration and forgiveness or as a silly hoax, filled with clumsy improbabilities by a playwright nearing the end of his creative powers. Obviously, neither of these is true in any simple sense. Just as the Ovid of the erotic epyllia was held in suspension with the Ovid of the moralized tales, so any choice to believe a play so like an "old tale" must be conscious, a temporary agreement made in full awareness of the range of other possibilities not in any way negated by that choice. Ironically, this defense of theater finally rests on an acceptance of multi-layered reality which must take into account the coexistence of theater as hoax. This tolerance for coexisting contradictions, so familiar to Renaissance readers of Ovid, is essential for us to participate in this double vision in order to understand the argument of *The Winter's Tale* in the Ovidian terms in which it was couched.

NOTES

1. Major books on the subject include Richard A. Lanham, *Motives of Eloquence: Literary Rhetoric in the Renaissance* (New Haven: Yale University Press, 1976); William Keach, *Elizabethan Erotic Narratives* (New Brunswick, N.J.: Rutgers University Press, 1977); Shakespeare's *Sonnets,* ed. Stephen Booth (New Haven: Yale University Press, 1977). The spate of articles on Ovid and *Midsummer Night's Dream, Twelfth Night, Taming of the Shrew, Tempest* and others is too large to detail here. For articles on Ovid and *The Winter's Tale,* see note 2, below.

2. The Pygmalion myth as a source for the statue scene, stage-managed by Paulina, has been mentioned by Geoffrey Bullough, *Narrative and Dramatic Sources of Shakespeare,* vol. 8 (New York: Columbia University Press, 1975), 232–233; and mentioned with other possibilities in Kenneth Muir, *The Sources of Shakespeare's Plays* (London: Methuen, 1977), p. 273; the most complete discussion is Martin Mueller, "Hermione's Wrinkles, or Ovid Transformed: An Essay on *The Winter's Tale,*" *Comparative Drama* 5 (1972): 226–36; see also Adrien Bonjour, "The Final Scene of *The Winter's Tale,*" *English Studies* 33 (1952): 193–208; Northrop Frye, *A Natural Perspective* (New York: Columbia University Press, 1965), p. 112; for alternatives see H. Carrington Lancaster, "Hermione's Statue," *Studies in Philology* 29 (1932): 233–38. The most thorough discussion of Autolycus, especially in Renaissance allegories, is Merritt Y. Hughes, "A Classical vs. a Social Approach to Shakespeare's Autolycus," *Shakespeare Association Bulletin* 15 (1940): 219–26; for other associations see Christine White, "A Biography of Autolycus," *Shakespeare Association Bulletin* 14 (1939): 158–68; William T. Hastings, "The Ancestry of Autolycus," *Shakespeare Association Bulletin* 15 (1940): 253; David Kaula, "Autolycus' Trumpery," *Studies in English Literature* 16 (1976): 287–303. A few of many critics who oppose Paulina and Autolycus as artists include Patricia Southard Gourlay, " 'O my most sacred lady.' Female Metaphor in *The Winter's Tale,*" *English Literary Renaissance* 5 (1975): 375–95; Mary L. Livingston, "The Natural Art of *The Winter's Tale,*" *Modern Language Quarterly* (Seattle) 30 (1969): 340–55; Ellen Wright, " 'We Are Mock'd with Art': Shakespeare's Wintry Tale," *Essays in Literature* 6 (1979): 147–59; Robert Egan, *Drama Without Drama* (New York: Columbia University Press, 1975), pp. 77–78. William Blissett, "This Wide Gap of Time: *The Winter's Tale,*" *English Literary Renaissance* 1 (1971): 52–70, traces the influence of book 15 of the *Metamorphoses* on *The Winter's Tale.*

3. See Don Cameron Allen, *Mysteriously Meant: The Rediscovery of Pagan Symbolism and Allegorical Interpretation in the Renaissance* (Baltimore: Johns Hopkins University Press, 1970), pp. 163–199: Douglas Bush, "Ovid Old and New," *Mythology and the Renaissance Tradition in English Poetry* (New York: W. W. Norton, 1932, rev. ed., 1963), pp. 69–73; L. P. Wilkinson, *Ovid Recalled* (Cambridge: Cambridge University Press, 1955), pp. 399–438.

4. See Elizabeth Donno, *Elizabethan Minor Epics* (London: Routledge and Kegan Paul, 1963); William Keach, *Elizabethan Erotic Narratives* (New Brunswick, N.J.: Rutgers University Press, 1977). One H. A. was particularly amusing in his depiction of the Myrrha myth as a rank tale of incest without any redeeming value in his introduction to his own rendition, *The Scourge of Venus* (1613):

> Ye that have parents, or that parents be,
> Depart a space, and give not eare at all,
> To the foule tale that here shall uttered be.

(*Occasional Issues of Unique or Very Rare Books,* ed. Alexander Grosart [London, 1876], p. 5 [A4]). While *The Scourge of Venus* was written somewhat after *The Winter's Tale* (1611), it shows the climate of attitudes toward Ovid at around that time.

5. *The Winter's Tale,* ed. J. H. P. Pafford (London: Methuen for Arden Paperbacks, 1963; reprint, 1971); all subsequent citations will be taken from this edition.

6. This astrological interpretation of the myth appears in the widely-known commentary *P. Ovidii Metamorphosis, seu Fabulae Poeticae: Eárumque interpretatio ethica, physica, et historica Georgii Sabinii* (Frankfort, 1593), Aa6: this work was actually written by George Schuler (see Allen, p. 179) it also appears in English in Abraham Fraunce, *The Countess of Pembroke's Ivychurch, Part III,* ed. Gerald Snare (Northridge: California State University Press, 1975), p. 96.

7. *Shakespeare's Ovid Being Arthur Golding's Translation of the Metamorphoses (1567),* ed. W. H. D. Rouse (Carbondale: Southern Illinois University Press, 1961), 11.366–67. An excellent discussion of Golding is found in Gordon Braden, *The Classics and English Renaissance Poetry: Three Case Studies,* Yale Studies in English, vol. 187 (New Haven: Yale University Press, 1978), pp. 1–54; for Shakespeare's use of Golding, see pp. 3–7.

8. *Mythologiae* (Venice, 1567), L13; Hughes, p. 224.

9. *Metamorphosis Ovidiana Moraliter a Magistro Thoma Walleys Anglico* (Paris, 1511), 11, fo. 130 (this work was really a fourteenth-century allegory by Pierre Bersuire or Berchorius; see Allen, p. 168).

10. Thomas Heywood, *Apology for Actors* (London, 1612), B3v.

11. William Gager, *The Overthrow of Stage Playes* (London, ca. 1599), E3v.

12. *Measure for Measure* 3.2.44–47, in *The Riverside Shakespeare* (Boston: Houghton Mifflin, 1974), p. 569.

13. According to Sabinus, the Pygmalion myth shows that one should seek to be given a chaste and modest wife by praying to God (Y7). According to Pierre Bersuire, *Metamorphosis Ovidiana Moraliter a Magistro Thoma Walleys Anglico* (H7), the statue's transformation to living flesh represents the change undergone by a chaste woman after a sexual encounter, which transforms her "de bona in fatuam," from a good woman into a fool.

14. Phillip Stubbes, *The Anatomie of Abuses* (London, 1583), L7; I. G., *A Refutation of the Apology for Actors,* G2v; I. G. refers to Vives as the source for Ovid's "interludes." I. G.'s work is a little later (1615) to show influence, but it does show the moment of the debate continuing shortly after *The Winter's Tale*.

15. Ben Jonson, *Works,* ed. C. H. Herford, Percy Simpson, and Evelyn Simpson (Oxford: Clarendon Press, 1932), 4:209.

16. Two excellent articles on views of Ovid in Jonson and in the period include Joseph A. Dane, "The Ovids of Ben Jonson in *Poetaster* and in *Epicoene*," *Comparative Drama* 13 (1979): 224–34; James D. Milvihill, "Jonson's *Poetaster* and the Ovidian Debate," *Studies in English Literature* 22 (1982): 239–55.

17. Stephen Gosson, *Schoole of Abuse* (London, 1579), A5v; Henry Crosse, *Vertues Commonwealth* (London, 1603), Q2v–Q3. See also Arthur F. Kinney, *Markets of Bawdrie: The Dramatic Criticism of Stephen Gosson* (Salzburg: Institut für Englische Sprache und Literatur, 1974).

18. Thomas Lodge, *Defence of Plays* (London, ca. 1580), B3.

19. Ovid, *The Art of Love and Other Love Books* (New York: Grosset and Dunlap), p. 112.

20. Heywood, *Apology,* B4–C1; Jonas Barish, *The Antitheatrical Prejudice* (Berkeley: University of California Press, 1981), p. 118, calls Heywood's argument

"inept." Heywood's work, a little late for *The Winter's Tale*, shows the continuing power of this passage in the debate over theater.

21. Anthony Munday, *A Second and Third Blast of Retrait from Plaies and Theaters* (London, 1580), E2v. (*The Third Blast* only, which includes E2v, was Munday's original composition.) The same point is made by S. P. Zitner, "Gosson, Ovid, and the Elizabethan Audience," *Shakespeare Quarterly* 9 (1958): 206–8. For the possibility of real prostitutes soliciting at the theater, see A. J. Cook, " 'Bargaines of Incontinencie': Bawdy Behavior at the Playhouses," *Shakespeare Studies* 10 (1977): 271–90.

22. Gosson, *Schoole of Abuse*, A3–A3v.

23. Lodge, *Defence of Plays*, A2v.

24. Russell Fraser, *The War Against Poetry* (Princeton: Princeton University Press, 1970), pp. 4–28.

25. Harington, "Brief Apology for Poetry," *Elizabethan Critical Essays*, ed. G. Gregory Smith (Oxford: Clarendon Press, 1904), 2: 211.

26. Barish, *Antitheatrical Prejudice*, esp. pp. 92–93.

27. Richard A. Lanham, *Motives of Eloquence: Literary Rhetoric in the Renaissance* (New Haven: Yale University Press, 1976), pp. 48–64, 82–110.

28. Robert Greene, *Greene's Groatsworth of Wit Bought with A Million of Repentance* (1592), concluding letter; reprinted in *The Repentance of Robert Greene* (1592).

29. See, for example, Frank Kermode, *William Shakespeare: The Final Plays* (London: Longmans Green, 1963, reprint, 1973), p. 33, who calls Autolycus the "blackest rogue available," and David Kaula, "Autolycus's Trumpery," *Studies in English Literature* 16 (1976): 295, who calls Autolycus a "spiritual fornication", as opposed to Lee Sheridan Cox's formulation in "The Role of Autolycus in *The Winter's Tale*," *Studies in English Literature* 9 (1969): 288. "A seemingly unscrupulous rogue masks a man with a moral sense still alive and kicking"; and Hallett Smith, *Shakespeare's Romances* (San Marino, Calif.: Huntington Library, 1972), p. 110, who finds Autolycus "charming." This split response indicates the disparity between moral judgment and emotional appeal central to the presentation of Autolycus.

30. Bullough, *Narr. Sources*, 8: 214, and Muir, *Sources of Shakespeare*, p. 275, discuss Greene as source.

31. The moral content of Autolycus's ballads is discussed by Cox, "Role of Autolycus," p. 284; Roy Battenhouse, "Theme and Structure in *The Winter's Tale*," *Shakespeare Survey* 33 (1980): 132; see also Peter Berek, " 'As We Are Mock'd with Art': From Scorn to Transfiguration," *Studies in English Literature* 18 (1978): 299–300.

32. Cox, "Role of Autolycus," p. 288, discusses Autolycus as an "unwilling agent" of Providence.

33. Muir, *Sources of Shakespeare*, p. 277.

34. Battenhouse, "Theme and Structure," p. 131, asserts "both have an imagination limited to a world of the senses as interpreted by self-love."

35. Muir, *Sources of Shakespeare*, p. 274, discusses the success of this scene on stage; once almost universally criticized, the scene was defended by Nevil Coghill, "Six Points of Stage-Craft in *The Winter's Tale*," *Shakespeare Survey* 11 (1958): 39–40. For criticism, see Edwards, p. 149.

36. See, for example, the reaction of Arthur Colby Sprague, *Shakespeare and the Audience* (New York: Russell and Russell, 1935; reprint, 1966), p. 159; for a long time this statue scene was considered unplayable, a flaw in *The Winter's Tale*; performances in this decade have shown how playable it really is.

37. Possibly strengthening the somewhat squalid resonances of the Pygmalion myth of the time are Leontes' exclamation, "Her natural posture," (5.3.23) on first seeing the statue, and all the to-do about Julio Romano as the sculptor. Romano was best known for his sixteen sketches of "the various attitudes and postures in which lewd men have intercourse with lewd women," according to Vasari. See Eric Partridge, *Shakespeare's Bawdy* (New York: Dutton, 1969), p. 165, and James Cleugh, *The Divine Aretino* (New York: Stein and Day, 1966), p. 68, who quotes Vasari. The use of Romano's name is rationalized in Terence Spencer, "The Statue of Hermione," *Essays and Studies* 30 (1977): 39–49; Andrew Gurr, in a lecture at the Second Congress of the International Shakespeare Association and Ninth Annual Meeting of the Shakespeare Association of America, Stratford-upon-Avon, 3 August 1981, "Shakespeare's Audience," discussed the use of Romano's name as a "divisive reference" to be understood by the "cognoscenti."

38. Ovid, *Art of Love,* p. 135; this Ovidian Hermione seems more relevant than K. E. Duncan-Jones's Hermione, the daughter of Helen and Menelaus; see her "Hermione in Ovid and Shakespeare," *Notes and Queries,* n.s., 13 (1966): 138–39; see also Charles Frey, *Shakespeare's Vast Romance: A Study of The Winter's Tale* (Columbia: University of Missouri Press, 1980), p. 61.

39. Cox, "Role of Autolycus," p. 296, and Battenhouse, "Theme and Structure," p. 132, both see this oath as leading to Autolycus's repentance on, I think, very slim grounds, given the brevity of Autolycus's response and his ability as an actor to appear whatever is in his own best interests.

The Problem of "Context" in Interpretation

Richard L. Levin

It takes no great courage today to maintain that the interpretation of any literary work must always rely upon contexts external to that work. I think most critical theorists and practical critics would now regard that proposition as axiomatic. This is, however, a fairly recent phenomenon. Not so many years ago, in the heyday of the New Criticism, many of its practitioners were insisting on the absolute autonomy of the work "on the page" and were telling us that its meaning could only be explicated by a "close reading" of the text itself, without reference to anything outside the text. In fact they often argued that going outside the text was a critical fallacy or heresy that was irrelevant to the task of explication and might even interfere with it. They were, of course, reacting against the biographical-historical school of interpretation, which they were replacing; but this reaction carried them to an untenable position, though it won a very widespread acceptance at the time.

Although they disagreed with the New Critics on many other matters, this same position was held then by the Chicago Aristotelians, the school in which I was trained. Their earliest pronouncement, published in 1942, included Elder Olson's well-known analysis of Yeats's "Sailing to Byzantium," which was based on the principle that the poem is an "independent universe" that is "referable to nothing outside itself."[1] Thus he argued that the poet will "arbitrarily determine" the significance of his words, since they are not defined by "their dictionary meanings" or by any other external reference, but solely by their use within the poem. This would mean, if we were to take him literally, that the poem could be perfectly understood by someone who did not know a word of English. He also asserted, as another consequence of this principle, that Byzantium has no connection to "the historical city" of that name, but is defined, like all the other words there, by the poem itself, which would mean that the poem would remain the same if it were retitled "Sailing to Los Angeles." Needless to say, Olson no longer holds this view, nor do the other members of this school.

For it should be obvious that no literary work, or any other form of human communication, can ever be understood until it is placed in some prior and larger contexts. Indeed the first and largest of these contexts is that of communication itself. If an archeologist at a dig came upon a stone covered with markings, her first step in trying to understand it would be to determine whether those marks were made by a human being, rather than by an animal or some natural process. And if they were man-made, she would then have to determine whether they were placed there to convey a meaning, rather than for some other purpose, such as shaping a tool. And if they were intended to convey a meaning, she would then have to determine what language or sign system was employed. Without first establishing these contexts, she would have no hope of understanding what she was looking at.

Today when we look at a literary work we assume these contexts of communication and of a language; in fact we usually do not even think about them. Our problems begin when we proceed from them to other, more specific contexts that we must consciously choose and consciously apply to the work we are interpreting. For the real problem in interpretation is not *whether* a literary work requires a context to be understood, since it obviously does, but rather *which* contexts, or which kinds of contexts, should be chosen in order to understand *this* particular work. Of course, this only becomes a problem if we are trying to interpret the author's intended meaning, since the nonintentionalist critic is completely free to choose any context he pleases. (Often, however, it turns out that he is completely unfree when he is committed to a single, universal context that is supposed to explain all human activity and hence all literary works, a point I will return to later.) But I have taken an intentionalist position here, as have all the critics I will be discussing, so for us the choice of interpretive contexts presents a problem. It is a very complicated problem that I cannot possibly settle in this paper; but I would like to examine some of the kinds of contexts most often employed by intentionalist critics, in order to evaluate them and to derive from this evaluation some general principles concerning their reliability or utility. I should make it clear at the outset, however, that these principles can only be relative and tentative, because they must be based upon probabilities. In the choice of interpretive contexts, as in all other aspects of interpretation, there are no certain rules. All the examples except the final one will be drawn from modern criticism of English Renaissance drama, but they should apply, with the same caveat, to other fields as well.

Some years ago, while doing research on the thematic approach to this body of drama, I came upon an essay on *Troilus and Cressida* published in 1952. It was a typical product of thematics, which undertook to prove that the play is really about the conflict between reason and passion—one of those standard, all-purpose themes, like appearance versus reality, which used to be so popular. The author argued that the danger of allowing reason to be subordinated to passion was an "entirely traditional" doctrine of the Renaissance, which "any orthodox humanist would have understood at once," and that it is exemplified in the behavior of Troilus, Achilles, and Hector. The demonstration itself was a rather plodding, mechanical performance; but at the end it suddenly came to life when the author asserted that his interpretation had finally succeeded in placing *Troilus and Cressida* in its proper context and then concluded, in almost ringing tones, that to interpret it in any other way would be "to take the work out of its context—out of which it may mean anything."[2]

I know nothing about this author, but it is not difficult to imagine what he was like. He must have been trained in the old school of historical scholarship and undergone a long and painful initiation, embodied in his dissertation, before being admitted to the academic citadel of like-minded scholars. Then he saw that citadel invaded by a barbaric horde of New Critics, who not only lacked the historical knowledge that he had acquired with so much effort, but actually denied its relevance. And so in this article he was striking back in defense of scholarship and the historical context.

I do not think that his defense converted anyone, however. It was, as I said, a mechanical exercise that failed to convey any hint of the play's complexity or capacity to engage and excite us. Moreover, the kind of interpretive context he was arguing for has proved to be of relatively little use. It is an example of what I call "ideas-of-the-time" criticism, in which the interpretation is determined by some contemporary doctrine or attitude that is applied to the work. We are all familiar with other examples, which insist that we must interpret *Romeo and Juliet* in the light of Renaissance ideas about filial obedience or suicide, and *Hamlet* in the light of Renaissance ideas about revenge or ghosts, and so on. I have stated my objections to this approach at length elsewhere and will only summarize them briefly here.[3] It misrepresents the role of the playwright, since it assumes that he cannot ignore or even modify the designated "idea-of-the-time," but is simply a conduit through which this idea is transmitted from the historical context to the play. It misrepresents the role of the audience, since it assumes they will automatically apply this idea to the play, regardless of what the playwright has done. It misrepresents history, since it assumes there was a single "idea-of-the-time" about the passions or revenge or ghosts, etc. And finally, even if there were a predominant attitude on such subjects, it could not be demonstrated from the type of evidence adduced by the practitioners of this approach, for they usually find it in the homiletic literature of the period—the sermons and courtesy books and moral treatises of those "orthodox humanists"—

which sought to teach people how they should think, not to describe current thought. For these reasons, therefore, I would conclude that if we were to rank the possible interpretive contexts on a scale of descending reliability and utility, this use of the "ideas-of-the-time" would have to be placed somewhere near the bottom.

These objections to what I call the "ideas-of-the-time" approach do not extend, of course, to all uses of contemporary ideas as a context for interpretation. There is in fact one kind of employment of these ideas that is obviously essential to any successful interpretation, since it gives us the knowledge necessary to construe the very meaning of the words of the text and understand the social customs and institutions, the proverbial lore, the beliefs, and the like that these words allude to. This is the sort of context that is supplied for us by the footnotes in modern scholarly editions of works of the past and has always been relied upon by the interpreters of those works (including the New Critics and the Chicago Aristotelians). Indeed it should probably be considered an extension of the very general context of "language," which I said at the outset was assumed as a necessary preliminary to any interpretation. And for that reason it really does not enter into the problem we are examining here, since the interpreter does not have to decide whether or not to apply it (although he may certainly be ignorant of it). Like the language itself, it precedes the contexts that present him with conscious choices.

In addition to this application of contemporary ideas to elucidate the specific details of a text, there are other uses of more general moral and social ideas of the period—or what might be termed its intellectual climate—which do require conscious choices but escape the pitfalls of the "ideas-of-the-time" approach. One such use, in fact, proceeds in the opposite direction from that approach: instead of beginning with the contemporary ideas and applying them to interpret the play, it begins with the ideas found in the play itself and then applies them to this broader intellectual context, in order to "place" the play within that context. This type of study, therefore, does not assume that the playwright automatically followed the orthodox teachings of the time, since the nature of his relationship to those teachings, and to the other intellectual currents competing with them, is precisely what it is investigating. It has proved to be a very fruitful avenue of inquiry, but it is really more closely affiliated to what is usually called the "history of ideas" than to interpretation, at least in the narrower sense in which we are using this term, since it depends on a prior determination of the meaning of the play and the ideas in it. It is postinterpretive, in our sense, just as the use of the "linguistic" context discussed above is preinterpretive.

This general intellectual context is also invoked by several of the more recent approaches to Renaissance drama that have now become so popular—Feminism, Neo-Marxism, and the New Historicism. Despite the many differences between these approaches (and sometimes within them), they are agreed in rejecting the assumptions of the older "ideas-of-the-time" criticism. They all insist that there was no single, monolithic Renaissance attitude on the major issues of the day, since the orthodox doctrines expounded in those homiletic treatises were under various pressures, and as a consequence, they argue that any play of the period need not necessarily embody those doctrines but could relate to them in other, more complex ways (in their terminology, it could "contest," "subvert," or "recuperate," as well as "reproduce" them). These approaches, however, are usually not concerned with the author's intention and so do not produce interpretations in our sense (which some of their practitioners acknowledge). Moreover, while this nonintentionalist position would seem to free these critics to choose any general context in the period, it too often turns out, as I suggested earlier, that the ideology of their approaches commits them to a single, a priori context that all the plays are supposed to be "about." And that context is almost always some conception of "power," defined in terms of either class or gender. Indeed the themes of class and gender conflict seem to be just as pervasive in these approaches as those all-purpose conflicts of reason and passion or appearance and reality were in the older criticism, and just about as helpful in getting at the specific meaning of each play. There is, of course, no reason why the use of the general intellectual climate of the period as an interpretive context must necessarily lead to this kind of constriction. It can be employed much more flexibly to help us understand these plays in all of their rich variety, but only if we are able to determine which general ideas to apply to which plays, and in what way. For the ideas always stand at some distance from the plays, and so this kind of context will always present the critic with more difficult problems of choice and consequently must be regarded as less reliable and less useful than other contexts that are closer to the plays themselves.

We may seem to have reached a more reliable context of this sort if we proceed from these general contemporary ideas about social issues to the contemporary ideas about literature, especially when they bear upon the specific genre of the literary work we are interpreting. One of the best-known examples of this approach is *Shakespeare's Tragic Heroes: Slaves of Passion* by Lily Bess Campbell,[4] which sets out to explain *Hamlet, Othello, King Lear,* and *Macbeth* in terms of the Renaissance conception of "the purpose and method of tragedy." She begins by establishing, through extensive quotation from contemporary treatises, that tragedies were supposed to be "*exempla* by which men are taught the lessons of moral philosophy" on "how to avoid ruin and misery," which were supposed to be caused, once again, by the subordination of reason to passion.

She then applies this doctrine to Shakespeare's tragic heroes and discovers, not too surprisingly, that each is presented as the slave of some passion that causes his ruin, which thus teaches us how to avoid a similar fate. It should be evident, however, that this use of a literary context is open to the same basic objections as the more general "ideas-of-the-time" contexts we just discussed. It, too, assumes that there was a single "idea-of-the-time" about tragedy, that this idea can be demonstrated from those treatises, and that it would necessarily govern the dramatist in his writing and the audience in their response. And all four assumptions, I believe, are invalid.

These objections should become clearer if we compare Campbell's approach to another, very different attempt to interpret Shakespeare in terms of a contemporary literary context—Helen Gardner's essay on *Hamlet*.[5] She also applies a Renaissance conception of genre to the play; however, she defines that genre, not as tragedy in general, but as revenge tragedy, and she derives the Renaissance conception of it, not from theoretical treatises, but from the plays themselves. What she seeks to determine, therefore, is "how *Hamlet* appeared to audiences which had applauded *The Spanish Tragedy* and *Titus Andronicus*." I think most people would agree that the interpretation resulting from this kind of historical investigation is much more satisfactory than Campbell's. It enhances our understanding of *Hamlet,* because Gardner is able to illuminate crucial aspects of the play by relating them to the nature and requirements of the revenge plot and the revenger's role, to the expectations aroused by this form, and to the effect aimed at. And it enhances our appreciation of the play, since the investigation also enables her to demonstrate how "*Hamlet* towers above other plays of its kind through the heroism and nobility of its hero"; whereas Campbell's approach, because of its formulation of the context, seemed to reduce all tragedies to the same simplistic level of Morality plays (and to reduce all their heroes to negative *exempla* of "slavery to passion").

From this comparison I think it is possible to derive two tentative principles concerning the use of these literary historical contexts in interpretation. When we try to interpret a work in the light of this kind of context, it would seem better to use a more proximate or specific genre (or subgenre) than a more general one within the same period—to use Elizabethan revenge tragedy, that is, rather than Elizabethan tragedy, or Elizabethan tragedy rather than Elizabethan drama as a whole.[6] (Actually Campbell's approach is further removed from Gardner's in this respect than it might appear, since many of the Renaissance statements that she relies on are concerned not just with tragedy but with all forms of drama, to which they assign the same purpose of teaching those "lessons of moral philosophy.") And it would seem better to determine the contemporary conception of that genre from the actual practice of the time, as seen in the works written within the genre, rather than from the theory promulgated in treatises on the subject. This is especially pertinent in the case of the treatises cited by Campbell, because most of them were composed as *defenses* of tragedy (or the drama) against its enemies, who had attacked it as immoral, so that they were virtually forced to define it in moralistic terms as an edifying lesson in how not to behave, regardless of what contemporary tragic authors were really doing in their plays. Of course, some of these authors did write tragedies (invariably inferior ones) that fit the formula and ended with neat, aphoristic couplets warning the audience to "learne from this example, ther's no trust / In a foundation that is built on lust,"[7] and so forth. But most of the tragedies of the period, including all of Shakespeare's, do not end on such a note, and there is no reason to assume that this didactic conception of the genre must apply to them.

It is necessary, however, to emphasize the relative nature of these principles. Although I have argued that specific genres are better than general ones and that contemporary practice is a better definer of genre than contemporary theory, it does not follow that a specific genre defined by contemporary practice will always give us the best context for interpretation. This may be seen, for example, in a recent book by Joyce Peterson on *The Duchess of Malfi*.[8] She says that "Webster's Jacobean audience" would have immediately recognized that this play belonged to the genre of "commonweal tragedy," which was designed to show the "consequences of mis-rule," and therefore would have regarded the Duchess as a "curs'd example," a ruler who is condemned by the play and justly punished for "placing private desire above public responsibility." To support this claim about "the response of Webster's audience," she cites some contemporary plays that exemplify the genre (along with some contemporary treatises that state the "orthodox political theory" of the time concerning the duties of rulers), but ignores the best evidence we have of that response— the commendatory poems written for the first edition of the play (1623) by William Rowley and Thomas Middleton.[9] These men, who were of course not only practicing Jacobeans but also practicing dramatists, and so might be expected to have some understanding of dramatic genre and audience reaction, give not the slightest hint of such a view of the play or its heroine. Rowley's poem expresses his admiration for the way the Duchess defends her marriage: *"Yet my opinion is, she might speake more; / But (neuer in her life) so well before"*; and Middleton's ends by addressing Webster directly:

> *Thy Epitaph onely the* Title *bee,*
> *Write,* Dutchesse, *that will fetch a teare for thee,*
> *For who e're saw this* Dutchesse *liue, and dye,*
> *That could get off vnder a Bleeding Eye*

which does not sound like a response to the just punishment of a "curs'd example." Their testimony, certainly, provides a more reliable context for determining the contemporary perception of the play than the genre to which it allegedly belongs (and of which they seem to be unaware).

It should be evident that in this last example I have expanded the meaning of "context." All of the previous contexts—the ideas of the time about morality or literature and the genres of the time—were presumably present in the consciousness of the dramatist and the original audience, and therefore could have affected his composition of the play and their reaction to it, which is the claim of the critics who employ them. But obviously Webster and his audience could not have been affected by what someone was going to say about this play some ten years later. That was not part of *their* context. We are concerned here, however, with contexts for interpretation, and as interpreters of the play we can choose to make these contemporary comments part of *our* context, just as we can choose any of the other contexts discussed earlier. The question of interpretive context, as was said at the outset, is a matter of conscious choice, so if we wish to know how the play we are interpreting was viewed by its contemporaries, the best context to choose will be their stated responses to it that have come down to us. This in fact can be seen as another application of our second general principle, which placed practice over theory: in determining the Renaissance perception of a play, just as in defining the Renaissance conception of a genre, the actual practice of the time, represented by those responses (even when we only have a few of them), must be regarded as a more reliable or useful context than any number of theoretical treatises. It is very interesting, therefore, that these responses are ignored by the "ideas-of-the-time" critics. They are always invoking contemporary theory, derived from those "orthodox humanists," which they claim will tell us how people then *would* have reacted to the play (by condemning Juliet for disobeying her father, and so on), but they never refer to contemporary practice, to these comments on the play itself, which are the only evidence we have of how people then actually *did* react to it. And the reason for this, I suspect, is that these comments never seem to bear out the claims of those critics. But that is the subject of another paper.[10]

I think most people would agree that we have reached a more reliable interpretive context when we move from history to biography—from the ideas and practices of the time to the ideas and practice of the author himself. Indeed, the author is the most frequently employed context in interpretation, and with good reason, for our first general principle of "proximity" applies here as well. Just as the contemporary ideas about literature were closer to the work than the ideas about morality and religion, and the more specific genre was closer to it than the more general one, so the author is closer to the work than is any aspect of the period he lived in. Moreover, we tend to regard the work as the personal expression of its author and so feel that we can understand it better if we understand him, just as in real life we feel we are in a better position to understand the behavior of someone well known to us than that of a complete stranger. The authorial context therefore figures significantly in a great many interpretations, but it can become particularly important in cases that raise special problems, such as literary parody. If the "Pyramus and Thisbe" playlet in *A Midsummer Night's Dream* had been published separately, without any indication of authorship, we would have no way of knowing whether we were dealing with a bad play or a parody of a bad play. Of course, Shakespeare has provided a context for us within the larger play where it appears to tell us it is parodic; but even if he had not, we would still be reasonably confident that it is, so long as we knew it was written by him and not, say, by Thomas Preston or even by anonymous. (And if it were anonymous, the date could provide a useful context for addressing the problem: we would probably decide it was not parodic if it had been published in the 1560s rather than the 1590s.) The importance of this authorial context is confirmed, I think, in the actual case of *Eastward Ho,* for most critics (including myself) would be much less likely to argue that it contains a parody of bourgeois values if Heywood or Dekker had been named on the title page, rather than Chapman, Jonson, and Marston.

In such cases, however, the author's practice cannot be treated as a single, constant context. This was the point of a controversy I engaged in some years ago with Douglas Duncan on *The New Inn.*[11] In his article Duncan asserted that "the grotesque postulates" of the Frampul family relationships in this play "must, coming from Jonson, be interpreted as a challenge to the audience to swallow a camel if it will," and that the ending therefore must be deliberately "spoofing romantic comedy." I answered that if those grotesque postulates were "coming from Jonson" during the period of his comic masterpieces (1605–14), we might well suspect that he was spoofing. But they come from the Jonson of 1629, three years after *The Staple of News* and three years before *The Magnetic Lady,* so it is to *this* Jonson that the critic must appeal. And since in these two plays we find family relationships no less absurd than those in *The New Inn,* the argument from authorial practice points to the opposite conclusion: the grotesque postulates of *The New Inn,* coming from the same stage in Jonson's career as other plays based upon postulates equally grotesque, are not at all likely to be a spoof. Here again, it seems, our first general principle of "proximity" applies. When using the author's practice as a context for interpreting a work, we should narrow that practice down (just like the concept of genre) to the phase closest to this work. And even then, of course, we are still only dealing with probabilities, for authors can change their mode of writing radically within very brief periods.

According to our other general principle of the superiority of practice over theory, we would expect that an author's ideas about art will provide a less reliable context than the artistic works themselves. In the field of Renaissance drama, the use of this second kind of authorial context has been pretty much limited to studies of Ben Jonson, since he is the only playwright of the period who has left us a substantial body of aesthetic theory, principally in *Timber, or Discoveries.* In her book on Jonson, Gabriele Jackson undertook to interpret all of Jonson's plays in the context of his theory, with very uneven results. [12] Since the theory has a great deal to say about ethical instruction in literature and very little about laughter, her procedure worked quite well with the plays at the serious end of Jonson's spectrum, but those at the other end—especially *The Alchemist* and *Bartholomew Fair*—were distorted almost beyond recognition into grimly moralistic condemnations of the comic wits and their activities. Jonson's pronouncements in *Timber* simply do not explain these two plays. Moreover, if we are seeking to interpret them in the light of his own view of his art, he himself has provided a more useful context for this purpose in the Prologue to *The Alchemist,* which states that "Our *Scene* is *London,* 'cause we would make knowne, / No countries mirth is better then our owne," and in the Induction to *Bartholomew Fair,* which promises the audience a play that will be "merry, and as full of noise, as sport: made to delight all." So it appears that here, again, the principle of "proximity" applies in determining the better context—in fact it applies doubly, since the Prologue and Induction are closer to the plays in question than *Timber* is in two distinct senses: they are about these specific plays, whereas *Timber* is about literature in general; and they were written at the same time as these plays (1610 and 1614), whereas *Timber* was compiled many years later (between 1623 and 1635). Indeed, of all the possible contexts for interpretation that we might derive from an author's views (as opposed to his practice), the most proximate, and therefore most reliable, would be a direct comment of this sort about a particular work that he was then writing or had just written. This does not mean, however, that we can always rely on such comments, as anyone can testify, for example, who has tried to cope with Tennessee Williams's conflicting explanations of *A Streetcar Named Desire.* [13] Authors may change their ideas about what they have written (or even deliberately misrepresent them), just as they may change their practice in writing, as was noted earlier. The principles I am trying to develop here, to repeat once more, can never give us certainty because they are only probable and relative. All we can say is that the author's ideas about a specific work supply a more useful interpretive context than his ideas about art in general, since they are closer to that work; but this context is not infallible.

The same principle of "proximity" indicates that an author's ideas about art, while less useful than his comments on a given work, will still provide a better context for interpretation than his ideas about morals and religion and life, or what is sometimes called his philosophy, which is the most remote of all authorial contexts from the work and therefore the least reliable. Although it has been invoked in a few studies of Renaissance drama, such as the attempts to interpret Marlowe's plays in the light of his "atheism" and Chapman's in the light of his "stoicism,"[14] for my example here I have gone outside the field to consider Wordsworth's "A Slumber Did My Spirit Seal," which has generated what must now be the best-known controversy on the use of this kind of authorial context. Since the poem is very short and its details will be essential to my argument, I am quoting it in full:

> A slumber did my spirit seal;
> I had no human fears:
> She seemed a thing that could not feel
> The touch of earthly years.
>
> No motion has she now, no force;
> She neither hears nor sees;
> Rolled round in earth's diurnal course,
> With rocks, and stones, and trees.

Interpretations of this poem have tended to divide into two opposing positions. On one side we have what might be called the inconsolable reading, associated with the New Critics and exemplified by Cleanth Brooks. According to him, the poem is built on a contrast between the speaker's former feelings about his loved one and his feelings now that she is dead. The first stanza presents his earlier

blind[ness] to the claims of mortality . . . [as] a slumber, immersed in which he thought it impossible that his loved one could perish. . . . [The second stanza presents his] agonized shock at the loved one's present lack of motion . . . [at] her utter and horrible inertness. . . . The girl, who . . . seemed a thing that could not feel the touch of earthly years, is caught up helplessly into the empty whirl of the earth. . . . She is touched by, and held by, earthly time in its most powerful and horrible image.[15]

Opposed to this is what I will call the consoling reading, which is associated with the biographical critics and exemplified by Frederick Bateson. He says that

the final impression the poem leaves is not of two contrasting moods, but of a single mood mounting to a climax in the pantheistic magnificence of the last two lines. . . . The vague living-Lucy . . . is opposed to the grander dead-Lucy who has become involved in the sublime processes of nature. . . . Lucy is actually more alive now that she is dead, because she is now a part of the life of Nature, and not just a human "thing."[16]

The most influential attempt to adjudicate this controversy is that of E. D. Hirsch, whose argument bears directly on the issue we are discussing. He begins by asserting that the two readings are both "coherent and self-sustaining . . . within the context which [each critic] adumbrates," so that the best way to judge between them is "to show that one context is more probable than the other." Then he continues:

> When the *homme moyen sensuel* confronts bereavement such as that which Wordsworth's poem explicitly presents, he adumbrates, typically, a horizon including sorrow and inconsolability. . . . Brooks' reading, therefore, with its emphasis on inconsolability and bitter irony, is clearly justified not only by the text but by reference to universal human attitudes and feelings. However, . . . the poet is not an *homme moyen sensuel.* . . . Instead of regarding rocks and stones and trees merely as inert objects, he probably regarded them in 1799 as deeply alive. . . . Physical death he felt to be a return to the source of life, a new kind of participation in nature's "revolving immortality." From everything we know of Wordsworth's typical attitudes during [this] period, . . . inconsolability and bitter irony do not belong in its horizon.

And he concludes, therefore, that "since Bateson grounds his interpretation in a conscious construction of the poet's outlook, his reading must be deemed the more probable one."[17]

Now it has probably become evident that I usually find myself in agreement with Hirsch, but in this argument I think he is wrong. The context that he is relying upon—Wordsworth's pantheism—seems to me one of the least reliable for interpreting this poem. The connection between a person's professed philosophy or theology and his actual feelings can be very tenuous, especially when he is reacting to such a violent shock as the death of a loved one. After all, not only pantheism but virtually all of the more orthodox religions preach a very consoling view of death, but this has not prevented even the most devout believers from feeling inconsolable grief at such a time, and there is no reason to think that authors are any different in this respect from the rest of mankind. In fact, some of them have portrayed this very human discrepancy between belief and emotion. We are all familiar with the delightful episode in *Joseph Andrews* where Parson Adams, after explaining at length to Joseph that Christian doctrine requires us to bear the loss of our dear ones "peaceably, quietly, and contentedly," is informed that his favorite child has drowned. He "began to stamp about the Room," Fielding tells us,

> and deplore his Loss with the bitterest Agony. *Joseph* . . . endeavour[ed] to comfort the Parson; in which Attempt he used many Argu-

ments that he had at several times remember'd out of his own Discourses both in private and publick, (for he was a great Enemy to the Passions, and preached nothing more than the Conquest of them by Reason and Grace) but he was not at leisure now to hearken to his Advice. . . .—'My poor *Jacky,* shall I never see thee more?' cries the Parson.—'Yes, surely,' says *Joseph,* 'and in a better Place, you will meet again never to part more.'—I believe the Parson did not hear these Words, for he paid little regard to them, but went on lamenting.[18]

There is a more serious episode of this sort in *Antonio's Revenge* by John Marston, where Pandulpho, who has been wandering through the play expounding Stoic maxims on the need to remain impervious to the blows of fortune, is finally overcome by grief at the sight of his son's corpse, and when asked why he is weeping, replies, "Man will breake out, despight Philosophie."[19] In fact, we know of such an episode in Wordsworth's own life. According to Henry Crabb Robinson,

> when his beloved daughter Dora . . . died, it was nearly a year before he could quiet his grief. James, the faithful servant, 'took the liberty' of saying to his master: 'But Sir, don't you think she is brighter now than she ever was?' Wordsworth's response was to burst into a flood of tears.[20]

Apparently he did not then find much comfort in his belief that the dead become involved in the sublime processes of nature and participate in her revolving immortality, because for him, too, man could break out, despite philosophy. It is certainly possible, then, that he was expressing such a feeling of inconsolability in "A Slumber Did My Spirit Seal" (and for the purposes of this argument, it makes no difference whether he had actually experienced a loss of this kind, or was only imagining the reaction of someone who had). Of course, this does not disprove the consoling reading of the poem, since that is also a possible human response to death. But I believe it does disprove any argument for that reading which relies on the context of Wordsworth's pantheism.

We have, however, a very different kind of authorial context for interpreting this poem that seems much more reliable: the other "Lucy poems" written by Wordsworth. There are four of them—"Strange Fits of Passion I Have Known," "She Dwelt Among the Untrodden Ways," "Three Years She Grew in Sun and Shower," and "I Travelled Among Unknown Men"—all composed during the same period as "A Slumber" (1798–1801) and all concerned with the death of a young woman. And in every one of them her death is viewed as an unmitigated loss, with no hint of anything that might be called consolation, pantheistic or otherwise. Moreover, these poems can be shown to provide a better interpretive context for "A Slumber" than Wordsworth's pantheism on the basis of *both* of the general principles I have been developing. They embody the author's actual artistic practice at the time he wrote "A Slumber," which is a more reliable context than his theory of life (or of art, for that matter); and they are more proximate to "A Slumber" than the compositions that state Wordsworth's pantheistic beliefs, since they belong to the same genre (or subgenre) as that poem, in terms of their form and their subject. Indeed these two principles tend to converge here, which should increase our confidence in the use of this authorial context. It will not give us certainty, because there is always the possibility that in the middle of this period Wordsworth wrote a poem expressing an entirely different reaction to Lucy's death. But in terms of the probabilities, it is superior to the context employed by Bateson and Hirsch.

There is, finally, one nonauthorial context that seems relevant to the interpretation of "A Slumber" and strengthens the case for the inconsolable reading—a letter written by Samuel Taylor Coleridge to Thomas Poole on 6 April 1799, where he comments briefly on the poem and quotes it. Coleridge must surely be regarded as an expert witness here (like Middleton and Rowley on *The Duchess of Malfi*), since he was a poet himself and an intimate friend of Wordsworth's, and so would have known about his pantheism. Yet he apparently did not notice its presence in "A Slumber," for this is what he has to say of the poem:

> Some months ago Wordsworth transmitted to me a most sublime Epitaph / whether it had any reality, I cannot say.—Most probably, in some gloomier moment he had fancied the moment in which his Sister might die.[21]

It is possible, of course, that he completely misread the emotional tone of his friend's poem (just as it is possible that Middleton and Rowley completely missed the point of their friend's play), but it seems less probable that he misread it than that Bateson did. For the principle of proximity applies here too, as it did to the contemporary responses to Renaissance drama discussed earlier, so that the context supplied by his letter reinforces that of the other "Lucy poems" to support Brooks's reading over Bateson's. Thus while I agree with Hirsch that the adjudication between these two readings depends on determining the more probable context for interpreting the poem, I believe, on the basis of the two general principles I have been arguing for, that he chose the less probable context and so ended up defending the less probable reading.

Now I could stop here, but in the course of writing this paper I suffered a sudden attack of intellectual honesty and was forced to admit to myself that even if the other "Lucy poems" and the Coleridge letter did not exist, I would still prefer Brooks's reading. And when I tried to account for this, I was forced to go to the poem itself. For it seemed to me that the per-

suasiveness of his reading does not depend on assuming the context of the
homme moyen sensuel, as Hirsch contended, since both the inconsolable
and the consoling readings represent possible responses of a normal
person to bereavement, as I noted earlier—in fact, they could represent the
responses of the same normal person at different stages of bereavement. I
found Brooks's reading more persuasive than Bateson's, not because it
seemed closer to my preconceptions about the nature of grief, but because
it gave me a more satisfactory account of the details of the poem, and
particularly of the sequential relationship of the two stanzas.

The poem is so brief, and so familiar, that we can easily overlook (or
forget) the fact that on a first encounter the opening stanza would raise
certain problems for the reader. She would wonder why the speaker refers
to his earlier view of Lucy, and specifically his lack of fear for her, as a
"slumber" that "sealed" him from something, and why he says that she
"seemed" impervious to time, and why this seeming imperviousness is
stated in such an unusual way, as that of a "thing" unable to "feel the
touch of earthly years." She would carry these problems over to the
second stanza, and would discover—if she read it as Brooks does—that
they are resolved there. For the speaker's shock on confronting the fact of
Lucy's death explains why he thinks of his earlier lack of fear for her as a
"slumber," an illusion, which "sealed" him from the harsh reality of
human mortality. And the details of his description of her present state
reflect back on, and so explain, his description of his earlier illusion. Then
she "seemed" a "thing" that could not "feel" time; now she really is a
thing and cannot feel anything. Then time could not "touch" her; now it
holds her forever. And the "earthliness" of that time has become the earth
itself, which she is now part of. This grimly ironic fit of the two stanzas—
noted by Brooks and some other critics who share his interpretation of the
poem—shows that the speaker's description in the first stanza, which is of
course stated retrospectively after Lucy's death, is intentionally ambiguous, so that it can refer both to his earlier belief and to his present
realization. And the reason for this ambiguity is also explained, since it
emphasizes how completely her death contradicts his earlier belief by
fulfilling it in this ironic way and so embodies his realization of how
completely erroneous that belief was. It even suggests the nature of this
error, because his mind was sealed against the other, ironic meaning of
that ambiguity (the fact of her mortality), which was, in this sense, present
before him all the time. Thus, in this reading, the second stanza explains
and justifies the first by resolving the problems that it raised.[22]

I do not see how this can be said, however, of Bateson's reading, which
insists that the poem does not present two contrasting moods, but a single
mood mounting to a magnificant pantheistic climax at the end. There is
then no opposition between the two stanzas, and hence, no ironic fit of

their details. For if the dead Lucy is grander and more alive than the living Lucy was, then the speaker really did have no reason to "fear" for her, and no reason to call this absence of fear a "slumber," and no reason to suggest that this slumber "sealed" him from something, and no reason to say that she "seemed" impervious to time, and no reason to describe that condition in the way he does. This reading, in short, cannot provide a satisfactory explanation of the first stanza, or, therefore, of the poem as a whole, and that is the real reason why I believe it is less probable than Brooks's.

Does this mean that we have come back full circle to the New Critics' position, stated at the outset, which held that the literary work is absolutely autonomous and must be explicated by a "close reading" of the text without reference to any external context? I do not think so. For it should be evident that my argument in favor of Brooks's reading, and against Bateson's, did assume a context external to this poem, and to *any* particular work. It was an assumption about the nature of literature itself. I was assuming that a literary work raised and then resolved certain specific problems or expectations, so that its ending accounted for and completed its beginning—or, putting it in the more usual way, that it was a coherent artistic whole. This was the context I relied upon in examining the poem, and in judging between the two readings. Like all other contexts, it is not infallible; but it does seem to govern the way we try to make sense of a work as we go through it and the way we arrive at a final interpretation after weighing other alternatives.

How does this context relate to the two principles I have been developing here? It could be said to conform to the second one in a very general sense, since it is not derived from some theory but from the actual practice of most authors and readers (and spectators, in the drama). But it certainly does not conform to the first principle, because it is not proximate to this work or to any other. It seems, rather, to be one of the most general contexts that we can apply in interpretation, like the context of communication itself. Indeed, it might be thought of as defining the special mode of communication that we call literature. However, this general context of artistic coherence is always subject to modification by the much more specific contexts dictated by our principle of "proximity," for our knowledge of the author's practice (again, not of his theory) in the subgenre and time period closest to the work we are interpreting (and also, in some cases, of the practice of other authors writing within the same subgenre and period) will determine the particular *kind* of coherence that we look for in this work and will even determine how hard and how long we will look for it.

This last consideration deserves some elaboration, because it involves another general principle of interpretation that seems to be very important, but that I have never seen discussed—the principle of knowing when to give up. As I just noted, when we confront a literary work we try to "make sense" of it by formulating an interpretation to see if it will yield a coherent whole. If it fails to do this, we assume that there must be something wrong with it and hypothesize another one, and if that fails we try still others. But at some point in this process, when we have apparently exhausted all of the likely hypotheses, it will seem more reasonable to give up and conclude that the lack of coherence probably does not lie in our interpretation of the work but in the work itself. And the location of that point, I am arguing, should be governed by the proximate contexts stated above, since these will determine the probability that the work really is coherent. Thus we ought to give up more quickly and more easily if we are dealing with one of Shakespeare's early plays, or one of Jonson's late ones, rather than with a play from the period of their greatest achievement. (By the same reasoning, we should look very hard and very long before giving up on "A Slumber," because almost all of the short lyrics written by Wordsworth during this stage of his career, including the other "Lucy poems," are coherent wholes.) Some of the most dubious new readings of our time, it seems to me, come from critics who ignore this principle and try to "save" the work at any cost, even when there is little reason to expect coherence in it, by adopting some highly improbable interpretation (as we saw in Duncan's essay on *The New Inn*).

Of course, the probability of this interpretation will itself be determined by the proximate contexts discussed earlier, for the general context of coherence has not cancelled them out or diminished their authority in any way. They must still be employed in establishing the meaning of the various parts of the work and of the work as a whole. We would naturally hope that the interpretation based on the most reliable of these proximate contexts will also conform to this more general one by giving us a coherent work of art (that is, when we expect such a work from this author at this time). If it does not, we are in serious difficulties. For a real contextual problem in the interpretation of "A Slumber" would arise, not if the other "Lucy poems" and the Coleridge letter disappeared (in the situation I imagined previously), but if they supported Bateson's reading—if the poems all presented a very consoling, pantheistic response to Lucy's death, and Coleridge found this same meaning in "A Slumber." Then we would have to choose between the interpretation that is historically more probable, in terms of the proximate contexts, and the one that is artistically more satisfying, in terms of the general context of coherence. It would be a very tough decision, but I said at the outset that I could not possibly settle all the problems involved in the role of contexts in interpretation, and so I will end here.

NOTES

1. R. S. Crane, Norman Maclean, and Elder Olson, "Two Essays in Practical Criticism," *University Review* 8 (1942): 209–19. Compare his later view in "An Outline of Poetic Theory," *Critiques and Essays in Criticism, 1920–1948,* ed. Robert Stallman (New York: Ronald Press, 1949), pp. 281–88, reprinted in *Critics and Criticism, Ancient and Modern,* ed. R. S. Crane (Chicago: University of Chicago Press, 1952), pp. 563–66.

2. Robert Presson, "The Structural Use of a Traditional Theme in *Troilus and Cressida,*" *Philological Quarterly* 31 (1952): 180–88. At the end he adds to this context a biographical dimension (of a type to be discussed below) by claiming that the same central theme appears in Shakespeare's later plays.

3. *New Readings vs. Old Plays* (Chicago: University of Chicago Press, 1979), pp. 148–66.

4. (Cambridge: Cambridge University Press, 1930), sect. 1.

5. *The Business of Criticism* (Oxford: Clarendon Press, 1959), pp. 35–51. She first rejects the use of the "idea-of-the-time" about the ethics of revenge.

6. Compare the more general principle of "narrowing the class" in E. D. Hirsch, *Validity in Interpretation* (New Haven: Yale University Press, 1967), chap. 5.

7. Massinger's *The Duke of Milan;* for other examples, see the final lines of *Locrine, A Warning for Fair Women,* Alexander's *Darius,* Barnes's *The Devil's Charter,* Marston and Barkstead's *The Insatiate Countess,* and Fletcher and Massinger's *Sir John van Olden Barnavelt.* The connection between these moral tags and the plays that they conclude is sometimes not very clear.

8. *Curs'd Example: "The Duchess of Malfi" and Commonweal Tragedy* (Columbia: University of Missouri Press, 1978), chaps. 1–2.

9. There is a third poem by John Ford, which praises Webster in general terms without indicating any attitude toward the Duchess. In his Dedication to the 1708 edition, the publisher, Hugh Newman, refers to the "just Cause" of "the Injured and Oppressed" Duchess; and in the Prologue he wrote for Lewis Theobald's *The Fatal Secret,* an adaptation of Webster's play produced in 1733, Philip Frowde records that "An ancient Bard, a Century ago. / Chose out this Tale of soft, pathetick, Woe. / Then, as they say, Beaus could Attention keep; / And injur'd Virtue force the Fair to weep."

10. For two such cases where these recorded responses to a work clearly contradict the assertions of certain critics who claim to know, on the basis of some other historical context, how the contemporary audience would have viewed it, see my "The Ironic Reading of *The Rape of Lucrece* and the Problem of External Evidence," *Shakespeare Survey* 34 (1981): 85–92, and "The Contemporary Perception of Marlowe's Tamburlaine," *Medieval & Renaissance Drama in England* 1 (1984): 51–70.

11. *Essays in Criticism* 20 (1970): 311–26; and 22 (1972): 41–47.

12. *Vision and Judgment in Ben Jonson's Drama* (New Haven: Yale University Press, 1968); in addition to *Timber,* she makes use of the conception of the poet found in the two *Every Man* plays, *Poetaster,* and *Cynthia's Revels.*

13. Some of them are reported in Randolph Goodman, *Drama on Stage* (New York: Holt, Rinehart and Winston, 1961), pp. 278, 308–11, and in Foster Hirsch, "The World Still Desires *A Streetcar,*" *New York Times,* 15 April 1973, sec. 2, pp. 1, 3. Many New Critics would declare his statements out of bounds for the

interpreter, but it is not clear whether this ban would extend to prologues and inductions, which are part of the "text" (see W. K. Wimsatt and Monroe Beardsley, "The Intentional Fallacy," *Sewanee Review* 54 [1946]: 468–88).

14. See, for example, Paul Kocher, *Christopher Marlowe: A Study of His Thought, Learning, and Character* (Chapel Hill: University of North Carolina Press, 1946), and John Wieler, *George Chapman: The Effect of Stoicism upon His Tragedies* (New York: King's Crown Press, 1949).

15. "Irony and 'Ironic' Poetry," *College English* 9 (1948): 235–37.

16. *English Poetry: A Critical Introduction* (London: Longmans, Green, 1950), pp. 32–34, 80–81.

17. *Validity in Interpretation,* pp. 228–30, 239–40 (an earlier version appeared in "Objective Interpretation," *PMLA* 75 [1960]: 471–72, 476–77). For some later discussions of the two readings and Hirsch's adjudication of them, see John Oliver Perry, *Approaches to the Poem: Modern Essays in the Analysis and Interpretation of Poetry* (San Francisco: Chandler, 1965), pp. 13–15; Don Geiger, *The Dramatic Impulse in Modern Poetics* (Baton Rouge: Louisiana State University Press, 1967), pp. 132–45; Monroe Beardsley, *The Possibility of Criticism* (Detroit: Wayne State University Press, 1970), pp. 27–31, 44–48; Spencer Hall, "Wordsworth's 'Lucy' Poems: Context and Meaning," *Studies in Romanticism* 10 (1971): 159–75; Gordon Mills, *Hamlet's Castle: The Study of Literature as a Social Experience* (Austin: University of Texas Press, 1976), pp. 125–26, 163; James Phelan, *Worlds from Words: A Theory of Language in Fiction* (Chicago: University of Chicago Press, 1981), pp. 92–97; and "Validity Redux: The Relation of Author, Reader, and Text in the Act of Interpretation," *Papers in Comparative Studies* 1 (1981): 80–111.

18. 4.8, p. 309, ed. Martin Battestin (Middletown: Wesleyan University Press, 1967).

19. 4.5, p. 121, ed. H. Harvey Wood (Edinburgh: Oliver and Boyd, 1934). See also Feste's dialogue with Olivia in *Twelfth Night,* 1.5.51–64.

20. Melvin Rader, *Wordsworth: A Philosophical Approach* (Oxford: Clarendon Press, 1967), p. 172, based on *Henry Crabb Robinson on Books and Their Writers,* ed. Edith Morley (London: Dent, 1938), 2:482.

21. *Collected Letters of Samuel Taylor Coleridge,* ed. Earl Leslie Griggs (Oxford: Clarendon Press, 1956), 1:274.

22. For a number of the preceding points I am indebted to an unpublished essay by Bruce Bashford.

PART 2
Stage

Theatrical Plots and Elizabethan Stage Practice

Bernard Beckerman

Since W. W. Greg made his exhaustive examination of *The Battle of Alcazar* in 1922[1] and then his comprehensive analysis of extant dramatic documents from the Elizabethan playhouses in 1931,[2] few scholars have felt the need to restudy the seven surviving theatrical Plots, or schematic outlines of plays from the 1590s.[3] Recently, however, T. J. King, as part of a larger project on *Actors and Their Parts in the Time of Shakespeare,* has reviewed four of the Plots in order to discern patterns of doubling. Thanks to his example, I too began to reexamine these intriguing remnants of Elizabethan stage practice, in my case in order to determine whether or not the Plots had anything more to tell us about staging than what Greg had so scrupulously extracted. Happily, I think they have, and this occasion for honoring S. F. Johnson seems an appropriate time to suggest, in a preliminary manner, what that is.

A Plot, as students of the Elizabethan stage well know, is a skeletal outline of a play's sequence. Written on sheets of paper measuring roughly twelve by sixteen inches, which were then mounted on the front and back of thin pulp board, a Plot, we have excellent reason to think, was hung backstage on the day of a performance to assist the actors in running through the play. Considering the fact that the actors never played the same show on successive days and that they probably added a new play to their repertory every other week, some sort of reminder such as this must have been desirable. What a Plot supplied was the division of the play according to scenes, the sequence of entrances for the actors, and, in most copies, the assignment of roles. It might also give sound cues and list properties. More a guide to memory than a thoroughly detailed set of instructions, Plots probably were standard items in the working tools of the principal London companies.

Of the seven extant Plots, two appear to belong to the years 1590–91. Greg assigns *2 Seven Deadly Sins* to the company of Lord Strange's men, mainly because of the presence of the young Richard Burbage in the cast, arguing that the play was given at the Curtain in 1590. The relative simplicity of the Plot for *The Dead Man's Fortune* leads him to assign that play to the Admiral's men at the Theatre during the same period.[4]

The remaining five Plots, all belonging to the later Admiral's Men, come from the period 1597–1602. One, *2 Fortune's Tennis,* exists only in the most fragmentary form. Hence my remarks upon it will be negligible. The Plot of *Troilus and Cressida* is badly mutilated, but enough remains so that some evidence can be drawn from it. Likewise, what survives of *The Battle of Alcazar* is also mutilated, though in different ways. This Plot is fairly complete through nine scenes and substantially decipherable through four or five others, taking us well into the fourth act of the play as it is preserved in the extant Quarto of 1594. The outline of the fifth act, which occupied the back of the board, has disappeared. The last two Plots, those for *Frederick and Basilea* and *1 Tamar Cam,* are complete. Unfortunately, we no longer possess the original Plot for *1 Tamar Cam.* Our knowledge of it comes from a transcript made by George Steevens and printed in the 1803 'Variorum' Shakespeare. Reassuringly, the transcript exhibits the same characteristics as do the other Elizabethan Plots. Greg dates the last four of them in the following order: *Frederick and Basilea* in 1597; *The Battle of Alcazar* between December 1598 and February 1599; *Troilus and Cressida* in May 1599; and *1 Tamar Cam* in 1602.[5]

As Greg has shown, the Plots, while not absolutely uniform, do exhibit certain common features that indicate general playhouse practice. All Plots are laid out in vertical columns. Some sheets have two columns, others only one. Usually to the left of each column, whether one or two, is a margin that may contain sound cues or, rarely, a note on properties. Invariably cutting across each column are horizontal lines that, with one exception, mark out the scenes of a play. Only the Plot of *The Dead Man's Fortune* has any other sign of division, rows of crosses that seem to designate act endings. Otherwise, these horizontal lines confirm the generally accepted opinion that the scene was the basic unit in Elizabethan play production.

Among the most consistent features of the Plots is the use of the word "Enter." With some trifling exceptions, it comes at the beginning of a scene, indicating to the actor that he is to come out upon a cleared stage. For entrances within a scene the common locution is "to them," or, less frequently, "to him" or "to her." So consistent is this use of "enter" that Greg regarded "this rigid observance of a purely arbitrary rule in all the extant Plots [as] rather remarkable."[6] I cannot stress the importance of this consistency too much. It demonstrates that entries received careful attention and that the plotter or scribe—Greg calls the writer of a Plot sometimes one, sometimes the other—was precise in what he put down. So much Greg has already established. But there are other implications of this principle that remain unexplored.

Before proceeding to those implications, I should like to make some observations on Greg's orientation. As I have already noted, he calls the writer of a Plot either a plotter or a scribe. So far as I can discern he uses these two terms interchangeably. But the tasks performed by persons of such dissimilar titles would certainly differ. The scribe, we can presume, would record decisions made by others. On the other hand, the plotter, as the name suggests, would plan stage business and arrange the disposition of the roles, especially of those not taken by the sharers. The widespread practice of doubling parts would make this part of his task extraordinarily important. Yet Greg's use of the terms *scribe* and *plotter* indifferently obscures not only their separate functions but also the peculiar functioning of a theatrical company.

This confusion of terms is further aggravated by Greg's observation that what the players required for the preparation of a "fundamental Plot" were "the Book or prompt copy of the play [and] a second document, namely a Cast showing the distribution of the characters among the available actors."[7] Undoubtedly, these materials were necessary, but though the former was certainly a written document, the second may or may not have been one. The rapidity with which plays were put into the repertory, rarely taking more than two or three weeks from the conclusion of composition to first performance, argues for a fluidity of operation. Whether there were understood arrangements that determined who played what roles or whether the sharers met to divide the parts, we do not know. We do know, though, that the company gathered together to hear a playwright read a script after he finished it, and it may very well have been after such a reading that the sharers divided the roles among themselves. In other words, a Plot came out of active production. It embodied a process, not a system of recording.

Once we look at the Plots from the point of view of rehearsal and performance, certain anomalies strike us forcibly. The most startling has to do with the feature that is most regular: the designation of entrance. A Plot, as everyone agrees, is a practical document. Its value is in its utility. Primarily, it served to inform the actors when they were to enter the stage and, whenever this was relevant, as which character. In the course of supplying this information, the Plot reminded the actors of the parts they were playing. By comparison, the specification of exits was irregular. And as for other elements of staging, such as the timing of sound cues or the bringing in of properties, they might appear in one Plot and not in another. As an instrument for staging, then, a Plot concentrated almost entirely on entrances.

Seen in this light, the Plots are most curious. Let us imagine an actual performance. The players gather in the tiring house, dressed in their costumes for the first entrance. They face the back of the stage façade on the other side of which is the great platform and the near circle of playgoers. They prepare to make their entrances from one of the two doors in the backstage wall unless the Plot instructs them otherwise. That Plot hangs in a convenient place where they can consult it either before or during a scene, whenever they need to. From it they can readily tell *when* to make an entrance. But wait, how do they know *where* to make the entrance? What does the Plot say about that? For most scenes, it says nothing. Here are the players, behind the two or possibly three entryways that pass through the stage wall, and the Plot gives them no guidance as to which door to use.

The absence of such guidance is all the more astonishing when we realize that an individual player made eight or ten entrances in a play— Edward Alleyn made at least eight as Muly Mahamet in *The Battle of Alcazar.* To compound the difficulty, the lesser actors, who doubled in many roles, made appreciably more entrances during a performance than the leading players. R. Cowly in *Seven Deadly Sins* made eleven entrances in six different parts; in the same play Thomas Goodale made nine entrances in four parts. Likewise, in *Alcazar* W. Kendall had ten entrances divided among four parts and Robert Tailor, eight entrances for three parts. This volume of entrances would not be overwhelming were it not that the players had to remember entrances for as many as twenty or thirty plays at one time. In a typical two-week period of eleven performances, a company would play about eight different plays, making a total of sixty to eighty entrances for a journeyman actor. Can we assume that he needed help in remembering the sequence of entrances but did not need assistance in identifying the doors through which he entered?

So far as I know, no one has raised this question before. Yet as one examines the Plots with it in mind, one makes some interesting discoveries. Of the six Plots under discussion, the majority of all scenes follow the rule of beginning with the word "Enter." All eighteen scenes of *Frederick and Basilea* begin this way. Fourteen of the twenty-five scenes in *Seven Deadly Sins* and eleven of the fifteen scenes in *The Battle of Alcazar* observe the rule. But widespread as this rule is, there are some exceptions that point to subsidiary rules. Three of the six Plots contain directions for entries onto a higher level. In *Alcazar,* the stage direction reads, "Enter above Nemesis" or "Enter Nemesis above."[8] In both dumb shows where this occurs, the character relates to others on the platform below.

In *Troilus and Cressida* and *Frederick and Basilea,* where the stage directions occur within a scene, they specify entrance "on" or "upon" the walls. Interestingly, in two cases the direction indicates that the entrance is to be made "to them," that is, to the characters already on stage. This indicates that from the perspective of the actor, an entrance above was not to an autonomous part of the stage but to the action in progress. The agreement on this matter between *Troilus and Cressida* and *Frederick and Basilea* suggests that this type of direction was a secondary rule.

More frequent is another variant of the simple entrance. This occurs in five of the six Plots. With the exception of *Frederick and Basilea,* all contain scenes that direct the actors to enter from different directions. Some are to enter "at one dore" and some "at another." This is the most common form of the instruction. A companion form is the direction to enter at "severall doores." Given the care with which entries are marked, these exceptional directions must reflect deliberate staging practice. A clue to what that might be is suggested by the Plot for *Seven Deadly Sins.*

In the Plots for the other plays, the specification of two entrance doors occurs only once or twice. In *Seven Deadly Sins,* amazingly, it occurs five times. Moreover, it occurs in a strikingly significant way. As scholars have long recognized, *Seven Deadly Sins* is the second part of a two-part play. Together the parts must have treated seven historical or mythic incidents, each of which exemplified one of the sins. The extant Plot for *2 Seven Deadly Sins* dramatizes the sins of Envy, Sloth, and Lechery, in that order. Framing the action of these individual playlets is the drama of an imprisoned Henry VI visited by the poet Lydgate. Assumedly, Lydgate moralizes upon each sin and its story.

The first sin, Envy, is illustrated by the story of Gorboduc and his two sons, Ferrex and Porrex. Exemplifying Sloth in the second story is Sardanapalus. Finally, the tragic tale of Philomele follows to show the horrors of Lechery. The framing action begins and ends the play and separates each of the stories.

To dramatize the last two stories, the play employs seven and five scenes, respectively. All of these scenes strictly follow the rule for "enter" as defined by Greg. Not so the third story. That follows different principles. Like the play about Sardanapalus, the story of Gorboduc is divided among seven scenes. These scenes, however, have a notable symmetry, at least so far as entrances are concerned. The first scene, beginning with a dumb show, and the last have conventional entries: that is, in the first scene the opening direction reads, "Enter King Gorboduk" and his court; in the last, it reads, "Enter Porrex sad wth Dordan his man." The five scenes between have a pyramidal structure. At the center is a battle scene upon which Lydgate comments. Before and after, as the envy of Ferrex and Porrex grows, the scene directions all specify entrance from different doors, either by instructing Ferrex to enter "at one dore Porrex at an other" or by directing them to enter "severally." Since the central scene of battle consists of the single direction "A Larum with Excurtions After / Lidgate speakes," we can safely presume that entrances there too involved both doors. As a result, the entry plan of the Gorboduc play consists of two-door entries flanked by conventional entries at the beginning and end of the action.

The specification of two-door entries in the Gorboduc playlet and no similar specification in the latter two playlets argues that the distinction in entry schemes had a dramatic purpose. What that purpose might be is suggested by action in the first scene of the play. It is here that the first direction for two doors occurs. Henry lies asleep in a tent. To him come a lieutenant, a purcevant, and a warder. Then, "to them Pride Gluttony / Wrath and Covetousnes at one dore at an other / dore Envie Sloth and Lechery The Three put / back the foure and so Exeunt." In this struggle of the sins is prefigured the struggle between Ferrex and Porrex. The fact that all the subsequent directions for divided entrances pertain to these two characters alone shows that the staging is emblematic; that is, the use of two doors objectifies the envious conflict between the brothers. Further reinforcing this effect is the recurrent passage of the emblematic sin from one side of the stage to another preceding each playlet.

As we shall see with *Alcazar,* the two-door entrance may be employed for other purposes than those shown here. The mutilated portion of the Plot for *Alcazar* has two scenes where the surviving text is sufficiently clear to indicate that entries are made from alternate doors. Both scenes involve Sebastian, the King of Portugal. In the first (scene 10), Sebastian receives the ambassadors from the Spanish king, Philip. Its alternate entries accentuate the formality of the reception and the protestations of Philip's adherence to Sebastian's crusade, an adherence that the Presenter, according to the Quarto (818–20) has already told us is false. The second scene of alternate entries (scene 12) is another formal meeting. Here I rely on Greg's reconstruction of the text. Sebastian and his train enter "at one dore" with drum and colors. Apparently, the Governor of Tangier enters at the other door welcoming the King of Portugal to the city. Into their midst, that is, from a center entry, come Muly Mahamet and his family—he, Greg assumes, in a chariot since the Plot indicates that Muly Mahamet makes his first entrance in a chariot.[9] Like the first use of the two-door entrance, the second accentuates the formal spectacle of reception. In both instances the ceremony is hollow, a testimony to vainglory and deceit.

Of alternate entries in the other plays, the information is too scant to make reliable guesses. The one example from *Troilus and Cressida* seems to occur at the beginning of the play in a scene where the Trojans receive an embassy from the Greeks. If that is so, such usage agrees with that in *Alcazar.* Occurring twice in *Dead Man's Fortune* and once in *Tamar Cam,* this two-door stage direction is explicit, but the context does not allow us to speculate on the circumstances of the action. Nevertheless, from what we have been able to garner, it is evident that a switch from "enter" to entrance at alternate doors had theatrical purpose, in the interests either of emblematic significance or of spectacle, or, as is more likely, of the one with the other.

What then of my initial question? What does all this tell us about the Plot's call for entrance without identifying the location of the entrance? At this point, all we can do is speculate. My own view is that one of three conditions must have existed. Perhaps it was a matter of indifference to the company which door was used, and so there was no need to mark it down. The fact that the alternate doors were not identified in the two-door instruction lends some weight to this proposition, slight though it might be. Possibly the actors could remember all their entrances and wrote them down on their sides. But if so, why did they need the Plots at all? If Plots were needed to tell them when to enter, why not where? So many scenes begin with groups of characters entering together that there must have been some way of assuring that all the actors would assemble in the same place at the same time. Far more likely, it seems to me, is the existence of some convention governing usage of the doors. Perhaps—and I offer this conjecture in the most tentative way possible—it was understood that entrances were made at one conventionally designated door and exits at the other unless the actor was specifically instructed otherwise. In such a system, all actors knew that when the Plot indicated an entrance for them, they were to go to one place and one place only. When they saw the direction "at one door . . . at another," then they knew the first entry was to be made through the conventional entrance door and the second through the usual exit door. So was it with passage over the stage, the entry and exit being strictly regularized. Such a system, if it did exist, facilitated rapid mounting of a play and erased the pressures on actors who might have to juggle upwards of fifty roles during a single "season."

Of entry other than through one or through alternate doors there are some limited signs. Among the Plots the one explicit direction for a third entry occurs in scene 5—that is, the third scene of the Gorboduc story— of *Seven Deadly Sins*. Following the direction for the entrance of Ferrex and Porrex "severall waies" with drums and powers occurs the direction "Gorboduk entreing in The midst between." Like the other instances, one from *Alcazar* and one from *Troilus and Cressida,* where central entrance is indicated, the entryway is not a door. In the case of *Alcazar,* three furies, who are instructed to lie "behind the Curtaines," enter with whip, bloody torch, and chopping knife. It is from behind these curtains that Muly Mahamet emerges in his chariot in scene 12, according to Greg's reconstruction.[10] Since here the direction clearly specifies the use of two doors, we have to presume that Muly Mahamet, like Gorboduc, enters in "the midst between" Sebastian and the Governor of Tangier.

The one possible use of a central entrance in *Troilus and Cressida* comes in scene 9, when first Diomed, then Menelaus and Ulysses enter. "To them [comes] Achillis in his Tent." The tent could very well be represented by the stage curtains, and so the stage direction "Achillis in his Tent" might merely specify that Achilles enters from behind the curtains. The one doubt about this interpretation is raised by the opening direction in the Plot for *Seven Deadly Sins*. That reads: "A tent being plast one the stage for Henry the sixt he in it A sleepe." Like the tents in *Richard III* (5.3), this one appears to be a mansion-type set property. So may Achilles' tent. But if Henry's is such a mansion, then the very fact that he appears in it "asleep" suggests that it was placed before some entryway that enabled the actor to enter the closed tent unseen and seem to sleep. Since the tent is distinct from the two doors that are required in this scene, it appears to confirm this existence of a third entry.

Altogether then, the evidence from the Plots supports the widely accepted thesis that the Elizabethan stage had two doors plus a curtained area. The latter served as an entrance as well as a discovery place, as in *Seven Deadly Sins*. To this recognized picture of the stage, I would now add the proposition that standard usage was for actors to enter regularly through one door and exit through the other. So common was this practice, I imagine, that directions for these regularized entrances were minimal. Where the actors varied their entrances for theatrical purposes, the variations were noted in the Plot to remind them of the special arrangement.

This attempt to reconstruct Elizabethan staging practice, however, goes beyond the matter of entry, important though that is. There are the further questions of how a play was staged and who determined the staging. Unfortunately, all but one of the Plots has very little to tell us about these questions. The one Plot that is of use is, of course, that for *The Battle of Alcazar*, the only Plot for which we have a parallel script. What we make of the Plot or script principally depends on how we interpret the relationship between them.

Two facts govern that relationship. First, as Greg has so convincingly shown, the cast named in the Plot of *Alcazar* consists of members from the Lord Admiral's company as it existed in the winter of 1598–99.[11] This was some four or five years after the play was first published in 1594 and about ten years after it first made its appearance on stage. Both Greg and John Yoklavich, who follows Greg,[12] date the composition of the play from 1588 or 1589. The second fact pertains to the state of the Quarto text of 1594. Greg has pretty clearly shown it to be an abridged version,[13] a conclusion that Yoklavich accepts in his edition of *Alcazar*.[14] It is on the basis of these two facts that Greg has explained the relationship between the Plot and the Quarto.

His full analysis of this relationship appeared in a 1922 publication for the Malone Society entitled, *Two Elizabethan Stage Abridgements: "The*

Battle of Alcazar" and "Orlando Furioso." In the section on *The Battle of Alcazar* Greg finds that the Plot requires a larger cast than does the Quarto text and that many scenes in the Quarto are defective, exhibiting awkward transitions and at times, incoherence. From this he concludes:

> the text of *Alcazar* printed in 1594 proves to be a version drastically cut down by the omissions and reduction of speeches, by the elimination and doubling of parts, and by the suppression of spectacular shows, for representation in a limited time by a comparatively small cast, with a minimum of theatrical paraphernalia.[15]

Ineluctably, these conclusions lead Greg to the assumption that the Plot embodies the staging of the play in its "original" form. The Quarto text, on the other hand, he regarded as an abridgement of that original and therefore not as the source from which the plot was directly derived. Naturally, such a theory severely limits the information one can draw from the connection between the two documents since it posits a third, nonextant document separating them. Yet despite the weight of Greg's authority, his theory does not account entirely for certain features of the documents as we have them, and therefore they deserve careful review.

That the Quarto text of *Alcazar* contains an abridged version of the play there can be little doubt. But that the abridgement was for the purpose of accommodating a smaller cast and a less spectacular production is less certain. Unquestionably, the Plot lists more characters in some scenes than are called for in the Quarto, but with few exceptions these additional characters are supernumeraries. Indeed, it is not always evident that the numbers differ so much. For example, act 2, scene 1 of the Quarto calls for an entrance of five characters "with Moores and Ianizaries," (362–64). The parallel direction in the Plot specifies, besides the same five characters, Zareo and three attendants. Since Zareo is a Moor and the plural "Moores and Ianizeries" suggests at least four extras, it would appear that the numbers for the scene are identical. In other instances the Quarto calls for more people than the Plot supplies. For the first entrance in act 1, scene 1, the Quarto stage direction reads "enter Abdilmelec with Calsepius Bassa and his gard, and Zareo a Moore with souldiers." The Plot, however, indicates that despite this direction in the text, Calsepius alone had a guard of three; Zareo, on the other hand, entered without soldiers.

A close comparison scene by scene between Plot and Quarto reveals that the claim that the Quarto requires substantially fewer actors is illusory. A key case is act 1, scene 2. Greg remarks that "this scene affords some of the clearest evidence of revision in the Quarto."[16] The initial stage direction for this scene has "Enter the Moore [Muly Mahamet] in his Chariot, attended with his sonne. Pisano his captaine with his gard and treasure." The stage direction makes no mention of the Moor's wife,

Calipolis, although in the dialogue he addresses her as "Madame" (221). Neither does she speak in the scene, something that Greg regards as so unreasonable that he concludes the part "has been deliberately cut out of the Quarto version."[17] Yet the same sort of situation occurs in act 3, scene 4, where Calipolis is once again addressed although she does not speak. In that scene, moreover, it is evident, as Greg admits, that "her presence is intended though her part, if any, has been omitted."[18] But her presence is her part, at least in this instance, and the mere fact that she does not speak does not mean she is not on stage. In short, Greg's argument that Calipolis was eliminated from 1.2 in order to save an actor is shaky, made more so by his statement that this was done in order to allow two boy actors to play ladies in the previous scene. How this can be is puzzling, since Calipolis, as Greg admits, is the chief female role. It would appear to be the height of dramaturgic incompetence to cut out her initial appearance, one that identifies her as queen to the Moor, in order to double the women who greet Abdilmelec's return.

Not only in this scene but elsewhere the argument for a smaller cast for the Quarto is not convincing. It rests on the twin assumptions that the text of the play in its original form must have listed every character who appeared on stage, and that the Plot as a redaction of the Book should agree. This view reaffirms Greg's tacit assumption, discussed earlier, that staging is a matter of transference from one document to another rather than an interaction between players and text. From *Alcazar* we know this is not the case. In one scene (3.1), an illuminating one in this respect, the Quarto stage direction reads "Manet Stukley and another" (871). The Plot discards the neutrality of the other figure and assigns the scene to the Duke of Avero. Evidently, the author was indifferent to which character served as Stukley's confidant. It was the plotter, whoever he may have been, who selected the character and thereby the actor.

This is not the only point where the Quarto stage directions are imprecise, that is, "literary" rather than "theatrical." Throughout the Quarto there occur directions that indicate the general size of the cast or the general tenor of the action without providing the specifics that staging requires. Over and over again various contending kings enter "with their train" or "with others." It is left to the players to fill the train or company with whatever numbers they can muster. As we saw in the case of Zareo, according to the Plot he entered without soldiers despite the stage direction in the script calling for them. At other times the vaguely worded "others" can result in a retinue of three or four attendants. As a result, there is no way to tell from a comparison of the Quarto and the Plot whether the Quarto required fewer actors than the Plot. One could easily prove the contrary.

When it comes to comparing Quarto and Plot in terms of spectacle, the results are not nearly so clear-cut. The stage directions for most scenes in the Quarto are too vague to tell us much about the intended staging. The scenes from which we can learn most are those describing the dumb shows. The combined evidence of Plot and Quarto reveals that *Alcazar* contains five dumb shows. These shows divide the play into five acts. Neither Quarto nor Plot provides the data for all five, but together they give a complete picture of these shows. No doubt they were the most spectacular scenes of the play, exhibiting a triple murder in the first instance, an unloosening of ghosts and furies in the next, a judgment of the three chief characters by ghosts, furies, and possibly devils in the third, a feasting at the bloody banquet of war in the next, and finally the promise and loss of fame.

Insofar as the dumb shows are concerned, the comparison between Quarto and Plot is peculiarly difficult. No two dumb shows offer the same order of evidence. For the last dumb show, depicting Fame's appearance to hang crowns upon a tree, we can rely only on the Quarto. On the other hand, the Quarto includes only a short speech for the induction to act 3, a speech that contains no allusion to what must have been an elaborate pantomime of Nemesis standing above urging on three Furies to bring forth scales in order to judge King Sebastian, Tom Stukley, and the villainous Muly Mahamet. But we cannot conclude that the Plot regularly requires a more ambitious staging of the dumb shows than does the Quarto. In the induction to the first act, the Quarto dumb show is divided into two parts, the first calling for a curtained bed in which two young boys can lie and the second for a chair. In the parallel description of the Plot, the dumb show seems to unfold in an unbroken sequence. Mention is made of neither bed nor chair. The Quarto calls for seven actors, the Plot for eight. The difference is in a single attendant. From this comparison it is impossible to say which version is more spectacular.

Judging from the Plot, the two dumb shows that are the most ambitious in scope are the third and fourth. Both involve Nemesis overseeing the punishment of criminals. They require fourteen and ten (or possibly twelve) actors, respectively. Unfortunately, as I remarked previously, neither the speech of the Presenter nor an extant stage direction shows any trace of the third show in the Quarto. For the fourth, however, though the Presenter's speech is the shortest by him in the play, it contains a general description of what the Plot directions imply. In addition, a Quarto stage direction explicitly calls for a "bloudie banket," (1067). It is therefore reasonably certain that the Quarto demands a display similar to that represented by the Plot.

In the second dumb show, moreover, the action of the Plot is so exactly described by the Presenter that there can be no question that the Quarto requires substantially the same production as does the Plot. That being so, only the brief third speech by the Presenter lacks evidence of a parallel dumb show. That curtailment might reflect a deliberate cut or it might have resulted from defective copy. Whatever the reason, the other dumb shows, as described in the Quarto, show that there was no substantive difference between the versions in the Plot and in the play text.

In brief, then, I believe we cannot account for the cuttings in the quarto of *The Battle of Alcazar* by reason of adaptation for a smaller company. The text may have been cut to provide a shorter performance, but it is hard to believe that so short a performance could have proven profitable. Or the text, as preserved in the copy available to the printer, was defective. Whatever the reason, here is not the time nor place to try to resolve so elusive a matter. For my purpose it is sufficient to observe that the Plot and the Quarto agree structurally.

If then, as I believe, we cannot regard the relationship between Plot and Quarto as merely indirect, that is, each as a partial embodiment of an original copy, what is the relationship? One other feature of the Quarto throws some light on that question. Greg, following Dover Wilson, points out that of all the Quarto stage directions, the majority are printed in italics, though "over a score" appear in roman type. He regards the italics as representing the Italian hand of the "transcriber" of the original text and the roman print as reflecting the English hand of a "reviser."[19] Although he does not press this argument too far, he does conclude that "the roman directions are consistent with the revised text, the italic often are not."[20]

By referring to the writer of the Italian hand as the transcriber, Greg avoids the question of the source of the italic stage directions. Elsewhere, however, he notes that quite a few of them have a literary character. He notes, for example, that the printed text retains the sort of vague directions that "an author might be expected to write."[21] And in this observation I believe he is correct. When we examine the distinction between the italic and roman stage directions, we find that the latter almost invariably deal with practical stage considerations. Of the eighteen roman stage directions (as I count them), eleven include alarums alone or alarums followed by stage business. Of the remaining seven, two separate the first half of the initial dumb show from the second half (24, 35). Three pertain to fighting or dying (1335–37, 1450, 1504), one to flight in battle (1386), and only one is a straightforward direction for actors to enter (701). The italic directions, by comparison, rarely mention sound (only twice in the play) and then in connection with ceremonial entries (68, 978). The bulk of the directions specify entries, often with the tag of an indefinite number of supernumeraries.

What we appear to have in the Quarto copy are three layers of text. Much of it is as it came from the author's hand, the italics embodying his own words. This original copy was shaped into a prompt copy by the addition of nearly a score of stage directions (that were printed in roman type). It was an abridged version of this copy that reached the printer and that makes up the Quarto. But the abridgement was largely confined to the speeches and in essentials did not materially alter the staging requirements of the play. The Plot then, despite being prepared from what appears to be a fuller version, is an abstract of the stage requirements as they appeared in the original.

It has been necessary to deal with these issues at such length in order to argue that the Plot embodies the process by which the actors translate the demands of the playwright into the practical results of performance. If the italics express the writer's intention, then the Plot expresses the players' adjustment to that intention in 1598–99, or just about the time that Peter Streete was tearing down the Theatre in order to salvage timber for the new Globe. According to this thesis, the roman stage directions reflect the initial staging of the play, some features of which were adopted by the later production.

The complexity of the issues raised by this argument cannot be completely explored in this paper. At best, I can indicate one or two ways in which the players prepared the script for performance. Because the play has so many processional or ceremonial entrances, the plotter or "director" had to decide how many people were to make up soldiers, attendants, or janiseries and which characters they were to accompany. At times he used his discretion to add attendants. He also determined the manner of staging, in the case of the third dumb show introducing vials of blood and a sheep's gather to sensationalize the violent deaths of Sebastian, Stukley, and Muly Mahamet. Further, since the insert of alarums in roman type agrees for the most part with the sound cues in the Plot, we can assume that the plotter of the revival retained the staging of the earlier production in this respect.

A different sort of relationship is reflected in the staging of the second dumb show. As the reader will recall, this show describes in detail what happens according to the Plot, although the Quarto has only one rudimentary stage direction. The Presenter describes Nemesis arousing Alecto and the other furies with a thundering moan and drawing them from their "cave as darke as hell" (325). From the Plot we know that this cave is represented by curtains behind which the furies lie, one with "a whipp : a nother with a bloody torch : & the 3d with a Chopping knife," the precise properties described by the Presenter as the furies come forth. This placement of a "cave" supports the oft-expressed theory that an exotic locale is frequently represented by a conventional part of the stage. It also makes one wonder how the lost portion of the Plot dealt with the tree upon which Fame hung the crowns in the last dumb show.

A last illustration best reveals the dynamic relationship between text and performance in the Elizabethan playhouse. According to the stage direction in the Quarto for act 1, scene 2, Muly Mahamet makes his first entrance accompanied by his son, his captain Pisano, and a guard with his treasure. From the dialogue we learn that his wife Calipolis is also present. Since the direction appears in italics, we have to consider the likelihood that it was the author who inadvertently omitted Calipolis's name. The next significant business concerns Pisano. Although the Quarto does not contain an explicit exit for Pisano, he does make one in response to Muly Mahamet's order that he carry the Moor's treasure to safety. Some fifty lines later, after Muly Mahamet mocks the forces against him, a man rushes in, calling upon the king to flee and reporting the loss of his treasure to the enemy. Printed in roman type, the stage direction for this entrance reads: "Sound an alarum within, and enter a / messenger," (278–80). In line with Greg's argument, we conclude that this direction came from the reviser's hand and was therefore a theatrical modification of what the author originally wrote. Both the initial direction and this one belong, of course, to performances given in 1594 or earlier.

The later revival of 1598–99, embodied in the Plot, supplies an explicit exit for the actor playing Pisano as well as an explicit entrance for the man reporting the capture of the treasure. In the Plot he is one and the same person, the player and sharer in the Lord Admiral's company, Sam Rowley. From the Plot it is evident that Rowley exits as Pisano. But as whom does he return? The entrance in the Plot reads: "to them mr Sam a gaine." Greg believes that we have here a case of doubling, that Rowley departs as Pisano but returns as a different character entirely, the messenger. He bases his conclusion on the claim that Pisano must have been captured along with the treasure.[22] But the speech reporting the loss of the treasure makes no mention of Pisano's capture, and therefore does not rule out Pisano's return. Instead, I would suggest that in the parallel Quarto and Plot directions we have two contrasting stagings. In the initial production, two different actors may have been involved, one playing Pisano, the other playing the messenger. The revival, however, ignored this staging and used Pisano at both points. Whether the change was a reversion to an original stage direction that had been erased by the first plotter or was a new interpretation, we cannot say. It could very well have been that in the first production Pisano, who so far as the text shows did not speak in the scene, was played by a supernumerary. When the same part was taken by a sharer in the revival, it may have been convenient as well as theatrically effective for the sharer to return as the fleeing Pisano. By substituting the defeated captain for the anonymous messenger, the actors could make the danger for Muly Mahamet more immediate and dramatic.

The picture I am trying to draw is that of an active interchange between player and playwright. Fortunately, the extant theatrical plots give us some insight into the way in which that interchange took place. So far as the evidence goes, it suggests that staging did not transform a play but that it filled it out, occasionally modifying the way in which a writer conceived an action, but generally moving expeditiously to realize the physical requirements. Without being entirely conclusive, the Plots indicate that the physical elements of the stage, doors and curtains explicitly, were used sparingly but consciously for emblematic or spectacular purposes. The handling of entrances was particularly important in the running of the production, at times providing a fairly neutral sequencing for scenes, at other times supplying unusual accent.

More remains to be learned from the Plots. Inconclusive as the evidence is and fragmentary as the records may be, these half dozen surviving sheets and the one copy from Steevens still offer the best information we have on the workings of the Elizabethan playhouse. We owe W. W. Greg an enormous debt for having studied them so thoroughly, and we should not neglect that debt by failing to build upon the foundation he laid.

NOTES

In this paper, submitted posthumously, thanks are owed Martin Meisel for checking references.

1. W. W. Greg, *Two Elizabethan Stage Abridgements: "The Battle of Alcazar" and "Orlando Furioso"* (Malone Society, 1922).

2. W. W. Greg, *Dramatic Documents from the Elizabethan Playhouses: Stage Plots: Actors' Parts: Prompt Books,* 2 vols. (Oxford: Clarendon Press, 1931).

3. Of the seven theatrical Plots discussed in this paper, five are in the British Museum, bound in a volume classed as MS. Additional 10449. These five include the Plots for *The Dead Man's Fortune* (fol. 1), *Frederick and Basilea* (fol. 2), *The Battle of Alcazar* (fol. 3), *2 Fortune's Tennis* (fol. 4), and *Troilus and Cressida* (fol. 5). A sixth Plot, *2 Seven Deadly Sins,* is located at Dulwich College, catalogued as MS. 19. For the Plot of *1 Tamar Cam* we have to rely on the transcript made by George Steevens as printed in the Prolegomena to the 'Variorum' edition of Shakespeare published in 1803. Copies of the Plots are most readily available in W. W. Greg's collection, *Henslowe's Papers* (1907) and in his first volume of *Dramatic Documents from the Elizabethan Playhouses* (1931). The *Papers* contain transcripts of the Plots: *Dramatic Documents* includes both facsimiles and reconstructions. For a summary of the history of these documents, see the Commentary volume of Greg's *Dramatic Documents,* pp. 1–11.

4. Greg, *Dramatic Documents,* p. 19.

5. Ibid., pp. 123, 146, 139, 161, respectively.

6. Ibid., p. 76.

7. Ibid., p. 73.

8. All quotations from *The Battle of Alcazar* come from the reprint of the Quarto edited by W. W. Greg and published by the Malone Society in 1907.

9. Greg, *Abridgements,* pp. 34, 36.

10. Ibid., p. 34.

11. Greg, *Dramatic Documents,* p. 146.

12. George Peele, *The Battle of Alcazar,* ed. John Yoklavich, in *The Life and Works of George Peele,* gen. ed. Charles T. Prouty, vol. 2 (New Haven: Yale University Press, 1961).

13. Greg, *Abridgements,* pp. 94 ff.

14. Peele, *Life and Works,* p. 281.

15. Greg, *Abridgements,* p. 15.

16. Ibid., p. 104.

17. Ibid., p. 105.

18. Ibid., p. 115.

19. Ibid., pp. 99–100.

20. Ibid., p. 100.

21. Ibid., p. 98.

22. Ibid., p. 53.

John a Kent and John a Cumber
An Elizabethan Playbook and Its Implications

William B. Long

Anthony Munday's holograph of *John a Kent and John a Cumber,* 1590 (Huntington Library MS. 500) is the earliest surviving manuscript playbook from the Elizabethan theater. Its existence has long been known, and for more than six decades it has been readily available for study in a Malone Society Reprint. Yet like so much other accessible theatrical material from the period, little attention has been paid to it. Especially because it is the earliest, *John a Kent* warrants particular attention to discover not only what it can reveal about how a playwright prepared his manuscript for a company of players but also about how the players readied it for production: what details did the playwright include? what alterations did the players make to aid production? what can be learned from these disparate small details about larger questions concerning the relationship of playwright and players, about aspects of staging and the physical features of the playhouses themselves, and about what a knowledge of surviving playbooks can show both of playhouse practice and of what thus can be inferred from early printed texts.

John a Kent has not been ignored entirely, of course; it is mentioned several times in survey discussions of playhouse manuscripts.[1] But like the other plays so mentioned, details are extracted to provide examples for the construction of hypothetical history of what happened to a playwright's manuscript in the theater rather than being used to offer a full examination of a specific play. The great danger, then, is that the exception is made to seem the rule. Sir Edmund Chambers and Sir Walter Greg obviously were trying to make some sort of sense out of the surviving threads of information that constitute what was once the fabulously rich fabric of Elizabethan-Jacobean-Caroline drama. In attempting to give explanations, however, they necessarily had to wrench details out of their contexts in the plays in which they occurred. The value of constructing a coherent story is obvious; but the problems that such a history engenders are not so readily observable although they are quite dangerous. For instance, some detail of a manuscript alteration which may occur only once in a handful of plays suddenly is made to seem illustrative of regular playhouse practice. Chambers and Greg conflated evidence from widely scattered sources. The assumption was made, and Greg came to believe it more strongly as he grew older and to enunciate it more emphatically, that there were regular patterns of alterations made to playwrights' manuscripts in the theater and that there were certain things that a theater "prompter" would and would not do.

A second problem (perhaps unavoidable) is that Chambers and Greg were too much the products of their own times; that is, they assumed that the Elizabethan stage, its playwrights, players, and dramatic manuscripts were very similar to those of the late nineteenth- and early twentieth-century theaters with which they were familiar. In spite of their possessing enormous amounts of historical knowledge, Chambers and Greg failed to adjust the historical perspective from which they applied it. They assumed that the passage of three hundred years had not significantly altered theatrical practice.

Chambers and Greg had a third problem: not being theater people, they made assumptions about the nature and use of theatrical documents that are unnecessary, perhaps even baseless, and that have misled generations of similarly insular scholars. Greg strongly believed, in spite of his own researches, that a play manuscript used in the theater would be carefully inscribed and meticulously written, with all revisions neatly done so that the "prompter" could follow the text word-for-word, resolving whatever ambiguities remained in stage directions and speech heads. This is a logical supposition, but it did not happen. Those manuscript playbooks that survive not only do not bear out such expectations, but also they directly contradict them.[2]

The final problem with Chambers and Greg can hardly be laid at their feet. Whatever their limitations, Chambers and Greg were in many ways very fine scholars—so good, in fact, that all too many succeeding researchers have followed their interpretations of evidence almost slavishly, rarely bothering to consider attitudes or perspectives that might reveal problems if only someone looked. And therein lie the difficulties that have stalled productive research in a number of aspects of English Renaissance drama.

Greg's assumptions of close similarities between sixteenth- and twentieth-century playing practices begin with the labeling of the manuscripts as "promptbooks" and of those who used them as "prompters." To employ these terms in referring to the theater of the late sixteenth and early seventeenth centuries is teleological and highly prejudices any attempt to determine earlier practices. The Elizabethan terms "playbook" and "bookkeeper" are at once more literally accurate and much less likely to lead an investigator to unwarranted assumptions.

If a researcher begins an inspection of an early playbook with the assumption that both the playwright and the players knew what they were doing in terms of their theaters—no easy position to find among the many supercilious researchers and editors—then what is found there may help to construct an understanding of how Elizabethan-Jacobean-Caroline playwrights and players worked. It is an extraordinarily important corollary that such an investigation will also necessarily challenge much that has been assumed about the nature and provenance of the texts that lie behind the printed versions of the plays of Shakespeare and his contemporaries.

The surviving manuscript playbooks are by no means necessarily neat and orderly; playwrights' stage directions are very seldom changed in the theater; speech heads are not regularized; copious markings are not added to handle properties, entrances, and music. Regularization and completeness simply were not factors in theatrical marking of a playwright's papers. Theatrical personnel seem to mark the books only in response to specific problems, not all of which are presently decipherable. Despite the widespread belief in wholesale alteration and scribal recopying to create a "fair copy," it seems very rarely to have taken place. So infrequently do theatrical alterations occur that, if a stage direction exists in an old text—manuscript or printed—it is most likely the playwright's.

If a rule is needed for judging what happened to a playwright's manuscript in the theater, it should be, "as little was done as was possible." Actually, this should not be surprising. Playbooks were prepared for a small group of professional players performing in repertory, who must have been well aware of each other's capabilities. Such a situation does not require the minutely inscribed promptbooks prepared for the very different theatrical worlds of the last two centuries. Thus Elizabethan players regularly enter and leave the stage clad in the proper costumes and with the requisite properties without any changes being made in the playwright's instructions. When playhouse marginalia are added, they solve a problem—generally that of ensuring proper timing. This involved adding a notation (most often in the left margin) emphasizing an off-stage sound, or making sure that a crucial entrance occurred when it should, or (much less often) that a particular property was available. Even with such instances, modern researchers must be careful. One cannot dare to expect regularity. What may have caused a problem at one point in a play, often did not in a similar situation at another point in the same play. Nearly all playhouse markings were made to ensure the smoothness of a production, but there is no infallible checklist of such situations.

Nor can it be assumed automatically that all directions inscribed by playwrights necessarily were played. However sensible such a proposition may seem, it does not reckon with the fact that the players were remarkably casual (by modern expectations) about how they regarded what was written in the books. Again and again it is obvious that these manuscripts cannot be used to reconstruct a performance with the relative assurance that a modern promptbook can. Great caution needs to be exercised also in treating what I have labeled "playwright's advisory directions"—directions in which a playwright details a player's location, movement, expression, or any combination thereof. These directions do not include mere entrances and exits, nor do they include indications of costumes or properties; rather, a playwright's advisory direction is one in which the playwright tells the player what to do and/or how to do it.

Within historical and theatrical contexts and with these specific cautions before us, *John a Kent* must be examined in some detail. Elizabethan playing companies grew out of the roving bands of entertainers that had existed for centuries.[3] Until the establishment of permanent playhouses, no other form of playing group could long sustain itself. The idea of players moving from place to place, performing on different kinds of playing areas, and changing the play to fit differing circumstances never entirely disappeared. Even after 1576, pestilence scares and special engagements drew the players from their accustomed stages. Plague times all too often forced the players into the provinces to be itinerants once again. Performances before the sovereign or at one of the Inns of Court were welcome monetary and publicity opportunities for the players, but these situations frequently must have required alterations in the text and adaptations of staging to suit the available facilities.

Moreover, these two conditions which would force or draw a company from its theater remained relatively constant throughout the period and must have influenced playbook preparations. For the players to bind their productions to an elaborate and difficult to change system of performance markings would have been more than unwanted. Furthermore, if it were traditional that clowns, and presumably others, extemporized to suit the occasion rather than to "speak no more than is set down for them," a closely watched playbook was not as needed then as it was to become on more modern stages.

Given the small and financially insecure nature of the companies in the 1590s, especially during the plague-ravaged first half of the decade, it is highly doubtful that nonplaying functionaries would be wanted. Consequently, it is more than likely that prompting was the informal affair that it seems to have been traditionally—players holding book for each other while not on stage. It would follow that other aspects of production also would rely on the individual player's responsibilities.

The two earliest extant theatrical plots can be dated about 1590,[4] which is also the earliest year that a playbook can be dated. Presumably both of the plots (*The Dead Man's Fortune* [British Library, MS. Additional 10449, fol. 1] and *2 Seven Deadly Sins* [Dulwich MS. 19]) and the play (*John a Kent*) can be assigned to the apparently sporadic confederation of the Lord Admiral's and the Lord Strange's companies, which may have existed in some form from the winter of 1589 to the summer of 1594.[5] This grouping was enforced generally by difficult circumstances and particularly because Master of the Revels Edmund Tilney "misliked their plays."[6] There is, however, considerable uncertainty about the personnel who composed this company and how constant their association was. It would seem to have been an on-again-off-again affair.[7]

The difficulties of the times were aggravated during this period when outbreaks of the plague were of sufficient intensity to force companies into the provinces.[8] When this group was playing in London, it is not certain whether it used The Theatre, the Curtain, or the Rose. Because the material from Dulwich College came from the Henslowe and Alleyn papers, it seems to suggest a connection with the Rose. Greg, however, believed that for 1590–91, the Curtain would be the more likely choice.[9] This unusual uncertainty of not knowing which commmercial London theater would be used must have made flexibility of staging all the more important.

Greg assigned the plot of *2 Seven Deadly Sins* to Strange's Men at the Curtain about 1590 and the plot of *The Dead Man's Fortune* to the Admiral's Men at The Theatre, also about 1590.[10] The information contained in both supports the thesis that these players were responsible professionals who handled the productions themselves without the aid of additional backstage personnel. Functionaries to handle the calling of players and the readying of properties were necessities in the much more elaborately organized theaters of the eighteenth century. There was neither need for such persons nor evidence, except imposed speculation, upon which to presume that they existed in the early 1590s. It is far more likely that the players used the plots as an aid in watching for their approaching entrances, and that they were themselves expected to have needed properties in hand at the appointed time. In fact, the very existence of the plots argues this conclusion.

The plots for *Dead Man's Fortune* and *2 Seven Deadly Sins* break the action into the basic construction units of scenes (although the word itself is not used) simply by listing the entrances and occasionally mentioning the main components of the action to take place. In *Dead Man's Fortune* (writer unknown), few players' names are entered and only an occasional exit. There are playing directions only in an elaborate scene involving music and dancing. The players' concern here is with ensuring the proper chronology and timing of the scenes, not in how they were played. This plot is additionally divided by rows of *X*'s into five sections with "Musique" noted in the left margins to be played at what might have been four act breaks.

2 Seven Deadly Sins is in the hand that I have labeled "Bookkeeper 1." The plot itself, although generally similar to *Fortune,* is different in that most of the characters (both major and minor) are also identified by the names of the players taking the roles and in that there is no indication of inserted music.

The names of several players could be substituted easily for others if a few substitutions were needed at subsequent performances; indeed the whole plot could be redone quickly if required by many changes in cast. Thus these plots are the platform upon which the playing of the drama was built, but they are little more.[11] The nature of the plots demonstrates the considerable amount of competence demanded of the players both back-stage and before the audience. In a tradition of players' possessing only their parts, and where, indeed, there was only one complete copy of the play, such a document as the plot was almost a necessity, especially in a repertory company that repeated plays only every few days.

Once the player is on stage, he is on his own as far as the plot is concerned, nor is any effort made to direct which door should be used for his entrance; only if multiple entrances are to be employed is any mention made, and then it is merely "at one dore . . . at another dore"[12] or "at several dores."[13] These documents are geared for a specific company playing on a particular stage, but they reflect a staging situation that is extremely elastic, one that is capable of being modified easily to fit the area available for playing. The players who used these plots had to be resourceful. The plots are the playing abstractions of the playbooks themselves.

I. A. Shapiro's discovery that the playbook of *John a Kent* was written by December 1590 and may possibly be as early as August 1589,[14] and Sir Edward Maunde Thompson's chronology of Munday's handwriting strongly suggest that Munday must have written the basic text of the *Sir Thomas More* playbook by 1594,[15] ensuring a firm chronological foundation for the examination of theatrical habits early in the last decade of the sixteenth century. In view of the shifting alignment of players during these years, it is somewhat less certain for what group Munday fashioned his play and in which theater it was performed, but this redating makes *Kent* concurrent with the plot of *2 Seven Deadly Sins* (ca. 1590) which Greg had assigned to Strange's Men at the Curtain.

Greg's further identification of the writer of the plot as the same person who made the stage markings in the texts and endorsed the titles on the wrappers of the books of *Kent* and *More* as "Hand C" of the *More* manuscript unites both plays with the plot.[16] The name of the player Thomas Goodale was one of many to appear in Hand C's *Sins* plot, and his is the only player's name to find its way into either play, having been carefully noted in C's hand as a messenger in *More* (fol. 13*a), thus more firmly fixing the placing of the two earliest playbooks with Lord Strange's Men at the Curtain, 1590–93.

The manuscript of *John a Kent*[17] is "written throughout in the hand of Anthony Munday" and is tied to the *More* manuscript not only by Munday's being a major contributor to *More*[18] but also by the fact that both plays were bound with pieces of the same medieval manuscript, thus making it very likely that they were bound at nearly the same time.[19] Conclusive proof is attained by Greg's identification of the hand that elaborately endorsed the play titles on both wrappers as that of Hand C,[20] who becomes "Bookkeeper 1" here.

The nature of marginal notations by Hand C–Bookkeeper 1 is such they would seem to be of use only to someone concerned with production of the play; his writing of the plots is the logical extension of his efforts to ensure a smooth production, as is his care of the books when not in use, as evidenced by his preparation of the wrappers. However, that this figure was involved in these three nonplaying functions does not preclude, or even particularly hamper, his being a full-time player. Providing wrappers and storing the books would take no time at all; preparing plots would be a short and perfunctory task; working through the book to ease production difficulties would take some time, but unless significant alterations were needed, the amount of time required need not have been great. If the actual prompting were a cooperative venture, this "prompter" would be even more free to play than those members of the company who were in charge of wardrobe or finances. From the evidence of Hand C's activities, there is no reason to believe that he was a functionary hired specifically to handle these tasks. If a playbook were prepared by a person whose sole (or even principal) duties were prompting and related matters, it might reasonably be expected that the markings would be done in considerable detail with attendant complexity, as they were in the eighteenth and nineteenth centuries when such positions assuredly did exist.

But in turning to *John a Kent,* just the opposite is to be found. *Kent* contains 1705 lines, but there are only seven notations that have been added to the text by a hand other than Munday's. This other hand in all cases seems to be that of Bookkeeper 1,[21] even though five of the additions appear in two shades of ink, both differing from Munday's.[22] The location of these directions, the rationale for their being inserted, and the formation of the letters themselves are all more important factors than the color of ink, which is often, as it seems to be here, attributable to the entries being made at different times—the color of the ink varying from day to day.

Munday presented the company a carefully written book with the text in

Elizabethan secretary hand; he employs his version of Italian script for most of the speech heads and stage directions. The leaves of the manuscript have been folded to form four equal columns, and Munday is generally quite careful in using the central pair for text while reserving the left for speech heads and the right for exits. The folding of the leaves into four equal columns is a common feature of much Elizabethan manuscript preparation, for both nondramatic as well as dramatic writing.[23] Fourteen of the sixteen surviving playbooks, excepting only *The Soddered Citizen* (ca. 1630) and *The Lady Mother* (1635), still retain evidence of such folding. In *Kent,* Munday divides his text with extraordinarily long speech rules that, while varying with the length of the line, often extend through the third column. In *More,* Munday shortens them to the one to two inches common to the other surviving playbooks.[24]

That Munday consistently observed a generous left-hand margin, entering there only the speech heads even though long prose lines often cramped his directions in the right margin, would seem to indicate that theatrical custom dictated that this extra left-hand space be reserved for orderly reading and for playhouse notation if needed. That Munday, a professional writer but at this date only beginning to be a professional playwright, should be aware of these general practices (though faulting on minor details) adds strength to the theory of the continuing existence of a playing tradition that was "popular" or closely tied to considerable awareness on the part of the public. It is this sort of knowledge of theatrical functioning and also of terminology on the part of the audience that allows playwrights to use theatrical allusions for dramatic purposes.

Other than the often complex entrances (which he centered) and exits (always in the right margin), Munday additionally supplied forty-nine directions (about one for every thirty-five lines) to ensure the enactment of his purposes. Hand C–Bookkeeper 1 deletes none of these; presumably the players found them helpful and followed them. Munday has divided his text into acts; no effort was made to delete these breaks, possibly indicating that they were observed. Considerable caution must be used in deciding if a playwright's directions and indications of act breaks were followed by the players who rarely delete matter that they consider extraneous. There is no effort to indicate scenes even though the centered act-breaks for all but the third add "Scena Prima."[25] The reason for the playwright's notation of the initial scene probably came, like the five-act structure itself, from school-text familiarity with Latin drama, which, of course, did indicate scene-division.

The first use of left-hand marginal space for directions occurs on fol. 2b to ensure the proper timing of an important entry.

> Countesse   Cossen, his kindnesse soone will calme this greefe,
>   and therfore cast these cares behinde thy back.

Enter ───────────

> But what olde man is this comes toward vs?

> Enter Iohn a Kent like an aged Hermit
>
> (fol. 2b, 211–14)

This marginal stage direction is entered in the same colored ink as Munday's, but it is not his handwriting. To distinguish among the various hands found in the *John a Kent* manuscript, I have printed Elizabethan secretary in roman, Italian hand in italics, and additions by Hand C–Bookkeeper 1 in boldface italics. It is highly important that John a Kent enter at the exact moment indicated; the players obviously felt that an additional notation was needed to ensure this. The next marginal addition is similar in emphasizing timing; but it concerns music, rather than a character, which must be commented upon at a specific point in the dialogue.

> Enter Iohn a Cumber lyke Iohn a Kent.
>
> S. Griffin. See where he comes, deep pondering wth him selfe,
>   important matters, we must not disturb him,
> ***musique***   but giue him leaue, till his owne leysure him.
>   Silence, me thinkes I heare sweet melodie,   / **Musique whi<**
>   And see he sets the Castell gate wyde ope,   / **he opens the doore**
>   Stand we aloofe, and note what followeth.
>
> (fol. 6b, 773–79)

The ink is darker than Munday's, and it is not in his hand. An almost identical addition this time made in a greyish ink occurs near the conclusion of a speech of John a Cumber.

> ***Musique***   Sound musique, while I shewe to Iohn a Kent,
>   those hither come, for whom he neuer sent.

> whyle the musique playes, enters on the walles Llwellen
>   Chester wth his Countesse, Moorton with *Sydanen,* Pemb.
> with Marian, *Oswen* and *Amerye.*
>
> (fol. 7b, 916–20)

Both these instances involve the meshing of onstage actions with offstage accompaniment. The problem is not one of directing either party *what* to do, but *when.* Someone with a vantage point on both is needed to coordinate timing. If complete scripts had been available to all concerned, such notations would not have been necessary.

The most involved alteration occurs with the entrance of the boy Shrimp who by mischance of spacing on the page was scheduled to enter at the top of fol. 8b. Once again it is important for timing that the character be noticed by the figure on stage at the proper moment. For this reason

and probably additionally because Shrimp was played by a young boy, a
hand similar to that in the added direction on fol. 2b has written in greyish
ink "Enter Shrimpe" opposite the end of John a Kent's speech, three lines
from the bottom of fol. 8a. This entrance is additionally difficult to anticipate because it occurs overleaf.

An important entry similarly located might cause trouble for anyone
holding the book, but the likelihood of difficulty is greatly increased by the
irregular performance schedule of an Elizabethan repertory company and
the probability of not having the same person doing all the "prompting."
The only other entrance at the top of a page is that of Turnop and his train
on fol. 11a. There is no addition to the bottom of fol. 10b for at least three
reasons: Turnop is played by an adult player and presumably was more
trustworthy; he enters with a group, thus they all could watch for their
approaching entrance on the plot and act as a check on each other; and
more importantly, it is easier for someone holding book to switch his
attention from a "b" leaf to an "a" than vice versa. At most this switch
involves turning a folded book; while to move from an "a" to a "b"
necessitates the turning of a page, which could prove a costly expense of
time at a crucial moment, especially with someone not certain of his text
or the movements on stage. The problem of turning pages quickly is one of
several practical, theatrical factors that occasionally affect both stage
markings and the play-text itself and that need to be remembered by
persons investigating problems in both manuscript and printed plays. The
other three additions to the left margin are similar in intent to the earlier
markings. On fol. 8b, a slightly simplified version of Munday's direction is
added, again to be certain that John a Kent is on stage long enough that his
eavesdropping will justify his soliloquy that shortly ends the act. Thomas
the taberer is talking to John a Cumber.

Thomas.	Harkeye Sir, you are a Gentleman, and weele doo as
	much for < y
	Lord, the Earle as poore man may doo, If it be to doo or
	say any thing
Enter Iohn	agaynst him selfe, or any other, weele doo it, marie
a Kent	Thomas Taberrer
	will neuer meddle wth M^r. Iohn, no, not I.

Cumber. why sillie soules, Ile be your warrantise
Iohn shall not touche ye, doo
the best he can,   / En<   > Iohn
Ile make ye scorne him to
his very face.   /   a K<   >t listning.
And let him [how] vendge it, how he will or dare<   >

(fol. 8b, 1045–52)

The ink is the same greyish one used in the two immediately preceding additions. The "Enter" is in Italian characters, but they are not so well-formed as those of Munday's; the change allows John a Kent to hear a bit more, but the important reason for the addition is that the rambling prose speeches of the clowns extend into the right margin and obscure Munday's stage directions. The same greyish ink is used shortly to assure that music will be played at the proper time.

| Powesse. | The lyke dooth Marians presence yeeld to me, |
| *Musique Chime* | for all greefes past assurde felicitie. |

Euan. Listen my Lordes, me thinkes I heare the chyme,
  which Iohn did promise, ere you should presume: {A daynt<
  to venture for recouerie of the Ladyes. { of musi<

(fol. 9a, 1137–41)

The word "Musique" is written by the same hand that inscribed this word of fols. 6b and 7b. Later, using the same colored ink as Munday's (as he had on fol. 2b), the same hand that wrote "Enter" on fols. 2b and 8a again emphasized an important entrance.

Oswen. Breefely to answere all of ye together,
  . . . as it was tolde to vs,
  That Griffin, Powesse and S^r. Gosselen denvyle,
  reskewed them from vs, how or when we knowe not,
Enter so sayd a deuill or boy sent to vs from Iohn a Cumber.

  Enter Iohn a Cumber pulling of his foole coat, lyke Kent still.
Cumber ffrom me young Lordes? alas you were deceiu'd,
(fol. 11b, 1430, 1433–38)

The players want to be sure that Cumber hears the reference to him and/or that he reaches center stage on time; so Cumber is sent on stage moments before the text would have him there. Hand C–Bookkeeper 1 is quite precise with his lining, and that all these additions are his is easily seen in the manuscript. Instances of his handwriting are similarly formed and clearly are not Munday's. And such are the changes that Bookkeeper 1 thought needed to transform Munday's autograph manuscript into a workable playbook for the theater. If one is not to fall back upon the comfortable preconceived notions, the only remaining explanation is that such was all that was needed, and what is more, all that was wanted.

Other features that seekers after elaborately marked promptbooks might have liked to have found are conspicuous by their absence. There is no attempt to add the names of the players to the roles that they played. At one point Munday centers the following:

Enter Pembrook, Moorton, Oswen, *Amery,* to them this crew<
marching, one drest lik a Moore, wth a Tun painted with<
yellow oker, another with a Porrenger full of water an<
a pen in it, Turnop speaketh the Oration.

(fol. 3b, 369–71)

There is no attendant "prompter's list" ensuring that these properties
would be on hand at the proper time. It is well within the bounds of
reasonable conjecture that such helpful items might be transcribed onto
the plot or onto the player's part, thereby transferring responsibility to the
players involved.

Another problem (which seems to have been no problem to the company) is what might be labeled that of "alternative entrance." Act 2 begins:

Actus secundus. Scena Prima.
Enter at one doore Iohn a Kent, hermit lyke, as before, at anoth<e
enter the Countesse, *Sydanen* and *Marian*

(fol. 4a, 405–7)

If one is to place substantial reliance upon the usual reconstructions of
Elizabethan stages with a door at either side of the rear wall and some sort
of opening halfway between these, if in other words there were three
standard entrances to the main playing area, why are entrances not clearly
specified? More modern playbooks are exact, and surely even the most
vehement deprecators of players would admit that Elizabethans could
differentiate between left and right. There are several possible explanations: first, the playwright was unfamiliar with the inside of a particular
theater; or, especially in the uncertain times of *Kent,* the playwright was
unsure which theater might be used. Thus if either of these suppositions is
valid, there was not so much similarity in public theater stages as is
generally assumed. But this refusal to specify entrances continues
throughout the entire period in all the playbooks.

Second, there were more than three possible entrances. If the back wall
of the stage area consisted only of pillars that supported the superstruc-
ture but had no wall between them (the tiring house being blocked from
audience view by arras or curtains),[26] many entrances are possible. This
kind of stage-backing has at least literary support in woodcuts "illustrat-
ing" classical plays in Renaissance editions. The folio of Terence published
in Paris in 1552 has many such pictures. While it cannot be proved that
Elizabethan stages used this construction, it is a most flexible arrangement both for London stages and for playing elsewhere and should at least
be considered as a possibility.[27]

Third, regardless of the above, the directions were left vague purposely
by the playwright because that is the way the players wanted them. Staging
flexibility for touring performances was thus written into the play at its

conception; therefore playing in halls with only two entrances would offer no particular problem. It is important to note that Hand C–Bookkeeper 1 made no attempt whatsoever to alter this kind of direction. It was not only playable as it appeared, but (more important for this study) it was desirable to let it stand as it was. And all succeeding bookkeepers handle these entrances similarly. Given the repertory nature of performance and the short period (by modern standards) for rehearsals, it seems likely that the players would have an agreed-upon system for entering and exiting from certain places or sides of the stage—a habit of theatrical use that would not need written reminders unless something different were called for, such as "at several dores."

Munday does assume the availability of some sort of upper playing area, for he twice (fol. 7b, 918–20; fol. 11b, 1447–48) assigns no fewer than nine characters to enter "on the walles." This is a surprisingly large number, but the players apparently envisaged no problem; at any rate, nothing is altered in the book. The playwright does not indicate the precise numbers to be used in groups; obviously the customs and personnel facilities of the company would settle this detail. Munday asks merely for a "trayne" three times (fol. 2a, 140; fol. 4b, 472: fol. 11a, 1354) and for "some seruaunts" once (fol. 5b, 605). Both the evidence from the plot of *2 Seven Deadly Sins* and the scholarship of William Ringler show that two was the assumed, customary number for such unspecified groups.[28] Thus for the person preparing the playwright's manuscript for production to go through carefully enumerating every such group would be an exercise in point-lessness.

A remarkable series of entrances, perhaps more properly labeled "play-wright's advised entrances," appears early in the third act, immediately after Bookkeeper 1's first annotation:

> ffrom one end of the Stage enter an antique queintly disguysde
>   and cōming dauncing before them, singes.

(fol. 6b, 780–81)

followed by:

> ffrom the other end of the Stage, enter another antique, as the first.

(fol. 6b,798)

and later:

> ffrom vnder the Stage the third Antique.

(fol. 7a, 819)

finally:

> The fourth out of a tree, if possible it may be.

(fol. 7a, 836)

All these are totally untouched by Hand C–Bookkeeper 1. There is no attempt to aid the timing of the spirit under the stage although it apparently rises to speak and then exits. Quite noteworthy is the "tree," which supposedly gets set up on stage and remains there to be used again much later.

> Enter Shrimpe leading *Oswen* and *Amery* about the tree.
>
> (fol. 11a, 1393)

There are no "prompter's" directions for bringing it on or off; presumably there was no need for such notation in the book. If it was used, perhaps it was in place for the entire production.

The same sort of "permanent" property would seem to be indicated by Munday's unannotated series of directions referring to entrances and exits to and from the "Castell." Munday had directed each of the four Antiques to "*exit* into the Castell." After they depart, John a Cumber leaves with:

> . . . then Ile in to make vp the messe.   ⎰ the dore
>   *exit* into the Castell, & makes fast ∧
>   (fol. 7a, 847–48)

There are numerous additional references to the "Castell" in the dialogue. They could easily have been cut or altered if the players had wished; of course, they might have been used merely to conjure up the idea of a castle facade, but it is at least possible that the company was using something representational as well as functional here. It might well be that the company both in its London theater and in its performances elsewhere used the kind of portable structure suggested by Hodges.[29] If so, it must have been of a larger size (to accommodate nine persons) than is usually presumed.

Both the flexibility and the infinite convenience of such a moveable structure in traveling as well as in London argue for its presumed use. Munday seems to be writing with a tacit assumption of its employment. Hand C–Bookkeeper 1 makes no mention of it because it is not the sort of thing that has to do with timing between onstage actions and offstage sounds that are very much his business. If such a structure were wanted, it could be set up before the play began or even during an action break.

The last nonspecific call to be made by Munday is for Shrimp to enter beginning act 4 (fol. 9a) by "playing on some instrument." Whether this should be something as different in appearance and sound as a lute or a recorder is left entirely to the preferences or resources of the company. Hand C–Bookkeeper 1 does not deem it necessary to make any alteration in the playbook. There is no attempt to clarify this imprecise suggestion as there was no attempt to be specific about the numbers of attendants. This evidence is thus in direct contradiction to the unfounded assumptions like that of M. R. Ridley in the Arden *Othello* where he declares that no prompter would let such authorial vagueness stand.[30] Whether the plot would have been more specific about the kind of instrument is doubtful.

This kind of particularization does not seem to have been considered in making up the plots; for instance, in the sixteenth scene (4.2) of *The Dead Man's Fortune* plot (ca. 1590), an unspecified number of "satires" are instructed to enter "plainge on their instruments." Again the resourcefulness (or better perhaps, the professionalism) of the players is relied upon not only by the playwright in constructing his play, but also by the playing company itself in preparing its playbook and plot. This detail, like that of getting himself on stage at the proper moment, would be worked out by the player himself. Except in special cases, as above, where Bookkeeper 1 has felt obliged to add a caution in delicate instances of timing, such matters were the responsibility of the player, not the duty of a company functionary.

There are six instances of minor cutting in the text, four of which are quite unimportant; the final two are short; but because they eliminate minor characters' comments, they stop the action after a major character's important speech and thus sharpen the dramatic effect of the scene in which they appear.[31] The rejected words and lines all have been struck out in a darker ink than that of the text (except for the fourth cut, which is in the same color as the text); presumably these changes reflect rehearsal decisions and have been done by Bookkeeper 1 rather than by Munday.[32]

What is more easily demonstrable as Bookkeeper 1's work is the date inscribed at the end of the play; this follows Munday's signature, but it is not in his hand. The darker ink is again used; but far more importantly, the formation of the letters in "Decembris" can be compared very favorably with those in Hand C–Bookkeeper 1's writing of the *2 Seven Deadly Sins* plot.[33] What the date signifies is not known, although its being the date of company acquisition rather than of performance or of license is likely. Hand C–Bookkeeper 1, as the member of the company in charge of the book and of seeing it through part-copying, rehearsal, licensing, and storage, is the inscriber.

The final leaf of the manuscript, which bears the concluding eighteen lines of the play as well as Munday's signature and the date of inscription, is now a fragment, but supposedly it once bore the Revels Office license. There are no signs of censorship in this clear and uncluttered text; presumably the play was determined to be actable as it stands both by the censor and by the company.

On the basis of this earliest surviving example, the difference between the literary document—the fair copy of the play manuscript sold to the company by a fledgling playwright nevertheless aware of an ongoing theatrical tradition—and the theatrical document—the play as adapted to playing needs by the company—was merely seven short annotations indicating how few markings a given company felt it necessary to employ in its playbook. The nature of these seven annotations, usually noting when a crucial entrance or necessary music was to occur further reinforces the limited scope of such markings. Although *John a Kent* is but a single example, the mere knowledge of the existence of this manuscript as a "promptbook" should have forced reconsideration of previously held assumptions about Elizabethan-Jacobean-Caroline playbooks in general.

NOTES

1. For the "history" of playhouse manuscripts, see E. K. Chambers, *William Shakespeare: A Study of Facts and Problems,* 2 vols. (Oxford: Clarendon Press, 1930), vol. 1, chapter 4, "The Book of the Play," 92–125; W. W. Greg, *The Editorial Problem in Shakespeare: A Survey of the Foundations of the Text,* 3rd ed. (Oxford: Clarendon Press, 1954), chapter 2, "Theatrical Manuscripts," pp. 22–48; and *The Shakespeare First Folio: Its Bibliographical and Textual History* (Oxford: Clarendon Press, 1955), chapter 4, "Editorial Problems—2, pp. 105–74. Of course, Greg's most extensive work on manuscripts was his masterful survey, *Dramatic Documents from the Elizabethan Playhouses: Stage Plots: Actors' Parts: Prompt Books,* 2 vols. (Oxford: Clarendon Press, 1931).

2. The sixteen surviving manuscript playbooks are, in chronological order:

Anthony Munday, *John a Kent and John a Cumber,* 1590
Anthony Munday, et al., *Sir Thomas More,* 1592–93
Anon., *Thomas of Woodstock,* ca. 1594–95, and revivals ca. 1602–4 and ca. 1633
Anon., *Edmond Ironside,* 1590–1600
Anon., *Charlemagne,* ca. 1603–5
Anon., *The Second Maiden's Tragedy,* 1611
John Fletcher and Philip Massinger, *Sir John van Olden Barnavelt,* 1619
Anon., *The Two Noble Ladies,* 1619–23
Thomas Dekker, *The Welsh Embassador,* ca. 1623
Thomas Heywood, *The Captives,* 1624
Philip Massinger, *The Parliament of Love,* 1624
John Fletcher, *The Honest Man's Fortune,* 1625
John Clavell, *The Soddered Citizen,* ca. 1630
Philip Massinger, *Believe as You List,* 1631
Walter Mountfort, *The Launching of the Mary,* 1633
Henry Glapthorne, *The Lady Mother,* 1635

3. More and more records of the activities of players are being discovered and published. The Malone Society, *Collections,* vol. 8 (1969 [1974]) carries the *Records of Plays and Players in Lincolnshire, 1300–1585; Collections,* vol. 11 (1980–81) carries the *Records of Plays and Players in Norfolk and Suffolk, 1330–1642.* The REED project in Toronto continues to provide volumes of vital information. Analysis, of course, lags behind publication of source material; Glynne Wickham's efforts are still pioneering. His explorations of the antecedents of Elizabethan stages show that there were functioning traditions of many sorts, including a considerable division of labor among persons concerned with production. Wickham argues

for a strong degree of professionalism in miracle cycle production as early as the mid-fifteenth century; the evidence he cited from York, Coventry, and Chester proves that much care was given to matters of production and the quality of acting. *Early English Stages, 1300 to 1660,* vol. 1, 1300 to 1576 (London: Routledge and Kegan Paul, 1966), pp. 297–301.

4. Greg, *Dramatic Documents,* 1:11.

5. E. K. Chambers, *The Elizabethan Stage,* 4 vols. (Oxford: Clarendon Press, 1923), 2:136.

6. Ibid.

7. Essentially Chambers wished to view the amalgamation as being continuous; Greg did not, and he detailed his objections in "The Evidence of Theatrical Plots for the History of the Elizabethan Stage," *The Review of English Studies* 1 (July, 1925): 257–74.

8. Chambers, *Elizabethan Stage* 2:121.

9. Greg, *Dramatic Documents,* 1:111; see also Chambers, 2:125–26, 402, 406–9.

10. Greg, *Dramatic Documents,* 1:19.

11. For a discussion of plots, see Greg, *Dramatic Documents,* 1:70–93.

12. First, fourth, and eighth scenes of *2 Seven Deadly Sins.*

13. Fourth and thirteenth scenes of *Dead Man's Fortune.*

14. "The Significance of a Date," *Shakespeare Survey* 8, Allardyce Nicoll, ed. (Cambridge: Cambridge University Press, 1955), 100–5. Shapiro's rereading of the date subscribed at the end of the play as "1590" rather than the usually read "1595" or "1596" thus proved Celeste Turner Wright's conjecture that Munday had written *Kent* about 1590. *Anthony Munday: An Elizabethan Man of Letters* (Berkeley: University of California Press, 1928), p. 106.

15. The chronology of Munday's manuscripts was established by Sir Edward Maunde Thompson's meticulous examination of the changes in Munday's handwriting. "The Autograph Manuscripts of Anthony Munday," *Transactions of the Bibliographical Society* 14 (October 1915–March 1917): 325–53. Thompson suggested dates of about 1590 for *Kent* and about 1592–93 for *Sir Thomas More.*

16. Greg, *Dramatic Documents,* 1:225. Lord Strange died on 16 April 1594 (Chambers, *Elizabethan Stage* 2:126) thus necessitating a further reshuffling of the players who were under his patronage. Hand C's fragmentary plot of *2 Fortune's Tennis* (British Library, MS. Additional 10449, fol. 4) shows that at least by ca. 1597–98 (Greg, *Dramatic Documents,* 1:131) Hand C had followed Alleyn to the Lord Admiral's Men rather than joining those members of Strange's, including Burbage and Shakespeare, who moved to the new Lord Chamberlain's Men. Chambers connects Hand C with the Admiral's, but on other grounds (*Elizabethan Stage* 2:319); a fuller account of Hand C is given by Greg in *Dramatic Documents,* 1:45–46.

17. Anthony Munday, *John a Kent and John a Cumber,* edited by Muriel St. Clare Byrne and checked by W. W. Greg, Malone Society Reprints (Oxford: The Malone Society, 1923), p. vii. All further references are to this edition.

18. W. W. Greg, "The Handwriting of the Manuscript," in *Shakespeare's Hand in the Play of "Sir Thomas More,"* A. W. Pollard, ed. (Cambridge: Cambridge University Press, 1923), p. 48.

19. Byrne, *John a Kent,* p. vi. In a more detailed investigation, Alfred W. Pollard concurs, in "Introduction," *Shakespeare's Hand,* p. 9.

20. Greg, *Shakespeare's Hand,* pp. 55–56. The headings can be compared with the reproductions in the facsimile volume (2) of Greg's *Dramatic Documents* (unpaginated).

21. Byrne is exceedingly cautious about this: "It is possible that the hand of the prompt-directions in the left-margins of 6b, 8b, 9a, may be that of 'C' . . ." (*John a Kent*, p. vii).

22. "Munday's ink is darkish brown in colour, verging on yellow in light strokes or when faded. It is some shades lighter than the ink he used in the *More* manuscript" (Byrne, *John a Kent*, p. vii).

23. Greg, *Dramatic Documents*, 1:206.

24. For a reliable general survey of what selected pages from various playbooks look like, see the seven reproductions in the facsimiles volume (2) of Greg's *Dramatic Documents* (unpaginated).

25. The heading for act 1 is mutilated but discernible, and that for act 3 (apparently omitted in making a fair copy) consists only of a fragmentary "tertius" in Munday's hand in the left margin (fol. 6b, 739).

26. C. Walter Hodges touches on this problem. *The Globe Restored: A Study of the Elizabethan Theatre*, Second Edition (London: Oxford University Press, 1968), p. 17.

27. These woodcuts can be found in P. Terentii, *Comoediae* (Paris, 1552).

28. The inclusion of players' names in the plot of *2 Seven Deadly Sins* shows that "others" (scene 13) and "Lords" (scene 21) are to be played by two minor members of the troupe. William A. Ringler, Jr. in "The Number of Actors in Shakespeare's Early Plays" opts for two as the number of mute attendants in Shakespeare's pre-Globe plays of the 1590s, in *The Seventeenth-Century Stage: A Collection of Critical Essays*, Gerald Eades Bentley, ed. (Chicago: University of Chicago Press, 1968), p. 115. It is more than likely that Shakespeare was following an established custom.

29. Hodges, *Globe*, p. 55.

30. M. R. Ridley in his introduction to the Arden *Othello* wished to argue that the text for Q1 was based on Shakespeare's "foul papers" rather than on Greg's theoretical later transcript of the "foul papers." "There is . . . one clear piece of evidence. There are in Q1 two stage directions at 1.3.120 and 170, 'Exit two or three' and 'and the rest', which cannot, I think, be anything but authorial. Two stage-directions may seem slender evidence, but I think that though slender it is unbreakable and decisive; no prompter could let anything so imprecise stand in his prompt-book, even if it ever got there." The Arden Shakespeare (London: Methuen, 1958, rpt., 1967), p. xlii.

The two stage directions certainly do seem to be the playwright's, but to believe that no bookkeeper would let such stand simply betrays an ignorance of existing evidence. Clearly Ridley had failed to adjust his perspective from the twentieth-century theater to that of the late sixteenth. It is his erroneous assumption about what a "promptbook" should be that distorts his application of these directions in his attempt to ascertain the date and provenance of the copy-text. Because of his lack of knowledge of the context in which these directions exist, Ridley's interpretation is less than meaningless.

31. The deletions include fol. 5b, 608–10: the entire speech of a servant. This is his only speech in the scene, thus reducing the part to that of a mute. Fol. 8a, 958–59: most of two lines in a speech of John a Cumber; fol. 8b, 1060–68: the entire speech of John a Cumber, which is reported in essence in 1071–74; fol. 10b, 1340–44: the entire speech of Powesse which is largely repeated in the succeeding speech of Chester; fol. 12b, 1570–76: the replies of Powesse, Griffin, and John a Kent himself upon his just stated plans for resolving the difficulties of the plot; fol. 12b, 1597–1602: the entire comments of the Countesse, Sydanen, and Marian to Cumber's summary of his anticipated actions.

32. Munday made certain changes, but he had prepared his own fair copy; thus the corrections are those of a copyist. For instance, he once mistakenly wrote "of," deleted it, and interlined the correct "for" above the deletion (fol. 4a, 394). There are corrected letters and others reshaped for clarity. Copying play texts, even if not allowing for the guiding provided by the folded columns of the paper, tends to push the copyist (even though he is the playwright) to copy by columns, not by following each line entirely accross the page. Thus the play occasionally (most noticeably on fol. 3b, 325–33) shows the rather common curiosity of having speakers' names out of line with their speeches. Apparently this caused no prompting difficulties.

33. The majuscule "D" is almost half missing, but it looks very much as if it were formed by bringing the initial stroke from top to bottom, pulling a loop to the left, then coming to the right for the bottom of the letter, and then up and back across the initial downstroke; similar letters appear in line 5 ("Duke"), 14 ("Dumb"), and 18 ("Duke"). A matching internal "e" occurs in lines 3 ("being"), 4 ("sleepe"), 10 ("sincler"); "c" in 5 ("purceuaunt"), 8 ("Lechery"), and 37 ("Lucius"), medial "m" in 14 ("Dumb"), 37 ("Damascus"); "b" in 3 ("being"), 9 "back"), 20 ("bringe"); "r" in 3 ("Henry"), 5 "purceuaunt"), 8 ("Lechery"); "i" in 3 ("being"), 11 ("him"), 20 ("bringe"); final "s" in 7 ("Couetousnes"), 13 ("speakes"), and 15 ("Counsailers").

The similarities in letter formation between those in the *Sins* plot and those in the date inscription are very striking; there is no reason not to attribute the dating to Hand C.

The Versatility of Shakespeare's Actors

T. J. King

This paper demonstrates the versatility of Shakespeare's company, the King's Men, in ten of the plays they performed between 1611 and 1632.[1] Table 1, King's Men Identified in Principal Parts, summarizes the evidence about casting for these plays. Of the nineteen actors listed, twelve— Burbage, Taylor, Lowin, Ostler, Benfield, Condell, Robinson, Underwood, Rice, Tooley, Shank, and Gough—are among the twenty-six men named in the Shakespeare First Folio under the heading "Principall Actors in all these Playes."[2] This Folio list is the best single piece of evidence available about the men and boys who acted in early performances of Shakespeare's plays.

To the right of the actors' names in my table are eleven columns headed by the titles of ten plays with the probable dates of the performances for which actors and their parts are identified.[3] Of these texts, three are playhouse manuscripts with actors' names probably added by the prompter at rehearsal, two are manuscripts with actors and parts identified by the author, and five are early printed texts with lists identifying actors in principal parts.

The relative size of each principal male part is indicated by a numeral above it. For example, on the top line Richard Burbage is identified as Ferdinand, the second largest male role in *The Duchess of Malfi,* probably in the season of 1613–14. Burbage died in 1619, and Joseph Taylor, who replaced him as the leading actor for the King's Men, is identified as Ferdinand in the second cast list for this play, first printed in 1623. John Lowin is identified in both cast lists as playing Bosola, the largest male role. An *f* above the name of a character indicates a female role played by a boy. For example, Richard Sharpe is identified in the title role in both cast lists for *The Duchess of Malfi.*

On the subject of actors and their parts in the time of Shakespeare, a widely accepted study is T. W. Baldwin, *The Organization and Personnel of the Shakespearean Company.* On the basis of some but not all of the evidence considered in the present paper, Baldwin attempts to define the personal characteristics of each actor, and then to describe his type for what Baldwin calls a "line of parts," which, presumably, each actor played throughout his career. According to Baldwin, when Shakespeare wrote his plays, "the play was regularly fitted to the company, not the company to the play. . . . These men did not act; they were themselves."[4] But there is no direct evidence that Shakespeare wrote his plays to suit the characteristics of individual actors. Instead, it seems more likely that the author relied on the services of an extremely skillful and versatile acting company.

These actors show their versatility in several ways. First, we should note that boy actors play adult female roles and that when these same boys become young men they act adult male roles. For example, in 1611 Richard Robinson plays the Lady who kills herself rather than yield to the lustful Tyrant in *The Second Maiden's Tragedy*. About eight years later, Robinson plays the evil Cardinal who murders his mistress, Julia, by having her kiss a poisoned Bible in *The Duchess of Malfi*. John Rice was an apprentice to John Heminges in 1607;[5] about six years later in *The Duchess of Malfi*, Rice plays the Marquis of Pescara, who is described as "a noble old fellow" (I.v). In the earlier cast of this play, Robert Pallant, Jr. plays Cariola, a young woman; in the later cast he doubles in the minor adult roles of a Doctor and an Officer.

Richard Sharpe, who plays the Duchess of Malfi, probably became a sharer in the King's Men in 1624.[6] Thereafter, he plays adult male roles: Lysander, a young lover; Parthenius, a young man; Ferdinand, a general; Wittworth, a young lord; and the King of the Lombards.

John Honyman was baptized in 1613,[7] and at nine he plays Clarinda; at thirteen, Domitilla; at sixteen, Sophia. At seventeen, Honeyman plays the adult male role of Sly, a tricky servant; at eighteen, the First Merchant; at nineteen, the Young Factor.

Actors also show their versatility when they double, often in markedly different roles. In *The Duchess of Malfi*, John Underwood plays Delio, the good friend and confidant of Antonio, secretly married to the Duchess; Underwood doubles as one of the eight Madmen who torment the sleep of the Duchess when they "sing and Daunce And act their gambols to the full o' th'moone" (I3). Nicholas Tooley plays three roles: the cowardly Count Malateste; Forobosco, a comic servant, and another of the Madmen.

When a character assumes a disguise, he is in effect playing another role within the play. The audience is usually made aware of this double identity, but most of the other characters do not penetrate this disguise. For example, in *The Swisser* John Lowin plays Andrucho, who late in the play removes his false beard to reveal his true identity as the banished Count Aribert, the father of Eugenia, the long-lost love of the King.

In each of the plays considered here, each of the leading actors plays

Table 1
King's Men Identified in Principal Parts

	2nd Maiden's Tragedy 1611 MS.	Duchess of Malfi 1613-14	Duchess of Malfi 1619-23	Barnavelt 1619 MS.	Deserving Favorite 1622	Roman Actor 1626	Picture 1629	Soddered Citizen 1630 MS.	Swisser 1631 MS.	Believe as You List 1631 MS.	Wild Goose Chase 1632
R. Burbage	-	2 Ferdinand	-	-	-	-	-	-	-	-	-
J. Taylor	-	-	1 Ferdinand	-	2 Duke	2 Paris	1 Mathias	-	1 Arioldus	1 Antiochus	1 Mirabell
J. Lowin	-	1 Bosola	3 Bosola	-	4 Jacomo	1 Caesar	2 Eubulus	1 Undermyne	3 Andrucho	2 Flaminius	2 Belleur
W. Ostler	-	3 Antonio	-	-	-	-	-	-	-	-	-
R. Benfield	-	-	Antonio	-	3 King	7 Rusticus	6 Ladislaus	5 Makewell	5 Antharis	4 Marcellus	4 De Gard
H. Condell	f=female role	4 Cardinal	-	-	-	-	-	-	-	-	-
R. Robinson	Lady	-	Cardinal	8 Captain Ambassador	5 Orsinio	9 Aesopus	-	-	-	6 Lentulus	6 La Castre
J. Underwood	-	5 Delio 6 Madman	5 Delio 6 Madman	-	-	-	-	-	-	-	-
J. Rice	-	Pescara Madman	Pescara Madman	4 Captain Servant	-	-	-	-	-	-	-
N. Tooley	-	8 Malateste Forobosco Madman	Malateste Forobosco Madman	-	-	-	-	-	-	-	-
R. Pallant, Jr.	-	f Cariola	Doctor Officer	-	-	-	-	-	-	-	Comic Servant
J. Shank	8	-	-	-	-	-	5 Hilario	8 Hodge	-	-	-
R. Gough	Memphonius	-	-	-	-	-	-	-	-	-	-
T. Pollard	-	7 Silvio Madman	7 Silvio Madman	Holderus Servant	-	6 Stephanos Lamia	3 Ubaldo	2 Brainsick	6 Timentes	3 Berecinthius	3 Pinac
R. Sharpe	-	f Duchess	Duchess	-	1 Lysander	3 Parthenius	8 Ferdinand	3 Wittworth	2 King	5 Chrysalus	5 Lugier
E. Swanston	-	-	-	-	6 Utrante	4 Aretinus	4 Ricardo	7 Clutch	4 Alcidonus	-	-
A. Smith	-	-	-	-	7 Gerard	8 Philargus	7 Baptista	-	7 Asprandus	8 Jailer 2 Merchant	7 Nantolet
W. Penn	-	-	-	-	-	-	-	-	8 Clephis	1 Merchant	-
J. Honyman	-	-	-	-	f Clarinda	f Domitilla	f Sophia	6 Sly	-	-	9 Yng-Factor

only one major part, but over the years each of them plays a wide variety of parts. As noted, the first actor to play the evil Duke Ferdinand, the twin brother of the Duchess of Malfi, is Richard Burbage. His successor, Joseph Taylor, also plays Duke Ferdinand. Later, Taylor plays a noble Duke in *The Deserving Favorite*; Paris, the Roman Actor; Mathias, a faithful husband; Arioldus, a gentleman who leaves retirement to become a successful general; Antiochus, the deposed and aging King of Syria who has wandered in exile for twenty-two years; and Mirabell, a young Benedick who finally succumbs to love and marriage.

John Lowin, apparently skillful as villains and tyrants, also plays sympathetic parts. As noted, he plays Bosola, the villain of *The Duchess of Malfi;* Jacomo is also a villain, but Eubulus is an old windbag courtier reminiscent of Polonius. Undermyne is an unscrupulous citizen, but as noted, Andrucho is the sympathetic Count Aribert in disguise. Flaminius is a tyrannical Roman consul who persecutes Antiochus, but Belleur is the companion of Mirabell and the bashful lover of Rosalura.

There should be no need to multiply examples. Evidence shows that each of the other actors on this list plays a wide variety of parts. The most important consideration in casting a given part was *not* the type of role to be acted but the *size* of that part. It should come as no surprise that the leading actors of the company almost invariably play the largest parts, a practice that continues in the theater of our own day.

For the purpose of this paper, perhaps the most instructive play is Massinger's *The Roman Actor* (1626), in which the cast performs three distinctly different plays-within-the-play. With the first play, *The Cure of Avarice,* Paris attempts to help a young man, Parthenius, who has a miserly father, Philargus. Paris suggests that a possible remedy for his father's obsession with money would be to have him watch a play showing a character with the same obsession. In describing this process, Paris paraphrases Hamlet's lines about "guilty creatures sitting at a play" who "have proclaimed their malefactions" (*Hamlet* 2.2.590, 539):

> I once observ'd
> In a Tragedie of ours, in which a murther
> Was acted to the life, a guiltie hearer
> Forc'd by the terror of a wounded conscience,
> To make discoverie of that, which torture
> Could not wring from him. Nor can it appeare
> Like an impossibilitie, but that
> Your Father looking on a covetous man
> Presented on the stage as in a mirror.
> May see his owne deformity, and loath it.
>
> (D2)

The young man agrees. He pays Paris a fee for a performance of *The Cure of Avarice* and says that he will ask Caesar to command his miserly father to observe the play. In this, Paris plays the Doctor of Physic who attempts to cure the miser-within-the-play, but Philargus, the miserly father of Parthenius is not reformed.

Nevertheless, Caesar's wife, the Empress Domitia, in watching the play, becomes infatuated with Paris. After the actors leave, she says to Caesar:

> The Fellow
> That play'd the Doctor did it well by *Venus;*
> He had a tunable tongue and neate delivery,
> And yet in my opinion he would performe
> A lovers part much better. Prethee *Caesar*
> For I grow wearie let us see tomorrow
> *Iphis and Anaxarete.*
>
> (E3)

The next day Paris acts in the second play-within-the-play, and when Paris, as Iphis, is spurned by the hard-hearted Anaxarete, he threatens to hang himself. But the Empress Domitia becomes so frightened by this that she stops the performance. Before she leaves the scene, however, she says, "Come to me, Paris / Tomorrow for your reward" (G2). When they meet, Domitia says that she loves Paris and that he is worthy of her love because he must *be* like the noble characters he plays:

> Thou whom oft I have seene
> To personate a Gentleman, noble, wise,
> Faithfull, and gainsomne, and what vertues else
> The Poet pleases to adorned you with
>
> . . . .
> Thou must be reallie in some degree
> The thing thou dost present. Nay doe not tremble.
> We seriouslie beleeve it, and presume
> Our *Paris* is the volume in which all
> Those excellent gifts the Stage hath seene him grac'd with
> Are curiouslie bound up.
>
> (H2)

But here the Empress labors under the same misapprehension about actors and their parts that appears to have misled T. W. Baldwin when he asserts: "These men did not act; they were themselves." Paris, in his reply to the Empress, describes one of the qualities essential to the art of acting:

> The argument
> Is the same, great Augusta, that I acting
> A foole, a coward, a traytor or cold cinique
> Or any other weake and vitious person
> Of force, I must be such. O gracious Madam,
> How glorious soever, or deform'd,

I doe appeare in the Sceane, my part being ended,
And all my borrowed ornaments put off,
I am no more, nor lesse, then what I was
Before I enter'd.

(H2)

As the scene continues, Domitia attempts to seduce Paris—her stage direction reads: *"Courting Paris wantonly"*—but Caesar, who has been secretly observing them from above, intervenes. At first, Caesar seems merciful toward Domitia and Paris, and he asks Paris if the actors can perform a play called *The False Servant*. Caesar describes the argument: a great lord who suspects his wife of infidelity pretends to go on a journey, but he returns home to surprise his wife attempting to seduce a servant. Paris remembers the play and says that his actors are ready to perform it. In this, the third play-within-the-play, Paris is to act the Servant, and Aesopus is to play the Lord. But before the actors can begin, Caesar insists that he himself play the Lord:

We can performe it better.
Off with my Robe and wreath. Since *Nero* scorn'd not
The publike *Theater,* we in private may
Disport ourselves. This cloake and hat, without
Wearing a beard or other propertie,
Will fit the person.

(H4v–I)

But one of the actors asks Caesar to use a property sword instead of his real one:

Sir a foyle
The point and edge rebutted, when you act
To doe the murder. If you please use this
And lay aside your owne sword.

(I)

But Caesar insists on keeping his own sword, and apparently playing the part of the irate Lord, Caesar stabs Paris to death. Massinger's *The Roman Actor* requires the talents of several very versatile performers, and this play alone should serve to dispel Baldwin's erroneous notions about actors and their parts.

A more perceptive comment about the nature of acting is offered by William Hazlitt, who writes in *The Examiner* of 5 January 1817:

Players . . . are the only honest hypocrites. Their life is a voluntary dream; a studied madness. The height of their ambition is to be *beside themselves.* Today kings, tomorrow beggars, it is only when they are themselves that they are nothing. Made up of mimic laughter and tears, passing from the extremes of joy or woe at the prompter's call, they wear the livery of other men's fortunes; their very thoughts are not their own. They are, as it were, train-bearers in the pageant of life, and hold a glass up to humanity, frailer than itself. We see ourselves at second-hand in them; they show us all that we are, all that we wish to be, and all that we dread to be.[8]

These observations are appropriate not only for the great actors of Hazlitt's day but also for the actors of Shakespeare's company, the King's Men.

NOTES

1. In a slightly different form, this paper was read at The Fifth City University of New York English Forum, 25 March 1983.

2. William Shakespeare, *The First Folio: The Norton Facsimile,* prepared by Charlton Hinman (New York: W. W. Norton, 1968), p. 17.

3. Evidence about the places and dates of performance for these and other pre-Restoration plays that identify actors and parts is summarized by Gerald Eades Bentley, *The Profession of Player in Shakespeare's Time, 1590–1642* (Princeton: Princeton University Press, 1984, pp. 247–95. Grateful acknowledgement is here given to The Henry E. Huntington Library for microfilm copies of *The Duchess of Malfi* (Q-1623), *The Deserving Favorite* (Q-1629), *The Roman Actor* (Q-1629), *The Picture* (Q-1630), and *The Wild Goose Chase* (F-1652); thanks are also due to the British Library for microfilm copies of *The Second Maiden's Tragedy* (MS. 1611), *Sir John van Olden Barnavelt* (MS. 1619), *The Swisser* (MS. 1630), and *Believe as You List* (MS. 1631). Also cited here is *The Soddered Citizen* (MS. 1630), ed. John Henry Pyle Pafford (Malone Society Reprints, 1936).

4. (Princeton: Princeton University Press, 1927), pp. 197, 184.

5. E. K. Chambers, *The Elizabethan Stage* (Oxford: Clarendon Press, 1923), 2:336.

6. G. E. Bentley, *The Jacobean and Caroline Stage* (Oxford: Clarendon Press, 1941), 2:570.

7. Bentley, *Stage,* 2:476.

8. William Hazlitt, *Selected Essays,* ed. George Sampson (Cambridge: Cambridge University Press, 1917), p. 17.

Edmund Kean Onstage Onstage

Gerald Weales

"The life of a player is, assuredly, not the most important thing in the world," Bryan Waller Procter (Barry Cornwall) wrote at the beginning of *The Life of Edmund Kean.* "Nevertheless, it may be made amusing, and even useful in its way, if the vivacity of the writer or the misdeeds of his hero are sufficiently great."[1] Procter is easily the liveliest of the Kean biographers, and the actor's deeds and misdeeds are flamboyant enough to have attracted not only writers of fact and factoid,[2] but novelists, poets, playwrights. The *Morning Star,* in a passage that F. W. Hawkins used as epigraph to his biography of Kean, compressed the actor's career into a sentence: "So bitter and weary a struggle for a chance, so splendid and bewildering a success, so sad a waste of genius and fortune, so lamentable a fall, can hardly be found among all the records of the follies and sins and misfortunes of genius."[3] Even if one passes over the wealth of anecdote that surrounded Kean, there are verifiable events that seem to have been designed for melodrama: the death of his son Howard just as the actor got the long-awaited bid to play at Drury Lane; Alderman Cox's successful suit against Kean for *Criminal Conversation* with his wife, a trial that marked the beginning of the lamentable fall. Pain and peccadilloes aside, he *was* the most celebrated actor on the English stage in the nineteenth century.

Kean's life, in the generic not the specific sense, is familiar to anyone who grew up on American movie musicals. It is the account of the slum boy who tap-danced his way to stardom only to discover that the spotlight is bright without being beneficently warm. That story can be sliced according to need—can be played for the moment of triumph or the pathos of decline. *Ned Kean of Old Drury* (1923) is a play in that vein. "Mr. Arthur Shirley knows his way to the hearts of those popular audiences for whom he has been writing for some forty odd years," said the reviewer on *The Stage,* and *The Era* described the play as "a Drury Lane melodrama,"[4] a term that belongs to a kind of post-Kean Drury Lane play, which in its turn was dying out by 1923. Shirley gathered up the most usable of the Kean stories from the nineteenth-century biographies—the corrective works of Harold Newcomb Hillebrand and Giles Playfair would

151

not appear until the 1930s—to tell how Kean triumphs over his own weakness and the influence of evil companions to succeed on the London stage. The primly querulous Mary is here depicted as the perfect helpmate, and the death of Howard is the sentimental string on which Shirley threads his beads of pseudobiography. A single and rather lovely example that characterizes Shirley's method: Lord Byron, who did admire Kean but who was not at his London debut, is one of a number of personages who arrive at Kean's home to praise his instant success as Shylock; the poet does so in a variation on Coleridge's well-known line: "To see him act, is like reading Shakspeare by flashes of lightning."[5]

There is a scene in act 3 of *Ned Kean* in which the actor turns on his corrupt and corrupting drinking companions in a grand Shakespearean pastiche of insult and lament. Since, drunk or sober, he speaks in Shakespeare quotations most of the time, the surprise in the scene lies not in his choice of verbal weapons but in their being tailored to the emotional moment. Shirley intended nothing more complex than easy triumph for a third-act curtain—like the easy tears of Kean's performing the Animations of Harlequin for the dying Howard at the end of act 2—but the scene cannot help suggesting the other, more persistent stage Kean, the one who embodies a concern for the relation between performer and role. In *Play within a Play,* as a prelude to his provocative discussion of the *Keans* of Alexandre Dumas père and Jean-Paul Sartre, Robert J. Nelson indicates the change that overcame theatrical use of theatrical event in the late eighteenth century—the interior play no longer being used for plot, not to catch the conscience of the king but to reveal the consciousness of the actor.[6]

Heinrich Heine said that Kean was "inspired by that boundless, unfathomable and unconsciously diabolic-divine power which we are apt to call 'the demonic,' "[7] a description that has less to do with the often petty and manipulative man who emerges in the biographies than with Heine's having found onstage the vehicle for the Romantic concept of the actor—one endowed with or burdened by the twin qualities of Dumas's subtitle, *désordre et génie.* Kean may have been an admirable candidate for Heine's demonic actor, but—as performer if not as man—he kept his demon under tight rein. "Impulse was the spring of his greatness on the stage," insisted his friend Thomas Colley Grattan, but William Hazlitt, Kean's early and most articulate admirer, knew better. "Mr. Kean's style of acting is not in the least of the unpremeditated, *improvisatori* kind: it is throughout, elaborate and systematic, instead of being loose, off-hand, and accidental." What Hazlitt recognized in 1814 is obvious in the responses of other performers to Kean's work. James H. Hackett, through repeated observation of Kean during his American tour in 1825–26, "noted all the business and readings of *Mr. Kean*" in a prompt copy of *Richard III.* George

Vandenhoff remembered that "his delivery of Othello's 'Farewell' ran on the same tones and semitones, had the same rests and breaks, the same *forte* and *piano,* the same *crescendo* and *diminuendo,* night after night, as if he spoke it from a musical score."[8] A meticulous deviser of effects, Kean came finally to perform them by rote; it was this mechanical quality that allowed him to continue to play his most famous roles after his failing memory kept him from doing new parts. Yet he was celebrated for the natural style that drove John Philip Kemble's classicism from the stage, and his high emotional points were said to terrify audiences (Lord Byron is supposed to have fallen into convulsions at his Sir Giles Overreach in the last scene of *A New Way to Pay Old Debts*). Grattan's recollection says more about the way Kean was perceived than the more interesting testimony of the experts. For audiences, interested in the emotion received rather than the method of communication, Kean's performances might have seemed the result of inspiration, not careful preparation. Whatever later playwrights might have known about the workings of the theater, it was this public sense of Kean that was useful to them, particularly when they were on the trail of "the demonic."

The "diabolic-divine power" that drove the actor onstage also drove him offstage, and Kean's not very private private life obviously qualified him for Romantic actor on these grounds, too—his excessive drinking, his very visible affair with Mrs. Cox, his wild rides on his black horse Shylock, his pet lion, his fondness for dressing up in his Huron chieftain's costume, his rumored descents into madness. Grattan compared him to Napoleon and Byron: "And what Byron was to Buonaparte, Kean most assuredly was to Byron. . . . And, after all, which was most a stage-player of the three?" Kean became and stayed "the Myth of the Actor incarnate," as Jean-Paul Sartre called him.[9]

This idea of the actor is valuable to any writer interested in creating a work more complex than a simple show-business tale. It allows a consideration of the actor as a special case among artists, the confusion of the man and his roles. On the simplest level, this can be seen whenever an audience responds to a line as though it belongs to the performer, not the character. The nicest example among the Kean anecdotes has to do with his playing the title role in John Howard Payne's *Brutus* for the benefit of his son Charles after the two had become reconciled; when Kean/Brutus said to Charles/Titus, "Embrace thy wretched father," the audience is said to have broken into wild applause.[10] The actor can, of course, play to a single member of the audience, as Dumas's Kean says actors do when they choose a particular woman as "the inspiring angel of our genius."[11] In *The Royal Box* (1897), his adaptation of Dumas's play, Charles Coghlan has a note at the end of act 4, "Clarence [his name for the Kean character] plays the Balcony scene to Helen [Eléna] not to Juliet"—not at all the way

Dumas conceived the scene—and Raymund FitzSimons gets closer to home in his biography when he says that Mrs. Cox hurried from sex in the dressing room to Kean's box where "she would watch him make love to Ophelia or Desdemona, knowing that the words he spoke on stage were addressed to her."[12] There seems to be no hard evidence for FitzSimons's pretty picture—surely such a transfer of a love object would have been chronicled in the letters read out at the trial[13]—but it is a good example of the way in which a character's words can escape their dramatic context.

More interesting is the less conscious confusion between actor and role that Amy conjures in Sartre's *Kean* when she says, "Kemble plays Shakespeare. And I have the feeling that it is Shakespeare who plays Kean." To Amy, this is just a witticism. To Sartre, I assume, it is a recognition of the actor's difficulty in distinguishing between illusion and reality. This takes a variety of forms. An actor can so identify with his characters that he has no existence outside of them. He can be so uncertain about where the stage begins and ends that he can respond only to what we think of as real life in terms of stage gesture and conventional scenes. He can so use the material of his own life to feed the creation of his characters that the power that goes into the creation turns on him and destroys him as a man. Kean was ripe for transformation into any or all of these conceptions of the actor. He died on 15 May 1833. Dumas's *Kean* opened at the Théâtre des Variétés on 31 August 1836.

Alexandre Dumas's Kean was Frédérick Lemaître, who had already played his Napoleon (1831). Lemaître called Dumas "a coquette whom one is obliged to accept with his virtues and his faults, his enthusiasms and his frivolities," and Dumas more than once compared Lemaître to the real Kean so that he could emphasize how difficult he was despite his immense talent. Whatever the tensions between actor and author, they managed in *Kean* to create a play that fed the reputations of both men. Gautier wrote, "Never has a more suitable role been written for Frédérick, who himself has a number of affinities with the English actor." He was like Kean in the ostentation and the excesses of his behavior, in his sense of his own importance, in his occasionally taking to the stage while drunk, even in his early days in pantomime at the Funambules to balance Kean's early success in the provinces as Harlequin.[14]

The play began with Lemaître. Early in 1836, he signed a contract with the Variétés, and M. E. G. M. Théaulon de Saint Lambert, whom Robert Baldick describes as one of that theater's "accredited authors," began work on a play about Kean; he conceived it as "a mixture of all the genres," he said in a letter to Lemaître, which also indicates that it was Théaulon who came up with the subtitle that is so often used to define the nature of the play. The script then passed through the hands of Frédéric de

Courcy, a follower of Scribe whom Sartre called "the renowned hack." According to Lemaître in *Souvenirs,* their version lacked dramatic continuity (putting together a play for the Boulevards was rather like getting a workable script in Hollywood), and the authors were sent to Dumas who did not, as he did on some occasions, work as a silent play doctor or discreetly as one of a group.[15] *Kean, ou désordre et génie* has become Dumas's play. I rehash this theatrical history not to discredit Dumas, but to indicate that the promise of Kean as theatrical subject was very much in the air at the time.

If Jean-Paul Sartre is correct when he says that Lemaître went drinking with Kean when he was performing in Paris in 1828,[16] the French actor may have had direct experience of Kean's talent for debauchery, may have heard the visitor "d——n——g 'lords' with all the vigour of a sincere hater," to use Procter's phrase,[17] and in a maudlin mood, predicting that he would have to go back to playing Harlequin when the public turned against him. Whether the behavior and the attitudes of the real Kean came to Dumas from Lemaître or Procter's book, which was published in 1835, or the general store of trans-Channel theatrical gossip, the play uses them, as it does references to Kean's lion, his fondness for a tavern called the Coal Hole,[18] his loyalty to old friends (although it is difficult to imagine the real Kean's being moved by Salomon's saying that if he failed to perform in the benefit for "le père Bob" and his troop of *saltimbanques,* it would be the first time he had gone back on his word). Despite this circumstantial window dressing, Dumas is not interested in the real Kean. He forgets that the actor had a wife, as Kean often did, and he seems indifferent to the roles that made Kean famous. Although there are references to Othello and Hamlet, Dumas has Kean play Romeo, a character with which he was not successful. The other role most often referred to is Falstaff, which Kean never played at all. One can hardly expect biographical care from a playwright so casual about the English background of the play. Dumas's Prince of Wales speaks twice of his brother the king, although it is impossible for a Prince of Wales—always the firstborn son—to have a brother on the throne. Dumas was probably thinking of William IV, who had recently succeeded his brother on the English throne and who was never Prince of Wales. The anonymous translator of the 1847 edition of the play silently changed the *frère* to "my royal father,"[19] thus turning the character into the Prince Regent, a more likely royal figure for Kean's glory days after his success in 1814. The Prince Regent did give Kean a hundred guineas to celebrate his triumphant first season,[20] but he and the actor were hardly drinking, whoring buddies, as the translator indicated when he commented crossly on "the exquisite innocence of English life and manners which M. Dumas evinced at that time."[21]

Dumas could not have cared less about accuracy. He had his own Kean

to create. There are two sides to Dumas's Kean and they do not always
seem at home in a single figure. One is the actor in search of experience
that he can turn to stage use; the other is the man who would like to be
accepted for himself and not for his celebrity or for the roles he plays. The
idea informing the first of these can be seen in some remarks of Talma,
which Hawkins thought so appropriate to Kean that he wrongly imagined
the French tragedian to have spoken them at a banquet he gave Kean on
his visit to France in 1818: "The observations which [the actor] has made
on his own nature serve at once for his study and example."[22] Dumas's
Kean says much the same thing when he admits to his friend Salomon that
he may be killing himself through his excesses: "An actor must know all
the passions in order to express them well. I study them on myself; it's the
way to know them by heart." Lemaître, who is supposed to have said
something similar ("If I didn't live like that, I shouldn't be able to act like
this!"),[23] may have been able to play the line so that it sounded less like an
actor's maxim than it looks on the page. Not that the play is that rich in
passionate experience. We see Kean recovering from a night of drinking
with the actors who play the "rude mechanicals" in *A Midsummer Night's
Dream* (Kean's taste for low companions?), and he punches out a professional boxer at the Coal Hole. Yet in the double plot that provides the
main action of the play, he behaves impeccably toward the innocent Anna
Damby and fails to bed Eléna, the almost willing wife of the Danish
ambassador.

The second Kean is more in evidence in the two plots. One is a melodrama in which he saves Anna from the wicked Lord Mewill, who wants
to marry her against her will to get his hands on her fortune; the other is a
comedy of intrigue in which he and the Prince of Wales are rivals for
Eléna, and the three of them manage to outsmart her husband. In the first
of these Anna admits that she fell in love with Romeo, Othello, and Hamlet
watching Kean perform, which is why she turned to him for help, and
Mewill declines a duel because an English lord would never fight with a
mountebank. There is a nice ambiguity in Kean's long speech at the end of
act 3, in which he dismisses Mewill after having developed at length "the
distance between us," the dishonorable honorable man and the self-made
man of the people. It should be Kean the man speaking, but the speech is
impressively histrionic, and the final gesture—the toast to Anna and the
husband of her choice—is pure theater.

The intrigue plot begins in what Lemaître correctly calls "un chef-
d'oeuvre de persiflage diplomatique"[24] (certainly the marvelously bitchy
exchange of compliments between Eléna and Amy at the beginning of act
1 is one of the best things in the play), and it is here that the actor's role in
society is defined. The count has invited Kean to dine "as a clown: we will

have him play a scene from Falstaff after dinner." The tone in this act is playful ("My lord, all men are equal before a secret," Kean tells the prince), but in the fourth act Kean seems really to want Eléna to love him for himself, not his stage image ("My Othello!" she says, faced with his jealousy) and the prince to be his friend, not his patron. A contemporary reader might doubt his sincerity (he does want Eléna and to keep the prince from her) or suspect that he is practicing jealousy as an aid to his art, but for the sake of the plot and the man-versus-actor theme, we have to accept his appeals to love and to friendship—which Eléna and the prince, unable to separate him from his public image, cannot do.

Kean laments the unhappy lot of the actor forced to play against his feelings and denounces the audience, which "takes us for automatons having no passions but those of our characters," but he does go on stage and play his part until, turning to exit, he sees the prince and Eléna together in the box. "Who calls me Romeo?" he says to the attempts to whisper him off the stage. "I am not Romeo." this presumably to Eléna, and then for the prince, "I am Falstaff, the companion in debauchery of the English prince." His expansion of the Kean-Falstaff analogy is interrupted by Lord Mewill, who shouts abuse from the opposite box. "Falstaff?" Kean cries. "Oh! I am no more Falstaff than I was Romeo. I am Punch, the crossroads Falstaff," and calls for Punch's stick with which to beat Mewill. Then, overcome by the confusion among roles and the confusion between the player and the played, he collapses from "un accès de folie," as Salomon says, presumably meaning madness, not folly.

The fourth act is the emotional high point of the play; the fifth is a tidying up, dramatically and thematically. The prince, as a kind of deus ex machina, rescues Kean from the trouble the double plot has imposed on him and suggests temporary exile. Kean contradicts his life-upon-the-wicked-stage warning to Anna in act 2 by rejecting her sympathy: "Me! me! quit the theater . . . me!" Now he will go to New York with Anna, who has contracted to play there, and presumably marry her, since she has proved earlier in the last act that she loves him, not simply his roles. Besides, as a professional, she will be able to see, as the audience cannot, "what happens behind the backdrop." He says that she and Salomon are his only two friends, and when the prince calls him "an ingrate," Kean throws himself into the prince's arms, asking his pardon. Kean at the end is man and actor both, and although the emphasis is on friendship that penetrates theatrical disguise, it would not be out of place to resurrect a line from act 4 and let Kean speak it, not wryly as before, but triumphantly. When he buckles on his sword to play Romeo, he says, "Come on, workhorse, now that you're in harness, go plough through your Shakespeare."

The role of Kean is so invitingly flamboyant that Dumas's play became a staple in France, Italy, Germany. It was less popular in England and the United States, but it attracted a number of translators and adapters. Charles Coghlan "lacks the brutal strength and vivid coloring of the mighty earth-forces," wrote Willa Cather, reviewing *The Royal Box* in Pittsburgh, but she praised the actor's adaptation for doing something that the original never did, providing "the actual impression of a given time and society."[25] If it seems odd to do a play on Edmund Kean and turn him into someone identified as "Clarence, an actor," even odder things have befallen *Kean*. Henry L. Williams wrote a novelization of the play, *The Regal Box* (1902), which Street & Smith, as the title page indicates, sold as a work by Alexandre Dumas. The play does not surface at all until over a hundred pages of fruity prose have passed, and even then it can be seen only in mutilated bits, like French raisins in Williams's sentimental English pudding. *Moving Picture World*, reviewing *Kean, or The Prince and the Actor* (1910), praised "the superb acting of Kean on the stage," the idea of Shakespeare in silent film making one regret that the movie has disappeared. There was also a Soviet silent film version (1922) in which, so Jay Leyda says, Ivan Mosjoukine's Kean played not only Hamlet and Romeo, but Tristan, Werther, and Manfred.[26] I found in the Shubert Archive, New York, the incomplete script of an unproduced operetta called *Kean* (1912) with the attached report of a play reader: "This impresses me as very good material, and would be a play without the addition of the music." So it was, and by Dumas.

Non-Dumas Edmund Keans, ranging from parody to dramas, appear in catalogues of plays produced in England and France.[27] Most of these have disappeared, but if two typescripts in the Theatre Collection of the New York Public Library at Lincoln Center are examples even the most foolish concoctions could not quite escape Dumas. One is an unidentified work with "Edmond Kean" penciled in as title (he is Edmund in the text), said to be translated from the French and dated 18——. The other is a one-act *Edmund Kean* (1903), by Gladys Unger, who went on to do translations and musical libretti for Broadway and to work as a scriptwriter in Hollywood. Both plays have their roots in the Kean-Anna-Mewill plot—or in the kind of melodrama that Dumas borrowed for the occasion—since Kean in both instances has to rescue a maiden from a scheming nobleman. Although Unger does emphasize Kean as actor, at least to the extent of having her heroine fall in love with him as Hamlet ("I am not Hamlet now. I am Romeo and you are Juliet!"), in neither play is there any concern with the actor's dilemma as Dumas used it to give substance to his conventional plots.

Much later, in the 1940s, two works appeared that made no great stir in the literary-theatrical world but which may be seen as steps toward

Sartre's reworking of Dumas, although it is unlikely that Sartre knew either of them. One is *The Sun's Bright Child* (1946), a novel by Julius Berstl, the German playwright and novelist who worked in England and in English after he got out of Germany in 1936. Subtitled "The Imaginary Memoirs of Edmund Kean," Berstl's book fails aesthetically because he does not find a compelling voice for his actor-narrator. There is none of the convoluted platitudinizing, the too plausible sincerity, the occasional bluntness of the existing Kean letters. *Child* is one more trip through the Kean biography with some noticeable errors (presumably the "omissions and simplifications" Berstl speaks of in his preface) and a deal of scenic embroidery—local color in lieu of life. What Berstl is interested in is not biographical fact, but the forces that push Kean to triumph and self-destruction. Although he sets out to correct the sentimental distortions of Dumas, as he says in his preface, he admits his fascination with the play, and he harks back to the French playwright in his concern with the offstage roles of the actor and his inability "to distinguish clearly the illusions of the boards and the reality of the world." He is even more drawn to Heine, whom he quotes at length in the preface. The title, which he borrows from a poem on Kean that he wrongly attributes to Byron, is a promise of the fire/flame images that run all through the book, his metaphor for Heine's "diabolic-divine power." Berstl's Kean sees himself as "the sacred flame itself, and my God-given mission was to make it shine throughout the world," then as "a flame consuming itself," and finally as "a burnt-out crater where one could sense the once unbridled fire even in the greyness of the cinders."[28]

If Berstl is a late-blooming Romantic, at least in his attitude toward the actor, Peter Yates (William Long) is more modern in his approach to Kean. Yates, a somewhat mysterious figure, published a number of books of poetry, plays and murder mysteries in the 1940s, went suddenly silent after 1951, and emerged more than thirty years later with a new collection of poems. His *The Burning Mask* (1948) is more interesting as a play than Berstl's book is as a novel. There is a scene in the Coal Hole, a drunken gathering of the Wolves Club—Kean supporters as thuggish as the anti-Kean newspapers often said the real Club was. It is ugly, noisy, chaotic, as debauchery should be but seldom is in plays about the dissolute Kean, but it is also thematically important. Yates used Kean's biography, but he alters events and tinkers with time for both dramatic and thematic effect. The titular mask is a mask of tragedy that hangs on stage in each scene (except the one in the Coal Hole)—"the god / That's had my faith," Kean says—and it represents the transforming power of art, in this case of performance: "It is a burning Mask, transfiguring / The human features." Drunkenness offstage is often equated with possession onstage ("a kind of selfless drunkenness"), but Kean, acting onstage or off, never quite succeeds in escaping into his role. That the mask is an untrustworthy god is obvious in the way in which Yates uses Shakespeare. Kean triumphs as Shylock, which he did in fact, but for most of the play he is identified with Richard III, the real Kean's most famous role. When Mrs. Cox, in love with the actor not the man, asks him to "be Richard for me, Ned," he does a few lines of the "Was ever woman in this humour woo'd" speech, ending, appropriately enough, with "I'll have her, but I will not keep her long." In the Coal Hole scene, the Wolves, proclaiming Kean King of Drury, have brought Richard's crown from the theater, and at the end of the scene, carried away by drink and the occasion, Kean forces the Drury officials to kneel to him before he will consent to play. In 3.1 Kean faces down the hostile post-trial audience, as he did not in fact, and at the end of the scene we can hear the play beginning. A triumph for Kean, but a deceptive one since the winter of his discontent is not at all made glorious summer. At the end of the last scene, Kean speaks brokenly, moving from his own words to fragments from 4.6 of *King Lear*. Lear was never one of Kean's greatest roles, but it is fitting that, having lost his family, his friends, his celebrity, his memory, he becomes Shakespeare's unthroned king—a "ruin'd piece of nature," one might say, if the final image, in which Kean faces the audience, the mask held in front of his face, were not so obviously an emblem of art. He says, "This is the actor's fate . . . to feel the Mask / A lie, and yet to know . . . the Mask is all. . . ." With these words, we are ready for Sartre, or at least his *Kean* under the rubric Robert J. Nelson gave it: "The Play as Lie."[29]

Sartre's Kean was Pierre Brasseur, and according to the playwright, it was the actor's idea that a new adaptation of Dumas be made. Although Sartre emphasized *Kean* as an actor's play in the program note for the Paris production (1953), it is plainly Sartre's despite his avowal, "There is no philosophical theme of any sort in the play."[30] Sartre retains Dumas's two plots—the melodrama and the love intrigue—but they are altered in tone and in detail. Sartre is more overtly funny than Dumas (and occasionally more tedious when he works his say-it-one-more-time vein), and the characters are changed. Sartre's Kean has some of Dumas's identity problems, but he is far too knowing to suffer from Romantic afflatus. Eléna has become more brittle, the prince even more playful, and the count is now a cross between Pantaloon and the tired businessman (he sleeps through most of Kean's big scene). Anna has become an aggressive virgin who would not be out of place in F. Hugh Herbert's *The Moon Is Blue,* and she plays Desdemona to Kean's Othello where an anonymous actress was Juliet to Kean's Romeo in the analogous scene in Dumas.

In at least two interviews at the time the play was first produced, Sartre insisted that his *Kean* is not parody.[31] Nor is it. It does, however, tease the original, using direct and indirect references to have affectionate fun at the expense of Dumas and his hero. Sartre drops the famous subtitle; yet, when Anna suggests that she marry Kean to bring order to his life, he says, "And genius—what would become of it if I had order?" Earlier in his first scene with Anna, he says, "Don't be surprised if Romeo turns into Falstaff," which is what the Romeo of Dumas's Kean does. In the tavern scene, when Anna turns up with Mewill's forged letter and the kidnapping plot revives, Kean says, "I haven't a chance; I leave the theater only to step back into it." The most extended gloss on Dumas comes in the Kean-Eléna encounter in act 5, which is the most amusing scene in the play and the key to the philosophical drama that Sartre assured us he did not write.

In Sartre, as in Dumas, Eléna wants to end their affair, which in the later version seems rather more established than the flirtation in Dumas. She has come for her letters, but she and Kean have to get through a great deal of verbal foreplay before her mission can be consummated. At first, she urges that for his sake, for her sake, for the sake of the child she has never had with the count, he leave London, but he, obstinate in his presumed love, demands that she go with him. "If you must ruin my life," she says, "first make me lose my head." When he takes her in his arms, she says, "Not like that! Speak to me, get me drunk on words." Her appeal to the stage lover in Kean ends with, "Show me that I am the universe for you and that you will be able to hold me above everything." When he does not respond, she repeats the end of the sentence, and he snaps, "Don't prompt me." He explains, "I no longer act, that's all" (he has earlier told Salomon that he is "a merchant named Edmond," not "the great Kean"), and calls, "Curtain!" Outraged ("I playact!"), she playacts a denunciation of him ("you are only an actor"), which ends when he sweeps her into his arms to carry her off and she has to come up with new excuses not to go. When he says, "Be frank: you come to ask for your letters back," and puts them on the table, she cries, "For shame!" He then does an extended bit on the emotional value of the letters, beginning "Have I been too quick? I admit that in a modern play, I would have refused to return them at first," and ending in an imitation of Eléna and what she would have said: "You will love another woman and these letters which are now mementoes of love will be no more than trophies of conquest." The line is almost word for word the one that Eléna does speak in Dumas's play when she asks for her picture back. Keans within Kean: the "modern play" of Sartre's actor is the home of Dumas's. Sartre's two characters fall out laughing at themselves and their pretended earnestness, and when they hear the count, now awake enough to be jealous, noisily demanding admittance, Kean says, "What superb delivery! He is certainly not in the same play we are. . . . That is pure tragedy."

Sartre differentiates between the player, "who becomes a person like anyone else when he has finished work," and the actor, who " 'plays himself' every second of his life."[32] Kean is an actor, of course, and never more so than in the scene with Eléna in which, adept at improvisation, he responds to her cues (even while he denounces her for delivering them) with abrupt switches that make her work to keep up with him. She is no slouch as an actor herself, having learned her skills in the drawing room and the correct responses from her box in the theater, but she is more eager than Kean to restrict their scene to a single genre. "Let's stay in sentimental comedy," she says; "we women, we rarely risk farce." Earlier, Kean plays a scene with Anna in which he asks her to improvise a meeting between an aspiring ingenue and a celebrated actor, and they go in and out of their imaginary encounter, never sure whether the lines come from themselves playing themselves or themselves as conventional show business clichés. These are only the most overt instances of the kind of performing self that Kean displays from his first entrance to the final curtain.

In his angry scene with the prince in act 2, after his long speech about how society has turned a potential man into a trompe l'oeil because "serious men need illusion," he makes a gesture as though to strike the prince and shrugs it away with, "It is only Kean, the actor, playing the role of Kean." The line is meant sardonically, but the truth in it is emphasized by the onstage scene in act 4. Kean plays Othello, a better role than Dumas's Romeo for a jealousy scene, but the attention here is split between Anna's ineptitude and Kean's presumed distress. He has told her to say "I love you" if she forgets her lines, and we have an almost farcical scene in which she clings to Kean, repeating "I love you" over and over, she trying to protect him, he torn between helping her and confronting the prince. He does manage to insult the prince, Eléna, Mewill, and the audience (for applauding his fake Moor but not his real Kean), but how we are to respond to the scene depends on how seriously we take M. Edmond in the next act. The way in which Kean uses his anti-Kean self in scenes with Salomon and Eléna suggests that it is just another role. Waiting for the police, he strikes a pose in Richard III's chair, and when Salomon indicates what he has done, he shows how he sits as Richard, stands as Shylock. Was what I did last night a gesture or an act, he wonders. "It was an act because it ruined my life," he decides, but it has not ruined his life; he will go to New York with Anna and the blessings of the prince.

The confusion of *geste* and *acte* is so prevalent in this play that the prince's line at the end of act 4 has its own ambiguity. When the count, who has just awakened, asks how the prince liked Kean, he says *in the tone one uses to congratulate an actor on his performance.—*He was, quite simply, admirable." As a man? As an actor? I do not think there is a choice. "But one should absolutely not conclude that everyone is putting on an act," Sartre says.[33] Yet Eléna and Anna are clearly performers. "You play the role of the Prince of Wales, don't you?" Kean asks the prince in act 2. Mewill comes masked and under a fake name (Kean's) in his attempt to carry off Anna in act 3. Amy is self-consciously witty, as in her speech in act 1 about how boring society is, and the count is like an actor uncertain of what part he is cast for. Sartre finishes the sentence quoted above, "and especially not derive a theory from it." The last line of the play, in which Kean offers the prince the curtain speech while taking it for himself, reminds us that this play is a play. And perhaps something more. It is not necessary to propound a theory to suspect that Sartre's *Kean* is about role-playing more extended than that of the actor.

One of the jokes in *Kean* is that Anna has been hired by a New York theatrical representative who took her incompetence for art. One of the jokes on *Kean* is that Sartre's play did not make it to New York at all until it was turned into a musical comedy in 1961. Without the help of their dead collaborators, Grieg on *Song of Norway* and Borodin on *Kismet,* Robert Wright and George Forrest turned out an innocuous score. The play had to be opened up to provide street scenes—choral numbers—but for the most part Peter Stone, who did the book, stuck close to Sartre. He did add a scene in which Kean apologizes to the prince from the stage, using snippets of Shakespeare as his vehicle. It sounds less like Kean than like Peter Stone's rummaging through a quotation book, particularly when the prince protests "Let us be keen," and the actor cites his reference: *Measure for Measure,* 2.1. The real transformation of Sartre comes in the somewhat soupy song, "Man and Shadow," which frames the action. At the beginning, Kean sings his confusion about which is the real, which the illusionary world; in the final scene, he sings the end of his confusion. He stands in the shadow while on the backdrop we see blowups of him as Othello, Hamlet, Richard. "I know—you create *me*—you alone make me real." On the original cast recording of the show, Alfred Drake (it is appropriate that this Kean be played by a musical comedy star who is also a Shakespearean actor) repeats the final phrase, breaking breathily on "make" and drawing out the "me real" in a sentimentally significant elongation.[34] If Dumas's Kean found the man in the actor and Sartre's Kean found only the actor, offstage and on, Broadway's Kean, settling for truth in illusion, found the man in the role.

Of all the theatrical evocations of Edmund Kean, the one that Kean himself would have wanted to play is the most recent one, that of Raymund FitzSimons. It is not that FitzSimons's *Edmund Kean* is a more accurate portrait of the actor, although the playwright, who is also a biographer of Kean, would insist that he has come closest to the true Kean. It is that FitzSimons's play is a monologue for one actor, the ideal vehicle for a performer who wants always to be center stage, and Kean was notoriously impatient with competition in his own theater and at rival ones. All the biographers testify to this, from Procter, with his funny, presumably fictional tale of Kean's swift departure from Paris to avoid seeing Talma in a second of his celebrated roles, to FitzSimons, who said of the youthful, unknown Kean, "he had nothing but contempt for other actors and admitted no talent but his own."[35]

Although FitzSimons's play was performed in London and later in New York in 1983, there is no finished script.[36] Unless the playwright decides to head off in some unsuspected direction, it is unlikely that the final version of *Edmund Kean* will differ greatly in form or in substance from those I saw in New York and on television. Like most one-character plays about celebrity writers and performers—Emily Dickinson, Gertrude Stein, Paul Robeson—this one is a combination of confession and lecture in which chat with the audience becomes a substitute for the traditional drama of character confrontation. FitzSimons's Kean, speaking in his own voice, is blunt, coarse, direct, but he moves regularly from the actor in the dressing room to the performer onstage, using his most famous roles to illuminate his private life. Thus he can let Othello indicate his love for and then his suspicion of Charlotte Cox, and his memory of his dead son can call up Lear's "My wits begin to turn / Come on, my boy. How dost, my boy? Art cold?"

The Kean of this play, as FitzSimons said in the "Author's Notes" he prepared for the director and the actor, is "a monster, stinking, drink-sodden and syphilitic," but also "the first great Romantic actor and the matchless interpreter of Shakespeare." This double-natured Kean comes directly from FitzSimon's biography. In fact, Kean in the play often seems to be paraphrasing the biography, and once I think I heard him speaking Hazlitt's defense of Kean—or was it Leigh Hunt's—with the pronouns changed from third person to first.[37] The difficulty with the play is that the strong narrative line of the biography does not transfer comfortably to the stage when the genre forces the protagonist to be his own explicator. At the end of the play, when the dying Kean opens his Othello robes to show the Harlequin costume underneath, FitzSimons provides a potentially moving visual image, but it does not stand for a destruction/revelation of character that has been created dramatically. It is the last slide in the presentation.

In his "Author's Notes" FitzSimons says that his play is "not about a fantastical Kean" like those of Dumas and Sartre. Oddly enough, it is in one way similar to another "fantastical Kean," that of Arthur Shirley in *Ned Kean of Old Drury*. Although FitzSimons's play is different in form, intention, tone, and quality, both he and Shirley concentrate on a specific Kean and use Shakespeare to decorate or to elucidate the figure they present. FitzSimons's use of the passages from Shakespeare may show the way in which an actor's life affects his reading of a part, but he does not generalize as Dumas and Kean do. FitzSimons is interested in Edmund Kean; Dumas and Sartre are interested in "the Myth of the Actor." Their work suggests that the Procter quotation which opens this essay might be expanded to suggest another and more fascinating way in which the "life of a player . . . may be made amusing and even useful."

NOTES

1. *The Life of Edmund Kean* (London: Edward Moxon, 1835), 1.v. No author is given in the book itself.
2. Norman Mailer's neologism for a fact that has "no existence before appearing in a magazine or newspaper, creations which are not so much lies as a product to manipulate emotion." *Marilyn* (New York: Grosset & Dunlap, 1973), p. 18.
3. F. W. Hawkins, *The Life of Edmund Kean* (London: Tinsley Brothers, 1869). The epigraph appears on the title page of both volumes.
4. *The Stage,* 10 May 1923; *The Era,* 16 May 1923. Clips in the *Ned Kean of Old Drury* file, Theatre Collection, New York Public Library, Lincoln Center, New York.
5. *Specimens of the Table Talk of the Late Samuel Taylor Coleridge* (London: Murray, 1835), 1:24. Entry for 27 April 1823. *Ned Kean of Old Drury,* act 4, p. 20. Typescript, Shubert Archive, New York.
6. Robert J. Nelson, *Play within a Play* (New Haven: Yale University Press, 1958), p. 89.
7. Quoted in Julius Berstl, *The Sun's Bright Child* (London: Hammond, Hammond, 1946), p. 7.
8. T. C. Grattan, Esq., "My Acquaintance with the Late Edmund Kean," *The New Monthly Magazine* 39 (1833 pt. 3): 7; *Hazlitt on Theatre,* ed. William Archer and Robert Lowe (New York: Hill and Wang, 1957), p. 22; *Oxberry's 1822 Edition of King Richard III with the descriptive notes recording Edmund Kean's Performance made by James H. Hackett* (facsimile), ed. Alan S. Downer (London: Society for Theatre Research, 1959), Hackett's line written opposite the title page; George Vandenhoff, *Leaves from an Actor's Note-Book* (New York: Appleton, 1860), p. 23.
9. Grattan, "My Acquaintance," p. 14; *Sartre on Theater,* ed. Michel Contat and Michel Rybalka, trans. Frank Jellinek (New York: Pantheon, 1976), p. 243.
10. Hawkins tells the story (*Life* 2:329), but he unhappily misquotes, his "Pity thy wretched father" being less appropriate for a reconciliation than Payne's actual line. Later biographers used the story and corrected the line. Harold Newcomb Hillebrand, *Edmund Kean* (New York: Columbia University Press, 1933), p. 298; J. M. D. Hardwick, *Emigrant in Motley* (London: Rockliff, 1954), p. 4; Raymund FitzSimons, *Edmund Kean—Fire from Heaven* (New York: Dial, 1975), p. 228.
11. The edition of the play I used is the one published with Jean-Paul Sartre's adaptation (Paris: Gallimard, 1954), pp. 219–305. It is essentially the same as the one published in *Magasin Théatrâl,* vol. 14 (1836) and collected in Dumas's *Théâtre Complet,* vol. 5 (Paris: Lévy, 1876). The translations from Dumas, Sartre, and any other work cited in French are my own.
12. Charles Coghlan, *The Royal Box,* typescript, Theatre Collection, New York Public Library, Lincoln Center, New York: FitzSimons, p. 142.
13. *Cox vs. Kean* (London: Fairburn, [1825]). Account of the trial with the letters that Kean wrote Mrs. Cox.

14. *Souvenirs de Frédérick Lemaître* (Paris: Ollendorff, 1880), pp. 219–20; Alexandre Dumas, *My Memoirs*, trans. E. M. Waller (London: Methuen, 1908), 5:116, 452; Théophile Gautier, *Histoire de l'art dramatique* (Paris: Hetzel, 1858), 2:249–50. Gautier is not being chummy; Lemaître was known professionally as Frédérick.

15. Robert Baldick, *The Life and Times of Frédérick Lemaître* (London: Hamish Hamilton, 1959), p. 152; *Sartre on Theater*, p. 238; Lemaître, *Souvenirs*, pp. 218–19.

16. *Sartre on Theater*, p. 238. There is no reason why one should believe Sartre. His account (pp. 243–44) of the Boston riot over Kean, rich in imaginary detail, has less to do with the real event than with his desire to illustrate "certain constants in the American character."

17. Procter, *The Life of Edmund Kean* 2:156.

18. Act 3 of Dumas's play takes place at the Trou de Charbon, which Barnett Shaw, a recent translator who knows even less about Kean than Dumas did, retranslates as The Coal Bin (*The Great Lover and Other Plays* [New York: Ungar, 1979]). The name had already undergone a variety of changes as adapters got farther and farther away from Kean's own time. Charles Coghlan renamed it the Cat and Fiddle, and Henry L. Williams, in his novelization of the play, *The Regal Box*, played it both ways by calling it "the Fox-under-the-Hill, facetiously known as 'the Coalhole'" (New York: Street & Smith, 1902), p. 191. Sartre called it the *Coq noir*, which Kitty Black, perhaps nervous at how a direct translation might sound, changed to the Black Horse (*The Devil and the Good Lord and Two Other Plays* [New York, Knopf, 1960]). Frank Hauser, apparently unnervous, stuck with The Black Cock Inn in his translation (London: Davis-Poynter, 1972]). It became The Green Frog in the musical comedy version of the play, presumably for the sake of an idiotic song, "The Fog and the Grog," in which a frog is a central figure and/or rhyme (in typescript, Theatre Collection, *New York Public Library*, Lincoln Center, New York).

19. *Edmund Kean, or The Genius and the Libertine* (London: n.p., 1847), p. 16. The translator slipped up on the second *frère* in 5.9 (Dumas's 5.11) and used "brother" (p. 114).

20. Letter from Susan Chambers, Kean's sister-in-law, quoted in Hillebrand, p. 136.

21. Unpaginated preface to 1847 translation.

22. Talma, *Reflexions on the Actor's Art* (New York: Dramatic Museum of Columbia University, 1915), p. 39. Hawkins used a very different translation (2:53–54), but clearly the same passage is intended. Talma's essay was published in 1825, so it is possible for him to have made some such remarks at his earlier meeting with Kean. Yet no other biographer alludes to any such remarks and the essay, Talma's response to the autobiography of Lekain, makes no reference to Kean.

23. Baldick, *Life and Times*, p. 245.

24. Lemaître, *Souvenirs*, p. 220.

25. Lincoln *Courier*, 30 April 1898. In *The World and the Parish, Willa Cather's Articles and Reviews, 1893–1902*, ed. William M. Curtin (Lincoln: University of Nebraska Press, 1970), 1:481.

26. *Moving Picture World* 7 (26 November 1910): 1250; Jay Leyda, *A History of the Russian and Soviet Film* (London: Allen, 1960), p. 117.

27. Charles Beaumont Wicks, *The Parisian Stage* (University: University of Alabama Press, 1950–1967); *The Stage Cyclopaedia, A Bibliography of Plays*, compiled by Reginald Clarence (London: The Stage, 1909).

28. Berstl, *Bright Child*, pp. 9, 32, 40, 176.

29. Peter Yates, *The Burning Mask* (London: Chatto and Windus, 1948), pp. 16, 56, 39, 71; Nelson, p. 100.

30. *Sartre on Theater,* pp. 240, 239, 242.

31. *Combat,* 5 November 1953; *Les Lettres françaises,* 12 November 1953. *Sartre on Theater,* pp. 240, 245–46.

32. *Sartre on Theater,* p. 240.

33. *Sartre on Theater,* p. 241.

34. Columbia KOL 5720.

35. Procter, *The Life of Edmund Kean* 2:171; FitzSimons, *Fire from Heaven,* p. 11.

36. Letter from FitzSimons 23 June 1984. He also sent me the "Author's Notes," quoted below.

37. FitzSimons the biographer quotes both, *Fire from Heaven,* p. 226.

The Humanist and the Artist

Robert Brustein

In *Theatre Notebook,* the celebrated theater critic Jan Kott confesses to an attraction to actresses. He was still a schoolboy, he tells us, when he found himself backstage for the first time in his life, clutching a bunch of flowers at the dressing room door of the beautiful Polish actress, Lena Zelochowska. Her invitation to enter the room so terrified him that he threw the bouquet on the floor by her feet and fled.

One hears that, in the intervening years, Professor Kott somehow managed to overcome his terror of the histrionic female animal. But what I find most interesting about this story is not his early shyness around women, but rather that his first experience of theater was of flesh, not language or scholarship. Looking at Lena Zelochowska with his young, amorous, awestruck eyes, he knew from the beginning that the theater was something tangible, material, alive.

That is the infinite sadness of the theater, indeed of all the performing arts—that it is written in flesh and the flesh is mortal. The actresses who so enchanted the young schoolboy Kott are now all either dead or very ancient; and while the plays in which they performed may have survived in published texts, the performances themselves are now only a fading memory in the minds of the surviving spectators. We in the theater work always in the knowledge that our work is transient. The months of preparation, the weeks of rehearsal, the days or weeks or months or (if the play is a hit) even years of performance—intense as they may have been at the time— lose their physical life the moment the show closes. And that is why a disbanded company of actors, meeting in reunion after many years of separation, find themselves left with nothing to talk about, except to retell anecdotes about performances past. They are trying to stop time, to reconstitute a lost reality, to give some value to a transparent, abandoned episode. "Ephemera, ephemera," says the old actor in David Mamet's play about the stage, *A Life in the Theatre,* as he looks over the vast, empty expanse of empty theater seats. For ephemeral is precisely what a life in the theater is doomed to be.

We have methods in our technological society by which to preserve the memory of performance—film and videotape, photographs, and audio cassettes—none of them very satisfactory. The essence of theater, which is its presence and immediacy, is invariably lost on celluloid or tape, and in some ways this is a blessing. Styles of theater change so rapidly that records of performances often seem embarrassing. Marlon Brando is said to have revolutionized naturalistic acting when he first appeared on stage as Stanley Kowalski in *A Streetcar Named Desire*. Looking at the filmed version of that performance today, admirable as it is, makes us conscious not of a new naturalism, but of a stylization so special it attracted dozens of imitators. In the same way, the voice on record of a Forbes Roberston reading Hamlet or of John Barrymore acting Richard III now sounds surprisingly cracked and hammy, though both were considered models of "natural" acting in their time. And that has been the awful fate of the theater—to claim to be providing a model of truthfulness and reality for one age that invariably strikes the next age as stilted and false. Actors are, in a very real sense, what Hamlet called them—"the abstracts and brief chronicles of the time." Abstract and brief they are indeed. It is immediate time, in all its fleeting, changing evanescence that they are doomed to chronicle.

So we should be grateful that the theater leaves no adequate permanent record of itself. We are spared the embarrassment—an embarrassment often expressed by filmmakers—of encountering a work of which we once were proud but which now looks yellow and crumpled, like a piece of fading parchment. It remains true, of course, that the literary side of production is more likely to withstand the ravages of time than the acting or production; the text is often still readable after the performance has died. It is a paradox of the theater that a text has no real life until it is acted; but the text is the one thing about the performance that manages to survive.

This is one of those paradoxes that obsessed the Italian dramatist, Luigi Pirandello, a paradox that both attracted him to and repelled him from the stage. Only in the spoken performing arts could something fluid and spontaneous have a formal impact on something fixed and immutable; only in the theater could we simultaneously satisfy our hunger both for permanence and for change. The words he wrote were etched in stone, but the actor's art had the capacity to change these words through an improvised action, an extemporized speech, an accident of memory, perhaps even in a catastrophe in the physical theater itself. "We are not free," wrote the French theater theorist, Antonin Artaud, "and the sky can still fall on our heads. And the theatre has been created to teach us that first of all."

This distressed Pirandello as a writer who valued his own words; it also fascinated him as a philosophical animal playing with ideas. So much so that, in his three plays about the theater—*Six Characters In Search of An*

Author, Tonight We Improvise, Each in His Own Way—he experimented with the conflict between his written language and the actors who were pledged to speak it but who sometimes preferred to substitute their own words, their lives, expressions, gestures.

Tha actor's resistance to the playwright is traditional—perhaps it is influenced by a residual memory of the most primitive form of the theater, when thespians, not playwrights, dominated the attention of the audience, when not plays held the stage, but mimes, interpolations, scenarios, improvisations. Perhaps this resistance reflects the feelings all of us have about hardening into a fixed character determined by others, which others are then in position to analyze and catalogue and dismiss. It is a resistance to cause-and-effect thinking, to predestination, to determinism, to the sense that we are not free. In a late play, *When One Is Somebody,* Pirandello dramatizes the sadness of an aging, famous writer (very probably himself), whose every work is acclaimed in the same way, no matter how original or innovative it is, and who therefore feels trapped in a persona or mask he finds false to his authentic self. His solution is to publish his next volume of poetry under a pseudonym and to pretend it has been written by a young man. For a while the subterfuge succeeds, and the author is hailed by critics and readers alike as a new, vital source of youthful energy, whose poems vibrate with life. Eventually, of course, the poet is found out and treated exactly as before—as a distinguished, venerable man of letters with absolutely nothing new to say. In the final scene, he gives a formal speech at a solemn ceremonial occasion; his words are chiselled in stone behind him as he speaks.

So the theater's greatest failing is also its most triumphant quality—its vulnerability to Time. Like all living flesh, it yields, but also like flesh, it is pulsing and alive. It is this bridge of flesh that has the capacity to span the wide gulf that has traditionally existed between humanism and art, between what is completed and enshrined, and what is ongoing, developing, in process. It is its capacity to be in time and of time that gives the theater the potential to unite two species—the humanist and the artist—who normally behave towards each other like two mutually hostile and antagonistic carnivores.

In stating this, perhaps I am suggesting something that is not generally acknowledged or openly admitted—namely, that the humanist and the artist, whom one would expect to be natural allies, often tend to ignore each other, when they are not trying to tear each other's hair. This surprising chasm between two professionals whose interests overlap worries me more about the future of American art, particularly its future in the university, than almost any other problem. And if the chasm is not bridged, then neither will be able to function in our society with the fullness and amplitude and intelligence that each profession needs in order to flourish.

One thing I have learned over the years is that the ultimate division in this nation is not between conservative and radical, or Democrat and Republican, or elitist and populist, or middle class and working class, or technologist and primitive, or black and white. It is rather a split between those who love the imagination and wish to advance its potential, and those who scorn and fear it. This may sound as if I am pitting artists against the rest of humankind. Quite the contrary, there are a large number of people currently practicing theater, music, literature, painting, and, of course, criticism, whom I think of as chief among its enemies. Where you stand in this adversary relationship is determined not by what you do, but by how you respond—which is to say, by the nature and quality of your spirit. It is determined by how you appreciate the talents and capabilities of others, by whether you are open or closed to what may seem strange and unfamiliar. And I'm not speaking of a fixed condition, either. I know many people who once had a tendency to close themselves off from imaginative experience and who later developed extraordinary capacities of response.

So it is possible to be a carpenter or an insurance agent and love the creative imagination, just as it is possible to be a university professor and despise it. I have known a number of distinguished faculty members, many of them in English departments teaching the imaginative literature of the past—Blake and Yeats, Dostoyevsky and Tolstoy, Dante and Machiavelli, Proust and Joyce—who have always been curiously indifferent to modern artists attempting to create work of an adventurousness and quality similar to that they were teaching and studying. If they went to the theater, they usually chose escapist Broadway commodities, and if they attended classical plays, they invariably preferred conventional revivals. When I was at Yale, running a theater predominantly designed for a university audience, our most alert, demanding spectators, oddly enough, came not from the English department but from the school of medicine: epidemiologists, pharmacologists, psychiatrists, internists, doctors, and nurses.

I can only guess at an explanation of this curious situation. One is that those who consider themselves custodians of the past sometimes have an impulse to preserve the past in formaldehyde. Considering themselves trustees of literature, some scholars seem to feel at ease only with what is authorized and established, and this means they are generally conservative in their theories of art, and particularly suspicious of modernist heresies. Classics are regarded with awe and reverence, and new interpretations are often a source of unease and disquiet. I suspect the relationship between the teacher of literature and the practitioner is not so different from that between the art historian and the painter, or between the musicologist and the composer. Those engaged in practice seem to constitute a threat to those engaged in curatorial, pedagogical tasks.

I am generalizing wildly, and all generalizations admit of exceptions, but I hope I am describing something you recognize. In the university, there are no wars more savagely fought than those between the literature and theater departments and no appointment more fiercely resisted than that of a creative writer or a practicing artist. And the resistance I am describing comes not only from the cloistered academic but from some of the more adventurous literary minds of the age. My revered teacher, the great critic of literature and society, Lionel Trilling, once astonished me, after hearing of my interest in the theater, by wrinkling up his nose and expressing disapproval. It was an inferior art, he informed me, slightly vulgar, not worthy of a serious person's attention. I presumed that he, as an expert in nineteenth-century English literature, was commenting on the admittedly inferior dramas of his period; but no, his disdain was more far ranging than that. He considered the whole of drama to be a poor stepsister of literature. I reminded him, feeling very impertinent, that the greatest writers of all time—the Greek dramatists, the Elizabethans, Molière, Racine, Ibsen, Chekhov, Beckett, Brecht, Shakespeare himself—had all written for the theater; so, admittedly with less success, had most of the English authors he admired. It was astonishing to me that this brilliant teacher, whom I revered above all living critics, could exclude from his consideration a form of literature so preeminently creative and imaginative.

Only later did I learn that Trilling's disdain masked an early passion that he now considered somewhat shameful; he had hung around theaters as a young man, perhaps like Jan Kott, watching actresses, and he had even written an approving essay about the early works of Eugene O'Neill. When he began doing textbook anthologies toward the end of his life, Trilling included a fair share of plays in the table of contents and wrote some striking introductory essays about them. I took this to mean that he no longer felt antagonistic to the theater. Still, what Trilling was expressing in his earlier remarks to me was the suspiciousness felt by the literary profession in general toward the products of the stage. It was first expressed by Plato in *The Republic;* it was spread throughout Sir Philip Sidney's *Defense of Poesy;* it animated the Puritan hostility that closed down the English theaters for eighteen years following the Cromwellian Revolution. The only way one could put on a play during the Puritan Interregnum was to call it an opera, which perhaps explains why the theaters built in this country in the nineteenth century were usually called opera houses, even though the works done there were spoken, not sung. It may even explain why the most popular offering in the American Repertory Theatre season near Puritan Boston was an opera, *Orlando,* and why the theater in which it was staged—Harvard's Loeb—is not called a theater at all, but rather a Drama Center.

This Puritan hostility toward the stage, recently documented by Jonas Barish in an excellent study called *Anti-Theatrical Prejudice,* has left residual effects up to the present time, especially in the academy. In many English departments, there remains a deep distaste for that which has been "staled" on the stage or "clapper-clawed" by the general public; to many literary academics, even Shakespeare and Sophocles are considered private writers whose poetry is best scanned in the contemplative quiet of the study—writers who would probably have composed prose fiction if the form had been invented in their time.

Now I am a professor of literature myself. But first as an actor, and later in a double role as director of a theater and head of a conservatory of training, I developed the same conviction as Jan Kott during that moment he dropped his flowers at the feet of Lena Zelochowska—that the great works of dramatic literature have no reality whatever until they have found their life on the stage. Although the performing arts continue to be unwelcome at many major American and English universities—it was a professor at Harvard, I believe, who saw the same value in an acting course as in a course in meat-butchering—I believe that without the performing arts no university can be complete. If a library is a quintessential research facility, where students of Hellenistic poetry or Idealistic philosophy can investigate the primary and secondary sources of their disciplines, then surely a theater or a concert hall is a living library, where the works of drama or music are in a position to find their true, significant form. It is true that many of these performances are of poor quality; so are many works of scholarship. The important thing is that both scholar and artist should be striving to achieve the highest standards of excellence.

On the other hand, it is a curious aspect of university life that the same people who value professionalism in the humanities often tend to prefer amateurism in the arts. A distinguished professor of philosophy who takes a stern attitude toward the research papers of his students, recently announced publicly that the best Shakespeare production he had ever seen was one done by an ad hoc student group in a residential house. Now we have all enjoyed extracurricular student productions, just as we have often appreciated student recitals and concerts. But the difference is that while most undergraduate pianists are trained, most undergraduate actors are not: the vitality and imagination and energy of student performance do not sufficiently compensate for an incapacity to speak verse, or interpret, or characterize, or move gracefully on stage. To say that amateur theater production is preferable to that done by people with training is really to express contempt or indifference toward the stage. It is another way of saying that the closet is the most congenial place to examine a play.

So a drama, like a musical composition, really has no ultimate meaning until it has found some embodiment in the fleshly corporality of gifted, trained performers, and this may explain why women and physicians generally constitute the largest audiences for serious theater. In addition to their intellectual and emotional concerns, both groups stand in a special relationship to the human body. The one by nature, the other by profession, the one through childbearing and nurture, the other through healing and care, have managed to develop a special sensitivity to the kind of natural shocks that flesh is heir to. It is true that one of these shocks, sometimes, can be produced by the size of the doctor's bill, and I don't want to idealize a profession that has often been an appropriate subject for anger and satire, both in the past and the present. But perhaps in recognition of the special nature of women and doctors in regard to physical matters, the modern theater, at least, has tended to treat both groups as the true humanists of modern times.

It is not Serebryakov, the overindulged Professor in Chekhov's *Uncle Vanya,* who understands the misery of the household or protests the plunder of the forests; he is too busy plagiarizing his books, when he is not exploiting his brother-in-law's free labor. No, the sympathetic humanist in that play is the humane doctor, Astrov. It is not the intellectuals, in the plays of Ibsen, who represent the vanguard of thought and action; it is his female characters: Nora Helmer in *A Doll's House,* Mrs. Alving in *Ghosts,* and Hilda Wangel in *The Master Builder,* just as it is his doctors—Rank, Relling, Stockmann—who are able to perceive the rotten foundations of the social order. Shaw had no use for doctors; he believed, like his predecessors, Ben Jonson and Molière, that they are paid to flay a man before they kill him; but he had no use for orators or liberal intellectuals, either. The soft spot in his heart was reserved for what he called the "unwomanly woman"—Candida, Major Barbara, Ann Whitefield in *Man and Superman*—whom he believed to be most closely in touch with the life force.

Still, as I cautioned earlier, art is not happy with rigid classifications, and ultimately even this generalization will not hold. A love for the creative imagination is no more a matter of sex or profession than it is of class or educational level, or economic status, or color. It is rather a gift enjoyed by anyone with psychic generosity, with spiritual expansiveness, with the capacity to face and accept the unknown. Those who reject the imagination are really afraid of life, in all its unkempt, untidy, unpredictable disorder. They resent what cannot be categorized or pigeonholed, what cannot be organized into principles, channeled into theories. And this may help to explain why the university is still likely to be somewhat hostile to the performing arts. Like most institutions, it tends to attract those who want security and order, to whom the unconditioned nature of a living art can sometimes constitute a threat.

And what about artistic institutions, even those in universities? Are they not subject to the same kind of dangers? Of course they are, and they frequently attract the same kind of security-minded people. The pressures in our culture are simply enormous to channel the rough, ruffled waters of art into navigable streams and smooth, sheltered harbors. These are pressures that come from without; they are also pressures that come within. How tempting it is to yield to them when they promise peace and tidiness and serenity and approval. And how dangerous, too, for yielding can only lead to a rigidified, conventionalized, safety-conscious art.

The professional theater today, like all professional organizations, is peopled with automatons of precision, both in the artistic and managerial areas, who have been spawned by the incredibly complicated procedures of bookkeeping and fundraising, and the compulsion of institutions to bureaucratize themselves. As a result of the severe economic problems afflicting the performing arts, such people have begun to dominate the profession, for they sing a siren song of stability and salvation, perhaps even solvency. Such people are important and valuable, but only as long as they are willing to accept a subordinate rather than a ruling role. The danger is that they will rise to the surface and dominate the arts, precisely because they are willing to perform the tasks that others find onerous.

Because these onerous tasks have multiplied recently, performing arts groups are currently dominated by these people and their procedures. Some theaters now determine their season choices by sending questionnaires to their subscribers, inquiring after their favorite plays; others base their programs on the kind of fare likely to find favor with the current fashions in public and private funding; one theater I know, a large, prestigious institution, once considered replacing its current artistic director with a computer—programmed to measure, on the basis of what proved successful with audiences in the past, what combination of plays and players would work in the future. These are theaters run by human calculators—practical, hardheaded people—who can justify their procedures by reference to ledgers and balance sheets. But if the management of an artistic institution does not love the imagination first and foremost, if it does not dedicate itself to the growth of its artists and the development of its public, if it prides itself only on being a self-perpetuating machine, then it might as well be running a processing plant or a fast food chain.

For the primary function of a theater is not to please itself, or even to please its audience; it is to serve talent, even when that talent is unruly and disorderly (not, however, when it is destructive, for that ruins the work of the whole). Why this emphasis on the individual talent at the expense of the institution? Because the institution was originally founded—though it sometimes forgets this—for the sake of that talent. It is the destiny of institutions to become routinized, just as it is the fate of successful revolutionaries to turn conservative, authoritarian. As the French philosopher Charles Peguy phrased it: "Tout commence en mystique et finit en politique." But what use is the practical expertise, the *politique,* unless the institution preserves its *mystique,* its animating idea? And what keeps the fleshly theater alive but a passionate idea, which is its very mystical breath of creation?

I do not mean to sound disrespectful of all the important administrative tasks required for the survival of a collective artistic enterprise. I believe these must be performed, and performed well—but only for the sake of the *mystique.* There is no question whatever in my mind that an arts group that clings stubbornly to its original purpose will eventually triumph, just as I have come to believe that there are forms of survival that almost make failure and defeat seem more desirable. I am saying nothing new in suggesting that it is the process of struggle, not the result of success or victory, that is most ennobling. Sophocles understood this, and so did Shakespeare and Ibsen. And Chekhov knew that the creative example, even if momentarily buried by the forces of darkness, would eventually seed itself and multiply. These playwrights are not only our material in the theater, they function as our mentors and guides. We must be nourished by their example—and multiply.

Let me mention another philosopher-guide, a man not normally associated either with the theater or the flesh—the Greek philosopher Plato. He disdained all "imitations," especially plays; he believed that artists should be excluded from his ideal Republic, but he was an artist himself and not a bad dramatist either, to judge by his account of Socrates' trial and death. Plato understood that the ultimate reality was not to be found in material things or institutions, but rather in the Idea, the *mystique.* This Platonic Idea is hard for us to swallow today because it is a spiritual concept, immaterial, as vaporous as thoughts. It is something independent of the physical life; yet it gives our physical life its meaning. It is the spirit that transforms and animates, that pushes us forward, that yields no rest. The institution without an Idea is a decaying institution, no matter how prosperous or popular it may seem at the moment. For it is flesh without spirit, body without soul, an organism with dead cells that prevent its vital growth.

To speak personally for a moment, there were years when I was at Yale—dark and difficult years—when we had an idea all right, but it sometimes seemed as if we had very little else. We were not a popular theater, we were failing to communicate our purpose to the public or the company or the students, and we were getting a little shaky in our own convictions, too. In a moment of despair, my wife turned to me and asked, "What are we doing it for?" And I, not certain what I meant, replied: "We're doing it for Plato." For thirteen years in New Haven, and now eight years in Cambridge, we tried to do it for Plato, and it was not long before we discovered that Plato was not a phantom, that his Idea was composed of flesh and blood, that it was in a lot more people than we ever dreamed. And it was in that Idea that spirit and flesh were unified, and the humanist and the artist held out their hands to each other and were one.

PART 3
Traditions

PART 2
Traditions

"Not or I see more neede":
The Wife of Noah in the Chester, York, and Towneley Cycles

Sarah Sutherland

Of the many references to the Flood in the New Testament, one seems to have a special pertinence to the cantankerous character of Noah's wife in the Chester, York, and Towneley mystery cycles. The passage is lengthy but worth quoting in full:

> Knowing this first, that there shall come in the last days scoffers, walking after their own lusts, And saying, Where is the promise of his coming? for since the fathers fell asleep, all things continue as they were from the beginning of the creation. For this they willingly are ignorant of, that by the word of God the heavens were of old, and the earth standing out of the water and in the water: Whereby the world that then was, being overflowed with water, perished: But the heavens and the earth, which are now, by the same word are kept in store, reserved unto fire against the day of judgment and perdition of ungodly men.[1]

This association of the Flood with Doomsday is one of several figural links between the Noah plays and the New Testament plays in the Corpus Christi cycles. It differs from others, however, in describing "scoffers" who doubt the promise of the prophets and apostles.

The scoffers and ungodly men in 2 Peter belong to a distinct biblical class; they are equivalent to the scornful and doubting men so ubiquitous in Proverbs and Psalms, and indeed throughout Scripture. Their absence in the account of Noah and the Flood in Genesis 6–9 is conspicuous in the light of figural interpretations of the event in the New Testament and patristic commentary. To the medieval dramatists, aware also of folkloric, iconographic, and literary versions of the Flood in which scoffers are supplied, the event proved rich in associative and typological traditions and fraught with dramatic possibilities.[2]

The nature of God's command to Noah allows ample room for scorn: while—as Rosemary Woolf notes—"One's first thought is that Noah is

181

being instructed to his own advantage and in a way that he could readily
see to be to his own advantage . . . , God's command did not seem
immediately attractive: the flood was not an apparent danger, the building
of the ark was a long and burdensome duty."[3] Woolf goes on to stress the
theological and typological importance of Noah's obedience, but the ambivalence she has observed actually appears in the plays in the form of
what most critics have called disobedience. The plays of the Flood do not
stress the unattractiveness of God's command to Noah, except in relation
to his aged weariness and the infusion of physical strength through spiritual grace that makes his task easier. Disobedience, scoffing, or even
hesitation on Noah's part would not only violate the authority of the
biblical source but also obliterate the dramatic impact of Noah's willing
obedience following the willful disobedience of Lucifer, Adam and Eve,
and Cain. The Noah plays do, however, stress the unattractiveness of
God's command to Noah's wife, a person whose presence has the authority of Genesis but whose character—about which Genesis is silent—
could be freely drawn. The dramatists of the Chester, York, and Towneley
cycles, aided by New Testament commentary and apocryphal tradition,
provided Noah with a wife who was a quintessential scoffer.

The importance of the role of scoffer in the Noah plays is primarily
dramatic. Uxor may function typologically as the unrepentant sinner who
will not enter the Church,[4] and in theological terms the parallel between
her relationship to Noah and Noah's relationship to God may well be
operative in the plays.[5] Much critical ink has been devoted to these
aspects of Noah's wife, and appropriately so; comparatively little space,
though, is allotted to Uxor's effectiveness as a dramatic character with a
particularly interesting and complex relationship to the audience. In a
sense, of course, the distinction just made is a tenuous one, since scoffers
have as much biblical authority as unrepentant sinners, and—in the New
Testament at least—a person who is one must necessarily also be the
other. Perhaps, too, the various categories of medieval audience response
are not so easily separated. On the other hand, the specifically theological
aspects of Uxor have a distance from the audience that her dramatic role
as scoffer does not. The complex and various affinities between Uxor and
the audience work in juxtaposition with aspects of historical, typological,
and psychic distance to provide the crucial elements in the dramatic
effectiveness of these plays.

The characterization of Uxor in the Chester *Noyes Fludd* is less complex than that in York or Towneley, yet the Chester Uxor shows a tendency
to vacillate between acquiescence and scoffing that has proved troublesome to several critics.[6] The play of the deluge opens with a long
speech from God, a justification for the destruction of the world. God
describes the ark that Noah must build, and Noah accepts his task joyfully

and gratefully. Noah then turns to his family, asking their help in fulfilling God's will. In what Woolf has called a "litany of obedient assent,"[7] each member of the group, including Noah's wife, cooperates readily. Uxor announces,

> And wee shall bringe tymber to,
> for wee mon nothinge ells doe—
> women bynne weake to undergoe
> any great travell.[8]

It is possible to hear these lines ironically in the light of Uxor's later refusal to join her family in the ark, but it seems unnecessary to do so. At this point, Uxor has been told only to "worche this shippe" (51); she has not yet been asked to leave her friends and enter it.

When the ark is completed, Noah turns to his wife and says, "Wife, in this vessell wee shalbe kepte; / my children and thou, I would in yee lepte" (97–98). But this time Uxor will not join in any litany of assent. Instead, she announces, "In fayth, Noe, I had as leeve thou slepte. / For all thy Frenyshe fare, / I will not doe after thy reade" (99–101). Her refusal is explained in her next lines: "By Christe, not or I see more neede, / though thou stand all daye and stare" (103–4). Inability to "see neede" is a trademark of the scorner; it is not necessarily the same thing as disobedience, and it is quite likely a point with which an audience could sympathize. Noah, as if anticipating sympathy for Uxor, turns to the spectators and complains of "crabbed" women of whom "non are meeke" (105–6). In Noah's eyes, and in the eyes of most critics,[9] this is usurpation of "maistrye" (111–12); this is disobedience. The situation is the first of several in the Chester *Fludd,* and one of many in the Noah plays collectively, in which Noah's wife appeals simultaneously to opposing responses in the audience. Her desire to "see more neede" is hardly inappropriate, yet her place in what Noah considers to be the scheme of things requires obedience to her husband and to the word of God. There is a reflexivity—to borrow an anthropological term—at work here, a reflexivity that summons from the audience precisely that spirit of scoffing which is being shown disapprovingly *to* the audience.

The argument breaks off while the business of loading the ark gets underway. All except Uxor enter the ship (160, s.d.). All, including Uxor, take part in an inventory of animals (173–76). Uxor's participation in the naming of the beasts seems inconsistent with her refusal to enter the ship and her protests of some seventy lines before. Yet it is possible that a distinction is again being drawn between a willingness to help build and load the ark and a willingness to enter it. This possibility becomes more probable a bit later, when the cataclysmic (to Uxor) consequences of joining the group in the ark are made plain. For when the animals are loaded and the time to take refuge has come, Noah's wife faces a new dilemma.

Noah makes a second attempt to get his wife into the ark. He terms her "frowarde," explaining that "tyme yt weare, / for feare lest that wee drowne" (194–96). Uxor's response amounts to a curse (198) followed by an ultimatum:

> But I have my gossips everyechone,
> one foote further I will not gone.
> They shall not drowne, by sayncte John,
> and I may save there life.
> The loved me full well, by Christe.
> But thou wilte lett them into thy chiste,
> elles rowe forthe, Noe, when thy liste
> and gett thee a newe wyfe.
>
> (201–8)

Leaving her "gossips everyechone" is Uxor's new difficulty, and it is a crucial one. Noah's wife sympathizes with them,[10] and in her sympathy she ignites an ambivalent response in the audience. The gossips are of the world that is about to be destroyed; as such, they must reveal a degree of corruption commensurate with the wrath of God. Uxor's attraction to a corrupt world is hardly admirable, and the audience presumably did not think it so. Yet the gossips are human—drunk, perhaps, but human—and Uxor's desire to save those who loved her full well is a plea on behalf of a humankind that includes members of the audience. The dramatic tension here defies single judgments:

> the Chester play establishes by other means a critical sense of evil—of a world deservedly lost—but it intends one to experience a sense of human loss as well. This stretching out of hands takes two forms in medieval versions of the Flood: one is an elegiac sadness for that which is to be destroyed; the other is a temporary participation through laughter in the corrupted world at its last moment of being.[11]

These two forms are merged in Uxor: she articulates the spirit of scoffing in the audience by embodying a sympathetic attitude toward those who must drown, yet her refusal to enter the ark betrays an independence intolerable to Noah and the audience alike.

In the end, of course, God and Noah win, though there is considerable ambivalence in the victory. Noah's sons use threats of force (221, 243–44) before they get their mother into the ark. As she enters, she apparently strikes Noah (246). The threats of force and Noah's acceptance of Uxor's blow ("yt is good for to be still") are typologically appropriate as well as dramatically potent: threatened force signifies God's vengeance on a wicked world, while the received blow stresses Noah as a type of Christ and foreshadows God's covenant with Noah after the Flood (301–28). Uxor's blow is also the final assertion of scorn; once she is in the ark and the waters have risen, all scoffing is purged. Though she probably joins in the singing during the Flood (252, s.d.), she does not speak again in the play. Her absorption into the realm of the saved is signaled as much by her own silence as by God's inclusion of her in the family's show of thanks to God (265).

The York Uxor does not remain silent during the Flood, but the general pattern of characterization is the same as that in the Chester play. At York, the story of the Flood is broken into two parts: the first deals with the construction of the ark, requiring only God and Noah; the second presents the Flood itself with Noah's entire family as witnesses and participants. The story was probably divided in order to provide each guild with a play in accordance with "trade symbolism":[12] the Shipwrights produced the first part, the Fishers and Mariners the second. But the break serves dramatic purposes as well: for example, the hiatus between the two parts can indicate the one hundred years Noah needed to build the ark. Noah's wife appears only in the second play; the first follows its biblical model and while theologically, typologically, and metasocially important, is a static piece of dramaturgy.

The second play begins with Noah's recounting of Lamech's prophecy that Noah would be a comfort to mankind. The opening lines also provide the audience with Noah's opinion of his family: "Thre semely sonnes and a worthy wiffe / I haue euer at my steven to stande."[13] Noah's "semely sonnes" (the phrase recurs in 45) indicate their readiness to obey their father (47–48), and one is dispatched to fetch his mother.

Uxor's first appearance in the York *Flood* reveals her native stubbornness: she refuses to join her husband before she knows anything at all about the command he has received from God. Uxor responds to her son's message that Noah has sent for her with a resounding "Ʒa! good sone, hy þe faste agayne, / And telle hym I wol come no narre" (61–62). But her curiosity soon gets the better of her, and a few lines later she is standing outside the ark.

Her response to Noah's invitation to enter the ark is a show of scorn for what she clearly perceives to be an absurd command. "Trowes þou," she asks Noah, "þat I wol leue þe harde lande, / And tourne vp here on toure deraye?" (77–78). This is the voice of another who needs to "see more neede"; this is the voice of scoffing. To Noah's "sothly þan mon ye drowne" (82) she replies, "In faythe þou were als goode come downe, / And go do som what ellis" (83–84). When Noah explains that a flood will destroy everyone except those in his family, Uxor concludes that he is mad (91). She turns to leave, but is forcibly restrained (97–102). Only after repeated reprimands from Noah does she offer an explanation for her position:

> Noye, þou myght haue leteyn me wete,
> Erly and late þou wente þer outte,
> And ay at home þou lete me sytte,
> To loke þat nowhere were wele aboutte.
>
> (113–16)

Here Uxor defends herself by shifting attention from her own scoffing to Noah's secrecy.[14] To this new accusation Noah makes the only answer he can: it was God's will, he says, and he alone has had to do the labor (121–34). Uxor, only partially convinced, registers another protest, this one the same complaint used by the Chester Uxor:

> Nowe, certis, and we shulde skape fro skathe,
> And so be saffyd as ye saye here,
> My commodrys and my cosynes bathe,
> Þam wolde I wente with vs in feere.
>
> (141–44)

Uxor's sympathy for a world lost just when obedience to an angry God is most necessary creates a double-edged appeal to audience response, which recalls similar patterning in the Chester play of the Flood. The York Uxor, however, is allowed a more dignified grief:

> Allas! my lyff me is full lath,
> I lyffe ouere lange þis lare to lere.
>
> (147–48)

> My frendis þat I fra yoode
> Are ouere flowen with floode.
>
> (151–52)

The ring of pathos is unmistakable.

Although the York text leaves unclear precisely when Uxor enters the ark, the use of the present tense in her lament suggests that the flood has come. Where the Chester dramatist used silence to show Uxor's conversion, the York dramatist uses speech. When the waters recede and Noah's family rejoices in God's mercy, Noah's wife gives thanks for a gift even more precious: "Loved be that lord þat giffes all grace, / þat kyndly þus oure care wolde kele" (197–98). "Kyndly" is, of course, of double import here. The dual adverbial force of the word, modifying both the grace of God and the newfound unity of the family God has chosen to save, is the measure of Uxor's transformation. So confident is the York dramatist in the clarity of that transformation that he allows Noah's wife one final reference to the world that is lost. After the dove has returned with an olive branch, after the hills have reappeared from under the receding waters, she asks Noah, "But Noye, where are nowe all oure kynne, / And companye we knewe be-fore" (269–70). Noah's answer is the only appropriate one: "Dame, all ar drowned, late be thy dyne, / And sone þei broughte þer synnes sore" (271–72). As the first play in the York version of the Flood emphasized, the annihilation represented by Noah's first line was rendered necessary by the "synnes sore" of his second. In these two lines lies the only possible resolution of a divided response to the Flood; it may seem an uneasy resolution, but uneasiness is the stuff of effective drama.

By dramatizing two perspectives on the Flood and allowing the inappropriate one to linger, the York play reflexively urges its spectators to confront their own uneasiness about another resolution, the second deluge to which the passage in 2 Peter referred, the ultimate destruction and the ultimate salvation. This typological aspect is reinforced when Uxor's lament for the predeluvian world is followed by a lament for the postdeluvian prognosis: "A! syre owre hertis are feere for þes sawes / That ȝe saye here, / That myscheffe mon be more" (303–5). If the corrupt world destroyed by the Flood is to be succeeded by one that, because of God's covenant with Noah (284–94) will only stand until the Judgment, then Uxor's fear is indeed well-founded. Noah's response is necessarily evasive; he assures his wife that the fire will not come for "many hundereth yhere" (306–8). The play's ending rests on that evasiveness and on the lingering fears of Uxor. The ways of God are finally no more comprehensible to the postdeluvian Uxor than they were to the predeluvian Uxor. This open-endedness in the York *Flood* has extraordinary significance, for it stresses the play's place in a cycle that will not be complete until the Judgment has put the fears of Noah's wife to rest.

The Towneley *Processus Noe cum Filiis* presents the same pattern of ambivalent characterization appealing to multiple audience responses, though in Towneley the variations are more complex than in Chester or York. Students of the mystery cycles have shown a preference for the Towneley play of Noah[15] comparable to their preference, among the cycles' shepherds' plays, for the Towneley *Secunda Pastorum*. This preference persists despite what some perceive as an unwarranted and inexplicable development in Noah's relationship to his wife: his return of the blows she gives him.[16] As with the inconsistencies in the Chester play, however, Towneley's troublesome aspects turn out to be more apparent than real when attention is paid to the carefully structured pattern of Uxor's scoffing.

The Towneley Noah play opens with a long monologue from Noah followed by Noah's exchange with God. This first segment establishes the biblical context, freeing the Wakefield Master to develop the domestic action in the remainder of the play.[17] This separation of the scriptural account from the invented action is important, although there are of course close relationships between the two sections in structure, interaction of characters, and language.

Surprisingly, Noah receives his orders from God before he knows that it is God who gives them: "What are thou," Noah asks, "Tell me, for charité."[18] Inability to perceive at once the divine origin of a command is one trait Noah shares with his wife. But when God reveals himself, Noah thanks him for appearing to "a symple knafe" (173) and shows his willingness to obey God's commands. Noah's obedience established, the domestic turmoil can begin. As he turns toward home, Noah anticipates the scene with his wife, telling the audience that

> My wife will I frast what she will say,
> And I am agast that we get som fray
> Betwixt us both,
> For she is full tethee,
> For litill oft angré;
> If any thyng wrang be,
> Soyne is she wroth.
>
> (183–89)

This is not the York Noah, grateful for a "worthy wiffe," but one who knows (unlike his counterparts in both York and Chester) that a fight will ensue. As Richard J. Daniels observes, "strife seems simply the common state of affairs in their marriage."[19]

But the battle—the first of three in the play—has nothing to do with the building of the ark, for Noah never gets a chance to tell his wife about God's visit. Uxor greets Noah with a harangue on his neglect of the family's needs (191–98). She cuts off his attempt to tell her his "tythyngys new" (199–207). Finally, she turns to the audience and delivers a complaint ending in a promise to "qwite" (216) Noah. The verb, so important to (and so variously interpreted by) Chaucer's pilgrims, is used by Noah during the fight proper: "And I shall qwyte the tho, in fayth, or syne" (228). "Qwyte" her he does not; what stops the fight is Noah's sudden recollection that he has work to do. "Bot I will kepe charyté," he says, "for I haue at do" (235). Noah goes off to build the ark, his wife turns to her spinning, and not a word about the impending flood has been uttered.

The characterization of Noah in this first scene with his wife deserves some attention, since it has bothered critics like Woolf who find the rest of the play extremely successful. Allowing Noah to return force with force seems a serious lapse; the dramatist appears to have "dispensed with the patience of Noah . . . : the pattern of Christ summoning the sinner into the church is therefore obscured."[20] To this criticism two answers have been offered. On an analogy with the efficacy of a sacrament, "the significance of the event of the Flood is a function of its relationship to the motif of salvation, and not of Noah's super-human righteousness."[21] Such a view, however, reduces the dramatic representation of the Flood to the figural significance inherent in it, rendering even the most inept dramatization— that in the Cornish *Origo Mundi,* for example—indistinguishable in intent and effect from the finest portrayal.

The other response to Woolf's objection is more convincing. The Noah-Christ figure is not the only one operating in the play, Howard Schless notes. There is also a clearly drawn parallel between Noah and God: "Like God's chastisement of disobedient man with its subsequent harmony of the new creation, Noah's human, realistic chastisement of his wife will reassert order and bring them into a completely harmonious relationship."[22] While one might wish for a more sensitive phrase than "human, realistic chastisement of his wife," it is worth noting that Schless speaks not of obedience in the marriage, but of order and harmony. The distinction is developed at convincing length in Josie P. Campbell's argument that the Noah play turns not on submission or obedience but on love: Noah's love of God, and Uxor's love of Noah and her family.[23]

The Towneley play, like Chester's and York's, emphasizes Uxor's affinities with the audience by stressing her inability to comprehend the commands of God. In Towneley, the form which that inability takes is one of fear. When the ark is completed, Noah is at last able to tell his wife of the flood (300–312). Uxor's immediate reaction is fright: "I wote neuer whedir; / I dase and I dedir / For ferd of that tayll" (313–15). She is so frightened that she follows her family to the ark; there her dread of the ship and what it represents to her emerge in the form of a scathing observation about Noah's nautical design:

> I was neuer bard ere, as euer myght I the,
> In sich an oostré as this!
> In fath, I can not fynd
> Which is before, which is behynd.
> Bot shall we here by pynd,
> Noe, as haue thou blis?
>
> (328–33)

No amount of persuasion from Noah or his sons' wives will get Uxor into the ark. She sits down to spin upon a hill, refusing to move even when told that she may spin in the ship.

Only when Uxor's fear of drowning becomes greater than her fear of the ship does she flee to the safety of the ark. The persuasive element is physical, the flood is actually felt: "Yie, water nyghys so nere that I sit not

dry; / Into ship with a byr, therfor, will I hy / For drede that I drone here"
(370–72). As she enters the ark,[24] Noah gives her a blow which leads to a
final, full-scale brawl. Noah chides her for hesitating and answers her
taunts with blows (373–87). The fight is interrupted when Noah and Uxor
in turn address the audience. Noah's concluding lines are an appropriately
timed reminder of God's punishment of scorn: "Bot I, / As haue I blys, /
Shall chastyse this" (40l–3). The echo of Uxor's earlier "Bot shall we here
be pynd, / Noe, as haue thou blis?" is clear; only after this last fight is her
question fully answered. The battle ends when Noah's sons intervene,
begging their parents to stop. The press of business and the exhaustion of
husband and wife signal the establishment of marital harmony:

> We will do as ye bid ys; we will no more be wroth,
> Dere barnes.
> Now to the helme will I hent,
> And to my ship tent.
>
> (418–21)

Note that this fight, like the first one, has no real victor. "Neither is the
loser, and both are the winners," Campbell writes. She goes on to observe
that

> Kolve is right in the sense that "mastre" is the key to the brawling; it
> shapes the farce that contains the dramatic action between Noah and
> his wife. But "mastre" does not mean that Noah restores (or gains)
> domination over Uxor, despite what may be the "standard" medieval
> idea that a wife owes submission to her husband, analogous to the
> Church's submission to her Head. What does occur in the play as a
> result of the final battle is the disappearance of this notion of "mastre";
> it simply drops out of the play as an irrelevance as a new spirit of accord
> takes over.[25]

The Towneley Uxor plays a more important role during the Flood itself
than do her Chester and York counterparts. In the Towneley play, she
takes the helm of the ship while Noah lowers a plummet (433–37), she
announces the reappearance of the sun (452–55), and she gives thanks for
God's mercy as the flood wanes (458–59, 463–71). Yet there is an ambivalence here, too: Uxor mistakenly chooses the raven as the bird which
will "come agane sone" (472–80).[26] As in the York play, she asks about
those whom God has destroyed: "From thens agayn / May thai neuer
wyn?" (548–49). To this plaintive question Noah can only respond by
reminding Uxor, and the spectators, of the promise of eternal grace and
salvation in "his light" (550–58).

The promise of salvation foretells the Judgment; Noah's final line emphasizes the position of the Flood as one part of a great cycle stretching

from Creation to Doomsday. In the Noah play in each cycle, Noah's wife helps to link the account of the Deluge with the plays that have gone before and those that will follow. The Chester, York, and Towneley cycles take pains to show that the tendency to scorn exhibited by Uxor will not finally be expunged until that deluge of fire described in 2 Peter. While the progress of Christian history demands that Uxor board the ark, the nature of Christian typology and the reflexive play between drama and audience allow her doubt, her fear, her scoffing to be dramatized again and again. The essence of Uxor's character is far less wifely disobedience than the need to "see neede." Noah's wife enacts a pattern seen in Eve, Joseph, Mary's midwife, Thomas, and countless others unnamed and unconvinced.

Within the individual plays of the Flood at Chester, York, and Wakefield, situations calling for a divided response to Uxor, a response that sees her as a redeemable scoffer, form the very structure of her progress from doubt to belief. The comic scenes of marital strife do indeed "efficaciously purge the spirit of rebellion from the characters, and through them, from the spectators,"[27] but in order to do so, the scenes must first summon that spirit of rebellion. Such moments of communion between drama and spectator are, like the Balinese cockfights so closely observed by Clifford Geertz, "not merely reflections of a pre-existing sensibility analogically represented; they are positive agents in the creation and maintenance of such a sensibility."[28] The movement from sympathetic portrayal of the scoffer to the purgation of scorn is the progress of Noah's wife, but each stage in the process is marked by an ambivalence never fully resolved. That ambivalence is crucial: it marks the position of the play within the cycle, and it is the essential element providing an engaged affinity between spectator and play.

There is a point in Chaucer's *Miller's Tale* when Nicholas is describing to John how the rains will come and destroy the world. Analogy with the tradition of Noah's recalcitrant wife serves Nicholas' purpose well:

> "Hastow nat herd," quod Nicholas, "also
> The sorwe of Noë with his felawshipe,
> Er that he mighte gete his wyf to shipe?
> Him had be lever, I dar wel undertake,
> At thilke tyme, than alle hise watheres blake,
> That she hadde had a ship hir-self allone.[29]

Chaucer's miller may have given us a fine comment on the Noah plays at Chester, York, and Wakefield, for this particular teller of tales sustains a double vision. That vision encompasses both Nicholas's realistic appraisal of the scorner and a wonderfully comic sense of the absolute necessity—discovered too late by John—of getting Noah's wife into that single ark.

NOTES

A version of this paper was read years ago by S. F. Johnson in connection with one of his drama seminars at Columbia. I appreciated his comments then and acknowledge gratefully now that his constant emphasis on audience response—which he insisted on studying long before it became fashionable—infuses this analysis. I am also and more recently grateful to my colleagues in the Mellon Seminar on the Arts and Humanities, who convened in the spring of 1985 at Mount Holyoke College to study three medieval texts, for giving me new ways to consider a character who had long intrigued me.

1. 2 Peter 3:3–7, King James Version.

2. See Rosemary Woolf, *The English Mystery Plays* (Berkeley: University of California Press, 1972), pp. 133–34, and Anna Jean Mill, "Noah's Wife Again," *PMLA* 56 (1941): 613–26.

3. Woolf, *English Mystery Plays,* p. 133.

4. Woolf, *English Mystery Plays,* p. 139.

5. The best discussions of this parallel appear in V. A. Kolve, *The Play Called Corpus Christi* (Stanford: Stanford University Press, 1966), pp. 146–51, in Alan H. Nelson, " 'Sacred' and 'Secular' Currents in the Towneley Play of Noah," *Drama Survey* 3 (1964): 399, and in Howard H. Schless, "The Comic Element in the Wakefield Noah," *Studies in Medieval Literature,* ed. MacEdward Leach (Philadelphia: University of Pennsylvania Press, 1961), pp. 237–38. But see, for an argument against this analogy, Josie P. Campbell, "The Idea of Order in the Wakefield *Noah,*" *Chaucer Review* 10 (1975): 76–86.

6. See Richard J. Daniels, *"Uxor* Noah: A Raven or a Dove?" *Chaucer Review* 14 (1979): 25; Woolf, pp. 140–41; and Oscar L. Brownstein, "Revision in the 'Deluge' of the Chester Cycle," *Speech Monographs* 36 (1969): 55–65. Brownstein concludes from linguistic evidence that the text combines an old play (OP), stanzas 1–12, 15–24, and 33–48, with a new play (NP), stanzas 13–14, 25–28, and 31–32. Uxor is disobedient in the NP stanzas, but obedient (like the Uxor of the *Ludus Coventriae*) in OP. Brownstein's discussion of "reviser's intrusions" is convincing but ultimately strays from the point, which is the authority of the text as we have it.

7. Woolf, *English Mystery Plays,* p. 141.

8. *The Chester Mystery Cycle,* ed. R. M. Lumiansky and David Mills, vol. 1, Early English Text Society, supplementary series 3 (London: Oxford, 1974), ll. 65–68. Lumiansky and Mills relegate to an appendix lines 257–304 (the raven and the dove scene) of the edition of Herman Deimling, ed., *The Chester Plays,* vol. 1 Early English Text Society, extra series 62 (1892; reprint, London: Oxford, 1968). At one point in my discussion I refer to Deimling's text; all other references are to the newer one.

9. E.g., Kolve, *Corpus Christi,* p. 149.

10. Woolf insists that "the authors manifestly do not intend" Uxor's attachment to her friends to be seen as a sympathetic sign of human feeling (*English Mystery Plays,* p. 140). If we can talk about dramatists' intentions at all, I think the authors manifestly do intend this, though not only this.

11. Kolve, *Corpus Christi,* p. 263.

12. Alan D. Justice, "Trade Symbolism in the York Cycle," *Theatre Journal* 31 (1979):47–58.

13. *Noah and His Wife, the Flood and its Waning,* ed. Lucy Toulmin Smith, *York Plays* (Oxford: Oxford University Press, 1885; reprint, 1963), ll. 5–6.

14. Cf. the Newcastle Shipwright's Play, in which Uxor is visited by the devil, who persuades her to administer a potion to Noah in order to determine God's

scheme for the salvation of the family. An interesting and typologically important variation of this motif occurs in the York play of Pilate's wife's dream, where the devil again uses a woman to try to thwart the redemption. The relation of both events to Eve's seduction by the serpent is obvious.

15. E.g., Daniels, "Raven or Dove."

16. See, for example, Woolf, *English Mystery Plays,* p. 143, and Nelson, "Sacred and Secular," p. 397.

17. Nelson, "Sacred and Secular," pp. 394, 401.

18. *Processus Noe cum Filiis,* ed. A. C. Cawley, *The Wakefield Pageants in the Towneley Cycle* (Manchester: Manchester University Press, 1958), ll. 163–65.

19. Daniels, "Raven or Dove," p. 26.

20. Woolf, *English Mystery Plays,* p. 143.

21. Nelson, "Sacred and Secular," p. 396.

22. Schless, "Comic Element," pp. 237–38. I am not sure this is as peculiar to Towneley as Schless insists. Force or threat of force is used against Uxor in York and Chester as well, as Schless himself observes on p. 236. The situations are different in each case, but the typology seems to turn on the same relationship.

23. Josie P. Campbell, "The Idea of Order in the Wakefield *Noah,*" *Chaucer Review* 10 (1975): 76–86.

24. The text does not indicate whether the fight takes place at the door of the ark or inside it, but the location may not be as crucial as Woolf and others think. The significance of the ark as a vehicle of human salvation depends on the coming of the flood, which, while near enough to frighten Uxor into the ship at l. 370, appears not to have deluged the earth until *after* the brawl (see ll. 424–26).

25. Campbell, "Idea of Order," p. 82.

26. Noah's comparison of the hungry, irrational raven to the gentle and trustworthy dove (499–506) may also serve as his metaphor for the two aspects of Uxor, one revealed before the Flood, the other during and after it. The possibility is attractive, but the text does not urge it. The scene does, as Daniels notes, illustrate "the charity and restraint which Noah and his wife [now] display toward one another" (p. 28).

27. Nelson, "Sacred and Secular," p. 400.

28. Clifford Geertz, "Deep Play: Notes on the Balinese Cockfight," *The Interpretation of Cultures* (New York: Basic Books, 1973), p. 451.

29. Geoffrey Chaucer, *Canterbury Tales,* ed. Walter W. Skeat (Oxford: Oxford University Press, 1927), A3538–43.

The Polemical Drama of John Bale

Rainer Pineas

S. F. Johnson has pointed out that Bale's *Kinge Johan* is a protestantization of the miracle play, just as in other plays Bale had protestantized the mystery play—and that the polemical drama of John Bale represents a deliberate attack on the "popetly playes" of the medieval church and an attempt to replace that drama with a Protestant substitute.[1] It is the purpose of this paper to examine the polemical content and technique of these plays and demonstrate that Bale's overriding and constant concern was anti-Catholic polemic; that, contrary to recent criticism,[2] to further this sole concern he sacrificed consistency, historical accuracy, dramatic forms and traditions, save those which served him polemically, any interest in biblical dispensations or periodization of prophecy except to use them as polemical weapons—and that he had no use for historical, philosophical, or theological investigations of the nature of evil other than to demonstrate that the ultimate culmination of all evil was to be found in the Bishop and Church of Rome.

Beginning probably with the "mystery" or biblical plays *The Chefe Promyses of God*,[3] *Johan Baptystes preachynge in the Wyldernesse*,[4] and *The Temptacyon of Our Lorde*,[5] all three written before 1538, Bale introduced into what has been seen as a deliberate "cycle"[6] progressively more numerous and more vehement Protestant colorations of his biblical material. *Chefe Promyses* sticks fairly closely to the biblical account of God's promises to Adam, Noah, Abraham, Moses, David, Isaiah, and John the Baptist. The audience is warned not to trust in "fantasyes fayned" (sig. A2); Adam is a good Protestant who makes the point that he is justified by faith and not by works (sig. A4), echoed by Noah (sigs. B1v, B3) and Abraham (sig. C1v); image-making comes in for heavy condemnation (sigs. B3, D1), but this play is unique in Bale's extant corpus in not being blatantly propagandistic at the expense of its ostensible "plot." Whether Bale wrote these plays in chronological sequence or not is impossible to determine, but by the time we come to *Johan Baptystes Preachynge*, the tone is decidedly polemical. There is greater emphasis on justification by faith alone (e.g., pp. 132, 140) and that only the Scriptures are authoritative (p. 131). The Pharisees and Sadducees of John's time have become the

Catholic clergy of Bale's (p. 137), sodomites[7] who corrupt Scripture to set up their own ceremonies and traditions for monetary gain (pp. 138, 147), who consider John a "heretic" (p. 141) and deride his doctrine as "new learning" (pp. 137, 139, 140, 142), a favorite pejorative term used by Catholics for the Reformed faith.[8] Lest any spectator should have missed the point, Bale appears in his own person at the end of the play to say:

> John was a preacher—note well what he did teach:
> Not men's traditions. . . .
> To say long prayers, nor to wander in the desert. . . .
> The justice of men is but an hypocrisy. . . .
> Hear neither Francis, Benedict, nor Bruno . . .
> Believe neither Pope, nor priest. . . .
>
> (pp. 148–49)

The last play in the series, *The Temptacyon of Our Lorde*, abandons completely any pretense that the dramatization of the biblical material is anything other than a convenient point of departure for anti-Catholic polemics, and nothing is further from the truth than the assertion that the biblical "source is faithfully though lengthily reproduced."[9] Bale thoroughly perverts his source for polemical purposes, and at one point has Satan—who had been disguised as a Catholic hermit and then unfrocked (sigs. D1v–D2)—prophesy to Christ that

> Thy vycar at Rome I thynke will be my frynde.
>
> (sig. E3)

Satan's approach to the Scriptures, furthermore, is not only typically Catholic but also as extrascriptural as his prophecy concerning the Pope (sig. D3v), while he claims the allegiance of "false prestes and byshoppes" (sig. E3). Jesus, on the other hand, is a model Reformer (sig. D1), opposed by the "byshoppes" (sig. D2v), who denounces the clerical celibacy demanded by the Act of Six Articles of 1539 (sig. E1v). The play also warns of persecution to come as a result of the Act and counsels Christians patiently to suffer—"Resyst not the worlde. . . ."[10] In view of the above, it is rather surprising to read about the three plays discussed that their "controversial elements are very subdued. . . . It is only when they are seen in connection with *Thre Lawes* that the biblical plays gain the controversial significance which, otherwise, is largely left to the imagination of the spectators."[11]

Into these biblical plays, then, Bale introduced Protestant colorations to make the point that the sixteenth-century Church of Rome was anti-Christian and that it was he and his coreligionists who were fulfilling the will of God. His methods were extremely simple. He anachronistically had the forces of good, such as Christ and John, preach Protestantism while attacking Catholicism and at the same time identified the forces of evil, such as Satan and the Jews, with the Church of Rome. Some of the specific techniques he used to accomplish this will be discussed later.

Even more important, in *A comedy concernynge thre lawes*[12] (before 1538) and *King Johan*[13] (ca. 1536), he transformed the morality play, which had been the specific vehicle through which the Catholic Church had inculcated doctrine, into a medium for advancing the Protestant viewpoint and denigrating the Church of Rome. Once again his technique was simple. As he had done in his biblical plays, so in his protestantization of the morality play he took advantage of a medium with ready-made good and evil characters—and it was this and only this facet of the morality that interested Bale—and merely turned the morality Vices into Catholics and the Virtues into Protestants, again by methods to be examined later. To these two essential tactics of his propaganda, he added in *King Johan* a dramatization of a Protestant version of history that he had inherited from the prose tracts of William Tyndale,[14] which portray John as the secular antipapal hero, just as in his biblical plays he had made Christ into the spiritual leader of the crusade against Rome.

The ostensible plot of *Thre Lawes* consists of the corruption of the Laws of Nature, Moses, and Christ by what are anachronistically identified in all three cases as Catholic Vices—thus making Bale's favorite and constantly reiterated point that the Church of Rome has always been the servant of God's archenemy, Satan, and that it is not merely the current manifestation of evil in the world but rather the culmination of all the evil there ever was. The very structure of the play is made to serve Bale's anti-Catholic purpose, since the Law of Nature is corrupted by the unnatural acts of idolatry and sodomy, which prepares the way for the parallel corruption of the Law of Christ, with the implication that Catholicism is also unnatural. Again, the Law of Moses continually declares its own inadequacy perpetually to atone for sin through "darke ceremonyes" (sig. C6v). Moreover, even a cursory reading of the play reveals that Bale is not really interested in the tracing of God's will through the various biblical dispensations, but only in anti-Catholic polemic. Well over ninety per cent of the play consists of outrageously anachronistic fulminations against the Church of Rome.

King Johan is a combination miracle-morality-history play, whose object is to demonstrate that what Bale regards as the treasonous activities of the Catholic Church in his own time are merely the current manifestation of an ancient Catholic conspiracy against European and especially English rulers. The "tragedy" of John, as Johnson has pointed out,[15] is brought about neither by Fortune nor any weakness in the hero, but rather through the machinations of the Church of Rome.[16]

Turning to examine some specific polemical techniques Bale employed in these plays, we find that they can be broken down into major and minor categories. The major category comprises the use of the mystery and morality play conventions, the polemical use of the morality play Vice, and the controversial use of history and the history play. Bale Protestantized the Catholic mystery play not by selecting biblical material different from that used by his Catholic predecessors but by utilizing the biblical material merely as a platform from which to launch anti-Catholic polemics. The intent of *Johan Baptystes Preachynge* is not to acquaint an illiterate laity with the Gospel narrative—no one was more insistent than Bale that one should search the Scriptures for oneself; it is, rather, to identify the Catholic clergy of his own day with those who killed Christ (pp. 137, 139, 140, 141, 142), who in their Mass and their claims for that ceremony perpetuate his murder and not his resurrection (p. 147), who vaingloriously seek to be justified by ceremonies and traditions with which they have burdened Christ's flock—not even motivated by a sincere belief in the corrrectness of their doctrine, but, hypocrites as they are, motivated by a desire for financial advantage (pp. 138, 147).

The fact that *The Temptacyon* scarcely deals with the biblical narrative as such might raise the question of why Bale bothered at all to tether his polemics to the Gospel account instead of dispensing with it completely and simply writing straightforward dramatic invective. To this question two answers suggest themselves. First, if the chronological order of his "cycle" is indeed the order of composition, then it would appear that Bale began his dramatic venture with relative caution, becoming increasingly polemical with each play. It would certainly have been prudent on Bale's part to be able to claim that he was doing nothing more than dramatizing biblical narrative.[17] But much more important than that, Bale vehemently insisted on his anti-Catholic polemic having its roots in the Scriptures, for this permitted him to claim that in opposing Rome, he was merely denouncing what the Scriptures themselves condemned, and as has been pointed out, in *The Temptacyon* this great Bibliolater did not scruple to add to the text of Scripture to make that point. And so the medium of the "mystery" play served Bale actually to create a biblical narrative which was as "pliable" as the Bible created by William Tyndale.[18]

Bale approached the conventions of the morality play in exactly the same spirit as he had those of the mystery: those he found useful for his polemical purposes he retained; the others he discarded, for he was completely uninterested in these conventions for their own sake, just as he had absolutely no interest in founding any new dramatic genres.[19]

The most important convention of the morality retained by Bale is the Vice and his function. In the pre-Reformation morality, one of these functions had been to aid the Virtues in the preaching of truth, but what had been mere artlessness and lack of verisimilitude in the medieval play was transformed by Bale in his polemical moralities into a highly effective technique of controversy by having even the opposition in its candid and unguarded moments condemn itself and declare itself actually in agreement with the viewpoint of the playwright—a powerful endorsement of his position and an impugning of his opponents' honesty. Again, just as in the medieval play the identity and traditional motivelessness of the Vice—who is evil by definition and not by cause or circumstance—was naively announced by the Vice himself, so in his moralities Bale transforms the Vice's original simplicity into self-condemnatory satire, in that the Vice is made to brand himself as a Catholic through techniques to be examined later.

Bale's modification of the traditional Vice role can be seen in the fact that in his two moralities all of the evil characters are Vices. Thus in *Thre Lawes*, while Infidelity is the common denominator to the corruption of all three Laws, Bale himself refers to "the six vyces, or the frutes of Infydelyte" (sig. G1v). In *King Johan*, it is not just one character, Sedition, but also Clergy, Dissimulation, Usurped Power, Private Wealth, and Treason who fulfill the Vice function. For what Bale has done is to discard all the traditional elements of that role which did not serve his polemical purpose and retain only those which did, leaving him free to saddle any and all of his Catholic characters with Vice attributes. It should be noted that this treatment of the traditional Vice role described above is entirely typical of his general polemical technique: his constant aim is to have the best not just of both but, preferably, of a multiplicity of worlds. A good illustration of Bale's selective use of dramatic convention is his handling of the Vice's traditional disguise of his name to dupe his victim. The reason Sedition does not attempt to hide his name from John is not, as one critic has thought, that Bale wants to show that it is not by stealth but openly and insolently that Antichrist walks the earth,[20] but rather that the Vice's concealment of his true identity is normally part of his technique of seduction; and in *King Johan* there is no attempt to seduce the hero, who—also counter to morality tradition—never falls from virtue and remains perfect throughout the play.

Another aspect of the Vice's attempt to disguise his identity from his intended victim was through use of costume, and Bale avails himself of this tradition when it suits his purpose—even in nonmoralities such as *The Temptacyon*, where, as has been noted, Satan was masquerading in the attire of a Catholic hermit. As will be seen, Bale often uses the "disguise" of the Vice actually to reveal his true nature to the audience, but perhaps his single most brilliant use of the entire convention is his suggestion— through the Vice Sedition in *King Johan*—that not as pretense in a play but in actuality all Catholic clergy are Vices who disguise their malign designs on mankind under a cloak of holiness—their clerical vestments (2571–72; cf. 66).

Again Bale breaks with the tradition of the Vice—who is supposed to be an allegorical abstraction—when he identifies the Vice Sedition with Stephen Langton, the historical Archbishop of Canterbury of John's time. However confusing this may be to some critics,[21] Bale has very clear polemical reasons for his melding of allegory and history. First, beyond the evident implications of the name itself, Bale makes sure that he has demonstrated Sedition to be a thoroughly evil character in the play before he is identified with the Archbishop, the Pope's puppet appointment to Canterbury. And second, the technique permits Bale maximum flexibility, in that his "confusion" of Langton with Sedition leaves him free to imply that certain actions he attributes to the former are historical, when in fact they never occurred.[22]

Bale's use of secular and ecclesiastical history is the third major element of his polemical drama, and as might be expected, his basic attitude to the "convention" of history was the same as that to all the other conventions he inherited: he retained what he thought would be polemically useful and discarded—or changed—the rest. The best illustration of this historical selectivity is Bale's choice of material for *King Johan*. It was this monarch's opposition to Rome that attracted Bale—and nothing else in John's reign.[23]

Bale approached English and European history with a very definite bias. Briefly stated, his theory of history—the rudiments of which he inherited from William Tyndale and which he perfected—maintained that for centuries the affairs of the European states had been conducted for the benefit of the Pope and that secular rulers were merely the puppets of papal policy, retained in power only so long as they obeyed the dictates of Rome, to be removed—as was King John of England—the moment they proved recalcitrant. Onto this secular conspiracy theory was grafted its ecclesiastical complement, namely, that the original purity of the Church of Christ—and of England—became corrupted insidiously and gradually through the machinations of Rome, which depended on Roman ritual, language, and dogma to achieve what sometimes force could not.

Clearly, Bale's most important polemical use of history in his drama was the creation of King John as the first English Protestant martyr, saint, defender of the divine right of kings, and champion of the English crown's claim to the title of Supreme Head of the Church of England. Bale's portrayal of John has puzzled at least one editor of the play, who finds that "what is not so clear is the motive or incentive that Bale had for 'whitewashing' King John and writing him up as against the Church."[24] As indicated previously, what is in fact completely clear is that the " 'white-

washing' of King John and writing him up as against the Church" is Bale's
only motive at all for treating the events of John's reign, and as the first
entry in a new calendar of English Protestant saints and martyrs, John had
to be as perfect in all respects as were Bale's nondramatic contributions to
this list, Anne Askew and Sir John Oldcastle,[25] or the later dramatic
"creations" of Thomas Cromwell and Queen Elizabeth in *Cromwell* (1602)
and Heywood's *If You Know not Me* (1605–6).[26] But Bale had an even
more important motive in the creation of John than to demonstrate that he
was a forerunner of those mentioned above and—especially—of Henry
VIII, of whom he was clearly meant to be the prototype. That motive was
to demonstrate the ancient nature of English Protestantism and how it was
extirpated for four hundred years through the machinations of the Church
of Rome.

   And so we get a picture of John, who is always concerned about the
welfare of his people, wishing "To reforme the lawes" and seek "trew
iustyce" (21–22), who rendered justice impartially to clergy and laity alike
(1280 ff.), who thinks of the welfare of "England" rather than his own
(527), and who eventually makes the supreme sacrifice of resigning his
office to the power of Rome for the sake of the people and the land he loves
(1705–12). He is a saint, in fact, sometimes almost a Christ-figure, married
to his Bride, England, as the Church is the Bride of Christ (1615). While his
Catholic murderer dies "for the churche with Thomas of Canterberye,"
(2132), John's final words are:

> There is no malyce to the malyce of the
>   clergye. . . .
> For doynge iustyce they have euer hated
>   me. . . .
> I haue sore hungred and thirsted
>   ryghteousnesse.
>
> (2158–67)

And he is above all a Protestant saint, surely the most Bible-quoting
monarch in all of English drama, an expert in the Pauline epistles (54–55),
equally at home in the Old Testament (1404–7), insistent on Gospel
preaching (1391), and, like Bale himself, with one sure touchstone for
Church doctrine and practice:

> Prove yt by scriptur, and than wyll I
>   yt alowe.
>
> (1435)

   Bale's selectivity in dealing with the historical material available to him
regarding John's reign goes far beyond ignoring neutral or negative aspects
and extends to a wholesale refashioning of events and his hero's character.

As Adams points out, Bale's claim that only the Catholic and "Roman" historian Polydore Vergil was responsible for John's negative reputation, and that all the other authorities he cites "attest to John's noble virtues . . . is at best highly misleading" (p. 27). In fact, as Adams goes on to demonstrate, the authorities Bale cites as ostensibly giving a more sympathetic—and, therefore, more correct—picture of John do no such thing, and "Bale was serving his own polemical ends in attempting to saddle him [i.e., Vergil] with the full blame for the traditional antipathy toward King John" (p. 30). Adams is entirely justified in adding that Bale's unwarranted citation of historical authorities here is "not out of keeping with his treatment of other historical authorities" (p. 29). In fact, it was one of Bale's favorite tactics in his polemical use of history.[27] Apart from the "creation" of the King John material, Bale's most striking polemical use of history in his plays involves his documentation of the conspiracy theory previously mentioned, namely, that the Catholic clergy have historically been a subversive element in England, and that if the Pope is momentarily unable to achieve domination of the realm by force, he will attempt to do so surreptitiously through the use of Roman rite, language, and doctrine.

As will be seen later, the oaths Bale assigned to his Catholic characters are of particular significance in themselves and merit separate treatment, but two are of special significance to his accusations of Catholic subversion, for they indirectly involve the greatest champions of the Church Bale opposed. The oaths are uttered by Infidelity in *Thre Lawes*, who first swears "by the blessed rode of kent" (sig. B5) and then "by the holy Nunne" (sig. D1v). These references by the Catholic Vice are clearly to Elizabeth Barton, the Nun of Kent, who was executed for treason after prophesying Henry VIII's death should he "divorce" Catherine of Aragon. But Bale is probably after a bigger catch than the unhappy Nun, namely, Thomas More and Cardinal John Fisher, the leaders of the Catholic opposition to the Reformation in England, who were executed for treason about the time Bale was writing his plays (1535). Both were implicated in the Nun's treason, and although More was eventually cleared—which Bale surely knew—he evidently could not resist the temptation to implicate the revered Catholic champion in treason even before the formal charge was made; for he accuses More of treasonous involvement with the Nun again in a later work.[28] To his list of prominent English Catholics who are current manifestations of the ancient Catholic conspiracy, Bale adds the name of Cardinal Pole (*L*, sig. F8v).

While the entire play dealing with the reign of John is meant to illustrate how Rome uses the threat of force to bring a recalcitrant monarch to his knees, even in that situation the point is made that this threat is credible only because of the hold Rome has over people through its doctrine and ceremonies. "I am Sedycyon, that with þe pope wyll hold" (90), proclaims

the character who was born in Rome and who will become Steven Langton. And it is through the priestly power to forgive or retain sin that Rome
shall rule England, he prophesies:

> *Quodcumque ligaueris* I trow wyll playe
> soch a parte
> That I shall abyde in Englond, magry
> yowr harte,
> Tushe, the pope ableth me to subdewe
> bothe kyng and keyser.
>
> (97–99)

The Pope promises remission of sins to all "Crysten princes" who will
undertake to invade England and slay John (1070–72). John's murderer is
promised eternal salvation for his deed (2123–26).

Bale and other radical Reformers—especially Bale's close friend,
William Turner[29]—took the position that Henry VIII had been duped by
his conservative bishops into halting the English Reformation when it had
scarcely begun. They contended that Rome had lost only a battle and not
the war, that through the retention of Roman custom and ritual in the
Church of England, Rome retained a foothold in the realm, a beachhead
from which to launch new attempts to restore the realm to Roman rule
should the opportunity arise. That is the point, for instance, of Sedition's
derisive question to John, who has just asserted that he intends to be
master in his own household, including the English Church:

> Ye are well content that bysshoppes contynew styll?
> K. John. We are so in dede. . . .
> Sed. Nay, than, good inowgh. Yowr awtoryte and powrr
> Shall passe as they wyll. . . .
>
> (235–38)

So long as Roman rite and custom is retained in the Church, Rome rules:

> Sed. In your parlement commaunde yow what ye wyll,
> The popes ceremonyes shall drowne the Gospell styll. . . .
> If your true subiectes impugne their trecheryes,
> They can fatche them in anon for sacramentaryes. . . .
> Get they false wytnesses, they force not of whens they be. . . .
> Parauenture a thousande are in one byshoppes boke,
> And agaynst a daye are readye to the hooke.
>
> (2522–37)

In the above lines Bale is very probably making a scathing reference to
the conservative provisions of the *Bishops Book* (1537), which "restored"
the full complement of the traditional sacraments to the Church of En-

gland—as well as intending the expression as a Bishops' proscription list
of Reformers. The juxtaposition of the two ideas is not unintentional. Bale
cleverly portrays the radical Reformers as the true loyalists and the con-
servatives as crypto-Catholics when he has Sedition tell Imperial Majesty,
i.e., Henry VIII:

> Ye gaue iniunctyons that Gods wurde myghte be taught,
> But who obserue them? Full manye a time haue I laught
> To see the conneyaunce that prelates and priestes can fynde.
> *I. Maj.* And whie do they beare Gods wurde no better mynde?
> *Sed.* For if that were knowne than woulde the people regarde
> No heade but their prynce. . . .
>
> (2508–13)

And by making the character Verity "a personification of Reformation
doctrine," as Adams describes him (p. 149), a servant of Henry VIII (2318
ff.) in *King Johan,* Bale flatters the King and perpetuates the useful
fiction—from which he never departed, even after Henry's death—that
Henry really favored the Reformers but was regrettably misled later by his
conservative bishops.

In the minor category of Bale's specific polemical techniques have to be
included his deliberate use of anachronism, ways of identifying the morality Vices as Catholics, and various techniques for condemning the opposition. Farmer's rueful comment that "Bale is not . . . always innocent of
anachronism" (p. 309) is not only extreme understatement but also reveals
a misapprehension of Bale's purpose, for the playwright's use of anachronism is so sustained and pervasive that it has to be regarded as one of his
most important polemical weapons. The anachronistic elements in his
mystery plays have already been mentioned. Ironically, by far the heaviest
use of anachronism occurs in *Thre Lawes,* the play in which Bale is
ostensibly treating the various dispensations of God's dealings with man.
The most obvious and constant anachronistic reminder to the audience of
what Bale's real subject was while the play was supposedly treating the
Law of Nature and the Law of Moses is the dress of the Vices. Bale was
very specific in indicating their attire (*L,* sig. G1v), and considering that
the Laws of Nature and Moses were subverted by Vices dressed as friars,
monks, bishops, and canon lawyers, it would have been very difficult for
the audience to miss the point.

The play has scarcely begun when into the Garden of Eden intrudes the
Catholic Vice Infidelity dressed as a friar and ready to peddle paxes and
images of Catholic saints, whose specific virtues he extolls, while swearing by the yet nonexistent "masse" (sig. A6 ff.). As previously mentioned,
how little Bale cares about consistency in general and biblical dispensations in particular in this play is demonstrated by the fact that one of the

figures who subverts Law of Nature is the Vice Sodomy, dressed as a
monk! It is fairly clear that in this instance Bale sacrifices overall consistency—not to mention verisimilitude—for the immediate polemical advantage to be gained by thus representing the opposition. And this is
absolutely typical of his polemical technique: his prime objective is always
and exclusively the polemical point. Bale is simply using the *form* of the
dispensations, not to make the tautological point that evil has always
existed, but specifically to show that the kind of evil that produces Catholicism has been present since the Creation. To reinforce this concept he
makes certain to have identifiably Catholic figures in the Garden of Eden.

The Catholic Vice Infidelity uses necromancy—"I coniure yow both
here" (sig. B2v)—to summon to his aid both Sodomy the monk, and
Idolatry, dressed as "an olde wytche" (sig. G1v). The anti-Catholic point
might be somewhat less obvious than is expressed by presenting a Vice
dressed as a monk, but it would undoubtedly be apparent to the audience,
for the charge of necromancy was a classic one made by the Reformers.
One of its cleverest applications was to the Catholic doctrine of the Real
Presence, which was the subject of ridicule of an entire Protestant play,
Jacke Jugeler.[30] But Catholic Eucharistic doctrine was not the only target
of the Reformers' charge of necromancy; the cult of the saints was another,
and this is the point of Sodomy's mock-encomium of Idolatry—all still
ostensibly in the dispensation of Nature:

> Mennys fortunes she can tell.
> She can by sayenge her Auemarye,
> And by other charmes of sorcerye,
> Ease men of toth ake by and bye,
> Yea, and fatche the deuyll from hell.
> She can mylke the cowe and hunte the foxe,
> And helpe men of the ague and poxe,
> So they brynge moneye to the boxe
> Whan they to her make mone.
>
> (sig. B3)

With the true economy of the master craftsman, Bale makes four points in
the satiric lines above: that Catholic saint worship is idolatry, that it is
either superstitious nonsense or else involves sorcery, and that, whatever
else it may intend, it makes money for the Catholic clergy, which is their
prime motive for encouraging the practice. Not too modest to sing her own
praise, Idolatry adds (and all this long before the birth of Christ):

> Yong chyldren can I charme . . .
> With crossynges and with kyssynges
> With blasynges and with blessynges,
> That spretes do them no harme. . . .

With holye oyle and watter,
I can so cloyne and clatter
That I can at the latter
Manye suttyltees contryue.

(sig. B3v)

Examples could be multiplied, but one in particular, taken from the dispensation of the Law of Moses, makes the point perhaps better than any other. The Catholic Vice Avarice, attired as a canon lawyer, says of the Israelites:

Lete the cloysterers be brought vp euer in sylence,
Without the scriptures . . .
Se the laye people praye neuer but in latyne. . . .
If they haue Englysh, let it be for aduauntage,
For pardons, for Dyrges, for offerynges and pylgrymage.

(sig. D3v)

Since Bale's Protestantization of the morality play consisted simply of his catholicization of the Vice, we will now examine how this process was accomplished. The simplest and visually most obvious method, that of costume, has already been discussed. In the case of the Vice's name, Bale once again turned what had been mere artlessness in the medieval moral-ity—where each character, including the Vice, was named according to his quality and announced that name to the audience—into a polemical weapon. For instance, Sedition's announcement at the opening of *King Johan*,

I am Sedycyon, that with þe pope wyll hold,

(90)

establishes not only a pejorative name but also simultaneously suggests an inevitable relationship for the remainder of the play. Again, the mere fact that a character with the name of Dissimulation is singing the litany at another point in the same play brands that action as parodic, in addition to parodic elements in the litany itself (639–41). The same effect is obtained when Dissimulation offers prayer to the saints; the very name of the suppliant bears a negative implication about the efficacy of such action (648). That the pope is called Usurped Power encapsulates the entire Protestant attitude to both the spiritual and temporal claims made by the Bishop of Rome (837). Further identification is achieved by what might be called the "parentage" device, which is simply an extension of the Vice's revelation of his name. When John asks England the reason for her distressed state, England replies:

The faulte was in þe clergye
That I, a wedow, apere to yow so barelye
K. John. Why in þe clargye. . . .
They are thy chylderne; þou owghtest
     to say them good.
Eng. Nay, bastardes they are, vnnatvrall. . . .
The wyld bore of Rome . . .
Lyke pyggys they folow. . . .

                                        (58–72)

Another method Bale used to identify the Vice as a Catholic was by
assigning him specifically Catholic oaths. While in the pre-Reformation
morality the Vice condemned himself first by swearing at all, and second
by demonstrating his allegiance to Satan by the nature of his oaths, Bale
identifies the Vice as a Catholic by having him swear by the Mass. The
frequent repetition of Catholic oaths in *Thre Lawes* (sigs. A7, C5v, C8, E1,
E2, F4) and in *King Johan* (ll. 50, 230, 280, 633, 916, 971) serves to remind
the audience of the Vices' allegiance after initially establishing it. But as
we have already seen, Bale also makes a more sophisticated use of the
Catholic oath than using it merely as a method of identification. The oaths
involving the Nun of Kent served to remind the audience of Catholic
treason in high places. The oath is associated with Catholic malice and
cruelty, when as the Vices are about to burn Law of Christ as a heretic in
Thre Lawes, Infidelity comments:

          By the messe I laugh, to se how thys
               gere doth wurke;

                                        (sig. F2)

and with murder, when John's poisoner is made to drink his own poison:

          By the masse, I dye, I dye!

                                        (2121)

Occasionally Bale uses the Catholic oath ironically, as when Sedition
swears "by Iesus" (43), and, even more clearly, "Be my fayth and trowth"
(47), to be followed shortly by "by þe messe, ye may beleve me!" (50).
     Having established the Vices as Catholics, Bale's next task is to demon-
strate that it is their Catholicism that is the specific origin of their evil. And
while—as in the pre-Reformation morality—some of the condemnation of
evil consists of straightforward denunciation by the good characters, most
of it, and by far the most effective, takes the form of having the Catholic
Vices inadvertently and unconsciously condemn themselves.
     One of the forms this self-condemnation takes is the Vices' parody of
Catholic ritual, through which Bale aims to make the original rite appear

ludicrous while implying that the parodic substitutions represent the cele-brants' true intent. Much of this type of parody in *King Johan* has been analyzed by Edwin Miller,[31] but at least one important example of parody seems to have escaped his attention. At a point in the play before they have succeeded with their plot against John, the Catholic Vices, Usurped Power and Private Wealth, sing the following:

> Us. P. *(syng this) Super flumina Babilonis*
> *suspendimus organa nostra.*
> Pr. W. *(syng this) Quomodo cantabimus*
> *canticum bonum in terra aliena?*
>
> (764–65)

The correct reading of Psalm 136:1–4 (Vulgate) is *canticum Domini,* for which Bale has substituted *canticum bonum.* The substitution seems harmless—and meaningless—until one remembers the convention associ-ated with the morality Vice and his song. As Bernard Spivack has pointed out,[32] the morality Vice typically sings a song of triumph in his perverse joy at being successful in his machinations or in anticipation of assured success. In his perverted scheme of values, his song celebrating evil becomes a "good" song. But at the point in the play where the parody appears the Vices have not yet succeeded, and their song is a song of frustration and complaint. They cannot yet sing their celebratory song in England (*"in terra aliena"*), because John has indeed made it a "strange land" for them by standing in the way of their malice and frustrating their evil intent. It is only when they have perfected their plan for John's downfall that they sing in gleeful anticipation of certain success (s.d. after 11. 828 and 1055), and then, finally, to celebrate that success itself:

> By the messe, Pandulphus, now maye
> we synge *Cantate,*
> And crowe *Confitebor,* with a
> ioyfull *Iubilate!*[33]
>
> (1692–93)

A similar pattern is followed in *Thre Lawes* (sigs. C1, D5, F6v). The foregoing is yet another example of Bale's highly selective utilization of the morality play tradition.

In his anti-Catholic polemical drama, Bale used as weapons against the Roman Church the very same dramatic forms he had inherited from that source. Whereas the Catholic mystery play had taught an illiterate laity the principal stories of their faith from the Old and New Testaments, Bale protestantized the mystery play to teach his audience justification by faith alone. While the medieval play taught the glories of martyrdom and the intercessory power of the saints, Bale adapted it to create the first Protestant "saint" in King John, martyred by that same Church because he held England dearer than life and believed that there was no intercessor but Christ. And Bale took the pre-Reformation morality play, the vehicle through which the Catholic Church taught that outside of that Church there was no salvation, and turned the play around to demonstrate that that very same Church was really the Synagogue of Satan, and thereby converted the morality into the single most potent anti-Catholic weapon in the Protestant arsenal.

As this study has sought to demonstrate, Bale was completely uninterested in the internal and overall consistency of his polemics or in historical or chronological accuracy—indeed, he fashioned anachronism into a deliberate device—or in dramatic forms and traditions other than those which he found useful polemically. But he was devastatingly consistent in the pursuit of his objective in all of his plays that have survived— which was to demonstrate that the Church and Bishop of Rome were the root cause and current repository of all evil.

NOTES

1. S. F. Johnson, "The Tragic Hero in Early Elizabethan Drama," *Studies in the English Renaissance Drama,* ed. J. W. Bennett et al. (New York: New York University Press, 1959), pp. 157–71.

2. See Thora B. Blatt, *The Plays of John Bale* (Copenhagen: G. E. C. Gad, 1968), pp. 35 ff., 71, 83–84, 107–8, 111–12, 127; Richard Bauckham, *Tudor Apocalypse* (Oxford: Courtenay Library of Reformation Classics, no. 8, 1978), pp. 1–89; Leslie P. Fairfield, *John Bale* (West Lafayette, Ind.: Purdue University Press, 1976), passim; John Bale, *King Johan,* ed. Barry B. Adams (San Marino: Huntington Library, 1969), pp. 62–63; Robert Potter, *The English Morality Play* (London: Routledge and Kegan Paul, 1975), p. 97. Thora Blatt's attempts to prove that Bale was consistent in his interpretation of biblical prophecy succeed only in accomplishing the opposite of what she intends. As proof of Bale's consistency, she cites a passage from Bale's *The Actes of English Votaryes, Part 2* where Bale is "explaining" a previous interpretation of the book of Revelation he now wishes to change:

> I tolde ye afore, that Sathan was tyed vp for that tyme. Not from doynge of myschefe, for that he hath wrought in all ages of the world. But he was sequestered from doynge thys greatest mischefe of all, in the Christen church. . . .
>
> (quoted in Blatt, p. 39)

Bale's "explanation" here is the most blatant sophistry. He has changed his original absolute "was tyed vp"—after he no longer needs it—to the now convenient relative "was tyed vp . . . . Not from doynge of myschefe. . . . But . . . from doynge thys greatest mischefe of all. . . ." Furthermore, the "different application of the Apocalypse in the two works" (Blatt, p. 38) is simply another device of Bale's to further his favorite polemical strategy of "eating his cake and having it too." In any case, Katherine Firth has established conclusively that Bale's identifications of the papacy with apocalyptic anti-Christian images do vary according to the polemical needs of the moment from one of Bale's works to another; indeed, that he is not even consistent with the same work—although this may not have been her intention. See Katherine R. Firth, *The Apocalyptic Tradition in Reformation Britain, 1530–1645* (Oxford: Oxford University Press, 1979), pp. 43, 51–53, 54, 55, 79.

3. The text used is that of *STC* 1305. Hereafter cited as *CP*.

4. The text used is in J. S. Farmer, ed. *The Dramatic Writings of John Bale* (London: Early English Drama Society, 1907). Hereafter cited as *JBP*.

5. The text used is that of *STC* 1279. Hereafter cited as *T*.

6. See Blatt, *Plays*, pp. 86–87.

7. P. 139. Contrary to Blatt's opinion, the anti-Catholic context makes it unmistakably clear that Bale is here using one of his favorite characterizations of the Roman clergy in both the literal and spiritual sense. See Blatt, *Plays*, p. 97.

8. An entire Protestant polemical play was written on this subject, with the ironic title *New Custome*. See Rainer Pineas, *Tudor and Early Stuart Anti-Catholic Drama* (Nieuwkoop: B. De Graaf, 1972), p. 8.

9. Blatt, *Plays*, p. 98.

10. Sigs. C4v–D1. Blatt (pp. 97–98) thinks that in this passage Bale is rebuking Henry, in that Bale refers to the persecution as coming from "rulers." However, as has been demonstrated elsewhere, Bale is almost certainly referring to "rulers" of the Church, i.e., the bishops. See Rainer Pineas, "John Bale's Nondramatic Works of Religious Controversy," *Studies in the Renaissance* 9 (1962): 220.

11. Blatt, *Plays*, p. 99.

12. The text used is that of *STC* 1291. Hereafter cited as *L*.

13. The text used is *King Johan*, ed. Adams.

14. See Rainer Pineas, "William Tyndale's Influence on John Bale's Polemical Use of History," *Archiv für Reformationsgeschichte*, 53 (1962): 79–96. Leslie Fairfield contends that it is "probably taking too narrow a view" to say that Bale derived his concept of King John for his play on that monarch specifically from Tyndale (pp. 155–56). His argument is less than convincing—if for no other reason than that he does not even attempt to account for those lines in Bale's play that are merely versifications of prose lines in Tyndale's *Obedience*.

15. See above note 1.

16. The fact that *King Johan* is both a morality and a history play seems to have caused certain critics some difficulty. For instance, Boas finds it puzzling that not only is there a mingling in the play of historical and allegorical characters, but that also in some cases these two sets of characters are identical. See Frederick S. Boas, *An Introduction to Tudor Drama* (Oxford: Clarendon Press, 1933), p. 113. This same situation leads Blatt to the conclusion that "it is evident that Bale thinks of the evil characters as being first and foremost perennial representatives of evil; their occasional appearance as historical characters in a specific situation is used by way of *exemplum* to lend credence to their existence on a 'higher' plane" (p. 112). To have missed the point here, as both Boas and Blatt have done, is to have missed the polemical purpose of Bale's play, which claims that the historical *is* the allegorical, that, for instance, Langton *is* the very personification of Sedition.

17. On the danger Bale faced, see Farmer, *Dramatic Writings*, p. 303.

18. See Rainer Pineas, "William Tyndale's Polemical Use of the Scriptures," *Nederlands Archief voor Kerkgeschiedenis* 45, no. 2 (1962): 65–78.

19. Blatt's judgment is that "Bale was not original enough to invent a wholly new type of play" (p. 127). Potter thinks he can detect in Bale's *King Johan* "some

experimental modifications in the dynamics of morality characterization. Not all of these are entirely successful. The potential effectiveness of the play's beginning is marred by the premature (dramatically unmotivated) diatribe which colors every attack upon the Church. Such violent rhetoric is untraditional and unseemly for sympathetic representative figures like England and the King. Moreover, the traditional encounter of tempter and mutable humanity loses its effectiveness when the tempter, instead of dissembling, proclaims his viciousness for all to hear" (p. 97). For a discussion of the polemical morality, see Rainer Pineas, "The English Morality Play as a Weapon of Religious Controversy," *Studies in English Literature* 2 (Spring 1962): 157–80.

20. Blatt, *Plays*, p. 108.
21. See Adams, *King Johan*, p. 165.
22. Cf. *King Johan* ll. 2000–4 and Adams's note to *King Johan*, p. 186.
23. While "John's early life, his relations with Richard, his dealings with Arthur, all afford matter for dramatic treatment," they do not afford matter for polemical treatment, and therefore one is not justified in claiming that Pafford and Greg were too hasty in assuming that "Bale has exhausted all the suitable historical material in the play which has survived" (Adams, p. 22). See also Honor C. McCusker, *John Bale, Dramatist and Antiquary* (Freeport, N.Y.: Books for Libraries Press, 1971), p. 89.
24. Farmer, *Dramatic Writings*, p. 320.
25. See Pineas's article cited in note 10, above.
26. See Pineas, *Anti-Catholic Drama*, p. 11.
27. See note 10, above, and Fairfield, *John Bale*, p. 114 ff.
28. See *The First Examinacyon of Anne Askewe* (Wesel, 1546), fols. 4v–5.
29. See Rainer Pineas, "William Turner and Reformation Politics," *Bibliothèque d'humanisme et renaissance* 37 (1975): 193–200, "William Turner's Polemical Use of Ecclesiastical History and His Controversy with Stephen Gardiner," *Renaissance Quarterly* 33 (1980): 599–608, and "William Turner's *Spirituall Physik,*" *The Sixteenth Century Journal* 14 (1983): 387–98.
30. See Pineas, *Anti-Catholic Drama*, pp. 7–8.
31. See Edwin S. Miller, "The Roman Rite in Bale's *King John*," *PMLA* 64 (1949): 802–22. Miller says that the attack on the Roman rite in *King John* is of three kinds: by "good" characters, by papal characters, and by parody (pp. 803–4). It would seem, however, that this analysis—which makes no distinction between sources and methods of attack—is incorrect and overlooks an important technique of controversy. For the use of the Vice and the use of parody are not two separate ways by which the Roman rite and Catholicism are being attacked in *King John*— or, for that matter, in other Protestant moralities. The whole force of the attack is derived from the fact that it is the papal characters themselves who are made to parody their own ritual.
32. Bernard Spivack, *Shakespeare and the Allegory of Evil* (New York: Columbia University Press, 1958), p. 121.
33. This explication corrects the interpretation of these lines in the article on the polemical morality play (see note 19, above).

John Pikeryng's *Horestes:* Auspices and Theatricality

Michael Shapiro

Most historians of drama regard John Pikeryng's *A Newe Enterlude of Vice Conteyninge, the Historye of Horestes with the cruell revengement of his Father's death, upon his one naturall Mother,* or *Horestes,* published in 1567, as a play written for and performed by professional adult actors. The evidence for assigning the text to an adult company rather than to a children's troupe, however, is not as strong as they have believed. A reconsideration of the relevant facts points rather toward production by one of the boy companies, probably one of the London chorister troupes accustomed to court performance. Whether or not it was a children's play, *Horestes* exploits the theatricality of the Vice figure of popular interludes in both traditional and innovative ways, establishing him basically as a theatrical presence rather than as a character in the plot of Horestes' revenge. Whereas one or two earlier critics have tried to integrate the theatrical and mimetic dimensions of the play, I prefer to accept the play's duality and regard it as an uneasy mixture of theatrical entertainment and classical legend.

1 THE AUSPICES OF PRODUCTION

Pikeryng's *Horestes* is generally thought to be one of the plays mentioned in the Revels Accounts for Christmas-Shrovetide 1567–68, a season rich in dramatic entertainment:

> Inprimis for seven plays, the firste namede as playne as Canne be, The second the paynfull plillgrimage [sic], The tthirde Jacke and Jyll, The forthe six fooles, The fyvethe callede witte and will, The sixte callede prodigallitie, The sevoenth of Orestes and a Tragedie of the kinge of Scottes, to the whiche belonged divers howses, for the setting forthe of the same as Stratoes howse, Gobbyns howse, Orestioes howse, Rome, the Pallace of prosperitie Scotlande and a gret Castell one the othere side Likewise. . . .[1]

For these seven plays, the Chamber Accounts for the same period record payments to one adult troupe, the Lord Rich's Men, and to the Masters of four children's troupes—the choristers of St. Paul's, the Chapel Royal, Windsor, and Westminster. Three of the titles mentioned in the extract from the Revels Accounts have been matched with extant texts:

1) "Wit and Will" is probably *The Marriage of Wit and Science* (Stationers' Register 1569–70). It has been assigned to the Children of Paul's on the grounds that it is an adaptation of an earlier unpublished play for the same troupe—*Wit and Science* by John Redford, Master of the Paul's choristers from 1534 to 1547.[2]

2) "Prodigality" has been identified with *The Contention between Liberality and Prodigality* (pub. 1602). It too was probably performed by the Children of Paul's, to whom the Revels Accounts record the loan of costumes and properties designated in the printed text.[3]

3) "Orestes" has been identified with Pickeryng's *Horestes* (pub. 1567), which requires techniques of staging used regularly for court productions at the time.[4]

Although these identifications are conjectural, they have been accepted by most scholars in the field.

Unlike the first two texts just mentioned, which have been assigned to the Children of Paul's, *Horestes* is generally attributed to an adult company, the Lord Rich's Men, largely because its title page supplies a casting list, i.e., a scheme for distributing the roles in the play among a small group of actors.[5] Up until 1576, the year professional adult troupes established permanent theaters in London, companies of four, five, or six toured the provinces, each actor of necessity playing several roles. By contrast, chorister and schoolboy troupes were larger and thus resorted less frequently to doubling of roles, a larger number of which were usually women and children. Most of the eighteen plays printed with casting lists before 1576 seem on internal grounds to be the work of adult companies.[6] The presence of such a casting list on the title page of *Horestes,* a list which divides the twenty-six roles among six actors, has seemed reason enough to David Bevington and others for classifying the play as the work of an adult troupe.

Unfortunately, this list is unworkable. The actor who plays both the Vice and Duty must change from one role to another between scenes. The casting list also specifies two "sodyers," but makes no mention of the extras needed to represent two armies. As T. W. Craik argues, the use of extras seems to have been unique to children's troupes, at least until the more successful adult troupes established themselves in London after 1576 and increased in size.[7] Finally, the list divides, or "halves," the role of Idumeus for two actors, and Bevington himself admits that no other examples of "halving" can be found in plays of the 1560s and 1570s, either in the explicit requirements of casting lists or in the implicit demands of the action.[8]

The inadequacies of the casting list for *Horestes* have led Craik to the plausible suggestion that the scheme was the work of the printer, who may have wished to sell his text to small adult companies. In any case, the scheme can bear little relationship to an actual production and should therefore be discounted as evidence of performance by a professional adult troupe. It was probably imposed on a play originally performed by or intended for a larger troupe, such as one of the inns of court, a company of choirboys, or students of a grammar school. If Pikeryng's play was the same as the play of *Horestes* performed at court in 1567–68, then it was probably performed either by Richard Edwards's Chapel Children, John Taylor's Westminster choirboys, or the Windsor choirboys.[9]

Even if Pikeryng's play was not the same as the one performed at court in 1567–68, a careful look at the text—without the influence of the casting list—reveals strong evidence for assigning it to a troupe of child actors. Its large number of female and juvenile roles leads one to draw an analogy with *Patient Grissell,* which Bevington has described as follows:

> The number of female roles is too large for a popular play [*i.e.* one performed by an adult troupe]. Of a total of twenty-five or twenty-six, ten or eleven characters are women and three are boys—a proportion like that in *The Marriage of Wit and Science.* At least five of the eight actors are obliged to undertake feminine or juvenile parts.[10]

In *Horestes,* ten of the twenty-six parts are women or children, nearly as high a proportion as in *Patient Grissell* and *The Marriage of Wit and Science.*

Furthermore, the two actors who took the leading roles of Horestes and the Vice (both juvenile roles) were probably the company's strongest players. It is highly unlikely that a troupe of professional adult players would have two boys as its principal actors.[11]

Horestes has certain features in common with other plays of the 1550s and 1560s performed by children's troupes. Whether choristers or grammar school pupils, the boys in such troupes ranged in age from nine or ten to fifteen or older, and so varied correspondingly in size.[12] In *The Marriage of Wit and Science,* which was probably produced at court the same season as *Horestes,* the page Will gives his own age as "betwene eleven and twelve" (467) and that of his master wit as "seventene or there aboute" (473), while Will's diminutive stature is verbally underscored at several points in the text.

Children's plays of the first part of Elizabeth's reign sometimes poke fun at the diminutive stature of these younger and smaller boys, as in Richard

Edwards's *Damon and Pithias* (performed at court by the Children of the Chapel Royal in 1564–65), in which Grim the Collier calls Will and Jack "my pretie cockerels" (1396) and "two suche little Robin ruddockes" (1420).[13] In scene 1 of *Horestes,* the Vice bristles when Rusticus refers to him as "this lyttell hourchet" (51), while in scene 3 Haltersick and Hempstring, whose names suggest wayward youth,[14] dispute the applicability of the word "boy":

> *Haltersick.* Nay but Jacke Hempstringe sease of this prate,
>   If thou caull me boye, then beware thy pate.
> *Hempstring.* What hould thy peace, as far as I se,
>   We be boyse both thearfore let us grée.
> *Haltersick.* Boye naye be god, though I be but smaull,
>   Yet Jacke hempstringe, a hart is worth all.
>
> (395–403)

From Udall through Lyly, Marston, and Dekker, the writers of plays for children's troupes frequently cast these younger, smaller boys as servants, and often gave them names befitting their size and age, e.g., Tom Truepenny, Snap, Half-penny, Minutius, Doit, and Dandiprat.

Sometimes two or more of these pert servants will have a short scene to themselves. In scene 3 of *Horestes,* Dick Haltersick enters singing a song in praise of soldier's life and meets Jack Hempstring. They quarrel briefly, as we have seen, about the word "boy," discuss sharing the cost of a laundress when they go to war in order to be able to offer "my master some dayntye mossell" (413–14), argue over who will make the better soldier, and finally attack each other with fists. In using these diminutive servants to shed an ironic light on the military preparations of the main action and in accentuating their inherent boyishness (here through their bristling truculence), the scene bears strong resemblance to similar scenes in plays known to have been performed by children's troupes.

Other children's plays use one, two, or more cheeky servants to discomfit a comic villain, often an older man, a pedant, or some other caricature of authority, or a stage rustic, as in *Damon and Pithias,* where Will and Jack "shave" Grim. *Horestes* opens with a single diminutive figure, the Vice, "this lyttell hourchet," outwitting Rusticus and Hodge, a pair of country bumpkins whose rural dialect is reminiscent of Grim's. A common variant of this device in children's plays of the period is to set the witty audacity of one of these pert, diminutive servants against the sobriety of his master, as in *The Marriage of Wit and Science,* for example, where Will's bawdy impudence sparkles against his master's shyness and naivete.[15]

In *Horestes,* a similar contrast between a small cheeky boy (the Vice) and a larger one playing an earnest but dull-witted protagonist of higher social rank is somewhat muted by the Vice's assumption of a false identity. As Courage, the Vice usually exhorts rather than ridicules his master, but he exhibits extreme audacity when Horestes' firm resolve momentarily gives way after his mother is brought onstage as his prisoner, the stage direction—"*Let Horestes syth hard*" (891)—indicating a great sigh. The Vice's mockery at this point is a tour de force of verbal agility, as in quick succession he speaks one line to Horestes, the next directly to the audience, and the third in mimicry of Clytemnestra's pleas, which we have just heard:

> Ounds of me what meane you man, begyn you now to faynt [?]
> Jesu god how styll he syttes, I thinke he be a saynt.
> O w w, you care not for me, nay sone I have don I warrant ye.[16]
>   (892–94)

Later in the play, the Vice's coarse cheekiness plays off against Fame's Latinate sobriety. Horestes has just sentenced his mother to death and led his troops off stage. Fame then enters in an elaborately iconographic costume, complete with wings and perhaps trumpets of iron and gold,[17] declares her determination to report both ill and good repute, and announces the arrival of Menelaus and Helen. She is soon interrupted by the Vice, who enters singing a song of "a new master." Fame continues with maxims from Ovid before the Vice notices her and greets her by asking for a kiss:

> Who *Saintie amen.* God morrowe mystres Nan,
> By his oundes I am glad to se the so trycke,
> Nay may I be so bould, at your lyppes to have a lycke.
>   (1043–45)

Fame apparently recoils from his advances, but the Vice perseveres:

> Jesus how coye, do you make the same,
> You neaver knew me afore I dare saye:
> In fayth, in fayth, I was to blame,
> That I made no courchey to you by the waye.
> Who berladye Nan, thou art trym and gaye,
> Woundes of me, she hath winges also,
> Who whother with a myschefe, doust thou thinke for to go?
> To heaven? or to hell? to pourgatorye? or Spayne?
> To Venys: to Pourtugaull? or to the eyles *Canarey?*
> Nay stay a whyle for a myle or twayne.
> I wyll go with the, I sweare by Saynt Marey,
> Wylt thou have a bote Nan, over seay the to carey.
> For yf it chaunce for to rayne, the weathers not harde,
> It may chaunce this trym geare of thine, to be marde.
>   (1046–59)

Fame continues to ignore his presence and goes on sermonizing, until the
Vice's ears prick up when he hears that the Greek kings have arrived. He
decides to pack up and clear out, and exits parodying Fame by offering his
own Latin tag and coarse translation:

> *Auxilla humilia firma, consensus facit,* this allwayes provided
> That consent maketh suckers most sure for to be.[18]
>
> (1088–89)

The use of smaller boys as agents (as well as targets) of ridicule,
combined with the number of women's and children's roles, suggests that
Pikerying's play, whether or not it is the *Horestes* seen at court in 1567–68,
was written for and probably first performed by a company of boy actors.

2   THEATRICALITY AND THE ROLE OF THE VICE

Like other children's plays of the period, *Horestes* shows the influence
of the moral interlude, a form associated with adult companies but by no
means their exclusive property. While it is true that adult troupes often
performed straight moralities, they also acted popular romances, as well
as various amalgams, while children's troupes preferred to draw plots from
literary sources and often to embellish them with dramaturgical techniques derived from moral interludes. In short, hybrid moral interludes
appear in the repertories of both adult and children's troupes. Like
Horestes, the plays classified under the rubrics "Christian Terence" and
"Christian Seneca," which account for the bulk of the plays acted by the
children's troupes before 1576, display at least two classic features of the
moral interlude—the use of personified abstractions and the prominence
of a Vice.

"Christian Terence," or prodigal-son plays, were probably performed
for parents and friends by provincial schoolboys or choristers rather than
by the London children's troupes for the Queen and her courtiers. At least
one of them, *Nice Wanton,* dramatizes the parable of the prodigal son by
adding personified agents of temptation to the biblical story. The universal
human protagonist is here split into three representative children (given
the biblical names of Ishmael, Dalila, and Barnabas), spoiled (as usual) by
an indulgent parent, their mother Xantippe. The two wayward children are
corrupted by Iniquitie, while their mother is afflicted—nearly to suicide—
by Worldly Shame. As we have seen, two of the plays presented at court
by children's troupes the same winter as *Horestes*—*The Marriage of Wit
and Science* and *The Contention between Liberality and Prodigality*—are
moral interludes entirely populated by personified abstractions.

Similarly, the extant "Christian Seneca" plays attributed to the children's troupes, which generally dramatize the plight of a pathetic heroine, also add personified abstractions from the morality tradition to plots derived from biblical narrative (as in *Godly Queen Hester* and Thomas Garter's *The Most Virtuous and Godly Susanna*), from Italian *novelle* (as in *Patient Grissel*), or from Roman history (as in R. B.'s *Appius and Virginia*). In the same fashion, Pikeryng uses characters named Nature, Fame, Nobles, Commons, Truth, and Duty to embroider the story of Horestes which he adapted from Lydgate's *Troy Book*.[19]

A more important feature of the moral interlude is the prominence of the Vice. A complex figure, he is (1) the chief or only seducer of the protagonist; (2) the agent of mischief, clowning, and mirth; and (3) the coarse popular performer, who addresses the audience directly—familiarly if not impudently—and who is not completely contained within the mimetic dimension of the play. As Bernard Spivack puts it, he is "homiletic showman, intriguer extraordinary, and master of dramatic ceremonies."[20]

Because of the Vice's strong farcical tendencies, both in his relations with other characters and his rapport with the spectators, scholars usually associate him exclusively with the popular tradition of small itinerant professional troupes of adult actors ("four men and a boy"). But the evidence is not so clear on this point. All four editions of John Heywood's *Play of the Wether* (pub. 1533), a play probably performed by one of the boy companies,[21] include "Merry Report the Vice" among the dramatis personae listed on the title page. Of the twenty extant moral interludes performed between 1547 and 1579 listed by Peter Happé, six (not including *Horestes*) were performed by children's troupes.[22] Whether or not the Vice originated in the plays performed by children's troupes, he was certainly at home there by the 1560s and 1570s.

In the case of *Horestes*, the publisher's sense of the importance of the Vice is reflected by the full title he gave the play—"A Newe Enterlude of Vice Conteyninge, the Historye of Horestes with the cruell revengement of his Fathers death, upon his one naturall Mother"—with the first seven words printed in larger, heavier type. The Vice in *Horestes*, "little hourchet" though he may be, is typical of other Vices in the moral interludes of the 1560s and 1570s in most ways, but not in all, as we shall see. Like other Vices, he derives entirely from the theatrical tradition established by his predecessors and can not be found in the play's narrative source(s).

Like his forebears, the Vice in *Horestes* uses several names to deceive other characters in the course of the play—Patience, Courage, and later Revenge—but establishes his primary identity in relation to the spectators. The text calls for him to enter first, alone, and to present both himself (as a theatrical presence) and the world of the play (in whose mimetic action he will function as a character). He seems to make his first entrance through

the audience, greeting the spectators, or rather singling out one or two of
them with coarse familiarity:

> A Syrra nay soft, what? let me see,
> God morrowe to you[,] syr, how do you fare?

He then begins to introduce his role in the world of the play but within a
few lines has singled out an individual spectator once again:

> Well[,] forwarde I wyll, for to prepare,
> Some weapons & armour, the catives to quell,
> I[']lle teache the hurchetes, agayne to rebell.
> Rebell? Ye syr, how saye you there to?

Throughout the opening speech of twenty-one lines, he alternately addresses greetings, insults or threats to individual spectators and imparts
information about Horestes and the rebels to the entire audience. This
oscillation between presentational and representational roles, between
self-conscious theatricality and mimesis, occurs throughout the play,
often—as here—within the same scene, even within the same speech. As
Robert Weimann has observed, the Vice's movement between ritualistic
self-expression and mimesis is facilitated by a distinctive verbal style—
characterized by colloquialisms, oaths, puns, proverbs, and bawdry.[23]

Like other Vices, he is the instigator of farcical stage business, such as
the combat indicated by the stage direction at line 175 suggests: "Up with
thy staf, & be readye to smyte, but Hodg smit first, and let the vice
thwacke them both and run out." Mock weeping, as in a passage already
quoted above, was a stock-in-trade of the Vice, a sign of his duplicity, as
well as an opportunity for comic business, as lightly suggested by the
stage direction at line 895: "Wepe but let Horestes ryse & bid him pease."
Like other Vices, he sings. His first song, "Stand backe ye sleepinge
jackes at home," which begins at line 777 and is sung to the tune of "The
Painter," is a patter song about the dangers of war and his ferocity on the
battlefield, and ends with a warning to the spectators about his Cousin
Cutpurse, an invention of the Vice in other moral interludes. His second
song, "A New Master," beginning at line 1018, is cut short when he sees
Fame ("Mistress Nan") already on stage, in the passage discussed earlier.

The Vice regularly changes costume as well as name during a moral
interlude, usually to indicate either an attempt at deception, or, as here, a
change in status, as well as to provide an opportunity for the Vice to joke
with the audience. In *Horestes,* the Vice makes his final appearance
dressed as a beggar: "Vice entrith with a staffe & a bottell or dyshe and
wallet" (1233). He tells the audience he has left Horestes, who has now
married Menelaus's daughter, although he also says that he has been

driven from his master's side and supplanted by "one caulyd Amitie," whom he can not abide. But this turn of plot is the merest peg on which Pikeryng hangs a ninety-line comic monologue. Shortly after the Vice enters as a beggar, he decided to seek employment as a servant and so, as the stage direction stipulates, "put[s] of the beggares cote and all thy thinges" (1250). He explains again the circumstances of his dismissal and appeals to the spectators for employment, especially to the ladies present, for "the most parte of wemen, to me [Revenge] be full kynde" (1278) and "do know . . . Revengys operation" (1283). In mock-scholarly fashion he offers to "veryfye" these assertions, and does so by telling how Socrates' shrewish wife "cround him with a pyspot" (1301). He hopes that such "dames be not in this place" and bids the audience farewell, with a special adieu to his Cousin Cutpurse.

As this summary suggests, Pikeryng's Vice not only performs traditional actions and bits of clowning like his counterparts in other moral interludes of the 1560s and 1570s, whether performed by adults or children; but, like them, he lives primarily in his presentational aspect—in the *lazzi*, or stock gags that have minimal if any connection with the plot. Indeed, Pikeryng goes further than other writers of moral interludes in limiting the Vice's role within the representational dimension of the play: he confines the Vice's participation in the material adapted from Lydgate's *Troy Book* to two scenes, and in neither of them does he exert any influence over the protagonist.

In the second scene of the play, for example, he appears in answer to Horestes' prayer as the messenger of the gods, urging the protagonist to do what he has in fact already decided to do, i.e. to punish his mother and her lover, and commenting with approval (in an aside) when Idumeus offers Horestes his assistance. In claiming to be Mercury, the Vice may be deceiving Horestes, but nowhere does the play (as opposed to the dubious title page) suggest that he seduces Horestes into committing an improper act. Later in the scene, Horestes receives Idumeus's endorsement of his intended actions, as he afterwards receives Idumeus's approval for executing Egisthus and Clytemnestra, as well as commendations from Nestor, Council, Nobles, Commons, Truth, and Duty. The only two characters who offer opposing views are refuted. In scene 4 Nature urges pity, but Horestes argues, as his supporters do throughout the play, that the laws of God and man supersede her claims, and tops her final argument by declaring his indifference to the report of Fame, who will later compare him to Nero. Similarly, Menelaus accuses Horestes of matricide in the eleventh scene, but is answered forcefully by Idumeus and Nestor, who invoke the laws of man and God. Nestor even throws down his gage as a challenge to anyone who wishes to make further accusations against Horestes. Menelaus retreats to a position of self-righteous superiority and allies himself with Nature (whom he cites by name)—"But yet I would for nature's sake have spard my mothers lyfe" (1190)—but is again overruled by Idumeus and Nestor and is even persuaded to give his daughter Hermione in marriage to Horestes. In the final scene of the play (immediately after the Vice has finished his comic monologue and left to seek employment) Horestes and Hermione pledge their love to each other, and the new King is blessed by Nobles and Commons and crowned by Truth and Duty. In short, the weight of the authority-figures in this play is solidly behind Horestes and justifies his actions against token opposition. Any ironies in the Vice's impersonation of the messenger of the gods turn back on him, for he has unwittingly encouraged Horestes to do the right thing.

The next direct contact between the Vice and Horestes occurs in the ninth scene and may be subdivided into two separate episodes. In the first of these, the Vice exhorts Horestes before the battle for Clytemnestra's city, rejoices at her capture, and—in a passage already considered—taunts the anguished prince with mock weeping. Much depends at this point on the nonverbal interaction between the actors playing the Vice and Horestes. The stage direction following the crocodile tears is vague: "Wepe, but let Horestes ryse & bid him pease" (895), but Horestes' next speech suggests that he has been able to overcome any weakening of his resolve to punish Clytemnestra by recalling her role in Agamemnon's death:

> By all the godes my hart dyd fayle, my mother for to se,
> From hye estate for to be brought, to so great myserey.
> That all most I had graunted lyfe, to her had not this be,
> My fathers death whose death in south, chefe causer of was she.
>
> (896–99)

The Vice's response—"Even as you saye"—is cryptic. It may be sarcastic but is more likely dismissive, as a more pressing matter attracts his attention: "But harke at hand, Egisthus draweth nye." The Vice apparently remains onstage during the battle with Egisthus and his soldiers, but says nothing until after Egisthus is hanged and Clytemnestra returns to plead for her life.[24] With raffish vulgarity, the Vice reminds her (and the audience) that she showed no such mercy to Agamemnon and will now receive her due punishment. He curses her—"A pestalaunce on the[,] crabyd queane" (999)—and follows or leads her offstage, leaving Horestes to end the scene with a short triumphal address to his troops:

> Now syeth we have the conquest got, of all our mortall fose,
> Let us provide that occasion, we do not chaunce to lose.
> Stryke up your droumes for enter now, we wyll the citie gate
> For nowe resestaunce none there is, to let us in there at.
>
> (1003–6)

It is surprising in view of Horestes' rhetoric of victory that the Vice returns to the playing area in the very next scene to inform us, in song and in speech, that Horestes now feels remorseful. Even more surprising is the absence of remorse in any of Horestes' subsequent speeches, particularly since the usual pattern in the moral interlude would require the protagonist to see the error of his ways and either express a deeply felt penitence or endure his punishment or both. The Vice in such a pattern may receive his punishment too at the end of the play, or he may escape it altogether, scoffing implicitly if not explicitly at the plot's inability to contain his comic and theatrical vitality.

In *Horestes,* this pattern is radically altered as the Vice has again outsmarted himself, this time in anticipating Horestes' remorse and so deserting his master in order to escape blame for leading him into sin. But there is no sin. The laws of man and God have been invoked to endorse Horestes' acts, and so there is no cause for remorse, no need for Horestes to seek pardon, and no reason for Vice to flee retribution. Horestes' perseverance in his cause and in his belief in its rightness is a novel element in the moral interlude, for the Vices usually inflict at least temporary harm on the human protagonists. But Horestes suffers no more than a twinge of anguish and emerges at the end of the play as (1) the dispenser of human and divine justice; (2) the founder of a new dynasty; and (3) the faithful ally of Idumeus, a powerful but benevolent neighboring king.

In terms of the plot, the Vice is no more than an amusing or diverting irrelevance, like such stock comic bits as the squabbling "boys," Hempstring and Haltersick, and the woman who captures her captor.[25] That is, he generates comic routines of dubious thematic and no narrative relevance. But restricting our analysis of his functions to the mimetic dimension of the play fails to account for his theatrical predominance in the play, for his rich rapport with the audience, and for Pikeryng's innovative adaptation of the usual pattern of the moral interlude.

Such disjunctions between theatricality and plot are not unique in the moral interludes of the 1560s and 1570s, but in most of them the Vice preserves something of his moral and homiletic function. The absence of any such element in *Horestes* suggests that the play is less concerned with exploring moral and political issues than modern commentators would like to believe. Defenders of the play try to integrate the disparate elements of the play in order to persuade us that it is a unified, organic work of art with a consistent attitude toward revenge.[26] But such arguments do not seem to accord with our experience, even as readers, of the theatricality of the play, for they rest on aesthetic axioms inapplicable to a work that is clearly an aggregate of distinctive elements. As a German critic puts it, the seemingly intrusive elements in such works serve "to expand the framework of the main action limited by the subject matter so as to provide a more comprehensive image, a generally valid image of the world, not conceived exclusively against the background of the central [serious] problem actually dealt with."[27]

In *Horestes,* the Vice's horseplay with the audience and the familiar gags of the clownish rustics, the angry boys, and the rebellious female prisoner may well provide a broader picture of the world than one could derive from the Horestes material alone. Denigrators of the play usually ignore what seem to be unassimilated episodes of comic theatricality, apparently (if mistakenly) confident that the Horestes material alone offers sufficient evidence of Pikeryng's confusion.[28] The usual complaint is that the play fails to resolve the moral issues of matricide or revenge, or the political issues inherent in tyrannicide. But this is to assume *Horestes* is the kind of play that resolves issues, when it is not even the kind of play that seriously attempts to raise them.[29] Such critics try to see Nature as a potent advocate for mercy and Menelaus as the prosecuting attorney in the trial of Horestes for matricide. But the text of *Horestes* as we have it allows Horestes to vanquish Nature well before the execution of Clytemnestra and permits Idumeus and Nestor to persuade Agamemnon with very little difficulty that the prince has done right in punishing his mother and deserves to be rewarded with the hand of Hermione. As we have already seen, Pikeryng also brings forth some heavy allegorical machinery in support of Horestes at the end of the play. If the play "raises" any issues, it does so only to flatten them with a steamroller.

NOTES

1. *Documents Relating to the Office of the Revels in the Time of Queen Elizabeth,* ed. A. Feuillerat, *Materialien zur Kunde des älteren englischen Dramas* 41 (Louvain: A. Uystpruyst, 1908; reprinted 1963): 119.

2. Trevor Lennam, *Sebastian Westcott, the Children of Pauls and "The Marriage of Wit and Science"* (Toronto: University of Toronto Press, 1975), pp. 34, 61, 90–101. I have used this text for quotations.

3. H. N. Hillebrand, *The Child Actors: A Chapter in Elizabethan Stage History* (Urbana: University of Illinois Press, 1926; reprinted 1964), pp. 128–30; and T. Lennam, *Sebastian Westcott,* pp. 64–65.

4. E. K. Chambers, *The Elizabethan Stage* (Oxford: Clarendon Press, 1923), 3: 44 and 466. G. R. Kernodle, *From Art to Theatre* (Chicago: University of Chicago Press, 1944), pp. 133–34. Richard Southern, *The Staging of Plays before Shakespeare* (New York: Theatre Arts Books, 1973), pp. 495–506, argues for the use of simpler staging techniques, such as might have been used in banqueting halls other than those at court, where the resources of the Revels Office were available. David Bevington, "Popular and Courtly Traditions on the Early Tudor Stage," in *Medieval Drama, Stratford-upon-Avon Studies* 16 (London, 1973): 105, argues, largely on the basis of the siege scene, that "an inn-yard served as the *original* theatrical environment" (italics added). Daniel Seltzer, ed., *The Interlude of Vice (Horestes),* Malone Society Reprints (Oxford: Malone Society, 1962), p. v, points out that Pikeryng's text does not require a structure that might be described

an "Horestes' house," as the Revels Account terms it, and so questions the connection between the printed text and the court performance. T. W. Craik, *The Tudor Interlude* (Leicester: Leicester University Press, 1958), pp. 127–28 n. 38, conjectures that some interludes may have been revised for court production without the extant texts reflecting those revisions. The quarto of *Horestes,* which bears the date of 1567 on its title page and may even have appeared before the play, perhaps in a revised version, was produced at court during the winter of 1567–68.

In quoting from *Horestes,* I have used Seltzer's text and line numbering, but I have also compared readings and used the commentaries in two recent editions: Karen L. Maxwell, ed., *A Critical Edition of John Pikeryng's "Horestes" (1567),* Ph.D. diss. (Harvard University, 1969); and Marie Axton, ed., *Three Tudor Classical Interludes* (Cambridge: Cambridge University Press, 1982).

5. David M. Bevington, *From "Mankind" to Marlowe* (Cambridge: Harvard University Press, 1962), p. 61. Marie Axton, *Three Tudor Classical Interludes,* p. 30, suggests that "The size of the cast is an argument in favour of 'private theatre' origins," but she seems to favor a performance at one of the inns of court on the grounds that the author of the printed text is John Puckering, Speaker of the House of Commons in 1584 and 1586 and Lord Keeper from 1592 to 1596, who lived in Lincoln's Inn in the 1560s. That identification is plausible but does not necessarily imply that he wrote the play for performance *by* other residents of the Inn. The Children of Chapel Royal, who performed at the Candlemas Feasts of Lincoln's Inn in 1565 and 1566, have at least as good a claim to having performed the play. See Chambers, *The Elizabethan Stage,* 2: 34.

6. I follow Bevington's list of plays "offered for acting" before 1603, i.e. those printed with casting lists, in *From "Mankind" to Marlowe,* pp. 265–73, eliminating those published after 1576 or existing only in manuscript.

7. Craik, *The Tudor Interlude,* pp. 35–36. Bevington argues that *Horestes* is exceptional among adult plays for requiring "extras" (pp. 102–3). Maxwell, *A Critical Edition,* pp. 137–39, contends that the play could be performed without extras, but must add another role to those designated for player 3 in the casting list in order to support her claim. The inadequacy of the casting list is also discussed by R. C. Johnson, *Thomas Preston's "Cambises": A Critical Edition,* Ph.D. dissertation (University of Illinois, 1964), pp. 19–20.

8. Bevington, *From "Mankind" to Marlowe,* pp. 89–90.

9. There is some evidence for excluding the Windsor choirboys from consideration. The concluding prayers for Elizabeth and her nobles, clergy, and magistrates in *Horestes* are quite conventional, but the addition of one for the Lord Mayor is extremely rare. Perhaps it indicates a troupe accustomed to performing under municipal auspices or before the members of inns of courts and guilds, as well as at court or in its own playhouse. No such performances are recorded for the Windsor choirboys. On the other hand, the Chapel Children performed at Lincoln's Inn (see note 5, above), while the Westminster choristers appeared in the Merchant Taylors' pageant for Lord Mayor's Day in 1561 and in the Ironmongers' pageant for 1566, and also entertained the Society of Parish Clerks in 1562. See Chambers, *The Elizabethan Stage,* 2: 72; and R. Mark Benbow, "Sixteenth-century Dramatic Performances for the London Livery Companies," *Notes and Queries* 226 (1982): 129–31.

10. Bevington, *From "Mankind" to Marlowe,* pp. 62–63. In fact, Bevington exaggerates the similarity of the proportion of feminine and juvenile roles in the two plays. In *The Marriage of Wit and Science,* fourteen of seventeen characters are either women or children (p. 23), a much higher proportion than in *Patient Grissell,* with thirteen or fourteen out of twenty-five or twenty-six. The imprac-

ticality of the doubling scheme in the latter play was first noticed by R. B. McKerrow and W. W. Greg, eds., *Patient Grissell*, Malone Society Reprints (London, 1909), pp. xiii–xiv. For other faulty schemes, see Craik, *The Tudor Interlude*, pp. 29–31; Bevington, *From "Mankind" to Marlowe*, pp. 62–63; and Johnson, *Thomas Preston's "Cambises*,*"* pp. 300–305.

11. Axton, *Three Classical Tudor Interludes*, p. 207, suggests that the frequent use of the word "hourchet"—"rascals, urchins (from hourchent: Hedgehog)"— may indicate performance by child actors. Bevington, *From "Mankind" to Marlowe*, p. 77, argues that the play could have been performed with a troupe having a single boy, as did most of the itinerant adult companies of the 1560s, but is puzzled by the large number of feminine roles assigned to other players. In citing "the battle scenes and sieges, the drums and trumpets" as additional evidence of performance by adult players (p. 61), Bevington overlooks Nicholas Udall's *Ralph Roister Doister*, performed either by schoolboys of Eton between 1536 and 1541 or those of Westminster between 1535 and 1556, probably at court. Maxwell, *A Critical Edition*, p. 83, sees the heavy use of proverbs in *Horestes* as a sign of its having been written for production by an adult troupe, but *The Marriage of Wit and Science* is characterized by Lennam, *Sebastian Westcott*, p. 105, as "a fairly rich repository of proverbial sayings, comparisons, and phrases not found in Redford's original." On the other hand, having found *Horestes* more sophisticated in its dramaturgy than most adult plays of the 1560s, Maxwell is finally unable to determine whether it was written for (and presumably performed by) men or boys (p. 142).

12. Michael Shapiro, *Children of the Revels* (New York: Columbia University Press, 1977), pp. 104–6, 148–49, 239–42.

13. I quote from the text edited by Arthur Brown and F. P. Wilson, Malone Society Reprints (Oxford, 1957), silently correcting a few obvious misprints.

14. The *Oxford English Dictionary* defines Haltersick as a variant of Haltersack, a gallows bird, and Hempstring as one who deserves the halter. The names seem to connote youthfulness. The *Oxford English Dictionary* cites Minsheu's *Ductor*, which defines Haltersick as "a knavish boy." In *Damon and Pithias*, a similar term, "crack ropes" (1344), refers to the diminutive pages, Will and Jack.

15. See especially 11. 550–68. According to Craik, *The Tudor Interlude*, p. 43, the humor of such scenes depends on the fact that Wit too is a child, here speaking to the court audience as an equal. This effect would still be possible—might even be enhanced—if Will were a smaller and younger child.

16. The mimicry of Clytemnestra would be even sharper if "sone" could be read as "son" rather than "soon," but as bizarre as the spelling and printing are in this text, "son" is consistently spelled "son" or "sonne," while the spelling "sone" is regularly reserved for the word "soon."

17. Craik, *The Tudor Interlude*, pp. 65-66.

18. One hesitates to make too much of orthography in a text as badly printed as *Horestes*, but the misspelling in both the Latin adage and its translation may be intentional. *"Auxilla"* may be a misprint for *"auxilia,"* but it could also represent a mispronunciation to contrast the Vice's colloquial style with Fame's more learned discourse. Maxwell, *A Critical Edition*, p. 75, traces the adage to Richard Taverner's edition of *Mimi Publiani* (published with *Catonis Disticha*, 1553), where the Latin and English occur in slightly different form:

Auxilia, humilia firma consensus facit.
Consente maketh small succours sure.

(sig. Fiii)

See also Axton, *Three Classical Tudor Interludes*, p. 221. The Vice may also be punning on "sucker" as parasite. See *Oxford English Dictionary* (s.v. suckers, 1.3), which quotes a relevant sentence from *Pap With a Hatchet* (1589): "I know there is none of honour so carelesse . . . that will succor those that be suckers of the Church." In *Horestes*, such a pun would subvert the platitudinous adage into a boast by the diminutive Vice that he can profit from any turn of events.

19. Karen Maxwell Merritt, "The Source of John Pikeryng's *Horestes*," *Review of English Studies*, n.s. 23 (1972): 255–66, refutes earlier arguments for Caxton's *Recuyell of the Historyes of Troye* as the play's primary source. See also Robert S. Knapp, "*Horestes*: The Uses of Revenge," *ELH* 40 (1973): 205 n.

20. Bernard Spivack, *Shakespeare and the Allegory of Evil* (New York: Columbia University Press, 1958), p. 151.

21. Bevington, *From "Mankind" to Marlowe*, pp. 40–41, classifies it as a court play. Heywood's association with the Children of Paul's offers some basis for assigning the play to that troupe: see A. W. Reed, *Early Tudor Drama* (London: Methuen, 1926), pp. 54–61.

22. Peter Happé, " 'The Vice' and the Popular Theatre: 1547–80," in *Poetry and Drama: 1570–1700, Essays in Honour of Harold F. Brooks*, ed. Antony Coleman and Antony Hammond (London: Methuen, 1981), pp. 13–31. See also F. P. Wilson, *The English Drama*, ed. G. K. Hunter (New York and Oxford: Oxford University Press, 1969), pp. 63–65. To this list should be added a manuscript play, *Misogonus* (1560–77), which Bevington, *From "Mankind" to Marlowe*, p. 64, excludes from the repertories of adult troupes despite the presence of a casting list. Jackson I. Cope, " 'The Best for Comedy': Richard Edwardes' Canon Complicates the Vice," in *Dramaturgy of the Daemonic* (Baltimore: Johns Hopkins University Press, 1984), pp. 35–49, argues that two interludes usually assigned to adult troupes— *Common Conditions* and *Sir Clyomon and Sir Clamydes*—were written by Richard Edwards, Master of the Children of the Chapel Royal from 1561 to 1566, and therefore may have been performed by a company of boy actors. Robert Potter, *The English Morality Play: Origins, History, and Influence of a Dramatic Tradition* (London: Routledge and Kegan Paul, 1975), p. 111, argues that Lupton's *All for Money* (1577), which Happé among others classifies as an adult play, lacks the doubling scheme and preponderance of male roles usually associated with such works.

23. Robert Weimann, *Shakespeare and the Popular Tradition in the Theater*, ed. and trans. Robert Schwartz (Baltimore: Johns Hopkins University Press, 1978), p. 116 ff. See also Happé, " 'The Vice' and the Popular Theatre," pp. 27–28.

24. The staging of Egisthus's hanging is discussed by John H. Astington, "Gallows Scenes on the Elizabethan Stage," *Theatre Notebook* 37 (1983): 3–9. As Karen Maxwell Merritt points out, "The Source of John Pikeryng's *Horestes*," p. 257, the play has Clytemnestra executed offstage, whereas in both Lydgate's and Caxton's versions, "Orestes kills her with his own hands by hacking her to pieces with a sword." Similarly, at the end of *Edward II*, Marlowe has young Edward III sentence Mortimer to death but order his mother confined in the Tower until her innocence or guilt for the "unnatural" murder of Edward II can be established. Prince Edward, like Horestes, must also resist his own tendencies toward "pity."

25. R. C. Johnson, *Thomas Preston's "Cambyses,"* pp. 20–23, finds close analogues of each of these comic bits in that play and tentatively concludes that Pikeryng is the borrower, although one could argue that both playwrights are drawing upon a common stock of farcical stage business developed by popular actors over a period of centuries.

26. E. B. de Chickera, "Horestes' Revenge—Another Interpretation," *Notes*

and Queries 204 (1959): 190, argues that Horestes is presented as an authorized agent of Divine, public, and private revenge, but offers no explanation for the problematic presence of the Vice. Robert Knapp, "*Horestes*: The Uses of Revenge," *ELH* 40(1973): 205–11, argues that the dual nature of the Vice embodies the moral ambiguity of revenge. Although Knapp seems a bit too eager to impose doctrinal consistency on the play, his attempt to incorporate the theatricality of the Vice into a thematic reading is an advance over earlier critics, who discuss the play either as a late Medieval morality or as an anticipation of later revenge tragedies. For the former tendency, see Rosemary Woolf, "The Influence of the Mystery Plays upon the Popular Tragedies of the 1560's," *Renaissance Drama*, n.s. 6, (1973): 99–103; Spivack, *Shakespeare and the Allegory of Evil*, pp. 279–84; Willard Farnham, *The Medieval Heritage of Elizabethan Tragedy*: (Berkeley: University of California Press, 1936; rev. ed. Oxford, 1956), pp. 258–62. H. Felperin, *Shakespearean Representation* (Princeton: Princeton University Press, 1977), pp. 63–64; and R. Broude, "*Vindicta Filia Temporis*: Three English Forerunners of the Elizabethan Revenge Play," *Journal of English and Germanic Philology* 72 (1973): 494–97.

27. Günter Reichert, *Die Entwicklung und die Funktion der Nebenhandlung in der Tragödie vor Shakespeare* (Tübingen: Max Niemeyer, 1966), p. 9, quoted and translated in Weimann, *Shakespeare and the Popular Tradition in the Theater*, p. 158.

28. See, for example, Eleanor Prosser's conclusion, *"Hamlet" and Revenge* (Stanford: Stanford University Press, 1967), p. 44: "Pickeryng is either a confused moralist or a very careless playwright."

29. Joel B. Altman, *The Tudor Play of Mind* (Berkeley: University of California Press, 1978), pp. 13–30, contrasts the "homiletic," or "demonstrative," play with the "explorative" play, a dramatized investigation of a problem from a number of viewpoints that may or may not reach a conclusion. *Horestes* may be too polemical even for the former category if—as has been argued—Clytemnestra and Horestes were intended to suggest Mary Queen of Scots and her young son James. See J. E. Phillips, "A Revaluation of *Horestes* (1567)," *Huntington Library Quarterly*, 18 (1954–55): 227–44; and *Images of a Queen* (Berkeley: University of California Press, 1964), pp. 45–58; and Marie Axton, *The Queen's Two Bodies: Drama and the Elizabethan Succession* (London: Royal Historical Society, 1977), pp. 58–60. The Revels Accounts already quoted refer to a tragedy of the king of Scots performed at court the same season as *Horestes*, which may also have referred to recent events involving the Scottish royal family. On the other hand, David Bevington, *Tudor Drama and Politics* (Cambridge: Harvard University Press, 1968), and Knapp, "*Horestes*: The Uses of Revenge," pp. 212–20, argue that the play—like most political dramas of the period—is far more concerned with general issues of governance than with specific events and personalities. However, personal satire of political figures was quite common in plays acted by children's troupes throughout the sixteenth and early seventeenth centuries; see Shapiro, *Children of the Revels*, pp. 4–5, 8–9, 27, 38–58, 177–78, and 194–96; and Robert Wren, "Salisbury and the Blackfriars Theatre," *Theatre Notebook* 23 (1969): 102–9. On the polemical nature of post-Reformation moralities, see Rainer Pineas, "The English Morality Play as a Weapon of Religious Controversy," *Studies in English Literature* 2 (1962): 157–80. S. F. Johnson, to whom I am indebted for suggesting that *Horestes* might be a play written for or acted by a children's troupe, has also proposed to me that the play may have been intended as a warning to the Scots of what might happen—intervention by a powerful neighbor on behalf of a young king—if they failed to deal with Mary themselves.

Monteverdi and the Immorality of Art

Russell Fraser

In Monteverdi's time, the early seventeenth century, forward-looking composers wanted to enlist music in the wars of truth. This was the beginning of our modern age, and Monteverdi counts among our prophets. In key with his time, he shared the impulse to soul saving and said in prefaces what he thought he was up to. Words and deeds aren't the same, though, and the music he made has no purpose but itself. Also, it looks backwards and forwards. Master of the Second Practice, a new style in his young manhood, he highlighted words, projecting their truth through his music. In the old-fashioned style, the music, imperious, rode over the words. Monteverdi, backward-looking, mastered the First Practice, too. One side of him knew it for the more capacious vessel. The secret of his genius, this contrariness makes him hard to pin down.

Primarily a secular composer, he left nine books of madrigals and fifteen dramatic entertainments. Seven survive, among them the first successful opera. He wrote sacred music as well, hoping to get on in a world where music and religion were still closely intertwined. Psalms, masses, responsories, motets, hymns, and so forth, the sacred pieces make an alphabet of forms. Some sound like Gregorian Chant—the *Missa da Capella,* for instance, and parts of the *Christmas Vespers.* But in the *Vespers* the swelling brass sounds like the Gabrielis, predecessors of Monteverdi in Venice. Then the music changes, becoming "baroque." The twenty-three motets, *Sacrae Cantiunculae,* "little sacred songs," conform to strict polyphony, not different to my ear from the music of Palestrina. But some of these motets, trembling almost erotically, return on themselves like the secular madrigals. You can hear this echo sound on the first side of the *Cantiunculae,* just in from the end of the record (Hungaroton SLPX 11937).

For his sacred music, Monteverdi didn't mind adapting popular tunes, "songs made before." That was backward-looking, a practice forbidden by the Council of Trent. This Council, in session for almost twenty years,

227

wound up its business shortly before Monteverdi was born. The voice of militant Catholicism in the Age of Reformation, it meant to answer the Protestant Reformers. But new Catholics and Protestants were more like each other than either supposed, an echo, not an opposition. Each thought that music, literature too, was one thing or the other, serious or frivolous. Monteverdi, "post-Tridentine" with a difference, made a repertory that is all of a piece. Having written his opera *Arianna,* now lost, he went back later to the heroine's lament, a famous set piece. Fitted with sacred words, his secular lament became a five-part "Lament of the Madonna." It wasn't that the old man was more pious than the young man. He wasn't conscienceless either, only, like many makers, an opportunist and provident. When he served as chapel master at St. Mark's, Venice, the procurators there, confirming his tenure, voted him a raise in pay. They meant this for an incentive, wanting him to devote himself "to the honor of God with a whole heart." That is what he did.

Dying in 1643, he was the oracle whose voice had been stilled. *Oracolo della musica,* they called him, but by the end of the century they had forgotten his name. Verdi, knowing who he was, couldn't recommend him. Working out a curriculum for younger composers, he told them to study counterpoint but not Monteverdi's. Things have looked up since, and in our time Monteverdi has had a revival. Pavarotti said on national TV that for Italian opera, Monteverdi and Verdi and Puccini were the best. His name chimes with theirs—but this is mere euphony. Popular composers, Verdi and Puccini belong to the million, and Monteverdi in their company seems odd man out. He made a great opera, *The Coronation of Poppea,* and you can hear it on Vox and Telefunken, but for every live performance there will likely be a hundred of *Aida* or *Boheme.* Cognoscenti decry this, saying how Monteverdi wouldn't stoop to conquer. No "Anvil Chorus," no elephants on the stage. But most of those we call masters want to please the million, a generous impulse. Monteverdi, a court composer, pleases the few. He has his intensities, though, worth a hearing.

He was Claudio Monteverdi of Cremona, born in May 1567, the oldest child of a barber surgeon. His mother died, probably of plague, when he was an infant. The barber surgeon remarried, but this second wife died young. Another stepmother followed. At thirty-two, Monteverdi took a wife, Claudia, a court singer. She bore him three children, one dying in childhood. The marriage lasted eight years, terminated by Claudia's death in 1607. Later his elder son fell foul of the Inquisition. No doubt these sorrows had their impact on Monteverdi, but his music, impersonal, doesn't record it. He never had a Dark Period. This likens him to Mozart, already sick to death when he wrote his last chamber piece, the Quintet in E-flat major, full of brio and technical surprise.

Unlike Mozart, Monteverdi, subject to spleen or vapors, ran on about himself. The passionate man had a demon, and the music, like damped-down fires, suggests that he knew this. His letters, not meant for the world's eye, harp on bad health and the pressure of meeting deadlines. A tardy composer, he said this pressure brought him "almost to death's door." However, he lived a long life, and maybe he was hypochondriacal. Toward the end of his life he took holy orders, a comfortable thing to do, but his famous old age was no more serene than his youth.

The great composers in the year of his birth were Palestrina and Orlando Lasso, in England Thomas Tallis. Masters of polyphony, they looked to the past. Victoria and William Byrd, heralds of the future, were young men; Gesualdo and Thomas Morley were boys. In letters and science, Monteverdi's contemporaries included Shakespeare and Galileo, each born three years earlier in 1564. Galileo, an active personality, changed the world, where Shakespeare celebrated the world in his fictions. Monteverdi belongs with Shakespeare. A great revolutionary, he tutored us in nice discriminations.

This description wouldn't have pleased him, and his theoretical writings stake out a grander claim. In 1605, introducing a book of madrigals, he said that "the modern composer builds upon the foundations of truth." A slippery word, he didn't define it, and the truth of his music isn't didactic, having no ax to grind. It isn't generic, either, but endlessly refracted. So far, this makes him old-fashioned.

His natal place, Cremona, a provincial town in the Po valley southeast of Milan, had its substantial cathedral, still there. From the *maestro di capella*, Monteverdi learned his craft. This chapel master directed the small choir, men and boys. They studied "note-against-note," Monteverdi said, but didn't take "the melodic factors" into account. Town musicians, *piffari*, played for weddings, banquets, and church festivals. A *piffaro* is a pipe, and these anonymous musicians were named after the instruments they played. Liking tunes you could carry, they honored the "Leading Note" in their canzonets and villanelles. Monteverdi's madrigals, end-lessly tuneful, say that he is their scholar.

In his young time, serious music was polyphonic, the different melodic parts combining simultaneously to make a tapestry of sound. You couldn't distinguish the threads in the carpet, though, and some thought this a scandal. Benevolent, they wanted to "move the affections," but polyphonic music spoiled their game. Interweaving the voices, it "lacerated the poetry." They meant it undercut the idea. Betting on ideas, they called for a new kind of music, monophonic or homophonic, characterized by a single melodic line. In their univocal music, Truth was the burden, maybe a little coarse. Capital-letter abstractions are like that.

These connoisseurs of clarity were upper-class gentlemen, modeled on the discussants in Castiglione's *Courtier*, and they canvassed their theories in learned discussion groups. Cremona had its group, the Accademia degli Animosi, "bold spirits." In Mantua, where Monteverdi first came to public notice, the academicians were Invaghiti, "impassioned ones." Being themselves and polemical, they made manifestoes, appealing to "the Greeks and Latins of that better age." This appeal wasn't retrograde, but progressive. They thought the ancients got the truth out front where the proximate past had obscured it.

People who write about Monteverdi range him with these modern men, and there is reason to do this. If you put him on the record player after listening to Thomas Tallis or Josquin des Prez, he seems light years distant from these older composers. Egalitarian, they don't honor the Leading Note but parcel out the melody among the different voices. For all the voices, the rule is "share and share alike." Also they value sound more than sense, a rough and ready way to put this, the sound being the sense for them. Tallis has a hopeful choral piece, *Spem in alium,* for forty voices segregated in choirs of five voices each (Musical Heritage Society recording 4827M). He wrote it for a royal birthday, maybe Queen Mary's in 1556 or her sister Elizabeth's a generation later. But the occasion, a point of departure, matters little, and the Queen and the birthday don't get much of a hearing. Monteverdi, more scrupulous or courtly, keeps his eye on the occasion. Where the English composer makes gorgeous sound, he expresses his title, "Tancred Fighting Clorinda," etc. This expressiveness isn't a virtue exactly, only the hallmark of a new style.

The new style declares for "perspective." Taking priority, the highest voice part or cantus relegates all the others to secondary roles. This makes music more cognitive. Listening, you know where you are, not between C and E-flat but between the "shining blades" of Saracen and Christian. Expressive music makes a domicile where the bounding lines are sharper than they ever were before. The domicile is smaller, however. In his *Combattimento di Tancredi e Clorinda,* lifted from Tasso's *Jerusalem Delivered,* Monteverdi has a story to tell. When the fighters grow weary, *stanco e anelante,* "tired and panting," the music, not wearisome but suggestive, reflects this. It changes, said the composer, "in accordance with the words." That is something new, and on this side Monteverdi looks to the future.

Wanting a better future, he defers in his letters and prefaces to Plato, the great rallying point for moderns in his time. Also, at a guess, this self-made man wanted to bolster his credentials. Plato's aesthetic holds that music, the other arts too, is instrumental. This means that Lydian and Ionian harmonies are out. Being relaxed, they aren't instrumental except as they slacken our fiber. Laying down the law, Plato tells composers to look for rhythms that express a courageous and harmonious life. He wants "a warlike harmony to sound the note or accent which a brave man utters in the hour of danger" (*Republic* 399a). Monteverdi quotes this passage (getting the reference wrong) in his preface of 1638. Following Plato and his epigones, he says that the end of music is to "move our mind." It "either ennobles or corrupts the character," and this modern composer is all for ennobling. He goes on to tell how the combat of Tancred and Clorinda gave him "an opportunity of describing in music contrary passions, namely, warfare and entreaty and death." This was his *stile concitato,* an "excited" style that mirrored agitation and conflict. He meant it for kinetic, but his descriptions, pleasing mightily, don't make us brave or better. Luckily, he didn't see this. Otherwise, like poor Tasso, he might have folded his arms.

A disinterested poet, Tasso gave trouble to the hardliners of the Counter Reform. They leaned over his shoulder, moralizing his text. Finally, they drove him mad, and he lapsed in silence. Monteverdi, thicker skinned, paid lip service to the new imperatives. That is partly the point of the prefaces. He wrote them from the heart but knew what side his bread was buttered on. In the music, another matter, he stumbled on his own reality. Harking back to two early operas of his, he said how Ariadne had "moved the audience because she was a woman, and equally Orpheus because he was a man." He sought to render their emotions, only that—a "true lament" for one, for the other "a true supplication." Not the same as enlisting music in the wars of truth, this implied a remoteness from programs and theories.

Already in his teens, the precocious young man was publishing motets, spiritual madrigals, and secular canzonets. This is the mixed bag by which you know him. At nineteen, with four books to his credit, he had outgrown his Cremonese beginnings. So he looked elsewhere, moving to Mantua, forty miles east of Cremona and a bigger world. He moved in 1591, about the time Shakespeare came up from Stratford to London. For twenty-one years, refining his craft, Monteverdi lived in Mantua. He was *suonatore di vivuola,* a violinist in the service of Vincenzo I, the ducal ruler. Stepping up the ladder, he became a singer, then in 1602 *maestro della musica,* composer to the court. Thirty-five by then, he held a post equal to any in Italy except for some in Venice and Rome.

Tasso in poetry and Rubens in painting distinguished this Mantuan court, also Guarini, the author of the first pastoral play. "The play's the thing," Hamlet said, but Italians doubted this, titivating their plays with music and intermezzi, colorful "business" between the acts. Monteverdi and others wrote the music for Guarini's big success, *The Faithful Shepherd,* published in 1590 and premiered at Ferrara five years later. Like a tone poem by Respighi, this music was representational, "of the earth, the sea, the air, and the heavens." Monteverdi didn't like it. Years later, when they told him to create a "maritime fable," a musical extravaganza per-

formed on the water, he threw up his hands. "I have observed that the
personages of the drama are winds," he wrote morosely, "also that the
winds—the west winds and north winds—have to sing." A vulgar imitation, it was more than he had bargained for. He liked to paint words in
music but winds that talked dejected him. He wasn't an imagist. Call him a
humanist, if you understand by this not the glorifying of man, only that
people absorbed him. He cultivated truth to nature, not imitative but
mimetic, nature adjusted. Respighi, in the third section of his *Pines of
Rome,* puts us up on the Janiculum where we hear a nightingale singing.
This song is from the life, an actual recording. Monteverdi's music, lifelike,
keeps the real world at art's length.

Over in England, they knew about Guarini's *Pastor Fido.* Translated into
English, it inspired Shakespeare's junior colleague, John Fletcher. But
"inspired" isn't just the word, and Fletcher and Guarini share a lot of
blame between them. The sexy hodgepodge they made, mixing hot and
cold, dry and moist, tragedy with comedy, did as much harm to morals,
Cardinal Bellarmine said, as Luther and Calvin had done to religion. Art,
not morals, is what they did harm to. After the Restoration, when the King
came back and Fletcher's pastoral had a revival, Pepys the diarist went to
see it. He said the new production was "much thronged after for the
scene's sake." This is literary criticism. The scene is the thing, and the
pastoral, not really a play, is a pretext, on the way to something else. For
the playwright the something else is hothouse entertainment, for the
régisseur who produced him it is a *son et lumière.* Making their art a
vehicle, they aren't all that different from the academic theorizers, pro-
moters of truth. Collaborating with both, Monteverdi sailed his tricky
passage between these highbrows and lowbrows. Like that English milord
who wrote "The Character of a Trimmer," he adjusted at need, a good
thing to do if you have an end of your own worth pursuing.

"We used to have intermezzi to serve the plays," said one disgruntled
playwright in this time. "Now we have plays to serve as excuses for
intermezzi." Already before Monteverdi was born, streets, palaces, bizarre temples, loggie, and "various kinds of cornices" were materializing
on stage, all so well executed, Vasari says, that they seemed "not counterfeited but absolutely real." This reality, sponsored by the designer,
crowded the play into a corner. "Painting and carpentry are the soul of
masque," said an irascible Ben Jonson, crowded by his collaborator, the
designer Inigo Jones. What you saw convinced the eye, though, like the
words in the new homophonic music, convincing to the ear. The audience
went wild when the curtain going up showed Ariadne abandoned by
Theseus on her rocky island in the middle of waters. In the farthest part of
the "prospect," the waters were seen to move. No one had to ask the
heroine if she could hear the sea. A barefaced character in Shakespeare,

raising this question, goes on to paint the sea in words. The new theater, illusionistic, dispenses with this.

In these early years of the seventeenth century, the important question for the playwright was, Which deserved priority, the eye or the ear? For Monteverdi the question, apparently different, comes down to the same thing: Which counts more, the message (words) or the music? Another and harder way to put this question is to ask in what the "message" consists.

The Gonzaga duke—a lecher, gambler, and brute—patronized the arts, luckily for Monteverdi. This Vincenzo I looks forward to the Emperor Nero in *The Coronation of Poppea,* not a moral bone in his body but compelling when he opened his mouth. For his provincial Maecenas, Monteverdi turned out memorable music, most of it on demand. The Carnival season of 1607 wanted something up-to-date, Duke Vincenzo thought, perhaps a "musical fable" (*favola in musica*) like the story of Orpheus, or Apollo and Daphne "with her thighs in bark." Friends of Monteverdi's, Caccini, Peri, and Gagliano, Florentine composers, had tried their hand at these *favole.* Their early entertainments, less operas than intermezzi, showed Monteverdi a way. Not a plagiarist, he plundered royally as by right of conquest. His *Orfeo,* the cornerstone of Italian opera, was produced at the Accademia degli Invaghiti in 1607. In this year he lost his wife. She wasn't Eurydice, though, and *Orfeo,* like *Macbeth,* written at the same time, is partly a *pièce d'occasion.*

The conjunction in time of Monteverdi and Shakespeare is surprising, anyway to me. Monteverdi "sounds" later, not expansive or discursive like a maker of the blank verse line but constricted like Augustan poets, makers of the heroic couplet. Psychologically, that is the company he keeps. English poets in the eighteenth century, reining in, prefer the couplet, and Monteverdi mines his riches in a little room. Doing this, he is often at odds with his material, a fruitful contention. The Orpheus myth, a poignant fable of love lost, found again, then lost forever, offers him the whole gamut of emotions. The hero's virtuoso aria in the underworld exploits this. Mostly, however, Monteverdi declines to run the gamut. Artistic temperament, reticent, is uppermost here, as when Orpheus, despairing, bids goodbye to the earth, sky, and sun. "Addio, terra; addio cielo, e sole, addio." These are words for Verdi's Violetta or Puccini's Mimi, expiring on wings of song, and reading the libretto we know what to expect. But expectation is baffled, nineteenth-century bravura being still over the horizon.

For the ending of *Orfeo,* Striggio the librettist brought the Maenads and their savagery on stage. This ending Monteverdi excised, not caring for very much reality. Instead, he made an apotheosis, sending the hero and the god Apollo up to heaven. Up there all sorrows end, and the chorus and full orchestra proclaim this. The ending is *non troppo,* though, faithful to the beginning. So what has happened between the prologue and the end of act 5? The answer is involved with calibrating or nuance. A chiaroscuro painter among the great composers, Monteverdi works with half-lights or half-tones. His imagination isn't seized by the dramatic difference between kinds but the modest difference between degrees. A limitation, it suggests his range. But the limitation, acknowledged, frees him for his appointed thing, the study of inflections.

Written many years later, *The Return of Ulysses to His Homeland* is like this. Every chance for the big curtain is there, but put by. The day of joy has come, and the hero, wandering many years, clasps Penelope, a wife of sorrows, to his heart. They have their final duet: "Yes, my life, yes! Yes, my heart, yes, yes!" "Si, si, vita! Si, si, core, si, si!" But the heyday in the blood is past for these two and their duet is muted, all passion spent. This is the enthusiasm reserved for middle age.

Even at his artistic summit, in *The Coronation of Poppea,* Monteverdi, knowing his demon, declines to unloose it. Some musicologists, not trusting their ears, want to deny him his masterpiece, but he is Ulysses come into his kingdom, and no one else had strength to draw the bow. Handed back and forth, a few words and phrases compose the great duet that ends the opera. We hear Poppea first, saluting Nerone: "O mio tesoro," then the Emperor repeating this: "My treasure." Crowded by passion, these lovers vie with each other and the notes intertwine. But passion is bridled and they keep a saving distance, "two distincts, division none," like Shakespeare's chaste pair in his "Phoenix and Turtle." Joining together on the same beat and word, then diverging again, they enact a formal pattern, not hearts beating wildly but contracting and releasing. Systole-diastole is how I "see" this. The hero and heroine get the same words but the notes they sing are different, not all that different, Monteverdi being true to himself. Melodic range is modest, the melody proceeding by whole tones and half tones. For Poppea's "O mia vita," the range is D, E-flat, F, C; for Nerone, singing the same phrase, it is B-flat, C, D, B-flat. Jejune, they think a century later.

Handel thinks this. Specializing in bold contours, he jumps a full octave in the middle of a phrase, sometimes in midsyllable, as when the altos and sopranos invoke "the Lord God omnipotent," beginning the "Hallclujah Chorus." Monteverdi, less audacious, lets his dramatic intervals wait on the ending or beginning of a phrase. Between "o mia vita" and "o mio tesoro," he moves up a fourth from D to G. Earlier, Poppea, beginning on F ("pur t'anno" in the libretto), gets there from B-flat, another fourth. Nerone, in the same part of the score, overgoes her, moving from C to F, a fifth. The range, not negligible, gets our attention, but for sheer pyrotechnics Monteverdi is to Handel as one to ten.

That is by choice, as we see when he tries the high wire. Fittingly, he reserves this to the moment of climax. Poppea, moving up the scale, reaches high F above middle C. At the same time, Nerone, moving down, meets her an octave below. Then they go their separate ways again. "O mia vita," she sings, and waits for him to echo her. He does this and they resume, beginning their new phrase on G. Once more a full octave separates and unites them. Two thrilling conjunctions across the tonal scale but needing their complement, subsidence. For the final phrase, "o mio tesoro," Nerone's voice ascends, Poppea's descends, each seeking the other or seeking resolution. Where they join, on B, the opera concludes, diminishing, says the libretto, "to nothing."

Repetition stales, and the love duet is one of a kind. Characteristically the music, austere beneath the florid melismata, vocal passages sung to one syllable of text, doesn't soar or swoop, and when emotion is up front it grows softer. This is Monteverdi's bias, possibly his need. Remembering a line from Wallace Stevens: before you heard him you never knew that fluttering things had so distinct a shade.

Partly the narrow range is expedient, an index of technique. *Orfeo,* the first opera, illustrates the technique. When the Messenger, a fatal bellman, brings the news that Eurydice is dead, his grief doesn't bear much emphasis, and that is true for Orpheus responding. A single bass line accompanies the hero's solo, emphasizing declamation. Venturing on the underworld at the end of act 3, he brings this basso continuo with him. A simple figured accompaniment in the bass clef, it emancipates the singer, allowing wider expressive intervals than polyphony allows. But the basso continuo, introduced in the first years of the seventeenth century, is a double-edged blade. Heightening the word, it depressess the music, and I think that is why it got a welcome from truth-telling composers. Monteverdi's friend Schütz, a German Lutheran composer, has the Evangelist, declaiming, take center stage in his Easter Oratorio for 1623. You hear the Word all right, and in the interstices the dead level accompaniment. But this isn't an *agon* where voice and music oppose each other. Taking priority but only by default, the Word falls on deaf ears. At least, my ear says so.

For Monteverdi, the basso continuo, promoting vocal virtuosity, insures the triumph of art over ideas. Pope's art of the closed couplet offers an analogy. In this stricter kind of poetry, meter torments the poet. Pope is conscious, step by step, of the clink and fall of the meter, and Monteverdi, by analogy, of the music master's baton, a tyrannical presence. Most people grudge the tyrant, but for these makers constraint is the warrant of freedom. Monteverdi's music enacts a proposition. It says that if you go free or naked, you aren't free but diffuse. Dissolving like "the life / That wants the means to lead it," the ungoverned composition leaks into thin air. The quotation is Shakespeare's, his point being to the maddened King Lear. Monteverdi, understanding how all art is privation, estimates his confinement, then works out a modus vivendi.

Where the next generation of opera composers, Lully and Scarlatti, use the orchestra to frame the voices, Monteverdi gives them alternating roles. Except in his choral sections when the two get together, he scores a verse for singing, following this with a short instrumental passage, the *ritornello,* "returning" on the text. Then comes another verse, then another ritornello. Freestanding, the rondo clamors for support, and the solos, duets, and trios, missing the orchestra, need a tether to restrain them. This the basso continuo provides. Rising and falling with each verse the composer sets, the music wants to be free as the wind. Jealous of freedom, the bass line opposes this. It presents the normative thing, letting the composer know where he came from. Like it or not, he can't range very far. Compensating, though, he does exacting stunts and turns within his narrow compass, more exacting for the limits imposed and accepted.

Monteverdi, unlike Shakespeare, doesn't thunder and lighten, or the lightning, a fitful incandescence, comes and goes. Listening to his operas is like reading a long poem by one of the lesser masters, e.g. Spenser in his *Faerie Queene,* if this near-contemporary had written in couplets. For the big things, "the spirit-stirring drum, the ear-piercing fife," you have to wait patiently. This means that when they come you like them better for waiting, or better for the calm before the storm. In the meantime, little things are going on in the music, but you have to pay attention to hear them.

Much opera before Mozart is like this, Handel's *Semele,* for instance. An opera in English, it ends when the heroine, getting beyond herself, has to pay the piper. A chorus of Priests, homiletic as usual, sings how "Nature to each allots his proper sphere, / But that forsaken we like meteors err." The propriety isn't moral but melodious, however, and Semele, being in voice, doesn't err. "Happy, happy," says the music, approving all that's artistically just. Not much happens in Handel's opera until the last act. We jog along equably, and I wouldn't want to claim much more. This isn't the *Messiah.* Then, like a rocket, the great aria begins: "Where e'er you walk." The excitement is in the difference, first the metronomic thing, then this startling exuberance of sound. The privation, anterior, sponsors the yield. That is how it is in Monteverdi's entertainments.

Orfeo made his name, but in Mantua they paid him in plaudits. Complaining to the Duke, he said how his pay was five months in arrears. The neglect soured him, and he groused about it for the rest of his life. In 1612, the money stopped altogether. Duke Vincenzo died this year, and his son, wielding a new broom, swept Monteverdi from court. He left Mantua with twenty-five *scudi* in his pocket, what he had to show for two decades of service. The *scudo,* a gold coin, was worth about five lire.

This cloud had a silver lining, however. The *maestro di capella* at St. Mark's, Venice, dying in 1613, Monteverdi put in for the job and got it. He spent the rest of his life in Venice. When he died at seventy-six, a contemporary guidebook describing the Frati church where he is buried, singled him out as "a great theorist of vocal and instrumental music." Incidentally, said the guidebook, he was famous for his valor and his compositions.

* * *

Theory, laying a heavy hand on baroque and Renaissance composers, told them that the words had to fertilize the music. First, though, you had to hear the words. The Council of Trent, legislating this, got the support of Protestants and Catholics. Victoria, Spanish and Catholic, tried in his Masses for the rhythm of the spoken word. His word was Latin and most of us don't understand it any more. For his considerable music, this seems not to matter. In King Henry's England, Cranmer, a Protestant, said that composers ought to give every syllable a note. "Important" syllables got high notes or greater time value. That was how it was in classical times, Thomas Campion said. Born the same year as Monteverdi, he reinvented the solo song, "a naked air without guide, or prop, or color but his own." Nakedness, he thought, cast the truth in relief. His music, like his "measured" poetry, is artificial in high degree, a word meant in praise and another instance of art bringing in its revenge on the artist.

Some reformers, root and branch, wanted music out of the church— Erasmus, for one, a great scholar with a tin ear. He said the church wasn't a theater where you went to be entertained. Anyway, the faithful couldn't understand what the people in the choir were singing. In St. Paul's time, there wasn't any music. Also "words were then pronounced plainly." There is something to this critique, and you can estimate what there is and isn't by pleasing your ear with the songs in the Fayrfax MS (Musical Heritage Society 4649). This early Tudor miscellany, not indifferent to words exactly, uses them partly as an occasion. Taking off from the text, the swirling vocalizes (long melodies sung on a vowel) have their abundant meaning, but the meaning is "metrical." You understand a fury in the words, not the words. People who put their money on meaning, as when they ask for the moral of the piece, deplore this.

In Monteverdi's time these people had a program, "Greek ethical theory." Boiled down, it said that the message took priority. Afterwards came the musical notation. Plato said this first in his *Republic*. Suave, he took it for granted that right-thinking composers would want to "adapt the foot and the melody to words." Seventeenth-century composers throwing in with this prescription didn't need to be bullied. The capitulating of the artist, in their time and ours, doesn't depend on violence but the seductive power of a noble ideal.

William Byrd, for instance, may be England's best composer. He wrote stunning vocal music but withheld approval unless it was "framed to the life of the words." Composers before Monteverdi, disputing this requirement, made words subordinate to number. John Dunstable was one of them, a servant of the Duke of Bedford, brother of Henry V. After five hundred years, the repertory still honors his music. In his own country this prophet went unhonored, though, and the English in the next century made fun of him for "dittying." They meant that he fitted his words to the music. Dunstable, said Thomas Morley, "treated words like a dunce." Strange when composers lust after words.

Coming out in this nervous time, *Orfeo* succeeded hugely, the critics making it conformable to precept. They gave high marks to the "poetry," Striggio's libretto, but liked the music too. It "serves the poetry so fittingly," one of them said. Not listening, he skewed the relation. "Two stars keep not their motion in one sphere," says Shakespeare's character, and Monteverdi's truth is more influential than Striggio's. Where the librettist thinks that Fame falls short of the truth, "Nè giunge al ver," the music doesn't doubt this; only it adds a whole new dimension as when, quitting a tunnel, we emerge into the light of day.

Depending on notes, the music is abstract or concrete beyond paraphrase. Unless you are tone deaf, you can't ward it off. Not open to rebuttal, unlike discursive prose, it assaults the senses, enlarging or corrupting the meaning of the text. "Corruptio optimi pessima," and the greatest composers, greatest all round, are necessarily the most corrupting. Wagner, so luscious, doesn't corrupt, his music not being economical. Less patient of himself, Monteverdi is more efficient, the reward of the parsimonious style. In the love duet for *The Coronation of Poppea,* he has it all together. This means that moral guidons go down.

One of the great old men, he wrote this opera at seventy-five. A portrait made in his old age shows a narrow, cadaverous face, big ears and big Italian nose. Above the short beard, the mouth is twisted, the eyebrows, arching, are Mephistophelian, and the deep-set eyes, taking everything in, give nothing away. Saving his best for last, the dogged old man is like that William Blake "Who beat upon the wall / Till truth obeyed his call," but the truth he mastered in age is indigenous, so gets nothing done. Devoid of anxiety, he antedates sin. His opera poses choices, not ethical, though, and the music, making a sequence, isn't causal, only linear, not "if . . . then" but "and . . . and." This is the triumph of the paratactic style.

For moral men and women, most of us by intention, virtue is itself and the apple of our eye. On his composing side, Monteverdi has a different equation. Virtue means vigor. Gesualdo, Prince of Venosa, Monteverdi's twin star, still lives in his music where a hundred lesser fry, better men than he was, are dust. The author of madrigals whose beauty spites the mills of time, this Neapolitan composer murdered his wife. Two hundred years later, Salieri, some say, murdered Mozart, but his C Major Concerto for flute and oboe is fantastic.

An erotic tangle like Shakespeare's "story of the night," *The Coronation of Poppea* gives its verdict for Eros. Love makes the world go round, and the persons of the play attest this. Drusilla, a lady-in-waiting, loves Ottone and he would like to reciprocate but has Poppea in his heart. Her heart belongs to Nero, who ought to love his wife but doesn't. Seneca, a philosopher, speaks for the proprieties, and he and Nero have their back and forth, musically exciting. A moral monster, Nero is an aphorist too, studying Villiers de l'Isle-Adam. Law, he tells his old teacher, is for servants. In the context of the opera, circumscribed ground, this seems right.

Showing their maker's mark, Monteverdi's characters elude classification. A cento of pretty sayings, Seneca, blowing his nose, pretends to utter moral truths. The music, sardonic, mocks him for this. Elsewhere, however, it grants him equanimity. So Seneca, a humbug, is a kind of hero, too. Octavia, the cast wife, is onion-eyed, evoking pity, also a virago, evoking contempt. Either way, Monteverdi finds her useful. "Farewell, Rome," she sings, leaving for exile. Her aria, deeply poignant, ends on the word "Addio," and dying, begets another. This other, *sempre staccato,* goes to the nurse Arnalta, saluting the coronation of Poppea, her charge. You can pick up the aria near the start of side ten on the old Telefunken recording. No better than she should be, the nurse is elated. Trumpets and oboes share her elation, and Monteverdi goes along with it, too.

The doubtful priest is catholic, maybe to a fault, discriminations, even sexual, reducing for him to caloric content. Nero is a soprano, in other days a castrato, while a tenor takes Arnalta's part, the role of the "funny old woman." An apologist for "fruitful sinning," this ambiguous person gets applause, her act 1 aria, jocose, suspending moral judgment. Later Ottone, down at the mouth, summons this judgment. "Basta!" says Poppea, a woman on her way, and the music tips the scales in her favor.

The notorious courtesan ought to be evil. Busenello, Monteverdi's librettist, thinks she is. Behind them both is Tacitus, who makes no bones about it. But the music, plaintive or exultant, enters a different claim. "Dead to finer feeling," Poppea meets her match in Nero, everybody's idea of the villain. Muffle the music and you have the Macbeths, a "butcher and his fiendlike queen." But that is only paraphrase speaking, absurd to sense. Celebrating their triumph, the Emperor and his consort, two bad ones who deserve each other, are two lovebirds on a branch. If we feel aberration, this is from the musical line. The last word being "Yes," no ending in opera is happier.

I still have my program for a long-ago performance of *The Coronation of Poppea.* After the credits comes a note from the director, telling what the opera is about. "A stinging indictment of absolute dictatorship," the director calls it. But he is taking the wish for the deed.

Orfeo, a tragedy, is happy all through, "doleful matter merrily set down." In the underworld they listen, compelled by a greater harmony than they can contradict. Dryden's phrase for this, in his St. Cecilia's Ode, is "sequacious of the lyre." You follow the lyre whether you want to or not. This power from harmony is disordering or makes new orders, hard to come to terms with. The chorus tells how life, short-lived and frail, soon disappears, "che tosto fugge," but the music, inconsequent, finds this gloomy saying a theme for laughter. Shakespeare's art is like that, a bitter sky, a winter wind, and "heigh-ho, the holly!" "How can it be that I live?" Monteverdi's hero wants to know. Echoing his question, blithe brass and horns say that living is better than dying. "Sweetly lamenting to himself," "soavemente lamentarsi," the hero sucks up sorrow like a sponge. Charon, a "powerful spirit" barring access to Hades, offers him his chance, artistic. "Spirto formidabil," he sings, playing with the words, and a violin, all tenderness, ornaments his phrasing. While this is going on, gloom and doom melt away.

Blurring the story line, the music sows confusion. Plot goes in one direction, downward to darkness, but the affect is withershins, taking a contrary course. The hero, foiled or dying tragically, undergoes a sea change. Handel, in his entertainment *Acis and Galatea,* turns him into a river. In Milton's *Lycidas,* a "monody," he becomes the Genius of the Shore. The becoming-something-else, a laurel tree, a hyacinth, a constellation in the heavens—Pope's happy resolution for his *Rape of the Lock*—works partly as metaphor, and the real transformation is from life into art.

In *Orfeo* and elsewhere, Monteverdi, impartial, is his own best auditor. He gives ear to Proserpina, pleading for the hero, then to Pluto, rejoining. Or he estimates Ottone, the unlucky suitor, then Nero, whose suit is successful. Handel's masque has a character, Damon, who speaks or sings to Monteverdi's case, aloof from partisanship. Improbably, this Damon plays the role of confidant to the hero and villain. Endlessly receptive but a stern critic, he makes us feel how the ultimate censor is the ear.

Even in his nondramatic work a dramatic composer, Monteverdi takes fire from conflict, the element he lived in. *Combattimento* offers a good all-purpose title but the conflict is aborted or its resolution is technical. Someone wins a victory, the composer. It turns on an "if" clause, "s'adoprerà suo ingegno": "if he will use his talent." This being art, not life, the career belongs to the talents. Like Orpheus, the artist as hero, Monteverdi has a golden plectrum, also a magic cittern, making the difference for the health of the piece. Inducing sleep in the boatman who guards the black stream, the cittern, plucked cunningly, nips us into wakefulness. "Now you need a stout heart and a good song," they tell the hero. Most of all, he needs a good song.

Taken as a type of morality play, this opera ends at the end of act 4. Tempted to look back, Orpheus succumbs and a chorus of Spirits moralizes his falling: "Only he who shall have victory over himself / Can be worthy of eternal fame." The contention isn't moral, though, between right and wrong, but aesthetic, between harmony and discord. In the vindication of harmony bitterness is discharged, and the hero, much falling, is acquitted. This is better than life, altogether less formal.

For Monteverdi's music, point counterpoint is the rubric, joy after woe and the other way round. "The tunes change, now gay, now sad." For Orpheus just now, sighs were food and tears were drink, but this changes, and "today" he is happy. Sorrow being a mine worth working, he doesn't stay happy for long. "Benedico il mio tormento," he sings, blessing his torment. This is pragmatic. The torment breeds, and the yield, musical, is pleasing. "Whoever sows in sorrow," the chorus instructs us, "reaps the fruit of every grace."

Fructifying musically, this sorrow makes mischief, however. Pluto rejoices when Proserpina, singing, remembers the rape, a "sweet deceit," that brought her to Hades. But her singing, harmonious, doesn't free him from passion. On the contrary, it renews "the ancient wound" of love in his heart. That is thanks to Monteverdi and a reason for inviting him out of the commonwealth. His music roused the passions, said a friar in Mantua, calling down the wrath of God on *Orfeo*. The fire and brimstone seem much, but this judgment isn't out of the way.

Or not altogether. Donne has a poem, "The Triple Fool," that tells how the poet draws his pains "through rhyme's vexation," meaning to allay them. Bringing grief to numbers will tame it, he thinks. But some other, it might be Monteverdi, sets and sings his grief and by delighting many, frees it again. This art of Monteverdi's, augmenting grief or love, is unexpectedly kinetic. However, you can't enlist it in the wars of truth, and the friar-critic—he has his modern avatars—works himself up to no purpose. Calming every troubled heart, the music does the other thing, inflaming the most frozen minds. But the calming or inflaming make a well-tuned concord, winning assent, the death of activity.

In the whirlwind of passion, even there, says Hamlet to the players, "you must acquire and beget a temperance that may give it smoothness." Not the same as the naturalistic representing of passion, this smoothness, oil on troubled waters, gives passion the lie. You see this in Monteverdi

and his successors to the present. Indifferent to morality, they don't have
our good at heart, or the good they appeal to, like an axiom set, is only
"satisfiable." For example, Donizetti in *L'Elisir d'Amore*. The male leads,
at swords' points, are full of themselves, and tragedy for both is just
around the corner. But it all goes into harmony as they join in their great
act 2 duet. Not reconciled but getting outside themselves, these rivals
make a final claritas beyond moral censure or approval.

Intellectual pressure, mandated by the theorizers, isn't felt much in
Monteverdi's music. Madrigals from his ninth book (Musical Heritage
Society 941) are only exemplary. Content as such absorbs them less than
its ordering or disposing, as when you push the ink blots around on the
page, wanting to see what will happen. A good way to go, in music and the
arts generally, this outrages modern notions of what comes first. "A great
work of art demands a great thought," some modern person said, but
thought for Monteverdi is mostly a given, having value only as it enables.
Gracefully disposed in an artificial landscape, make-believe shepherds
celebrate the beauties of nature. "È null' altro desio," one tells us. "And I
have no other wish." Where Schütz's Evangelist craves redemption and
Guarini's Pastor Fido wants to tickle the viscera, art for prurience' sake,
this shepherd's business is delighting, which may be self-delighting. Eurydice in the opera, self-delighting, dies while gathering flowers,
"cogliendo fiori." Merely adverbial, this fact seems off the point, but the
music, playing on "fiori," lets us know that the flowers are themselves and
need attention.

Static like all art when it isn't impure, Monteverdi's madrigals look like
dialogue, a dynamic form. Voices answer each other, but "Hic" and
"Ille," our protagonists, take the same line. Conclusions are rhetorical,
managed by the refrain, an arbitrary cinching. Adjusting it gives you the
ending. Like an echo or rhyme in poetry, the refrain, "gioir . . . languir,"
joyful or doleful, convinces us sonantally. This isn't what theory means by
sound mirroring sense. Monteverdi knows what theory means and holds
the mirror up to nature when he wants to. *The Coronation of Poppea*
shows him on his "expressive" side. Pledged to kill his wife, Ottone blurts
out the truth, and the notes, descending and gravid, mimic his *secreto
gravissimo.* Meanwhile the Empire is going to the dogs, and Nero, a
feckless ruler, laughs about it. Gleeful, the music laughs with him. But
here he comes, the soldiers sing, so "let us keep quiet." Mirroring the
words, the music says "Hush!" Sometimes, though, the music, impatient
of "views," lumps them together, composing their difference. Surprising
in the madrigals, this is shocking in the hymns and motets.

For his sacred song *Ut Queant,* a hymn to Saint John, Monteverdi sets a
Latin text that varies from stanza to stanza. Now the saint's "devoted
servants" and now "guilty sinners," we move without ado from one role to

the next. But the music doesn't notice these important transitions. Discriminating thoughtfully, "through-composed" music provides a new melody for every new stanza. Monteverdi's setting is "strophic," however, and the melody for every stanza is the same. Ignoring our little lapses and our efforts to do something about this, perhaps he discounts them, like Shakespeare's Clown in *Twelfth Night*. "Anything that's mended is but patched," says the Clown. "Virtue that transgresses is but patched with sin, and sin that amends is but patched with virtue." Not an intellectual, Monteverdi, intelligent, has this skeptical notion of things.

Careless of discriminations, he modifies the sense, or you can say he redefines it. *Uccide* and *ride*, "killing" and "laughing," answer each other, and *clamor* answers *amor*, opposites by convention. This is echo music, like certain poems of Sidney's. Dissolving old connections, it argues for new ones we hadn't noticed before. A joiner or carpenter, the composer takes in hand the clashed edges of words. Making a join, he fits them together, and yesterday's oxymoron is today's familiar truth. The new thing perplexes, though. Relationship is everything, Monteverdi seems to say. Mirroring sense with a vengeance, the music, ambiguous through and through, reflects this. "To hear with eyes belongs to love's fine wit," says Shakespeare in the sonnets. In Monteverdi's music, you see with your ears.

Under the composer's hand, words, fragmented or agglutinated, lose their integrity. This happens across the board. Striking the ear, *che sete*, "what thirst," comes through as "kay-say-tay," a jingle. *Questo mesto giorno* translates as "this sad day," but if you English the Italian you impoverish the "sense," mnemonic like nursery rhyme. "Ah, great gods," a shepherd sings, *Deh, sommi dei*. Evaluating these homonyms, one an interjection, the other a substantive, the ear, helpless, can't tell them apart. Point of view is implicit in this baffling of distinction.

The ghost of polyphony haunts the new music. Fresh from his reading in Plato and Boethius, Monteverdi might have laid this ghost, writing solo songs whose truth is open and shut. But doubt nagged him or old loyalties, or his truth wasn't simple, and the madrigals that made him famous stuck to polyphony, lacerating the words. Even in the sacred music he does what Plato says he shouldn't, "puts his ear before his intelligence." He thinks it makes a better arbiter. Setting the Psalms (Period SPLP 536), he divides the line of text between male and female voices, but each infiltrates the other's part, and individual words are bones of contention, too. Emphasizing sound, not sense, or saying that sound is sense, this music resembles magic, where meaning, mysterious, isn't open to rational inspection.

The new declamatory style gives priority to meaning, and you hear it in the madrigals; but its uses are surprising. Oddly for the man who builds on truth's foundations, Monteverdi employs this style for "neutral" words that don't signify or shouldn't. Chanted, they come clear, and evidently he wants this. But "important" words don't get chanted, and the music obscures them. Consulting his own eccentric version of truth, he decorates neutral words with a melisma. He doesn't do this all the time, though, and the sobbing trill occurs impartially on conjunctions, prepositions, and big words like "love" and grief." Intellectually, I don't know where this leaves us.

Modern form is organic form. Polemical, it wants to reveal the shape beneath the skin. Innocent of this shape or detecting another, Monteverdi makes music like the exponential curve, i.e. it could keep going forever. All art, it seems to me, invites this description, not modern deep down but obeying imperatives that antedate our new learning. In the madrigals, three stanzas are enough to do the business, but that isn't inevitable, only a rule of thumb. Though thesis meets antithesis, no synthesis, emerging, dictates the conclusion. Truth being the matter of the religious music, things ought to be different. But sacred and secular aren't that different for Monteverdi. The sonorous "Amen" that puts a period to Psalm III, *Beatus Vir,* comes pretty much by fiat. A final notation, it might have been entered before.

In his sense of an ending, musically exigent, Monteverdi resumes the antique style. But only middling art needs labels. For consequential art, staking out its own territory, a private preserve, labels are dispensable, and he sheds them easily, water off a duck's back. The larger, the less rationalizable, and if you want his quiddity you have to describe him in his own terms. The Monteverdi I listen to doesn't differ step by step from the "representative" composer of the textbooks or blurbs on record jackets, only in the sum of his parts.

Growing up in an age committed to theory, the child of his age accepted its prescripts, making "a kind of music by which men might talk in harmony." This meant rejecting "compounded" music, "bated" or vexed with fugue, and "the excessive passage-work with which they embellished it." Also it meant submitting "for the most part to a recitative style." In these quotations, contemporary theorists are spelling out the new imperatives. Monteverdi endorsed them, always "for the most part." His "arioso" vocal line, midway between aria and recitative, comes home more clearly than the music of his fathers, polyphonic composers. What his voices have to tell us seems not worth remarking, though, not in so many words, and it isn't for their saying that we remember Monteverdi.

Where the fathers in their First Practice made music mistress of words, he rebelled against this, building his new art on the ruins of the old. Partly his rebellion had less to do with theory than with being fully fledged, as when austere Francesco, the fifth Mantuan duke, rebelled against Vincenzo, his father, or Sidney against Petrarch and his "long-denizened woes." Sometimes Sidney takes truce with Petrarch, and Monteverdi, not draconian, makes a bad rebel. Like Orpheus in the Underworld, he can't help looking back.

Honoring words, he had his own sense of what this required. His contemporary Campion wanted to couple "words and notes lovingly together," another imperative, and Monteverdi took it to heart. Magnanimous, he did more than this, however, and his magnanimity, the cardinal virtue, is also a vice, making trouble for him and us. Coupling the text with notes, he transformed it, darkening truth.

Like Mozart and Shakespeare, he couldn't stint on beauty if he tried. In *Macbeth* a hired bravo speaks like a poet where a surly epithet is all you need, and the great aria in *The Magic Flute* glorifies an evil woman, the Queen of the Night. As Monteverdi received it, the story of Poppea provides the stuff for a cautionary fable. Shakespeare's given in his *Measure for Measure* is like this, and the Vienna he imagines—it stinks in some sort—puts you in mind of Monteverdi's Rome, a cauldron of unholy loves. Then these makers, impersonal or themselves alone, bend to the work. Unexpected things happen, not welcome to some. Vivifying the given, each enacts the triumph of our erected flesh.

First and last the opportunist, Monteverdi wants to get the job done. Moral purpose, avowed or otherwise, takes a back seat to this executive impulse. Opportunism, much maligned, is another word for the demiurge, a chthonic spirit whose activity is willful but lucky. Credentialed makers at their wit's end invoke this shaping spirit but do so at their peril, it being no respecter of preconceived ideas. Campion, anxious for truth, likened the demiurge to Procrustes. This old tyrant, careless of truth, lopped or stretched his victims, a summary procedure. But when he was done they fit his "procrustean" bed.

The result shows arbitrariness but makes a coherence, oddly as near to truth as we can get. Campion doesn't say this; that is what I think. Anyway, the approximation satisfied Monteverdi. He wasn't a theorist but a professional entertainer, with all this means for good.

Divine Right and Divine Retribution in Beaumont and Fletcher's *The Maid's Tragedy*

Ronald Broude

We are accustomed to regarding *The Maid's Tragedy* (ca. 1608–11) as a play about the divine right of kings. The immunities conferred by kingship have a prominent part in the play, and the dilemma faced by the play's central character, Amintor, depends upon a conflict between the code of personal honor and a concept of monarchy that holds the person of the king to be inviolable.

Surprisingly, in view of the importance that the theme of kingship—or, more specifically, regicide—is thought to have in *The Maid's Tragedy,* there has been little agreement about what—if anything—the play says about kings, their responsibilities, and their privileges. During the reign of Charles II, influential members of the court seem to have felt that *The Maid's Tragedy,* with its portrayal of a lustful king slain by the woman he has seduced, was a play inimical to the interests of the Crown, and, accordingly, Edmund Waller undertook to rewrite Beaumont and Fletcher's most successful tragedy, providing two alternative endings in both of which the King's life is spared.[1] On the other hand, Samuel Taylor Coleridge, at least partially on the basis of his reading of *The Maid's Tragedy,* characterized Beaumont and Fletcher as "the most servile *jure divino* royalists."[2] J. St. Loe Strachey, however, vigorously contested this view, observing that the portrayals of kings in the plays of Beaumont and Fletcher demonstrate attitudes quite different from the blind respect for royalty that Coleridge seems to have seen in works such as *The Maid's Tragedy.*[3] More recently, John Danby has sought to show that the royalist views enunciated by characters in the Beaumont and Fletcher plays were not necessarily the views of the playwrights themselves but were, rather, one of the several absolutes, conflicts between which furnished these proto-cavalier dramatists with dramatically effective situations.[4]

What Beaumont and Fletcher's original audience may have thought of the regicide in *The Maid's Tragedy* we cannot say with certainty, for we have no contemporary comment on this aspect of the play. This lack of comment, however, may in itself be significant, for it suggests that the killing of the King in *The Maid's Tragedy* was not viewed by Jacobean playgoers with undue alarm. Indeed, had *The Maid's Tragedy* contained any matter which could have been regarded as politically objectionable, it is highly unlikely that the Master of the Revels would have allowed it to reach the stage: James I was, after all, a sovereign particularly sensitive to the privileges of royalty, and, as the author *The Trew Law of Free Monarchies,* he had propounded one of the most extreme statements of the theory of divine right to have been published during the Renaissance.

Plays in which wicked kings are killed are not uncommon in the drama of the English Renaissance—witness Saturninus, slain in *Titus Andronicus;* Piero, in *Antonio's Revenge;* and Claudius, in *Hamlet.* What is unusual in *The Maid's Tragedy's* treatment of regicide is the stress placed upon the view that the royal person is sacred. Other plays in which regicide occurs adroitly avoid reminding their audiences of the idea—sanctioned by approved doctrine under James—that a subject raising his hand against his lawful sovereign is guilty not only of treason but also of impiety. Regicide—even tyrannicide—was simply too sensitive a subject to deal with directly on the Stuart stage.

Perhaps, however, it was just this "forbidden" element in the regicide theme that made it attractive to Beaumont and Fletcher—and that helped to make *The Maid's Tragedy* popular with their audiences. For the courtier playgoers for whom Beaumont and Fletcher wrote, *The Maid's Tragedy* may well have provided much needed relief from the pressures—both intellectual and psychological—imposed by an unnecessarily rigid and unrealistically restrictive theory of royal privilege, a theory that, given the circumstances obtaining in the English court, could be questioned by the king's adherents neither openly nor directly.

But to prove successful, a play dealing with regicide was obliged to maintain a delicate balance between the dramatically effective and the politically objectionable. In *The Maid's Tragedy,* such a balance is carefully maintained by diverting attention from the political implications of the killing of the King. In so far as possible, the King's death is "depoliticized": the conflict in which the King plays so important a part is treated as a private rather than a public matter, and his transgressions are represented as injuries to his victim's personal honor and sexual vanity instead of crimes that affect the welfare of the commonwealth. Character and motivation are also artfully manipulated, so that the question of regicide, having been exploited for maximum dramatic effect in the second, third, and fourth acts, is tactfully forgotten when the King is actually killed in the fifth. Finally, the central issue of the play—the entrapment of

Amintor into a tragic marriage intended to conceal the liaison of the King and Evadne—is portrayed as part of a larger complex of events over which the heavens preside and that they direct towards the punishment of the adulterous king. Here again, however, political questions are eschewed, for the heavens seem to be punishing not a king who is an adulterer but an adulterer who happens to be a king. As the heavens' program works itself out, Amintor is spared the cruel necessity of choosing between the dishonor of wittoldom and the guilt of regicide, and the King's death, when it does come, assumes a significance altogether different from that it would have had, had Amintor, after mature deliberation, elected to kill the King himself.

But if Beaumont and Fletcher were successful in their own day in making of *The Maid's Tragedy* a play that both is and is not about the rights of kings, their success has not been altogether able to withstand the passage of time. The strategies that they employed to render their treatment of regicide acceptable to their Jacobean audiences depended in large part upon the conventions of action and character that were peculiar to the Renaissance English stage and that did not survive the closing of the theaters in 1642. It is, therefore, not surprising that these strategies should have failed to have their intended effect when the theaters reopened after the Restoration. For audiences of the Restoration and succeeding generations, Amintor's forcefully expressed views on the inviolability of the royal person naturally suggested that *The Maid's Tragedy* was a play about the divine right of kings. Moreover, like much literature that seeks to exploit the sensational aspect of forbidden questions while avoiding the potentially embarrassing implications of their answers, *The Maid's Tragedy* has suffered from the weakening of the taboos that had made its carefully wrought equivocations so daring to the courtier playgoers for whom it was written; to modern audiences, the play may well seem wanting in the integrity of vision that is expected of great tragedy. To recover some measure of the meaning that *The Maid's Tragedy* may have had for its original audience, it is necessary to read the play within the context of both the Jacobean political theory upon which it draws and the Jacobean dramatic conventions within which it was conceived. The insight to be gained is well worth the effort.

The limits of royal power and the immunities and privileges attaching to kingship—the theme with which *The Maid's Tragedy* seems to promise that it will deal—were issues much in men's minds circa 1610, the approximate date of *The Maid's Tragedy's* composition.[5] The accession of James I had brought to the English throne a rigid theoretician who claimed for the Crown broader rights and greater privileges than had been either asserted in Tudor theory or implied by Tudor practice. Changes in the social

structure of England, however, had given new standing to a middle class that ascribed to Parliament and the Law powers at least as great as those of the Crown. Social differences, economic pressures, and political confrontations served to aggravate the conflict between the Crown and the institutions in which were seen to lie alternative sources of power. Eventually, this conflict—and the antagonisms that it reflected—was to prove a cause of civil war; during James's reign, however, rival claims were still in the process of being staked and basic issues were still only tentatively defined.

Sixteenth-century English political thought had consisted of disparate (and sometimes mutually inconsistent) elements drawn from a broad range of traditions—from theology, from law, from speculative politics, and from custom.[6] The views that had received official sanction—and that had been disseminated in forms ranging from learned treatises to simple sermons and homilies—had been those which supported the Tudors in their effort to establish a strong central government which would secure the Tudor dynasty from feudal upheavals of the sort that had toppled in turn their Lancastrian and Yorkist predecessors. Notwithstanding the sixteenth century's interest in—and astute application of—the principles of *Realpolitik,* approved Tudor theory had grounded its concept of kingship upon a medieval cosmology that represented the structure of the commonwealth as the political manifestation of the divine order that permeated and informed the universe. To each member of the commonwealth (as to each being in the universe) God was supposed to have assigned a place and a function. The place of the king in the commonwealth had been understood to be analogous to that of God in the universe: the king's function was to serve as God's deputy on earth, to maintain order in the body politic, and to punish those who transgressed the law. Theories that sought the mandate for kingship in the assent of those governed or in a system of mutual obligations between sovereign and subject had not been unknown in sixteenth-century England—indeed, they had been reflected in some of England's most venerable institutions[7]—but Tudor theorists had preferred to regard royal power as flowing directly from God: the king and the magistrates, it was asserted, held offices ordained by God, and the power that they exercised was therefore His.

Failure on the part of the king to seek out and prosecute all malefactors had been considered an extremely serious matter, for unpunished crime had been understood to lay upon the entire commonwealth a burden of collective guilt. Especially grave was the situation created when the king himself violated the laws that it was his duty to uphold. Nevertheless, Tudor theory, consistent with its emphasis on the importance of civil order and its fear of riot and insurrection, had assumed the position that no royal

malfeasance—neither negligence in the pursuit of malefactors nor misconduct by the sovereign himself—could justify the use of force against the legitimate king. The wicked king, it had been argued, was a punishment visited by the heavens upon an unworthy people; to resist such a king was therefore to resist the will of the heavens. The subject of such an evil sovereign was advised to accept God's will and to obey his lawful ruler. Only if his king commanded a course of action manifestly contrary to the word of God could the subject refuse to obey; such refusal, however, rendered him liable to whatever punishment the sovereign thus thwarted might choose to inflict. Called by modern scholars the "doctrine of nonresistance," this insistence upon the immunity of the king from reprisals by his subjects and the obligation of subjects to obey even tyrannical kings had been a prominent feature of "official" Tudor theory; it had been especially valuable in helping to maintain political stability during the uncertain early years of the English Reformation.[8]

With the accession of Mary Tudor in 1553, English Protestants, who for the most part had been staunch in their support of the doctrine of nonresistance under Henry and Edward, had begun to reconsider their position. The sources of royal power were reexamined, and the view that the king derives his authority from "the people," who, if he abuses the trust placed in him, may remove him from office, had been revived and elaborated. The duty of a good Christian living under an impious king had been studied, and it had been suggested, tentatively at first but later more forcefully, that passive resistance might not in all cases be a sufficient response to the ungodly exercise of royal power: tyrannicide had been openly discussed.[9] With the death of Mary in 1558, English Protestants' interest in tyrannicide had understandably waned, but on the continent Reformers and Counter-Reformers alike had become intensely concerned with defining the circumstances that might justify active opposition to a legitimate but despotic ruler; some of the Catholic documents in this bitter exchange of pamphlets and treatises had been unmistakably addressed to the Catholic subjects of England's Protestant queen.[10] Concern with tyrannicide had not, however, been purely speculative; events such as the deposition of Mary Stuart in Scotland and the assassination of William of Orange in the Netherlands had served to keep tyrannicide a topic of current if not continuously immediate interest for Englishmen.

The broad range of ideas on kingship to which Englishmen had been exposed during the sixteenth century all but precluded the possibility of a favorable reception for views on royal authority as militant as those professed by James I when he ascended the English throne in 1603. As James VI of Scotland, the new English king had waged a long and bitter struggle to impose upon the unruly Scots nobility the same sort of strong monarchy that the Tudors had created in England a century earlier, and,

accordingly, his conception of the divine right of kings had become too firmly fixed to permit comfortable adjustment to the very different political conditions obtaining in his new kingdom. James's views, which his subjects could read in his published speeches and in *The Trew Law of Free Monarchies,* went well beyond the familiar model presented by "official" Tudor theory.[11] For James, the king derived his authority directly from God and was therefore responsible to no earthly power. The king, James argued, stood above the law, for laws were established in the king's name, and might be altered, suspended or revoked at his pleasure. The king might obey his own laws if he chose, but he was under no obligation to do so, and he might without reproach ignore them when it suited him. To all intents and purposes, then, royal power was absolute, untrammeled by institutions of any sort: this, indeed, is what James meant by a "free" monarchy.

To be sure, the king would be called to account before God both for his own conduct and for the welfare of his subjects, and severe punishment would certainly be visited upon the ruler found to have failed in his duty. Sometimes, James admitted, invoking a commonplace of Tudor doctrine, this punishment would take the form of an insurrection raised by God among the subjects of the wicked sovereign; all good Christians, however, were urged not to participate themselves in such mutinies, for, they were warned, subjects who overthrow their king are instruments of God which, having served His purpose, will be delivered up to the punishments prescribed for rebels.[12]

Although *The Maid's Tragedy* draws upon political theories that would have been familiar to Englishmen during the first decade of James's reign, it does so in ways that effectively remove the play from the context of contemporary political controversy. *The Maid's Tragedy* presupposes no more than superficial acquaintance with either James's views or the premises of sixteenth- or early seventeenth-century political thought; it avoids serious discussion of both abstruse and controversial aspects of political theory; and it alludes to royal privileges and immunities only in the simplest and most general terms. No attempt is made to examine the issues most likely to be of current interest—the limits of the king's powers and the relationship of royal authority to the laws of the realm. Nor is there any balanced presentation of conflicting views: the broad yet vague claims made on behalf of royal privilege by Amintor, the King, and Evadne are nowhere countered—not even in 3.2, the crucial scene in which Amintor reveals his predicament to Melantius—by reference to the obligations inherent in the office of kingship or to possible (if not universally acceptable) courses of action open to subjects whose king fails in his duty.[13]

The concepts of kingship upon which *The Maid's Tragedy* draws are applied to a situation so apolitical and so unusual that they seem to have little if any relevance to the real world of politics. In *The Maid's Tragedy,* a

king and his mistress propose to make use of the privileges and immunities of the royal office in a cynical attempt to keep their illicit relationship secret: they depend upon the position of the King both to compel
a loyal subject's participation in their scheme and to shield them from the
subject's wrath when he discovers how he has been deceived. But Tudor-
Stuart political theory does not contemplate the flagrant and premeditated
abuse of royal authority in an essentially private matter such as this.
Traditional theory assumes that, unlike the King in *The Maid's Tragedy,*
most sovereigns whose subjects complain of them will have some measure—or at least some pretext—of justice on their side. Moreover, the
wrongs to which English political thought addresses itself are political
wrongs—abuses on a large scale involving the consciences, lives, or
property of substantial numbers of subjects. Aside from the scandal of his
personal life, however, the King in *The Maid's Tragedy* remains a cipher:
we do not know, in political terms, whether he has been a good king or a
bad one, whether his policies have been wise or foolish, his kingdom
prosperous or impoverished.[14] He seems, in fact, to exist in a political
vacuum; the sins for which he dies are private sins, and his death, in so far
as a king's death can be, is without political significance. The situation
presented in *The Maid's Tragedy* is, then, an artificial one sufficiently
removed from the realities of English politics to make the application of
political theory to it a harmless academic exercise, an exercise in the
tradition of the *controversiae,* which, as Eugene Waith has shown, play so
interesting a part in the drama of Beaumont and Fletcher.[15]

Although *The Maid's Tragedy* assiduously avoids discussion of specific
topics that might have been construed to have relevance to Jacobean
politics, the importance accorded the question of royal immunity in the
second, third, and fourth acts requires that, if the play is not to appear a
pièce à thèse on the limits of royal privilege, the killing of the King must
not seem the considered act of a morally responsible character who has
carefully reviewed the arguments both for and against regicide. The King
has committed serious crimes, and he must certainly be made to pay for
them, but Amintor, who has suffered most from the King's malfeasance
and has had to decide whether or not to revenge himself upon his sovereign, cannot be made the immediate instrument of the King's punishment: having affirmed his belief in the inviolability of the royal person,
Amintor cannot reverse himself without calling into question the ade-
quacy of the doctrine of royal immunity. The punishment of the King is
accordingly accomplished through the joint efforts of three characters
among whom the functions of exposing the King and putting him to death
are carefully distributed: Amintor reveals the King's crimes to Melantius;
Melantius plans and sets in motion the machinery of retribution, and

Evadne executes Melantius's instructions. Great care is exercised in managing the details of circumstance and character that would have shaped an audience's perception of the significance of the characters' actions, so that the likelihood of any incident's assuming embarrassing political implications is effectively minimized.

The character of Amintor and the circumstances in which he is placed are manipulated in such a way as to make his reluctance to proceed against the King both credible and acceptable to a Jacobean audience. The particulars that define the injury that Amintor has suffered are carefully selected and arranged so that he cannot take action against the King without changing from an innocent victim to a villain revenger. The conventions of the Renaissance English stage recognized only one sort of crime for which revenge might be sanctioned—a felony (usually but not always murder) secretly committed against an immediate blood relative.[16] Judged in accordance with these conventions, the injuries that the King has done Amintor—commanding him to break his vows to Aspatia and marrying him to the dishonored Evadne—although grave, would not have been regarded by a Jacobean audience as serious enough to warrant revenge. Thus the question of justifiable regicide does not really arise in *The Maid's Tragedy,* for regardless of whether Evadne's lover be a king or a commoner, Amintor lacks sufficient cause to take action against him.

Nor does Amintor's character—a skillfull blend of engaging virtues and serious flaws—suggest that he will be likely to repair the damage that the King and Evadne have done his honor. Amintor can be generous, brave, and steadfast in his loyalty to principles in which he believes, but he can also be petty, weak, and strangely indifferent to the demands of the honor he professes to value so highly. In 2.1, we see him—under great stress, it is true—disgracefully agreeing to act the role of satisfied husband for which the King and Evadne have cast him; he defends his decision with the thoroughly unacceptable argument that honor is merely a matter of appearances:

> Me thinkes I am not wrong'd,
> Nor is it ought, if from the censuring world
> I can but hide it—reputation
> Thou art a word, no more. . . .
>
>   (2.1.331–34)[17]

These sentiments are in perfect harmony with those which underlie Amintor's plea in 3.1 that Melantius not revenge himself upon the King lest it

> shame me to posterity. . . .
> It will be cald
> Honor in thee to spill thy sisters blood

If she her birth abuse, and on the King
A brave revenge, but on me that have walkt
With patience in it, it will fixe the name
Of fearefull cuckold.

(3.2.216, 223–28)

We are reminded by these speeches that Amintor has already compro-
mised his honor by acceding to the King's command and abandoning
Aspatia, already his troth-plight wife.[18] As we have observed, Renaissance
Englishmen were unlikely to have regarded royal authority as having
power sufficient to compel a subject to disobey the dictates of his own
conscience, nor were they likely to have regarded the plea of obedience to
a royal command as absolving a subject from responsibility for his own
actions. Amintor himself shares these views: as he acknowledges,

It was the King first mov'd me to't, but he
Has not my will in keeping.

(2.1.130–31)

Nevertheless, Amintor has allowed his honor to be stained because of his
undiscriminating allegiance to the Crown and because of an ignoble preference for present comfort—the King's favor, alliance with his friend Melantius, and marriage to a much admired woman—to the disadvantages of
incurring royal displeasure while keeping his word to Aspatia. For an
audience sensitive to such failings, Amintor's inability to redeem his honor
by taking action against the King would seem neither surprising nor out of
character.

The passive role that Amintor must play if *The Maid's Tragedy* is safely
to avoid politically compromising issues determines the course that his
career follows. Amintor's tragedy conforms to the pattern associated with
such similar tragic figures as Richard II and Lear, and audiences ac-
quainted with the persecutions that these noble but flawed characters
impotently endure must have found the shape of Amintor's tragedy familiar.[19] Like Richard and Lear, Amintor can see the immediate cause of his
misery in an ill-considered choice—in Amintor's case, the decision to obey
the royal command and marry Evadne instead of Aspatia. This decision—
like those of Richard and Lear, superficially tenable but tainted by elements of self-indulgence and moral irresponsibility—opens Amintor to
persecution by powerful and implacable enemies; it seems also to deprive
him of the ability effectively to take the initiative in determining his own
fate. Reduced to theatrical displays of self-pity and futile rage, Amintor
must look to others to right the wrongs he has suffered. Only when he has
been rescued from the consequences of his fatal choice is Amintor able to
regain the moral composure with which bravely to confront his tragedy.

Melantius, who provides the impetus for action against the King, is presented as a veteran warrior, less naive and more adept at intrigue than he would like others to believe, but nevertheless decidedly more comfortable with simple deeds than with complex ideas. Forced to choose between the rival claims of friendship and family solidarity, Melantius quickly decides upon the priority of his loyalties and acts in accordance with the decision he has made. His preference for action allows him little opportunity for the sort of prolonged meditation that might be construed as an embarrassing discussion of regicide, and this quality permits the playwrights to accomplish almost without our noticing it the dangerous transition from deliberation on Amintor's plight to action against the King.

Particular attention has been given to the details that show Melantius to be not only a gentleman concerned with the honor of his family but also a just and pious man who accepts the part he must play in the King's punishment fully aware of what will be required of him.[20] In depicting the revenge that Melantius effects, the playwrights are careful "to touch all the bases." Although quick to act, Melantius is not over hasty: having heard—and believed—Amintor's accusations, he nevertheless seeks confirmation of what his friend has told him: having bullied a confession from Evadne, he patiently allows her to corroborate Amintor's charges by herself identifying the King as her lover.[21] Assured of the King's guilt, Melantius rightly perceives that the King's crimes are offenses against the heavens and that the revengers are the agents of the gods' vengeance: "All the gods require it [i.e., the killing of the King]," Melantius tells his sister: "They are dishonored in him" (4.1.144–45). Finally, having successfully contrived the King's death and secured the safety of himself and his followers, Melantius casts aside the dissimulation that he has so skillfully employed, accepting responsibility for all that he has done and submitting his cause for judgment.[22] Melantius has sought no material benefit for himself from the King's death; he is prepared to serve the new king as a loyal subject. That his actions have been scrupulous and his cause just is suggested by the choric observations of Strato ("He looks as if he had the better cause, . . . I do beleeve him noble . . ." [5.2.14, 19]) and by the promptness of Lysippus in pardoning him.

Evadne, to whom falls the actual killing of the King, is a character so filled with contradictions and so lacking in moral substance that it is difficult to attach moral significance to the regicide she commits. When we first see her, she is proud of her position as the King's mistress, but she is not altogether comfortable with the burdens that the necessity of concealing her liaison have placed upon her. She pities Amintor, yet she is able cold-bloodedly to make him accept the cruel realities of the shameful position into which she has helped to maneuvre him. Her confession to Melantius is extracted by brute force instead of being freely given, and her "reformation" seems dictated as much by fear of her irate brother as by sincere repentance. Although Evadne accepts the killing of the King as a form of penance, she sees it also as a way of winning Amintor. Unlike Melantius, Evadne is quite unaware that the King has offended the gods and that in punishing him she is acting as the heavens' agent; instead, she sees herself as avenging her much-injured husband, her dishonored brother, and her own lost purity. Her suicide, which she regards as proof of her love for Amintor, is merely another indication of her emotional instability and inability to recognize the moral principles that should be guiding her actions; having substituted love for ambition as her *summum bonum,* she dies, like another "reformed" criminal who seeks belatedly to avenge his own victim, in a mist.[23] She is, to use the familiar image that James employs in *The Trew Law,* an instrument that the heavens have employed to scourge a wicked king and that, having served its purpose, will be cast into the fire.[24]

Perhaps the most effective means by which *The Maid's Tragedy* contrives not to be a play about divine right is by being a play about divine retribution. The chain of incidents by which the adultery of the King and Evadne is revealed and the adulterers are punished is conceived and presented in accordance with the formulaic sequence of events that on the Renaissance English stage was reserved for portrayals of the ways in which the heavens bring secret crimes to light and mete out justice to secret criminals.[25] There is the secret crime exposed by the miscarriage of the very scheme intended to conceal it; there is the twist of plot by which the criminals are made the instruments of their own undoing; and there is the liberal use of dramatic irony to underline the limitations of the cunning in which the criminals have trusted to help them escape retribution. For a Jacobean audience, the presence of these conventions of action and dramaturgy would have indicated unequivocally that *The Maid's Tragedy* belongs to the tradition of plays concerned with the implementation of God's Justice and the operation of Divine Providence.

All of the events that constitute the action of *The Maid's Tragedy* have their origin in the adultery of the King and Evadne. To provide against exposure should Evadne conceive, the lovers devise the ingenious stratagem of marrying Evadne to Amintor, a highly regarded young man whose respect for the Crown will, they cynically assume, protect them from his wrath when he learns how he is being used. This cruel ploy backfires, however, when Amintor, having discovered the truth about his bride, proves too transparent to hide it from his friend Melantius. Having satisfied himself of the King's guilt and his sister's dishonor, Melantius does not hesitate in deciding between his allegiance to the King who has betrayed him and his duty to the gods and his own honor; he binds Evadne by oath to kill the King, and sets about himself to secure support for his enterprise. When the King next commands Evadne to his bed, all the circumstances of their illicit relationship combine to aid her in fulfilling her vow. The courtiers who guide Evadne to the royal chamber are told that it is the King's pleasure that "none be neere," and, obeying what they take to be their sovereign's command, they are too far away to hear him when he calls for help. Tied to the bed lest his strength prove too great for Evadne, the King at first thinks his bonds part of a new amorous game; when he has at last been convinced of Evadne's fatal intent, it is too late for him to offer effective resistance. But the ultimate irony of the King's death lies in the fact that in summoning Evadne to his bed on this occasion, the King has been the instrument of his own punishment.

Evadne, too, finds that irony attends her end. Having sought to redeem herself before Amintor, whose merits she has belatedly recognized, Evadne finds him appalled by the regicide that she proudly confesses to him: the same uncritical respect for the royal person upon which she and the King had earlier relied now condemns her in Amintor's eyes. Disappointed by Amintor's unexpected yet predictable response, Evadne kills herself.

As is often the case in Renaissance English plays dealing with divine retribution, the plot of *The Maid's Tragedy* consists of a chain of incidents in which each link is a logical but not inevitable consequence of the preceding one. Events grow out of one another in obedience to rigorously applied principles of cause and effect, but at crucial junctures a higher power determines which course among several equally plausible ones events will follow. That the direction that events take at these crucial junctures is not only consistent but also yields a conclusion that affirms the very justice that the adulterers have sought to circumvent suggests that the higher power is not chance but Divine Providence.

The elaborate machinery of crime and retribution that the liaison of the King and Evadne sets in motion not only brings about the punishment of the two adulterers but also claims the lives of Aspatia, Amintor, and Melantius, the three characters who have suffered most from the adulterers' ill-conceived attempt at concealment. The tragedies of these "victims," who, with best meaning incur the worst, are shaped by the same principles of cause and effect and the same fatal combinations of character and circumstance that determine the careers of the King and Evadne.

Aspatia, who has never recovered from the severe depression induced by Amintor's betrayal, remains ignorant of the failure of Amintor's marriage. Resolving to seek her death at Amintor's hands, she disguises herself as her soldier brother and delivers a challenge to the unhappy young man to whom she had thought she would be married. Aspatia's motives are difficult to identify: on the one hand, she seems prompted by a sincere desire to end her suffering, but, on the other, she seems attracted by the idea of a perverse vengeance, which will fix upon Amintor the responsibility for terminating literally the life that his broken promise has already figuratively destroyed. Declining to defend herself, Aspatia receives the fatal wound she has sought; before expiring, however, she reveals herself to Amintor, and the two exchange expressions of love. Amintor, whose intense suffering has already suggested thoughts of suicide,[26] proves unable to withstand this latest blow; taking up the sword by which Aspatia has died, he slays himself. Melantius, seeing the corpse of the youth whose friendship he had valued more than his own family's honor, prepares to take his own life; restrained, he vows that

> I will never eate
> Or drinke, or sleepe, or have to doe with that
> That may presrve life, this I sweare to keepe.
>
> (5.3.288–90)

There is no reason to suppose that Melantius will not honor this oath.

It is the untimeliness of Aspatia's response to her painful situation that puts the seal of tragedy upon events that to all appearances might otherwise have yielded a happy conclusion. When Aspatia confronts Amintor with her challenge, the King has already met his death, and Melantius has already received his pardon; in another instant, Evadne, having been rejected by Amintor, will kill herself. The sense of tragedy is heightened by the feeling that a matter of moments has made the difference between the happy outcome that for a brief minute had seemed possible and the catastrophe we witness. Lysippus, who, intuiting the justice of his brother's death, had expressed the hope that "heaven forgive all" (5.2.22), now, surveying the bloody scene, realizes that his hope had been vain; soberly, he draws the moral implicit in the events we have watched unfold:

> May this a faire example be to me,
> To rule with temper, for on lustfull Kings
> Unlookt for suddaine deaths from God are sent,
> But curst is he that is their instrument.
>
> (5.3.292–95)

For a Jacobean audience, conditioned by religious training, by political propaganda, and by repeated exposure to plays embodying orthodox views on divine retribution and kingship, Lysippus's comments would have constituted an appropriate—indeed, a self-evident—interpretation of the tragedies of the King, Evadne, Aspatia, Amintor, and Melantius. The adultery of the King and Evadne has offended the heavens, and the adulterers must certainly be punished. The punishment of the King by means of human agents, however, necessarily entails a new offense. The deaths of Aspatia, Amintor, and Melantius make up the price required by the heavens in order to wipe out both the transgression of which the adulterers have been guilty and the transgression that must be committed in punishing them.

For a modern audience, skeptical about the operation of Divine Providence and reluctant to regard kingship as sacrosanct, the temptation is strong to dismiss Lysippus's curtain speech as post facto moralizing that has no organic relationship to the events of the play. To discount Lysippus's comments, however, is to run the danger of reading the play not as tragedy but as a study of neurotic characters who suffer the inevitable consequences of their own self-indulgence, weakness, and perversity.[27] It is, however, the validity within the world of *The Maid's Tragedy* of the principles that Lysippus invokes—the sanctity of kingship and the concern of divine Providence to affirm this sanctity even while punishing a wicked king—that creates the tragic predicament in which Aspatia, Amintor, and Melantius find themselves.

To acknowledge the operation of Divine Providence in *The Maid's Tragedy,* however, is not necessarily to acquiesce in the justice that Divine Providence is represented as upholding. Christian acceptance of the heavens' will is not the only possible response to the glimpse we are granted of an inscrutable power that insists that even criminal rulers may not be deposed without penalty and that exacts a terrible price in suffering and death in return for maintaining order in the universe. Horror and outrage are responses equally appropriate to the spectacle of stern laws being implemented pitilessly, and such responses are not necessarily incompatible with the pious awe and enlightened resignation that such "demonstrations" of God's justice were traditionally supposed to induce. In *The Maid's Tragedy*—as in similar Elizabethan and Jacobean plays important elements of our response depend upon the discrepancy between what, on the one hand, we, as mortals with limited vision, perceive as "just" with respect to particular characters and situations, and what on the other hand, we are asked to accept as the manifest will of the omniscient and omnipotent powers whose Purpose is by definition identical with Justice. The more rigid, repressive, and arbitrary seem the principles we are required to acknowledge as established by these powers for the common good or the glory of God, the greater is the potential for tragedy. In Jacobean England, the tension between the extreme and uncompromising views on royal authority that James espoused and the broad range of alternative positions readily accessible to well-informed Englishmen provided favorable conditions for the creation of tragedy, which, by portraying a universe which functions in strict obedience to royalist principles, could generate situations in which intense and seemingly unmerited suffering might be seen to confirm the criticism of these principles implicit in the existence of rival political theories. *The Maid's Tragedy* adroitly exploited this tension, simultaneously affirming and questioning the religious and political doctrines upon which the events it portrays depend for their meaning.

NOTES

1. Waller's two versions of *The Maid's Tragedy* were published within two months of each other in 1689. The first to appear was included in *The Second Part of Mr. Waller's Poems, containing his Alteration of the Maids Tragedy . . .* (London: Thomas Bennet); the second—and, if we may believe the prefatory remarks, the version representing Waller's latest thoughts—was issued in *The Maid's Tragedy Alter'd with other Remains of Edm'd Waller* (London: Jacob Tonson). On the fortunes of *The Maid's Tragedy* during the Restoration, see Arthur Colby Sprague, *Beaumont and Fletcher on the Restoration Stage* (Cambridge: Harvard University Press, 1926), pp. 58–63; on Waller's *rifacimento* and its political implications, see pp. 178–86.

2. *Lectures and Notes on Shakespere and Other English Poets*, ed. T. Ashe (London: George Bell and Sons, 1884), p. 429. Coleridge's observation is prompted by Amintor's speech (2.1.306–8), "Oh thou hast nam'd a word [the King] that wipes away / All thoughts revengefull, and in that sacred name, / The King, there lies a terror. . . ."

3. Introduction to the Mermaid edition of Beaumont and Fletcher (London: T. F. Unwin, n.d.: New York: C. Scribner's Sons, 1887), 1:xxv–xxxiv; similar sentiments are expressed by G. C. Macauley, *Francis Beaumont* (London: Kegan Paul, Trench & Co., 1883), pp. 135–37.

4. *Poets on Fortune's Hill* (London: Faber and Faber, 1952), pp. 184–206.

5. On politics and political theory during the reign of James I, see John Neville Figges, *The Divine Right of Kings,* 2d ed. (Cambridge: Cambridge University Press, 1914), pp. 137–267; J. W. Allen, *English Political Thought, 1603–1660,* vol. 1 (London: Methuen, 1938), pp. 1–47; W. Greenleaf, *Order, Empiricism and Politics: Two Traditions of English Political Thought, 1500–1700* (London: Oxford University Press, 1964), pp. 58–67; Alan G. R. Smith, "Constitutional Ideas and Parliamentary Developments in England, 1603–1625," *The Reign of James VI and I,* ed. Alan G. R. Smith (New York: St. Martins, 1973), pp. 160–76; and D. M. Loades, *Politics and the Nation, 1450–1660: Obedience, Resistance and Public Order* (Brighton: Harvester, 1974), pp. 327–38.

6. On Tudor political theory, see J. W. Allen, *A History of Political Thought in the Sixteenth Century,* 3d ed. (London: Methuen, 1951), pp. 121–270; Franklin Le V. Baumer, *Early Tudor Theories of Kingship,* Yale Historical Publications, 35 (New Haven: Yale University Press, 1940); and Greenleaf, *passim,* but esp. pp. 1–125. Classic statements of Elizabethan concepts of order are to be found in "An Exhortation Concerning Good Order and Obedience to Rulers and Magistrates" and "An Homily Against Disobedience and Wilfull Rebellion," both in *Certain Sermons or Homilies Appointed to Be Read in the Churches in the Time of the Late Queen Elizabeth . . .* (London: Prayer Book & Homily Society, 1852).

7. Such a "contract" theory of kingship is implicit, for example, in the coronation oath, whereby the sovereign swears (in the words of the oath taken by Henry VIII) "to kepe to the people of England, the lawes and the custumes to they, as of old tyme rightfull and deuout Kings graunted." On the history of the coronation

oath, see Joseph Pemberton, *The Coronation Service* (London: Skeffington and Son, 1902); for the oath of Henry VIII, see p. 14.

8. On the doctrine of nonresistance, see Allen, *A History of Political Thought in the Sixteenth Century,* pp. 125–33.

9. Among the works of the Marian exiles, see John Ponet, *A Shorte Treatise of politike povver, and of the true Obedience which subiectes ovve to kynges and other ciuile Gouernours* . . . ([Strasburg,] 1556), passim, but esp. Gv–[H7v] and Christopher Goodman, *How Superior Powers Ought to be Obeyed* ([Geneva?] 1558). On attitudes towards tyrannicide during the sixteenth century, see Harold Laski's introduction to his edition of *Vindiciae contra tyrannos* (London: Bell, 1924), pp. 1–60, and Roland Mousnier, *The Assassination of Henry IV,* trans. Joan Spencer (London: Faber and Faber, 1973), pp. 63–105, 213–28.

10. Among late sixteenth-century documents, see, for example, Stephanus Junius Brutus [Hubert Languet?], *Vindiciae contra tyrannos* (Edinburg [i.e., Basle], 1579) and *De Justa reipublicae christianae in reges impios authoritate* (Paris, 1590).

11. For James's political writings, see *The Political Works of James I,* ed. Charles H. McIlwain (Cambridge: Harvard University Press, 1918).

12. Note James's formulation of this commonplace at the end of *The Trew Law:*

But remitting to the justice and providence of God to stirre up such scourges as pleaseth him, for punishment of wicked kings . . . my onely purpose and intention in this treatise is to perswade, as farre as lieth in me, by these sure and infallible grounds, all such good Christian readers, as beare not onely the naked name of a Christian, but kith the fruites thereof in their daily forme of life, to keep their hearts and hands free from such monstrous and unnaturall rebellions, whensoever the wickednesse of a Prince shall procure the same at Gods hands: that, when it shall please God to cast scourges of princes and instruments of his fury in the fire, ye may stand up with cleane hands, and unspotted consciences. . . . (*Works,* p. 70)

13. Significantly, no attempt is made to invoke the tradition of the king's "two bodies," i.e., the distinction between the king as an abstract office and as a particular individual. On this tradition, see Ernst Kantorowicz, *The King's Two Bodies* (Princeton: Princeton University Press, 1957).

14. There is a single reference to corruption in the court of Rhodes—Evadne's reproach that "your curst Court and you . . . / Made me give up mine honor" (5.1.79–81)—but this seems more a conventional condemnation in the complaint tradition than an indication that the King's court is especially wicked.

15. *The Patterns of Tragicomedy in Beaumont and Fletcher,* Yale Studies in English, 120 (New Haven: Yale University Press, 1952), pp. 86–98.

16. On these conventions, see Ronald Broude, "Revenge and Revenge Tragedy in Renaissance England," *Renaissance Quarterly* 28 (1975): 38–58. In no Renaissance English play is the sympathy of the audience engaged on behalf of a deceived husband who seeks revenge upon his erring wife or her lover.

17. All quotations from *The Maid's Tragedy* are from the edition prepared by Robert K. Turner, Jr., in *The Dramatic Works in The Beaumont and Fletcher Canon,* vol. 2 (Cambridge: Cambridge University Press, 1970).

18. The list of "Speakers" that prefaces *The Maid's Tragedy* identifies Aspatia as "troth-plight wife to Amintor, and Amintor acknowledges that "she had my promise" (1.1.35). On relevant marriage forms, see J. W. Lever's introduction to

the Arden Shakespeare edition of *Measure for Measure* (London: Methuen, 1965), pp. liii–lv.

19. Amintor's career conforms to a tragic pattern shared not only by Richard II and Lear but also (to take characters from plays postdating *The Maid's Tragedy*) by the Duchess of Malfi and the Duchess Rosaura (in *The Cardinal*). Richard's decision to call off the duel between Mowbray and Bolingbroke and to banish both appellants turns Bolingbroke's thoughts to the rebellion that deposes Richard. Lear's decision to divide his kingdom between Goneril and Regan subjects him to the indignities that both visit upon him; he is eventually avenged by Goneril's husband, Albany. The Duchess of Malfi's decision secretly to marry Antonio draws her brothers' wrath and brings about her death; like Lear, she is avenged by her persecutors' former ally: Bosola. The Duchess Rosaura's decision to reject Columbo for Alvarez arouses the ire of the Cardinal and his nephew; Rosaura's cause is avenged by Hernando, who is at first a member of the Cardinal's party.

20. It is not surprising that a pagan such as Melantius shares with Renaissance Englishmen the idea that the heavens may select a just man to serve as the agent of their vengeance; Renaissance Englishmen found pre-Christian examples both in the Bible (Ehud and Jehu, for example) and in the classics (Orestes). *The Maid's Tragedy* depends upon its pagan characters' awareness of such concepts shared by pagans and Renaissance Christians; consider the importance in the play of the idea of the sanctity of kingship. For Renaissance Englishmen, what the pagan who shared such concepts lacked was awareness of their Christian significance.

21. The confirmation of Amintor's accusations that Melantius seeks and finds in Evadne's identification of the King as her lover is comparable to the confirmation of the Ghost's charges furnished for Hamlet by the play which catches the king's conscience, and to the confirmation of Bel-imperia's letter that Pedringano's confession supplies for Hieronimo. On the significance of such confirmation for revengers, see S. F. Johnson, "*The Spanish Tragedy,* or Babylon Revisited," *Essays on Shakespeare and Elizabethan Drama in Honor of Hardin Craig,* ed. Richard Hosley (Columbia: University of Missouri Press, 1962), pp. 29–30. Johnson connects the necessity of securing such confirmation with Numbers 35:30: "Whoso killeth any person, the murderer shall be put to death by the mouth of witnesses: but one witness shall not testify against any person to cause him to die."

22. Melantius's conduct is to be contrasted with the behavior of Maximus in Fletcher's *Valentinian,* who, in a parallel situation, having secured the death of the evil Emperor, conceals his part in the Emperor's death and succeeds to the throne; he thus becomes a secret criminal whom the heavens must expose and punish.

23. Insofar as Amintor and the Duchess of Malfi are both the passive victims of secret criminals, Evadne's role as a criminal who repents and avenges her victim corresponds to Bosola's. That both Evadne and Bosola set about in the way they do to avenge their victims upon their former accomplices indicates that their "reformation" has been imperfect.

24. For this image, see above, note 12.

25. On this formulaic sequence of events, its development and significance, see Ronald Broude, "*Vindicta Filia Temporis,*" *Journal of English and Germanic Philology* 52 (1973): 489–502 and "Revenge and Revenge Tragedy in Renaissance England," pp. 54–58. On the role of Divine Providence in Renaissance English tragedy, see H. H. Adams, *English Domestic or Homiletic Tragedy* (New York: Columbia University Press, 1943), pp. 18–24.

26. Amintor's suicide is carefully prepared. Evadne suggests that Amintor kill

himself (2.1.172–83); Amintor indicates that his suffering has driven him to consider suicide (3.2.181–83); and Melantius fears that Amintor "may doe violence / Upon himselfe" (3.2.261–62).

27. For an example of such a reading, see Robert Ornstein, *The Moral Vision of Jacobean Tragedy* (Madison: University of Wisconsin Press, 1960), pp.173–79.

The Authority of Honor in Lope's
El castigo sin venganza

Bruce Golden

At the beginning of act 3 of Lope de Vega's *El castigo sin venganza* (1631), Aurora, the discarded lover of Count Federico, the illegitimate son of the Duke of Ferrara, describes what she has seen taking place between Federico and Cassandra, his stepmother.

> In Cassandra's bedroom, there are two closets which have their walls covered not in tapestries, but in mirrors and portraits. Suspicion counseled me to tread stealthily, and to my horror, I saw reflected in a mirror the Count Federico measuring the roses of Cassandra's lips with his own. . . . As I watched, I fancied that the mirror's silver clouded so that it should not see their lust. But love was not so coy; he did not hide his face, but my eyes followed every embrace. I know all that has passed between them. (2067–77; 2089–96)[1]

Their love affair becomes known to the Duke (not however through any conversation with Aurora or Cassandra's father, or the Marquis of Mantua, to whom she has described what she has seen). He exacts a terrible punishment on the guilty pair while he, his act condoned by Cassandra's father, survives. In the last speech of the play, the *gracioso* Batín utters what suffices at first to be the kind of commonplace that seals all tragedies of honor in seventeenth-century Spanish drama: "Thus ends, wise jury, the tragedy of punishment without revenge. Let that which was a fearful wonder to Italy be now an example to Spain" (3018–21). But there is more to Batín's remark than the conventional close; his words suggest a source for the peculiar shudder that excites the beholder of Lope's work.

Lope's tragedy tells the story of the Duke of Ferrara, who in middle age after a youth of lecherous revelry, has apparently reformed and arranged to marry Cassandra. He has sent his natural son, Count Federico, to help escort her from Mantua to Ferrara. Federico rescues Cassandra from an accident on the road and returns with her. Act 1 ends with Federico fighting his erotic feelings for his new stepmother. After their marriage the

Duke, in a state of depression, neglects his new wife. Cassandra knows that any sexual transgression, if discovered by her husband, will be her undoing. Yet, driven by feelings of frustration and vindictiveness, she allows herself to be seduced by Federico at the end of act 2. Their affair flourishes in the Duke's absence, for he has gone to fight heroically in the Papal Wars. This experience has changed him truly; his wayward behavior and depression have vanished. He returns, is told of the affair between his son and his wife, and consequently feels that his honor has been destroyed. By eavesdropping on the couple, he discovers the charges to be true. The Duke then entraps his son by lying to Federico as he asks him to kill someone who has threatened the Duke's life. The criminal is helpless, he tells Federico, bound with his face covered to keep his treachery secret. As soon as Federico leaves to execute his father's request, immediately the Duke summons everyone to confront his son, who returns, horrified, having looked at the face of his victim. The Duke tells Cassandra's father, the Marquis of Mantua, that Federico has stabbed to death his daughter. Upon learning this, the Marquis, who knew of the affair between his daughter and Federico, in turn kills him. Afterwards, he declares that the Duke has successfully wrought punishment without revenge.

During the entire play, the audience has been spectator to the action. No lines have been delivered in direct address to the audience. The action has been safely played out within the frame provided by the seventeenth-century *corral*. Yet with the play's concluding lines, the comfortable aesthetic distance collapses, the audience cannot feel at ease watching the grisly bloodletting of Lope's Italian Duke; Batín's concluding admonition perturbs his audience. They watch with that peculiar combination of terror (or at least fear) and horror as the Duke of Ferrara—the embodiment of personal honor—cruelly and efficiently arranges the death of his own wife and son. Lope succeeds in affecting the theatrical audience because it is easy to disturb seventeenth-century Spaniards by reminding them of the importance and fragility of their own personal honor.

Something more disturbing depends upon a particular ingredient of Aurora's speech cited above. She not only sees her former lover committing adultery; the lovers are virtually displayed to Aurora through mirrors in Cassandra's bedroom. Such secret observing suggests some voyeurism, but more importantly a queasy surveillance of one's own honor may be suggested by the mirror reference, however architecturally accurate the description of the room may be. One's honor is always on display, so to speak. In the form of reputation, it is the part of the self constantly on view. Protecting one's good name, or reputation, then becomes the same as looking after one's honor. We will see that Lope's Duke knows that his honor has been sullied by his wife's betrayal with her stepson, and in his culture the only response he can make is to avenge this most humiliating devastation. That he does so in his successful, yet gruesome manner makes for the tragedy in *El castigo sin venganza.*

In the Renaissance, because concern about personal honor is ubiquitous, it need not always be explained or defined whenever a character believes his or her honor has been challenged. All that needs to be signaled is the shame, anger, or other emotional responses to the feeling of being insulted or violated. Lope knows that personal honor is not something easily or casually detachable from the texture of Spanish daily life; it has no separate ontological status. Thus he uses the subject as if it were a complex kind of commodity composed, however, of clearly distinguishable aspects affirmed and shared by the culture, which understands both its totality and its multiple intentions and effects. For Lope, as for other Renaissance writers, the separate segments of the honor code include the necessity to establish the hero's character as one who believes in honor and is ready to accept the necessity for revenge if he has been dishonored; the requirement to keep that insult and his resulting shame secret; the need to dissimulate while suffering before exacting a bloody retribution.

These segments form the plot of revenge and honor tragedies; more important, they also become traits of the hero's character. He believes that he must remain silent and dissimulate in order to continue to function. Everything he does, even while planning a murder, is explained in the dialogue like copybook maxims found in dozens of authorized texts. Indeed, as maxims they appear in approved texts that are used to exemplify as well as justify patterns of behavior to educated people in the Renaissance.

Looked at another way, characterologically, the maxims serve more basically as rationalizations to help explain the desperately extreme actions undertaken by the hero in his tragic effort to regain control over his own life. In the texts that dictate manners and morals of Renaissance life are found ways to justify even the most reprehensible deeds.

Honor heroes first proclaim their belief in their own personal honor. That is to say, they cast themselves in the role of those who choose to live according to the demands honor places upon the shoulders of the individual. Lope's Duke of Ferrara, along with everyone else in *El castigo sin venganza,* unquestionably thinks of himself as a man of honor. In a reflective speech tinged with melancholy that ends the first scene of act 1, the Duke invokes the commonplace, classical link between the theater and life, adding to it, however:

The play is a mirror in which the fool, the sage, the old, the young, the strong, the courtier, the King, the governor, the maiden, the wife, may all learn by example, concerning life and honor. (215–21)

Lope artfully elucidates and amplifies the familiar Ciceronian definition, "imitatio vitae, speculum consuetidinis, imago veritatis" ("imitation of life, glass of custom, image of truth") by adding particularly the concept of honor. As *El castigo sin venganza* proceeds, we are not surprised to discover that on the subject of honor, the Duke's addition becomes the single yardstick by which we are to understand his life, the customs, and the truth dramatized in Lope's *comedia*. The Duke's definition also adumbrates the mirror reference in Aurora's speech with which this essay opened. If a play mirrors life and honor, then it is a character's honor that is reflected in that mirror. If the most vital part of life is honor, and honor is crafted by the ego to be seen by others, the worst that can happen is to be dishonored visibly. One must always "watch" himself (or herself), or "look" to one's reputation. Cassandra and Federico have been spied upon, but the one who suffers the most from their adultery in *El castigo sin venganza* is the Duke. He feels most acutely the censure of dishonor. The basic conflict within the Duke suggested in this scene is underscored by this speech. By using the old topos of life as a play, the Duke reveals the tension between his role as a man of honor and his sense of self, which he feels still incomplete, unformed finally as he sits fitfully between youth and manhood—bachelorhood and husband, carouser and responsible ruler.

Before their adultery, in the scene where Cassandra and Federico simultaneously reveal and suppress their powerful attraction for each other, the Duke's wife demonstrates her own understanding of honor's importance to men: "Men should show a firm resolve and weep for one cause alone, the loss of their honor . . ." (1432–35). Her remarks become heavily ironical because the Duke's concern for his honor will bring about her own murder by the very man she is talking to. Indeed, something of a premonition lurks in her words, as she says further (after Federico has left),

> I should be most evil, savage, and bereft of honor if I should permit so unlawful a passion to overcome us. Merciful heaven drive all such thoughts from my mind. I have not yet offended, for if unspoken thoughts give offense, there is no man on earth whose honor goes unscathed. (1581–91)

With honor so preeminent a part of character, then, we cannot overlook its centrality in the play. Using the honor code as his guide, Lope's Duke of Ferrara declares certain actions to be not merely permissible but indispensible. Because he has chosen to be a man of honor, the importance and necessity of preserving his own personal honor become a reason (or rationalization) to get away (literally) with murder. Lope's Duke would understand Tolstoy, who described a psychological law "which compels a man who commits actions under the greatest compulsion, to supply in his

imagination a whole series of retrospective reflections to prove his freedom to himself."[2]

Early in the play, the Duke has proclaimed his reformation and decision
to marry, but we see that his conversion is incomplete as he neglects
Cassandra after they marry. Yet by act 3, in one measure he has matured.
One of the play's multiple ironies is that this change has come too late to
save his own sense of honor. The Duke, returning from the wars, is
presented to the audience as a responsible ruler collecting petitions from
his subjects. Among them is a letter passed to him by a servant:

> "Sir, look carefully to your house, for in your absence the Count and the
> Duchess . . . have offended with infamous boldness your bed and
> honor." What, shall I bear this? "If you are circumspect, your own eyes
> shall prove it to you." (2484–85; 2488–91)

The Duke considers the charge, underlining the uniqueness of his own
identity and situation by casting himself in a role whereby he suffers more
than his "type," King David.

> And yet there is no evil so base that human weakness cannot compass it.
> Or is this the wrath of heaven upon me? This is Nathan's curse upon
> David. So God punished him. Federico is my Absolon. Yet if this be
> heaven's anger against me, I suffer more than David. . . . (2506–11)

He spies upon his wife in order to obtain ocular proof of her betrayal.
Once he has his evidence, his duty is clear: "Honor, [you must be the
judge and execute both the] sentence and the punishment" (2747). Yet the
Duke goes angrily on, condemning the outrageous "laws of Honor." He
has realized that his most prized possession, his own personal honor has
never been in his control:

> Honor, cruel enemy of mankind! Who was the first to impose your harsh
> law upon the world? Who first ordained that you should reside in
> woman's keeping and not in men's? The worthiest man may lose you,
> though he commits no sin at all. A barbarous tyrant, and no man of
> discernment, invented this fierce stricture. To leave us such a legacy
> only proves that he who first lost his honor invented this inhuman code
> so that others should suffer also. (2811–23)

The Duke may also be taking to task his own inadequacies as husband and
ruler of his own house. He may not be himself guiltless. If his wife has
been unfaithful, it may be because he has not acted as a husband should.
This is to say at least two things: he has neither protected her from
temptation, nor has he satisfied her enough to prevent her from seeking
sexual fulfillment elsewhere. Both of these felt inadequacies plague Lope's
hero.

For his own ego, in its bitter articulation, to blame himself is impossible. The fault must lie elsewhere—in that irrational code of honor that the Duke accepted in his role as honor-bound hero and sufferer, like David, only more so. The conflict is deep. To resolve it, he appeals to an external, superior authority—God. As his secular respresentative on Earth, the Duke dutifully prays for justice to be heaven-sent to absolve himself from the responsibility he must own if he plays out the role he has chosen for himself.

> Oh, Heavens, this day only your punishment will be observed. Raise your divine rod to bless my action. I do not avenge my injury. I will not invite your divine displeasure by taking vengeance, for to do so against my own son would be a double cruelty. This must be Heaven's chastisement and nothing more. To win Heaven's pardon, rigor must be tempered with moderation. I must act as a father, not as a husband, and administer punishment without revenge to a sin that was beyond shame. The laws of honor demand that much. . . . Do not take from me the right to punish when honor presiding in the court of reason pronounces its implacable sentence. (2834–51; 2897–2901)

His conscious ego has accepted this code when it chose the role; we hear as much in his proclamation as a man of honor. Yet living under the burden of the code makes him feel crazy with the present threat of having lost control of his own wife, honor, and even of his own sense of self.

As historical and critical discussions continue, the grounds for understanding the nature of honor become firmer. Lope's Duke reveals that the appeal to honor only mystifies the urge to subjugate women—something that entreatics to honor have manifested at least as far back as the early Middle Ages.

By the twelfth century, the old Roman concept of *probitas* ("a valour of both body and soul that produced both prowess and magnanimity . . . transmitted through the blood")[3] became central to the aristocratic code of values. The belief that the blood of both husband and wife contributed to the character of an offspring gave men the reason to concern themselves with their wives' fidelity. Their own, of course, didn't matter, because what was at stake was nothing so abstract or basic as virtue as we understand it, but only the character of any legitimate male offspring. The male heir had to bear an honorable name and carry especially honorable blood. It was the woman alone, then, who would be responsible for any impurity in the blood line, for only her infamy could introduce an impure strain into the family.

While this kind of understanding was general as a basis for any aristocratic code of values in medieval Europe, in Spain the purity of blood issue multiplied in importance against the background of seven hundred years of

Moorish presence and Jewish influence. By the time of the Spanish Renaissance, concern over family honor and purity of blood reached nearly hysterical proportions. Controversy seethed publicly and privately over the status of anyone with Moorish or Jewish bloodlines. Christian Spaniards insisted upon their superiority and naturally "pure" blood and honor. This kind of personal honor gave the male Spaniard a sense of "being" that established him as a virile, prudent guardian of his family and his name.[4]

In his role as guardian, Lope's Duke acts outrageously. Yet he has, in advance, rationalized his outrage. As soon as he casts himself in the role to act as revenger of his own honor, all that remains for him to do is follow the code that, in the speech cited above, he had so thoroughly criticized as irrational. He embarks upon a course that will indeed rescue his own sense of honor, but at a tragic price.

The code dictates that knowledge of the dishonor to oneself harms the aggrieved as much as the insult itself. Thus the hero must suffer in silence. He must revenge his injury without revealing what has happened. The role places him in a position worse even than a Christian sinner, who at least can confess and gain absolution through penance. There is no confession for the man of honor; there is no absolution from above; the responsibility is his. This burden of silence almost dictates that dissimulation becomes a course of action. Lope's Duke deliberately lies and resorts to eavesdropping.

The topic of dissimulation was frequently discussed in the Renaissance. It may be that the writings of Machiavelli and subsequent controversy over the "reason of state" contributed to a growing concern about whether it was possible any longer to live by Christian precepts in a world rapidly being reexamined through secular eyes. Yet many writers were concerned to distinguish between mere expedient secular behavior and Christian prudence.[5] Diego Saavedra Fajardo, in his widely admired collection of emblems, *Idea de un principe politico cristiano,* has no difficulty in advising prudent circumspection while adhering to Christianity:

> Dissimulation and cunning are . . . lawful, when they don't drive to Knavery. . . . One may sometimes use indifferent and equivocating words, not with a design to cheat, but to secure ones self, and prevent being cheated, and for their lawful ends. Thus we see the Master of truth himself pretended to his Disciples, who were going to the city Emmaus, that he was going farther (Luke 24:28). The counterfeit folly of *David* before King Achis (1 Sam. 21:13); the pretended Sacrifice of Samuel (1 Sam. 16:2); the Kid skins fitted to Jacobs hands (Gen. 27:16), were all lawful Dissimulations, the intent not being to cheat, but only hide another design, nor are they less allowable, because one foresees that another will thereby be deceiv'd, for that knowledge proceeds not from malice, but a kind of caution. (306–7)[6]

With such evidence from a Spanish Knight of the order of Saint James, we can assume that the concept of prudent dissimulation had widespread interest off the stage as well as on.

While the Christian literature on the question of prudent action is extensive, nearly all of it is paraphrased or adapted from Saint Thomas Aquinas. He makes prudence basic to the practice of justice, fortitude, and temperance. Fundamentally, prudence directs man's moral actions by first determining the practical truth in a situation and then selecting the proper virtuous action. In the language of the English Puritan William Perkins, we engage in two actions, "The one, is *Deliberation*, whereby according to spirituall understanding, we advise what is good or bad. . . ." This is followed by "*Determination*, whereby we resolve upon former deliberation, to imbrace, to doe, to follow, and pursue the best things in every kind" (*Whole Treatise*, p. 114). Thus no one acts wisely unless he is prudent. Classical and Christian commentators alike emphasize the fact that the prudent man acts with full knowledge of past, present, and future. In short, he must be—with the full power of his own controlling ego—like God himself.

Saavedra Fajardo echoes the widespread commonplace when he defines prudence by these attributes:

> Prudence is the Rule and Measure of Virtues, without that these degenerate into Vices. Wherefore as other Virtues have theirs in the Appetite, this has its residence in the intellect, from thence presiding over them all. . . . The Virtue of Prudence consists of several Parts reducible to these three Heads; the memory of past, the Knowledge of present, and the Prospect of future times. All these differences of time are represented In this Emblem, by a Serpent, the Emblem of Prudence, upon an Hour-glas, which represents Time present, winding itself about a Scepter, and viewing it self the Two glasses of past and future; with the Verse of Virgil, translated from Homer, including all three, for the Motto: *What are, what were, and what shall come to pass.* which Prudence looking into regulates, and composes all its Actions. (306–7)

Baltasar Gracián, the Jesuit critic and moralist, also points out, "The most practical kind of wisdom consists of dissimulation" (120–21).

Along with dissimulation comes craftiness—more practical wisdom. Lope, like other playwrights, uses the crafty characteristics of the hero to advance the plot. Such dissimulation becomes, in fact, the only means to gain revenge in a corrupt society like that of Ferrara in *El castigo sin venganza*. Turning to Gracián once again, we read, "Candor flourished in the Golden Age; in this iron age, cunning is supreme" (216–17).[7] Lope's Duke hides in order to spy on Cassandra and his son Federico because this is no Golden Age for honesty.

The major problem confronting modern critics of *El castigo sin venganza* is how to respond to the play's bloody catastrophe. If it is difficult for us to admire Lope's Duke, then we may be surprised to find that characters left alive to survey the results of his revenge look upon the Duke's accomplishment with admiration. "Admiration" is a key word. As J. V. Cunningham points out, "The literal meaning of *admiration* in the Renaissance—it is the meaning of the Latin word *admiratio*—is wonder" (p. 188). Thus our meaning of the word, with its connotation of approval, should not be brought to bear too heavily in assessing this tragedy. However, if we see this tragedy as a drama that captures the imagination of a contemporary audience that marvels at it and the clever craftiness of its hero caught in a merciless dilemma, we will be closer to understanding than if we search for actions to condone or lessons to learn from what we have seen dramatized. The sense of wonder aroused in Lope's spectator by the outcome of the plot is epitomized by the final tableau before us on stage. Lope's Duke is indeed marvelous in the execution of his finale. He binds his adulterous wife, Cassandra, covers her face, and summons his son Federico. He contrives an elaborate fiction about a nobleman who has been plotting against him and has since been captured. Now the Duke, needing an executioner, has chosen Federico.

Duke. When a father gives an order to his son, whether it be just or unjust, should he bandy words with him? Go, coward, or I will—
Feder. Hold your sword, my lord. I am not afraid. There is no cause, since your enemy is bound. I know not why, but I tremble to the very soul.

. . . .

Duke. I shall observe you. —He is there. Now, Now the sword pierces her heart. He who wrought my dishonor now executes my justice. Ho, there! Captains! My men! Guards! Knights of Ferrara! Come hither!

Enter the Marquis, Aurora, Batín, Ricardo and all those who have appeared in the play. . . .

The count has killed Cassandra. His only reason is that she was his stepmother. She told him that she was to bear me a son to disinherit him. Kill him, kill him. The Duke commands it.
Marq. He killed Cassandra?
Duke. Yes, marquis.
Marq. I will not go to Mantua until I have his life.
Duke. Here comes the murderer, his sword still bloody.

Enter Federico

Feder. I uncovered her face. You told me it was a traitor.
Duke. No more. Silence. Kill him.
Marq. Die.

Feder. Oh, Father, why do they strike at me?
Duke. In the tribunal of God, you will learn the cause.

After Cassandra's father, the Marquis of Mantua, has executed his daughter's lover and killer, he speaks of the Duke:

Marq. He turns to look at a punishment without revenge *(un castigo sin venganza).*
Duke. Just punishment is no vengeance. My grief is too great, my valor too weak, to hold back my tears. He has paid for that crime by which he hoped to be my heir.
Batín. Thus ends, wise jury, the tragedy of punishment without vengeance *(castigo sin venganza),* which being a fearful wonder in Italy is an example in Spain.

(3.2957–65; 2972–78;
2981–99; 3013–24)

Everyone left alive knows that the honor hero's duty lies in restoring his own honor. The catastrophe will concern his own actions, for he will freely determine what to do and how to obtain his goal. His duty is personal, his motives psychological, his suffering personal. Lope deftly focuses such matters by making the hero's own wife the cause and object of his obligation, suffering, and finally his vengeance.

Another critical principle needs to be applied to Lope's tragedy.

According to the philosopher, the two principal parts of the compound plot are the Reversal and the Recognition, adding yet a third, that being the Disturbance or Perturbation [turbación] of the spectator's spirit. (Bentley, p. 290)[8]

If we compare *El castigo sin venganza* with *Othello,* Shakespeare's play most often compared to Spanish drama, a difference between English and Spanish tragedy becomes clear. In *Othello* the finale ends in a tragic stillness and completeness, which somehow mitigates the horror of the murder and suicide. The unhappy tale is fully told to its tragic end.

But in *El castigo sin venganza* we have no such feeling of calm finality. Instead of the tragic married couple united in death, we see the Duke of Ferrara, the cuckholded husband, still alive. Instead of calm, we feel disquieted. While Othello passes judgment on himself and commits suicide, the murder committed by the Duke is condoned by the Marquis of Mantua. Indeed, the Duke sends Aurora off to marry the Marquis with the executed Federico on stage before them as a warning to look after her (and his) own honor. Thus the Duke stands before the audience (both onstage and off) as an emblem of the unrelenting laws of the honor code. They, like Lope's hero, know that sudden tragedy can arise, shattering the peace of mind of any honorable man. Accordingly we feel the disquietude of those obliged to live by the rigid honor code: Lope's Duke must survive as its agent, who embodies its precepts.

As Batín's final words make clear, we have an example before us, but the example is not a simple moral. Lope has used his tragedy of honor as a way to reflect and interpret life itself. Honor becomes an effective and recognizable "play thing" because off stage it pervades daily, continuous encounters, rituals, and transactions. The dramatic presentation of honor allows the public to see what it accepts, but they see it played with, complicated, exaggerated, deepened; they see it closely scrutinized by dramatic characters so that what in the aggregate (or the abstract) is already acknowledged, assumed, and accepted subjectively is for the theatrical moment specifically and critically examined in terms of both its components and ramifications. On stage, Lope's audience sees facets of their own temperament or character played out, facets that determine their own behavior and beliefs. They may not wholeheartedly approve of everything they see, but the drama is after all designed to be woeful, evoke fear—thus to be disquieting while it is being awesome.

Lope's dramatization of what can happen by following the accepted honor code shows us that believing in the importance of personal honor makes people do things to protect a sense of ego that would otherwise be outrageous and unacceptable. The tragedy develops from mistaking personal honor for the whole self. For if one's self is one's honor, then character becomes a function of whether one preserves this vital part of the self; honor becomes metonymic for self. This quality is created and developed especially to be credited as "reputation." But other aspects of character lie hidden from this concept of self as seen by others. The "I" observed is the "I" fashioned by the conscious ego to be seen. The unconscious hardly rests content in this situation. It too needs to be expressed; felt if not seen, acknowledged if not obeyed. If the emotions in the unconscious insist upon expression but are repressed, they erupt easily into action. The omnipresent conscious controlling ego, the public "I" of honor, reacts in embarrassed horror and shame at this loss of control. It will then go to extreme lengths to regain control of character. In this state of mind, all sorts of actions begin to be seen as part of honor. The suspicion, dissimulating, eavesdropping, lying, and eventually murder become part of the ego's activity to reestablish authority and control over the unconscious.[9]

By representing this controlling ego in his drama as an authority figure, Lope dramatizes the continuous qualm Spaniards feel if they fail to please the figures or institutions (like the Church or State) who watch over them, judging them in their daily life. Something in their lives, something in themselves is always observing them. Federico and Cassandra have been under surveillance in their adultery. The Duke, too, has been under scrutiny. But his most terrible observer has been his own ego, his own reputation, his own sense of personal honor. He stands alive at the play's finale as the audience's reminder that they too are under surveillance. They too may suffer the same punishment if they are dishonored and caught up in the cruel complications worked out of the ever-threatening, egoistic, but nevertheless necessary code of honor.

NOTES

1. References are to *El castigo sin venganza,* ed. C. A. Jones (Oxford: Pergamon Press, 1966). Translations are based on those by Jill Booty, in *Lope de Vega 5 Plays,* trans. Jill Booty, ed. with an introduction by R. D. F. Pring-Mill (New York: Hill and Wang, 1961).
2. See Phyllis Rose, *Parallel Lives: Five Victorian Marriages* (New York: Alfred A. Knopf, 1983), p. 55.
3. See Georges Duby, *The Knight, the Lady and the Priest: The Making of Modern Marriage in Medieval France* (New York: Pantheon Books, 1983), p. 38.
4. Arguments over the background, development and significance of honor in Spain will probably never cease. A clear, succinct discussion as a basis for Lope de Vega can be found in Donald R. Larson, *The Honor Plays of Lope de Vega* (Cambridge: Harvard University Press, 1977). Larson discusses *El castigo sin venganza* on pp. 131–158, supplying a helpful bibliography for the play.
5. On the matter of expedience and prudence, see George L. Mosse, *The Holy Pretence: A Study in Christianity and the Reason of State from William Perkins to John Winthrop,* (1957; reprint with new introduction, New York: Howard Fertig, 1968). A subtler and wider reaching study of political aspects of prudence treated from the history of ideas is John G. A. Pocock, *The Machiavellian Moment: Florentine Political Thought and the Atlantic Republican Tradition* (Princeton: Princeton University Press, 1975). See note 6, below.
6. Diego Saavedra Fajardo is discussed in a valuable study by Monroe Z. Hafter, *Gracián and Perfection: Spanish Moralists of the Seventeenth Century* (Cambridge: Harvard University Press, 1966). Hafter discusses the history, development and consequences of the idea of Prudence. He cites an important essay by Gerard J. Dalcourt, "The Primary Cardinal Virtue: Wisdom or Prudence?" *International Philosophical Quarterly* 3 (1963): 55–79. Dalcourt points to Saint Ambrose as the first to replace wisdom by prudence as the most important classical virtue. See also Thomas N. Tentler, "The Meaning of Prudence in Bodin," *Traditio* 15 (1959): 365–84 (also cited by Hafter, p. 65). In addition, see Robert D. F. Pring-Mill, "La 'victoria del hado' in *La vida es sueño,*" *Hacia Calderón,* Tirada Aparte (Berlin: Walter de Gruyter), pp. 53–70.
7. Gracián is discussed in Hafter's study, cited above, note 6.
8. Gonzalez de Salas, *Nueva idea de la tragedia antigua,* published in 1633, quoted by Eric Bentley, *The Life of the Drama,* (New York: Atheneum, 1964), p. 290, and referred to by Raymond MacCurdy, "The 'Problem' of Spanish Golden Age Tragedy: A Review and Reconsideration," *South Atlantic Bulletin* 38 (1973): 3–14. See also E. C. Riley, "The Dramatic Theories of Don Jusepe Antonio Gonzalez de Salas," *Hispanic Review* 19 (1951): 183–203.
9. In *Calderón and the Seizures of Honor* (Cambridge: Harvard University Press, 1972), Edwin Honig discusses honor from a psychological point of view, but he addresses himself to Lope's younger contemporary and successor, Pedro Calderón de la Barca.

The Death of Pompey: English Style, French Style

Eugene M. Waith

The death of Pompey and the immediately ensuing events in Alexandria are treated in the two tragedies I am going to compare: *The False One* (of about 1620) by Fletcher and Massinger and *La Mort de Pompée* (probably performed in 1643) by Corneille. The first play is hardly ever discussed today, though in my opinion it has several claims to serious and even sympathetic consideration. *La Mort de Pompée* has suffered a tragic fall from the high place it occupied in the minds of Corneille's contemporaries, among whom it was rated as one of his four best plays. Today it has few admirers, despite its considerable merits. It is not in the least surprising that the merits of the two plays differ greatly; it is more surprising that the aims of their authors are in certain respects remarkably similar. Comparison should therefore tell us something about the dramatic means they chose to realize their interpretations of historical events and characters: their common indebtedness to Lucan's *Pharsalia* and Plutarch's *Lives* makes the project all the more feasible. As to the possible relationship of either play to other plays about Pompey, Caesar, or Cleopatra, I shall limit myself to a few brief references. I hardly need to add that Corneille was surely unaware of the play by Fletcher and Massinger.

Caesar is the structural center of both plays: his imminent arrival is largely responsible for Ptolemy's decision to murder Pompey; his reaction to the murder and his infatuation with Cleopatra occasion the rest of the action. For Lucan, the prime source of both plays, Caesar was the great villain of the civil war: in the purple passages of his abusive rhetoric Caesar appears as responsible for the carnage of Pharsalia (or Pharsalus); his dismay when presented with Pompey's head is presented as pure hypocrisy; Cleopatra, with whom he is enthralled, is "the shame of Egypt, the fatal fury of Latium, whose unchastity cost Rome dear."[1] Others who wrote about the famous conqueror, both in classical times and later, found in him at least some elements of true greatness. In the Middle Ages he was, after all, one of the Nine Worthies. So, by the time of the Renaissance, a playwright dealing with the aftermath of Pharsalia had to make a crucial decision about the characterization of Caesar. The Caesar of Fletcher and Massinger and Corneille's César[2] make a good point of departure for a comparison of the two plays.

In both Caesar is heroic, though the playwrights manage in different ways to include Lucan's unfavorable opinion. The first view of him in *The False One* is at the moment of his reception of the head of Pompey. It is presented by Ptolomy's minister, Photinus, the author of the plot against Pompey, and Achillas, the captain of Ptolomy's guard. Pointedly ignoring both of them and also the king, Caesar apostrophizes the head as "Thou glory of the world once, now the pity: / Thou awe of Nations, . . . Thou hast most unnobly rob'd me of my victory, / My love, and mercy" (2.1; pp. 318–19).[3] When some of his followers extol his grief and magnanimity the blunt captain Sceva, a commentator somewhat like Enobarbus, says, "If thou bee'st thus loving, I shall honour thee, / But great men may dissemble . . ." (p. 319). The possibility of hypocrisy is introduced without being endorsed. In fact, Caesar roundly rebukes Ptolomy and says that the utmost reward he can expect is to be forgiven.

The next scene in which he appears dramatizes the famous story of Cleopatra having herself smuggled into Caesar's presence wrapped in a mattress or rug. Before her arrival Caesar is given a long soliloquy in which he reproaches himself for undertaking a civil war. Then Sceva enters *"with a Packet,"* out of which Cleopatra emerges (2.3; p. 325). Caesar, like a hero of romance, sees her as a "heavenly Vision," and falls instantly in love. Once again Sceva counters with a cynical view of the situation, but he is dismissed, and the love scene continues, conducted with the greatest propriety. Caesar addresses Cleopatra as "Queen of Beauty" and promises to make her a queen indeed (pp. 328–30).

Her brother Ptolomy, who has been keeping her from the throne, now tries to extricate Caesar from her influence by dazzling him with an extraordinary display of treasure during the course of a lavish banquet. The device succeeds, and Caesar leaves the room saying: "The wonder of this wealth so troubles me, / I am not well" (3.4; p. 343). For the first time he clearly swerves from his noble course.

The remainder of the play presents his recovery. Photinus and Achillas, plotting to rid themselves of both Caesar and Ptolomy, lead an attack on the palace, but Caesar manages to escape by setting fire to it. At the end, having surmounted all obstacles, he is able to say to Cleopatra, "Look upon *Caesar*, as he still appear'd / A Conquerour, . . . we'll to *Rome*, where *Caesar* / Will shew he can give Kingdoms" (5.4; p. 371).

In *La Mort de Pompée* Achorée describes the reception of the head, imagining that César repressed a natural inclination to rejoice at his enemy's death, but he attributes the tears César shed to the conscious exercise of virtue, and states flatly: "S'il aime sa grandeur, il hait la perfidie" (3.2.781).[4] We first see César onstage in act 3, scene 2, where he says that his wish was to conquer Pompey and then pardon him (1. 916). He sternly repels the overtures of Ptolomée but puts the blame on flattering ministers (1. 935). For Pompée he decrees funeral honors. As in the corresponding scene of *The False One,* his behavior is exemplary.

He does not share a scene with Cléopâtre until act 4, scene 3. Corneille avoids not only the outrageous indecorum of bringing a queen onstage in a mattress, but any mention whatsoever of this anecdote. An initial interview already has taken place when César enters to assure the queen that a disturbance in the streets of Alexandria has been ended: "Reine, tout est paisible" (4.3.1241). His assurance and imperturbability anticipate those of Nicomède, who in a similar situation enters to say, "Tout est calme, seigneur." The quiet self-possession of both heroes is one indication of their superiority to their scheming enemies. César tells Cléopâtre, however, that he is almost angry at his *grandeur,* which has forced him to carry out his responsibilities as a ruler rather than to be with her. In the long love-speech that he addresses to her, *grandeur* is opposed to *amour,* though it is also what he hopes may make him worthy of her. He even claims that he has made himself master of the world in order to court her. This extravagant claim is difficult to accept today, but I suspect that Donald Sellstrom is right in suggesting that to anyone steeped in the tradition of epic as understood by Tasso it would "render the hero even more heroic."[5]

In what remains of the play César is, above all, magnanimous—notably so to his implacable enemy, Cornélie, the widow of Pompée, and to Ptolomée, whose life he tries unsuccessfully to spare for the sake of Cléopâtre. At the very end, recognizing that Rome would never countenance his marriage to her, César nevertheless reiterates his love and looks forward to the ceremonies of the next day, in which she will be crowned and the spirit of Pompée appeased. Thus in *The False One* the hero has a failing that makes him wander briefly from the path marked out by his ideals, but recovering his self-control, he comes to a triumphant end, confident of his future. In *La Mort de Pompée,* though his behavior is uniformly admirable, he comes at the end to recognize certain limitations. Renunciation rather than conquest underlies his final speeches.

If the presentations of Caesar reveal in themselves different emphases, the use of other characters and of strikingly different stagecraft combine to make of the two plays contrasting variations on what is essentially a single theme—the superiority of Caesar's nobility to the base scheming of Ptolemy and his minister Photinus.

Cleopatra is of prime importance in both plays, and in both she is a woman concerned mainly with regaining her throne—to be in fact what she already is in spirit: a queen. Fletcher and Massinger were very aware of the different Cleopatra portrayed by Shakespeare. In the Prologue they explain: "*We treat not of what boldness she did dye, / Nor of her fatal love to* Antony" (p. 372). Instead, the "judicious" will find "*Young* Cleopatra *here, and her great Mind*" (p. 371). Clearly, they were also aware of the long tradition affecting Shakespeare's portrayal of her as an infinitely various coquette until the time of her courageous suicide. Classical historians were hard on her—Lucan especially so—but in a famous ode (1.37) Horace struck a note that was taken up by many subsequent writers. After condemning her roundly for her ambition and lust he says: "Yet she, seeking to die a nobler death, showed for the dagger's point no woman's fear."[6] The word translated as "nobler" is *generosius,* pointing to that aristocratic greatness of mind to which Fletcher and Massinger refer in their prologue, and to the *générosité* of Corneille's character. By the Middle Ages a more generally sympathetic view of her than that of the older historians was beginning to be expressed. For Boccaccio's Fiammetta she is one of the women "who with the unexpected brunts of cruel fortune have been confounded"—Jocasta, Hecuba, Sophonisba, Cornelia, and Cleopatra.[7] (It is surprising to find Pompey's widow side by side with Cleopatra in this list.) Her grief, even more than her great mind, concerns Fiammetta. Chaucer, in *The Legend of Good Women,* pays tribute not only to her grief but to the constancy of her love for Antony. Later, certain Senecan dramatists, such as Jodelle in his *Cléopâtre Captive,* present her as at least partially admirable, but in all of these more sympathetic depictions of the Egyptian queen, the emphasis is on her last moments. Fletcher and Massinger make her a noble figure at a much earlier period of her life. In her very first scene she is too preoccupied with her brother's injustice in depriving her of the throne to respond to the entertainment with which Apollodorus tries to divert her. She is not robbed of her wiles: she plans the seduction of Caesar the moment she hears that he is headed for Alexandria, but this is a Cleopatra who is willing, as she says, to lose her virginity "if it bring home Majesty" (1.2; p. 315)—a woman who means business. In her next scene she is purposefully seductive when she emerges from the "packet," and is soon convinced that "He is my conquest now" (2.3; p. 329). So there is a pleasing irony in the line that closes the scene, when she answers Caesar's proposition with "I must, you are a conquerour" (p. 330).

At the banquet, when Caesar shows that he is tempted by Egyptian wealth, Cleopatra is outraged because he pays no attention to her and, as she later tells her sister Arsino, because he has showed himself to be "a meer wandring Merchant" (4.2; p. 346)—as who should say, "He is in trade!" In the immediately following interview with Caesar she reproves him so bitterly for his materialism, while repelling his advances, that he determines to win her again by whatever means he can: "The bravery of this womans mind, has fired me" (4.2; p. 349). It is then that news of the Egyptian assault prompts him to distract the enemy by burning the palace and with it the wealth that tempted him. Cleopatra, whose "great mind" makes her constant even when the attack of Photinus appears to be succeeding, is both an agent in Caesar's redemption and an embodiment of the ideal with which he is reunited at the end.

The picture Corneille paints is equally flattering and curiously similar in making her noble from the start. Both he and the English playwrights presumably responded to the generally more sympathetic view of Cleopatra that had become common in postclassical times, but they are unusual in glorifying her relationship with Caesar. It is generally supposed that the topic of Pompey's death was suggested to Corneille by a minor French author, Charles Chaulmer, whose play, also called *La Mort de Pompée,* was performed and published in 1638. The Cléopâtre of Chaulmer, however, approaches heroic greatness only in her desire for revenge when she is rejected by Pompey's son, Sextus, with whom she has fallen in love at first sight. Since the play ends with Pompey's death, her affair with Caesar is not treated. Like Fletcher and Massinger, Corneille imagined a noble attachment for which no model has as yet been identified. In the *Examen* he says that history does not show Cleopatra as the lascivious woman she is usually thought to have been. He has therefore made her only "amoureuse . . . par ambition" (1. 84), which some recent critics do not consider a compliment.[8] I suspect it was intended to be one. Ambition, as Cléopâtre explains to Charmion, whether a vice or a virtue, is the only passion worthy of a princess (2.1.434), and the *générosité* of those born to royalty subordinates everything to their *gloire* (2.1.373).

Corneille, taking advantage of a historical possibility, imagines that she went to Rome with her father in her youth, and that at that time César fell in love with her. At the beginning of act 2, hearing that he is coming to Egypt, she hopes not only that he will restore her to the throne but that one day he will marry her (2.1.424 ff.). Nevertheless, before the murder of Pompée, she has urged her brother to cancel the plot, since they are both indebted to him for his favors to their father. Thus Corneille distinguishes between the ambition of Photin, which is naked lust for power, and the ambition of Cléopâtre, which is combined with integrity and loyalty.

In this version a scene of sudden enamorment, such as the queen-in-a-mattress scene in *The False One,* unthinkable on the French stage, is also unnecessary. Instead, Corneille gives us in the fourth act the renewal of the mutual love of these two noble personages. Cléopâtre now appears less sanguine about marriage with César, since she knows that Rome disapproves of queens, and although César suggests that this may change, the ending is easily surmised.

By the final scene the political reality of their situation has become clear to both lovers. Rather than subject César to the animosity of Rome, Cléopâtre renounces all claims on him and even offers to lay down her life for him. César sees this beautiful but foolish gesture as the product of a "grand coeur impuissant" (5.5.1762). The disappointment of the lovers at the moment of César's military success and their acceptance of the need to subordinate personal feelings to the good of the state produce the mingled tone of sadness and transcendence that differs so markedly from the triumphant notes of Caesar's last speech in *The False One*.

The title of the Fletcher and Massinger play reveals what is most original in their treatment of the story—the importance they give to the renegade Roman soldier Septimius, whom Photinus uses to kill Pompey. Inspired, perhaps, by Lucan's outrage (*Pharsalia* 8.597 ff.), they make him the exemplar of falsity, more despicable than Photinus. In a way totally characteristic of Elizabethan dramaturgy this lowly character, who is the butt of humor in the play's comic scenes, becomes a symbolic point of reference. The stage direction at the opening of act 2, scene 1, *"Enter Septimius with a head"* (p. 315), could stand by itself as an indicator of how Elizabethan dramatic conventions differed from those of French classicism. The property head, a perfect example of the horrors classicism kept offstage, fits into the long tradition of emblematic spectacle found in the dumb shows of Elizabethan plays as in street pageants and masques. Unseemly from one point of view, the head has the instantaneous effectiveness of all visual images. The tableau of Septimius with the head places the murder of Pompey at the bottom of the play's scale of values. A more precise meaning is given to the spectacle by Septimius's speech, in which Fletcher[9] has dressed his foolish boasts in a kind of pseudoelevated style:

> 'Tis here, 'tis done, behold you fearfull viewers,
> Shake, and behold the model of the world here,
> The pride, and strength, look, look again, 'tis finished;
> That, that whole Armies, nay whole nations,
> Many and mighty Kings, have been struck blind at,
> And fled before, wing'd with their fears and terrours,
> That steel war waited on, and fortune courted,
> That high plum'd honour built up for her own;
> Behold that mightiness, behold that fierceness,
> Behold that child of war, with all his glories;
> By this poor hand made breathless, here (my *Achillas*)
> *Egypt*, and *Caesar*, owe me for this service,
> And all the conquer'd Nations.
>
> (2.1; p. 315)

The crime is made to seem not mainly an act of Machiavellian politics but an example of treachery on the part of a man both frivolous and amoral.

Rewarded by Photinus, Septimius reappears in the next act, ostentatiously dressed and attempting to buy the good opinions of three lame soldiers. His lack of intrinsic worth is combined, in a familiar pattern, with the love of wealth and display. When the poor soldiers discover who he is, they fling his money back at him.

It is just at this point that the underlying reason for developing this character emerges. Up to this time Septimius seems to be only a convenient symbol for everything that Caesar and Cleopatra despise, but immediately after the scene of his ostentation comes Ptolomy's plan to dazzle Caesar, and then the banquet scene, made visually splendid not only by the display of Egyptian treasures but also by a masque of Isis, Nilus, and three "laborers" of the Nile, who sing about the wealth of their fertile valley. The juxtaposition is telling and as typically Elizabethan as is the use of a kind of spectacle that Corneille would have considered suitable for a *pièce à machines* but not for tragedy. Fletcher and Massinger enforce a shocking parallel. Can Caesar be bought by Ptolomy as easily as Septimius by Photinus? Caesar seems to give an answer when Cleopatra's rebuke prompts him to say, "I'le be my self again" (4.2; p. 351), but we cannot be sure. Next comes a comical scene in which Septimius is shown repentant for his pride and ingratitude, but he is not so much the picture as the caricature of a reformed man, and he is soon lured by Photinus into the plot against Caesar (4.3; pp. 352–57). The argument that wins him over is another disturbing parallel: Photinus asks, if the great Caesar does not repent of the slaughter of thousands in battle, why should Septimius repent of the murder of one man? The parallel is false, but it casts a momentary shadow on Caesar's promise of reformation. Decisive proof of his sincerity comes only when he orders his men to set fire to the palace and its treasures, and shortly afterward condemns Septimius to be hanged. The hero's triumph over his alter ego is finally assured. It is as if the situation of Bertram in *All's Well,* between Parolles and Helena, had been given tragic seriousness in the situation of Caesar between "the false one" and Cleopatra.

Corneille chooses to complicate his version of Caesar's triumph and love affair by his boldest alteration of history—the introduction of Cornélie, who in fact fled immediately to North Africa after her husband's murder. The use Corneille makes of her is exceedingly adroit. Determined to avenge Pompée's defeat as well as his murder, and morally opposed to Cléopâtre, she provides conflict of a very different sort from that contrived in *The False One* between Caesar and Cleopatra. To Cornélie it seems that César is destroying the old Roman values represented by Pompée; hence she makes the play in some sense about *La Mort de Pompée.* Although she doesn't appear until midway through act 3, her presence from then on overshadows the action of the play.

Her arrival is announced just as César is about to present himself to Cléopâtre. "Ah! l'importune et fâcheuse nouvelle!" he exclaims (3.3.977). She loses no time in delivering a bitter and defiant tirade (in the English as well as the French sense of the word), always addressing him as "tu," as H. T. Barnwell notes (p. 45), whereas he invariably addresses her as "vous." His reply to her, full of praise for his dead enemy, is so magnanimous that she says, "O Ciel! que de vertus vous me faites haïr!" (3.4.1072). One way of describing the conflict between Cornélie and César is as a contest of *générosité*. Honor compels her to seek the death of César, though repeatedly she is obliged to admire his virtue. Since she despises the treachery of Photin, she refuses to take advantage of it and by warning César, saves his life. The emotional tensions of the scene in which she does so (4.4) make it a theatrical tour de force.

She is given another big scene with César almost at the end of the play, when she requests permission to leave and take with her the ashes and the head of her husband. A famous painting and an engraving based on it depict Adrienne le Couvreur in this role, dressed in mourning and carrying an urn with the ashes. Here a kind of visual symbolism, comparatively rare in Corneille, reinforces the emphasis in the dialogue on *la mort de Pompée*. César accords her everything she requests but asks her to delay her departure until there has been time for proper funerary ceremonies. She replies that when she leaves she will pursue her vengeance on him, but adds:

> Je t'avoucrai pourtant, comme vraiment Romaine,
> Que pour toi mon estime est égale à ma haine.
>
> (5.4.1725–26)

A superb balance of forces keeps each of these noble persons from winning out over the other in the ethical competition.

When Cornélie suggests to a servant that César's grief for the death of Pompée is hypocritical (5.1.1537–38), we recognize Lucan's accusation, placed by Corneille with perfect tact in the mouth of one who could be expected to question César's sincerity, but who need not be believed. Those who accept her view of the matter side frankly with her in a way that Corneille never does.[10] He allows us to consider, with Achorée, the possibility that César had a secret moment of delight when he saw the head of his rival, and, with Cornélie, the possibility that his magnanimous gestures toward a dead enemy were hypocritical, but, unlike Fletcher and Massinger, Corneille never gives us unmistakable proof of a flaw in the hero's character.

A detailed comparison of the styles of the two plays would provide material for another essay. Here it must suffice to say that such a comparison would show that, while the playwrights on both sides of the Channel, inspired by Lucan, wrote some rhetorically colorful and extravagant verse, the style of *The False One* is more varied, because it is a collaboration and—shall I say?—because it is a pre-Restoration English play. What is true of the language is also true of the play as a whole: compared to *La Mort de Pompée,* it offers a more varied theatrical experience. It has spectacle, humor, and a greater range of characterization, though every dramatic device is made to serve the play's serious purpose. Expert craftsmanship makes *The False One* a successful, and occasionally even brilliant, play in the Elizabethan mode. *La Mort de Pompée,* a more assured artistic success, seems, like so many French classical tragedies, to capitalize on the very narrowness of its range. The uniform style contributes to the singleness and hence to the intensity, of the impression it makes. All the principal characters, trapped, as it were, within the confines of a restrictive code of behavior as their speeches are confined by the rules of rhyming alexandrines, struggle to achieve their conflicting goals, and in their contest reveal the subtle differences between them, which can best be seen against a monochrome background. Delicate but important shadings distinguish the *générosité* of César, Cléopâtre, and Cornélie and underlie the tensions that produce the most moving scenes. In these scenes I believe that Corneille's contemporaries were correct in seeing him at his best.

NOTES

In an earlier form this paper was read at the Modern Language Association meeting in New York, 29 December 1982, for the session on "European Baroque Drama of the Seventeenth Century" organized by Professor Jonas Barish.

1. Lucan, *The Civil War,* trans. J. D. Duff (Cambridge: Harvard University Press, 1951), 8.235 ff.; 9.1032 ff.; 10.59–60. In the text I refer to *The Civil War* by its more familiar title, the *Pharsalia.*

2. In all references to the characters in the plays I use the spellings of the editions from which I am quoting: *The Works of Francis Beaumont and John Fletcher,* ed. Arnold Glover and A. R. Waller, 10 vols. (Cambridge: Cambridge University Press, 1905–12), vol. 3, and Pierre Corneille, *Pompée,* ed. H. T. Barnwell (Oxford: Oxford University Press, 1971).

3. Since the Glover and Waller edition has no line numbers, references to act and scene are followed by the page number in the third volume.

4. References are to act, scene, and the continuous line-numbering in Barnwell's edition.

5. "*La Mort de Pompée*: Roman History and Tasso's Theory of Christian Epic," *PMLA* 97 (1982): 837.

6. *The Odes and Epodes,* trans. C. E. Bennett (Cambridge: Harvard University Press, 1918), p. 101.

7. *Amorous Fiammetta,* trans. Bartholomew Young, ed. Edward Hutton (London: 1926), book 7, p. 325. Marilyn L. Williamson, in her *Infinite Variety: Antony and Cleopatra in Renaissance Drama and Earlier Tradition* (Mystic,

Conn.: Lawrence Verry, 1974), gives a comprehensive survey of the presentations by Shakespeare's predecessors of the last part of Cleopatra's story.

8. See, for example: Albert Gérard, " 'Vice ou vertu': Modes of Self-Assertion in Corneille's *La Mort de Pompée*," *Revue des Langues Vivantes* 31 (1965–66): 327; Octave Nadal, *Le Sentiment de l'amour dans l'oeuvre de Pierre Corneille* (Paris: Gallimard, 1948), p. 244.

9. The authoritative discussion of the division of labor between the collaborators is Cyrus Hoy's in the second part of his "The Shares of Fletcher and his Collaborators in the Beaumont and Fletcher Canon," *Studies in Bibliography* 9 (1957): 148–50.

10. See, for example, Gérard, p. 331, and Serge Doubrovsky, *Corneille et la dialectique du héros* (Paris: Gallimard, 1963), pp. 279–81.

The Premiere of Davenant's Adaptation of *Macbeth*

Arthur H. Scouten

An unusual amount of scholarship has been expended on identifying the music and establishing the date of the first performance of Sir William Davenant's alteration of *Macbeth,* with the music attributed to a variety of composers and dates suggested for a premiere ranging over an eleven-year period. What makes these divergencies so remarkable is that firm evidence on both subjects has been known for a long time, without seeming to have affected the discussions. Genuine difficulties exist in ascertaining the date of the premiere, as there are complications that do not seem to yield a solution. Information presented in Murray Lefkowitz's valuable article in the *New Grove Dictionary of Music and Musicians* provides an occasion to review the problems again.

A survey of the dates suggested by literary historians and musicologists shows not only disagreement but also the notion of different adaptations of *Macbeth* by Davenant. In the following lists, I have divided the various proposed dates into different categories in the hope of preventing confusion.

I. Dates suggested by proponents of the theory of both an early revision and a later, operatic version:

Furness Variorum Shakespeare	1673;	1674
A. Nicoll; E. L. Avery (in *The London Stage*);		
A Biographical Dictionary of Actors	1664;	1673
E. W. White	——	1673
R. E. Moore	1663;	1671–72 season
J. Dover Wilson	1663	1673

II. Dates suggested by adherents to the theory of a single adaptation:

Montague Summers		1663–64 season
C. Spencer		1663
C. Price		1664
M. Lefkowitz (in *New Grove*)		ca. 1663–1674[1]

To evaluate these various dates, a list of known performances is necessary.

Date:	Theater:	Documentation, and pertinent comments by Pepys:
ca. 1663–64		In a sequence of undated plays following an entry for 3 November 1663, Henry Herbert has "a Revived Play, Mackbette £" (Edmond Malone, ed., *Shakespeare*, 1.2, p. 268).
5 November 1664	Lincoln's Inn Fields	Pepys, *Diary:* "a pretty good play, but admirably acted."
17 December 1666	At Court	Warrant for payment in Lord Chamberlain's warrant 5/139, p. 125 in Public Record Office.
28 December 1666	LIF	Pepys, *Diary:* "Saw *Mackbeth* most excellently acted, and a most excellent play for variety."
7 January 1667	LIF	Pepys, *Diary:* "Saw *Macbeth,* which though I saw it lately, yet appears a most excellent play in all respects, but especially in divertisement, though it be a deep tragedy; which is a strange perfection in a tragedy, it being most proper here, and suitable."
19 April 1667	LIF	Pepys, *Diary:* "Here we saw *Macbeth,* which though I have seen it often, yet is it one of the best plays for a stage, and variety of dancing and music, that ever I saw."
16 October 1666	LIF	Pepys attended
6 November 1667	LIF	Pepys attended
12 August 1668	LIF	Pepys attended
21 December 1668	LIF	Payment listed in a Lord Chamberlain's warrant, now at Harvard; see W. Van Lennep, *Theatre Notebook* 16 (1961): 13. Pepys also attended.

15 January 1669	LIF	Pepys attended
5 November 1670	LIF	LC warrant at Harvard, for attendance of William, Prince of Orange.
18 February 1673	Dorset Garden	Warrant for payment for royal attendance, Lord Chamberlain's warrant 5/141, p. 2.[2]

Our primary information about Davenant's *Macbeth* comes from John Downes, prompter for the Duke's Company. His account appears in his list of plays offered by this troupe after it moved into Dorset Garden, its new playhouse, in November 1671. Downes says,

> The Tragedy of *Macbeth,* alter'd by Sir *William Davenant;* being drest in all it's Finery, as new Cloath's, new Scenes, Machines, as flyings for the Witches; with all the singing and Dancing in it: THE first Compos'd by Mr. *Lock,* the other by *Mr. Channell* and *Mr. Joseph Preist;* it being all Excellently perform'd, being in the nature of an Opera, it Recompenc'd double the Expence; it proves still a lasting Play.
>
> *Note,* That this Tragedy, King *Lear* and the *Tempest,* were *Acted* in *Lincolns-Inn-Fields; Lear,* being *Acted* exactly as *Mr. Shakespear* Wrote it; as likewise the *Tempest* alter'd by Sir *William Davenant* and *Mr. Dryden,* before 'twas made into an Opera.[3]

Some of these details have been independently verified. Pepys saw *Macbeth* nine times at Lincoln's Inn Fields, as has just been shown. Shakespeare's *King Lear* had indeed been performed at Lincoln's Inn Fields before Nahum Tate adapted it, as had the Davenant-Dryden *Tempest* prior to its operatic elaboration. From the juxtaposition of titles, the obvious inference is that *Macbeth* was not acted as Shakespeare wrote it; but it remains an inference. Downes's purpose in grouping these three plays is not at all clear.

Accurate information is needed on both the identifications and the dating of the music in *Macbeth,* as it will lead to the time of the original production. In the *New Grove,* Murray Lefkowitz states that the music for "A Jigg called Macbeth" was published in 1666, and "the Witches Dance" (which follows this song in the play) appeared in 1669.[4] Both of these identifications had been made by R. E. Moore in 1961 and by Roger Fiske in 1964.[5] As E. F. Rimbault had turned up "A Jigg called Macbeth" in 1876, one must wonder why this discovery was not used in more recent scholarship to refute the suggested dates of 1672 to 1674 for the initial performance. In the Restoration period, publication of the music in a new play is strong evidence for performance. All accounts of musicians in this period testify to the fact that payments for the king's musicians were constantly in arrears, and most composers languished in financial distress.

As a result, they regularly sought other sources of income. Thus the publication of the music used in a play is a pretty sure sign that the play had been acted. In the commercial theater, it is most unlikely that a proprietor commissioned music for a play that was not in active preparation for staging.

In the past, different music used in various early productions of Davenant's adaptation was not properly identified, being mis-attributed to Purcell or Eccles. Later, the score composed by Richard Leveridge was called the "Famous Musick," and it was often credited to Locke. This music was used in productions as late as 1888. With these errors cleared away, we are in a better position to examine the musical composition employed in Davenant's original production of his adaptation.

When Davenant was preparing to stage his revision, he inherited the music for the two songs, "Oh Come away" (in *Mac.* 3.5.33) and "Black Spirits" (in *Mac.* 4.1.43) which Robert Johnson had composed for their use in Middleton's play, *The Witch*.[6] However, Davenant added a song and a dance in a new scene of his own, in which Macduff and Lady Macduff meet the witches (2.5, in the 1674 quarto of Davenant's text). Then, as Downes explained, Matthew Locke was asked to compose new music. In *The Musical Times* of 1 May 1876, the veteran literary historian E. F. Rimbault reported a tune by Locke called "A Jigg called Macbeth," as printed in J. Playford's *Musick's Delight on the Cithren*, 1666.[7] R. E. Moore states that this music perfectly fits Davenant's song in 2.5 "Let's have a dance upon the Heath," an identification endorsed by Fiske and Lefkowitz.[8] C. Spencer found the text of this song, without the music, in *The New Academy of Compliments* (1669).[9] Then Curtis Price found the score in the 1672 edition of Greeting's *The Pleasant Companion* with the initials "M. L." (Matthew Locke).[10] The witches' dance that follows, entitled "The Dance in the Play of *Mackbeth*," is in John Playford's *Apollo's Banquet* of 1669, and the *New Grove* gives the location of six extant copies. Yet Curtis Price does not include this edition of 1669, and enters this dance as No. 13 in the 1678 edition. However, I examined the 1669 edition myself at the New York Public Library's music collection at Lincoln Center, where its shelf number is MS. Drexel 5614. This collection also contains the music by Locke for Etherege's *The Comical Revenge* (first acted in March 1664), entitled "Love in a Tub, or Luke Cheynell's Jigg." Price also lists this music in the 1672 edition of *Pleasant Companion*, where it is signed "M. L."[11] Even so, not all scholars believe that Locke composed the music for Davenant's adaptation. The recent *Biographical Dictionary of Actors* objects to this attribution and cites Rosamond Harding's *Thematic Catalogue of the Works of Matthew Locke* in support. R. E. Moore, on the contrary, points out that in the seven other instances in *Roscius Anglicanus* "where Downes names the composer to an opera or play we know that he is correct."[12] The main factor is the date, regardless of disputes over the authorship, and the appearance of both music and words in 1666 and 1669 is certainly a refutation of the currently favored date of 1673 for the premiere.

The concept that seems to have dominated efforts to date the premiere is that of a periodic evolution of the text. In 1873, the elder Furness presented the idea that Davenant had revised an earlier version. Alas, Furness was wrong on all counts. He chose the date of 1673 for Davenant's early version because he knew *Macbeth* was printed in that year; however, Q 1673 is Shakespeare's play, and Davenant's adaptation was first printed in 1674. Next, Furness did not realize that Davenant died in 1668 and could not have engaged in any further playwriting, even with the aid of additional witches. Unfortunately, Nicoll built Furness's idea into a process, saying "that many of the alterations date back long before 1673" and there was an "earlier acting version."[13] This notion of different versions of the adaptation remains in some of the most recent scholarly treatments of this play. There is of course some basis for the belief in periodic alterations. For example, why did Davenant need two choreographers for only two dances (as recorded by Downes)? Luke Channel was a prominent dancing master in the 1660s. According to *A Biographical Dictionary of Actors,* he became dancing master for Davenant's company in the 1664–65 season and was still with that troupe in 1672, whereas the first known appearance of Josias Priest was as a dancer in Dryden's *Sir Martin Mar-all* on 15 August 1667. Consequently, it is entirely possible that Channel arranged all the dances for Davenant's *Macbeth,* with Priest becoming choreographer for the United Company for later revivals of this opera much later in the Restoration period, when Downes was still the prompter. If so, in 1708 Downes simply conflated the different revivals.

However, the chief reason for proposing a more elaborate version of the original adaptation was the construction in 1671 of the Dorset Garden playhouse, equipped with adequate machinery for spectacular effects, such as the descent of the witches in 3.8 (in Davenant's text). We also know that spectacular staging effects constituted John Downes's definition of the term "opera." Also, a parody by Thomas Duffett in 1673 and numerous contemporary allusions to the spectacular staging suggest that something new was being done.[14] In addition, Davenant's *Macbeth* was first published in 1674, in two editions.

Nevertheless, all this circumstantial evidence is undercut and rejected by the existence of the Yale manuscript of Davenant's text and C. Spencer's valuable material in his edition of this manuscript in 1961. In a detailed analysis, too lengthy to quote here, Spencer demonstrates that Davenant made his alteration on a playhouse copy of Shakespeare's play, and that the Yale manuscript is a fair copy derived from this revision. He describes the changes and additions that Davenant made and concludes that the adaptation "is the consequence of a carefully thought-out plan systematically applied to the play."[15] Then Spencer cites parallel passages and similar patterns between Davenant's *The Rivals* and his revised text of *Macbeth*. These parallels or imitations, which are clustered in the opening scene of *The Rivals,* suggest that Davenant's mind was still filled with the sentiments, patterns, and imagery of his extremely recent alteration of *Macbeth.*[16] *The Rivals* was acted in September 1664, and the revision of *Macbeth* must have been done sometime earlier in that year, with Spencer inclining towards 1663.

If one examines Spencer's edition of the *Macbeth* manuscript, the whole idea of a later revision falls to the ground, as Davenant inserted stage directions for a spectacular production: "Exeunt flying" (1.1.12); "a Heath" and "A dance of Witches" (2.5.1, 81); "Machine descends" (3.8.20); and "Musick, the Witches Dance & vanish, ye Cave sinks" (4.1.119). It was not until November 1671 (after Davenant's death) that these ingredients could be fully utilized by the new equipment or machinery in the Dorset Garden Theatre, but they were there all the time.

If we return now to Pepys's *Diary* with the knowledge that the music and dances were in Davenant's version from the beginning, we will be better prepared to interpret his comments. For three consecutive visits in the 1666–67 season, he says, "variety," "divertissement," and "variety of dancing and music." Unfortunately, his comment on 5 November 1664 is baffling; he did not tell his diary whether the play had "variety" or not. This performance is itself puzzling. We do not know whether the players were offering Shakespeare's tragedy (as John Genest suggested long ago) or Davenant's alteration of it. As mentioned earlier, Davenant had a playhouse copy that descended from the old King's Company before the closing of the theaters in 1642, so that his troupe could easily have acted Shakespeare's play. If this is what actually happened, we can make some conjectures about the course of events. First, Davenant proceeded to make his alteration of *Macbeth.*[17] He had been staging a major production in each summer since his company had been formed (as the pattern of a season from October to May had not been developed). He had spent a good deal of money to mount Orrery's *Mustapha* in the spring of 1665, and his alteration of *Macbeth* was possibly scheduled for that summer. However, the great plague struck London, followed by the terrible fire, so that the London theaters were not opened again until December 1666, and it is in this month that we hear of a production of *Macbeth.* In any event, the true date for the premiere of Davenant's adaptation does not fall in the 1671–72 season or on 18 February 1673; it takes place in December 1666 or else back in November 1664, if the Duke's Company never played Shakespeare's text.

Pepys's *Diary* for 17 December 1666, when Davenant's adaptation was performed at Court, contains an amusing coincidence:

> Then comes Mr. Cesar, and then Goodgroome, and what with one and the other, nothing but Musique with me this morning, to my great content; and the more to see that God Almighty hath put me into condition to bear the charge of all this. So out to the Change I, and did a little business; and then home, where they [*sic*] two musicians and Mr. Cooke came to see me—and Mercer, to go alone with my wife this afternoon to a play. To dinner, and then our [corrected over "my"] company all broke up. . . .

Who were these guests, who engaged in "nothing but Musique"? "Cesar" was William Smegergill, alias William Caesar, a lutenist, music teacher, and composer; John Goodgroome was one of the royal musicians, a singing master and composer; Captain Henry Cooke was a lutenist, singer, and composer. This conclave of musicians gives the impression of a group beating time until the hour when they would attend the opera and hear their friend Matthew Locke's new music.

NOTES

1. H. Furness, ed., *Macbeth* (Philadelphia, 1873); A. Nicoll, *A History of English Drama* (Cambridge: Cambridge University Press, 1961), 1:401–02; E. L. Avery, ed., *The London Stage*, Part 1 (Carbondale, Ill.: Southern Illinois University Press, 1965); *A Biographical Dictionary of Actors*, ed. P. H. Highfill, Jr., Kalman A. Burnim, and E. A. Langhans (Carbondale, Ill.: Southern Illinois University Press, 1973–), 9:338; E. W. White, *A Register of First Performances of English Operas* (London: Society for Theatre Research, 1983), p. 12; R. E. Moore, "The Music to *Macbeth*," *Musical Quarterly* 47 (1961): 22–40; J. Dover Wilson, ed., *Macbeth* (Cambridge: Cambridge University Press, 1947), p. lxxix; Montague Summers, *The Playhouse of Pepys* (London: Kegan Paul, 1935), p. 158; C. Spencer, *Davenant's 'Macbeth' from the Yale Manuscript* (New Haven: Yale University Press, 1961), pp. 1–16, and "*Macbeth* and Davenant's *The Rivals*," *Shakespeare Quarterly* 20 (1969): 225–29; Curtis Price, *Music in the Restoration Theatre* (Ann Arbor, Mich.: University of Michigan Press, 1979), p. 198; *The New Grove Dictionary of Music and Musicians* (London: Macmillan, 1981), 11:107–17.

2. All performance dates (unless otherwise noted) are taken from Part 1 of *The London Stage*. All extracts from Pepys's *Diary* are from the new edition done by Robert Latham and William Matthews, 9 vols. (Berkeley: University of California Press, 1970–76), but they can be found under date in any complete edition.

3. John Downes, *Roscius Anglicanus* (1708).

4. 11:113.

5. Moore, "Music to *Macbeth*," pp. 26–27; Fiske, "The *Macbeth* Music," *Music and Letters* 45 (1964): 114–25.

6. J. P. Cutts, "The Original Music to Middleton's *The Witch*," *Shakespeare Quarterly* 7 (1956), 203–9.

7. See Moore, "Music to *Macbeth*," pp. 26–27.

8. Ibid.

9. Spencer, *Davenant's 'Macbeth,'* p. 13.

10. Price, *Restoration Theatre,* p. 198.

11. Price, *Restoration Theatre,* p. 156.

12. Moore, "Music to *Macbeth*," p. 27.

13. Nicoll, *History of English Drama,* p. 402.

14. For these allusions, see Pierre Danchin, ed., *The Prologues and Epilogues of the Restoration,* 1660–1700 (Nancy: Publications Université Nancy, 1981), Part 1, pp. 546–49, 559–66.

15. Spencer, *Davenant's 'Macbeth,'* pp. 1–74.

16. Spencer, "*Macbeth* and Davenant's *The Rivals*," *Shakespeare Quarterly* 20 (1969): 225–29.

17. The cast in Q 1674 provides no help in dating a performance. With the exception of the dramatist Nathaniel Lee, who acted Duncan for one night only, all the rest of the players were in the Duke's Company in the 1664–65 season and also in the 1671–72 and 1672–73 seasons. Cademan, who played Donalbain, was permanently injured on 9 August 1673, and Jane Long (Lady Macduff) left the company some time in 1673. This cast was probably written down when copy for the 1674 quarto was being prepared.

I am indebted to Philip H. Highfill, Jr., and Edward A. Langhans for sending me unpublished material from a forthcoming volume of their *Biographical Dictionary of Actors.*

Biographical Note on S. F. Johnson

S. F. Johnson was born in Pittsburgh on 22 July 1918. He was graduated B. A., 1940, from Haverford College (one of the last students there of J. Leslie Hotson); and M.A., 1941, and Ph.D., 1948, from Harvard University (where his teachers included, besides Harry Levin and Hyder Rollins, George W. Sherburn, B. J. Whiting, Douglas Bush, Howard Baker, and Theodore Spencer.) From 1942 to 1946, he served in the United States Army. In the Army's language program, he studied Russian in 1943–44 at Indiana University. In 1944–45, he served as Traffic Analyst in Signal Intelligence in England, France, and Germany. Following the war's end, he studied sixteenth-century French literature at the Sorbonne. Returning to Harvard, from 1946 to 1948 he was Proctor and Tutor in English, and in 1948–49 Instructor. From 1949 to 1954, he was Assistant Professor at New York University. In 1954–55, he held a Guggenheim fellowship, and in 1972, a summer residency grant at the Huntington Library. At Columbia University, from 1954 to 1984 he rose to the rank of Professor. There, his closest professional colleague was the late Renaissance scholar, William Nelson. At Columbia, in addition to teaching Shakespeare and other Renaissance literature, he devised and conducted, from 1976 to 1983, a sequence of courses: "Opera Libretti as Drama," selectively covering to 1893 the history of operatic literature.

Among his professional appointments have been posts as Assistant Secretary and Editor of the Modern Language Association, 1951–52; as Chairman of the Supervising Committee of the English Institute, 1959; and as Associate Editor of the *Renaissance Quarterly,* 1967–84.

His publications give but limited evidence of the range and depth of his Renaissance knowledge. The recent publication of his dissertation, *Early Elizabethan Tragedies of the Inns of Court* (Garland, 1987) has been noted in the Preface. Such contributions as his essay on *Hamlet* ("The Regeneration of Hamlet," *Shakespeare Quarterly* 3 [1952]: 187–207); and on Kyd's *Spanish Tragedy* ("*The Spanish Tragedy,* or Babylon Revisited," in *Essays on Shakespeare and Elizabethan Drama in Honor of Hardin Craig,* ed. Richard Hosley [Columbia: University of Missouri Press, 1962], pp. 23–36); and his Pelican edition of *Julius Caesar* (1st ed., 1960; reprinted in Alfred Harbage, general editor, *William Shakespeare. The Complete Works* [Baltimore: Penguin Books, 1969]) are frequently cited in the scholarship. These contributions reflect one of his major dramatic concerns: the role of the Elizabethan tragic hero. This concern appears more explicitly in his essay, "The Tragic Hero in Early Elizabethan Drama" (in *Studies in English Renaissance Drama in Memory of Karl Holzknecht*, ed. Josephine W. Bennett et al. [New York: New York University Press, 1959], pp. 157–71). His interest in the tragic hero has emphasized the audience's empathetic *admiratio* for the figure, rather than a "Christianizing" or reductively moralistic search for his tragic flaw. Indeed, his interest in the dynamics of audience-response has anticipated a direction of recent critical theory.

Detailed scholarly reviews, moreover, put his knowledge to judicious use: as in his critique of Charlton Hinman's *The Printing and Proof-reading of the First Folio of Shakespeare* (*Renaissance News* 17 [1964]: 224–230); of Matthew W. Black's New Variorum edition of *Richard II* (*Journal of English and Germanic Philology* 56 [1957]: 476–83); and of T. S. Dorsch's new Arden edition of *Julius Caesar* (*Shakespeare Quarterly* 8 [1957]: 391–95). Notable also are his critical studies: e.g., his pioneer essay on *The Return of the Native* ("Hardy and Burke's 'Sublime,' " in *Style in Prose Fiction*, ed. Harold C. Martin [New York: Columbia University Press, 1959], pp. 55–86), and his exchange on critical theory with R. S. Crane ("Critics and Criticism, a Discussion: The Chicago Manifesto," *Journal of Aesthetics and Art Criticism* 12 [1953]: 248–67).

But such mere listing cannot account for his extraordinary influence as teacher and for the number of students, colleagues, and other friends who responded to the request for contributions (too many, indeed, for this volume—and apologies are offered those whose essays could not, for reasons of space, be included). What cannot be reckoned are Professor Johnson's scholarship, his expertise, not only in literature but also in the other arts, especially music, and his uncompromising scholarly integrity.

W. R. E.

Contributors

Jonas Barish has taught English at the University of California, Berkeley, since 1954. He is the author of *Ben Jonson and the Language of Prose Comedy* (1960), *The Antitheatrical Prejudice* (1981), articles on Shakespeare and other English Renaissance dramatists, on Verdi, on Genet and Sartre, and has edited plays by Shakespeare and Jonson. He is currently at work on a study of closet drama.

The late Bernard Beckerman was Brander Mathews Professor of Dramatic Arts at Columbia University. In addition to his many articles, he was the author of *Shakespeare at the Globe, 1599–1609* and *Dynamics of Drama: Theory and Method of Analysis.*

Ronald Broude is Executive Editor of Broude Brothers Limited and Co-Trustee of The Broude Trust for the Publication of Musicological Editions. He has taught at several universities and has published in *Studies in Philology, Shakespeare Studies, Renaissance Quarterly,* and *Studies in the History of Music.*

Robert Brustein is Professor of English at Harvard University and Artistic Director of the American Repertory Theatre. His latest book is *Who Needs Theatre.*

Elizabeth Story Donno is a member of the Senior Research staff at the Henry E. Huntington Library, San Marino, California.

W. R. Elton is Professor of English Literature at the Graduate School, City University of New York, and was first Visiting Mellon Professor of Literature at the Institute for Advanced Study, Princeton, 1984–85. His *"King Lear" and the Gods* (Huntington Library, 1966, 1968) has been reprinted with additions by the University Press of Kentucky.

Russell Fraser is Austin Warren Professor of English Language and Literature at the University of Michigan. Recently he has edited *All's Well that Ends Well* for the New Cambridge Shakespeare, and he has completed a biography, "Young Shakespeare," taking him to 1594.

BRUCE GOLDEN is Professor of English at California State University, San Bernardino. He has written articles on Ford Madox Ford, Calderon, and published *The Beach Boys: Southern California Pastoral.*

T. J. KING, author of *Shakespearean Staging, 1599–1642*, is Professor of English at the City College of New York.

MARY ELLEN LAMB, Associate Professor of English at Southern Illinois University, has published articles on Shakespeare, Sidney, and women writers in the Renaissance in such journals as *English Literary Renaissance, Review of English Studies,* and *Shakespeare Survey.* Her book, *Writing Women in the Renaissance,* is forthcoming from the University of Wisconsin Press.

HARRY LEVIN is Irving Babbitt Professor of Comparative Literature Emeritus at Harvard University. His most recent book is *Playboys and Killjoys: An Essay on the Theory and Practice of Comedy.*

RICHARD L. LEVIN, Professor of English at the State University of New York at Stony Brook, is the author of *The Multiple Plot in English Renaissance Drama* (1971) and *New Readings vs. Old Plays: Recent Trends in the Reinterpretation of English Renaissance Drama* (1979). Currently he is a Fellow at the National Humanities Research Center in North Carolina and is working on a study on the newest approaches to Elizabethan drama.

WILLIAM B. LONG taught English Renaissance drama at Washington University in St. Louis and at the City College of New York and is currently Senior Editor at AMS Press, New York. He has been writing about English Renaissance dramatic manuscripts and textual problems for some years.

RAINER PINEAS is a Professor of English at York College of the City University of New York. He has specialized in the study of the dramatic and nondramatic polemical literature of the English Reformation.

ARTHUR H. SCOUTEN, one of the editors of *The London Stage,* is Emeritus Professor of the University of Pennsylvania.

MICHAEL SHAPIRO is Associate Professor of English at the University of Illinois at Urbana-Champaign.

SARAH SUTHERLAND, author of *Masques in Jacobean Tragedy,* is Dean of Studies and Lecturer in English at Mount Holyoke College.

EUGENE M. WAITH is Douglas Tracy Smith Professor of English Literature Emeritus at Yale University. He is the author of *The Pattern of Tragicomedy in Beaumont and Fletcher, The Herculean Hero,* and *Ideas of Greatness: Heroic Drama in England.* He has edited *Macbeth* for the Yale Shakespeare, *Bartholomew Fair* for the Yale Ben Jonson, and *Titus Andronicus* for the Oxford Shakespeare, for which he is currently editing *The Two Noble Kinsmen.* A collection of his essays, *Patterns and Perspectives in English Renaissance Drama,* is being published by the University of Delaware Press.

GERALD WEALES is Professor of English at the University of Pennsylvania. The editor of *The Complete Plays of William Wycherley,* he has most recently published a new edition of *Clifford Odets, Playwright* (Methuen) and *Canned Goods as Caviar, American Film Comedy of the 1930s* (University of Chicago Press).

Index

Anonymous works are grouped under that heading.